GARY A. DAVIS

University of Wisconsin

SYLVIA B. RIMM

Family Achievement Clinic, Oconomowoc, Wisconsin

EDUCATION OF THE GIFTED AND TALENTED

PRENTICE-HALL, INC., Englewood Cliffs, New Jersey 07632

Library of Congress Cataloging in Publication Data

Davis, Gary A., (date)
  Education of the gifted and talented.

  Bibliography: p.
  Includes index.
  1. Gifted children—Education. 2. Educational
acceleration. 3. Gifted children—Education—Curricula.
I. Rimm, Sylvia B., (date). II. Title.
LC3993.D38 1985   371.95   84-11476
ISBN 0-13-236597-9

Editorial/production supervision and
  interior design: *Marjorie Borden*
Cover design: *Lundgren Graphics, Ltd.*
Cover photo: *Ken Karp*
Manufacturing buyer: *Barbara Kelly Kittle*

Acknowledgments
Figure 10.3: From Ruth B. Noller, Sidney J. Parnes, Angelo M. Biondi, *Creative Actionbook.*
Copyright © 1976 Charles Scribner's Sons. Used by permission of Charles Scribner's Sons.
Figure 11.2: Adapted from *Applied Information* by Alex Osborn with permission of Charles
Scribner's Sons. Copyright © 1953, 1957, 1963 by Charles Scribner's Sons; copyright re-
newed 1981 Russell Osborn.

Printed in the United States of America

10 9 8 7 6 5 4 3 2 1

ISBN 0-13-236597-9   01

Prentice-Hall International, Inc., *London*
Prentice-Hall of Australia Pty. Limited, *Sydney*
Editora Prentice-Hall do Brasil, Ltda., *Rio de Janeiro*
Prentice-Hall Canada Inc., *Toronto*
Prentice-Hall of India Private Limited, *New Delhi*
Prentice-Hall of Japan, Inc., *Tokyo*
Prentice-Hall of Southeast Asia Pte. Ltd., *Singapore*
Whitehall Books Limited, *Wellington, New Zealand*

to our families—

    Cathy, Kirsten, Ingrid, and Sonja

    Buck, Ilonna, David, Eric, and Sara

CONTENTS

PREFACE

To provide programs designed to help meet the psychological, social, educational, and career needs of gifted and talented students.

To assist students in becoming individuals who are able to take self-initiated action . . . and who are capable of intelligent choice, independent learning, and problem solving.

To develop problem solving abilities and creative thinking skills; develop research skills; strengthen individual interests; develop independent study skills; strengthen communication skills; receive intellectual stimulation from contact with other highly motivated students; and expand their learning activities to include resources available in the entire community.

To maximize learning and individual development and to minimize boredom, confusion, and frustration.

To enable them to realize their contributions to self and society.

These are the goals of educational programs for gifted and talented students, and these are the purposes of this book. Gifted and talented students have special needs and special problems; they also have special, sometimes immense talent to lend to society. We owe it to them to help cultivate their abilities; we owe it to society to help prepare tomorrow's leaders and professional talent. Gifted and talented students are a tremendous natural resource, one that cannot be squandered.

It is no secret that since the mid-1970s interest in special educational services for the gifted and talented has climbed to a higher level and with greater public awareness than ever before. Federal statements, definitions, funds, programs, and professional staff now exist. States are passing legislation that formalizes the existence and needs of gifted children and provides funds for directors, teachers, and programs. Cities and districts are hiring program directors and teacher-coordinators who design and implement specific identification, acceleration, and enrichment plans. And in those schools and classrooms where help from the outside does not appear, enthusiastic teachers plan challenging and worthwhile projects and activities for the one or two most gifted children in each of their classes.

While the ball is indeed rolling, it is also no secret that as with every other social or technological change, (a) mistakes are being made, some elementary ones and some major ones; and (b) there is resistance—from those who believe that providing special services to gifted students is like donating money to the Rockefellers. This book may or may not change the minds of critics who feel that special education for the gifted is unfair, undemocratic, or elitist. The list of virtues at the beginning of this preface, plus the argument that a true democracy includes full individual opportunity, may not make a dent in their good-intentioned defenses.

However, this book can help minimize the mistakes that plague so many thoughtfully planned G/T programs. Mistakes are made at every step, from selecting program goals and student participants to evaluating program success. There are many issues to consider, and many alternatives to choose from. This book should help the reader make better, more informed decisions. There are few absolutely right answers for G/T program plans, since their "rightness" depends upon the specific student needs and the particular educational circumstances. However, there are many absolutely wrong answers and methods. This book should help the reader decide which is which.

This text was prepared as an introduction to the exciting field of gifted education.* It is suitable for college undergraduate and graduate readers, for in-service teachers in elementary or secondary schools, for school psychologists, counselors, and administrators, and for parents of those bright but often bored and ignored gifted children and adolescents. The text provides an introduction—sometimes an in-depth one—to virtually all aspects of program planning and development, from (a) formalizing a statement of philosophy, rationale, goals, and objectives, to (b) identifying students, (c) outlining theory-based acceleration and enrichment activities, and (d) evaluating the ongoing or completed program. Often, specific rating forms and questionnaires for identification or evaluation are presented

*The authors are aware that "gifted education" is not grammatically correct, since it is not education but *students* who are gifted. However, "education of the gifted and talented" is so unwieldy that *gifted education* has become a widely used and fully accepted abbreviation.

as models that may inspire the creation of specific, program-relevant instruments. Also, lists of philosophy and goal statements, enrichment strategies, acceleration plans, strategies for teaching creative and critical thinking, and other central matters are described. Curriculum models that direct program planning and models that guide program evaluation also are reviewed. In most cases, an underlying theory, or at least a good rationale, accompanies the strategies and suggestions.

Importantly, the book does not ignore the special identification and programming needs of *female* gifted students or *culturally different, economically disadvantaged, handicapped,* or *underachieving* gifted students. Many existing programs do not adequately accommodate the needs and problems of these children.

The authors wish to thank Julia Betlej, research assistant at Mount Mary College, for her library searches; Marian Carlson, our secretary, for her efficient and ever-helpful contributions; and Prentice-Hall editor Susan Willig for her encouragement and assistance with the manuscript. Most important, we wish to thank our families for their encouragement, support, and real-life experiences that helped enrich our text.

1

GIFTEDNESS:
An Introduction

Parents and educators alike are becoming more and more "gifted conscious," and for very good reasons. Tens of thousands of gifted and talented children and adolescents are sitting in their classrooms—their abilities unrecognized, their needs unmet. Some are bored, patiently waiting for peers to learn skills and concepts that they had mastered two years earlier. Some find school intolerable, feigning illness or creating other excuses to avoid the trivia. Some say that existing schools are obsolete, more of a tradition than a necessity (Torrance, 1976, 1984). Some feel pressured to hide their keen talents and skills from uninterested and unsympathetic peers. Some give up on school entirely, dropping out as soon as they are legally able.

Other gifted students tolerate school but satisfy their intellectual, creative, or artistic needs outside of the formal system. The lucky ones have parents who will sponsor their dance or music lessons, chemistry kits and telescopes, art supplies, frequent trips to the library, and home computers. The less fortunate ones make do as best they can, silently paying a price for a predicament that they may not understand, and that others choose to ignore. That price is lost academic growth, lost creative potential, and sometimes lost enthusiasm for educational success and eventual professional achievement.

Some educators—and many parents of nongifted students—are not swayed by the proposition that unrecognized and unsupported talent is wasted talent. A common reaction is, "Those kids will make it on their own," or "Give the extra help to kids who really need it!" The argument is that providing special services for highly able or talented students is "elitist"—giving to the "haves" and ignoring the "have-nots"—and therefore unfair and undemocratic.

Certainly, there are many students who need special help, and every state and school district in the United States has allocated funds for special-education programs. These programs include the "special ed" teachers; speech, reading, and language specialists; and school psychologists; along with special equipment, materials, tests, and so forth. The rights of learning disabled, physically disabled, and retarded students are vehemently defended, and they should be.

However, a good argument can be made that gifted students have rights too, and that these rights are often ignored. Just as with other exceptional students, students with gifts and talents also deserve an education commensurate with their capabilities. It is unfair to them to ignore or, worse, to prevent the development of their special skills and abilities and to depress their educational aspirations and eventual career achievements. Our democratic system promises each person—regardless of racial, cultural, or economic background and regardless of sex or handicapping condition—the opportunity to develop as an individual as far as that person's talents and motivation will permit. This guarantee seems to promise intrinsically that opportunities and training will be provided to help gifted and talented students realize their innate potential.

To those who argue that gifted students will "make it on their own," sensible replies are that (a) they should not be held back and required to succeed in spite of a frustrating educational system, and (b) some do not make it on their own. Nyquist (Nyquist, 1973; Lajoie and Shore, 1981), for example, reported that a full 19 percent of high school dropouts in New York State would be classed as "gifted." Almost invariably, gifted dropouts are underachievers, talented but depressed students who are unguided, uncounseled, and unchallenged (Whitmore, 1980).

It is not only the gifted students themselves who benefit from specific programs that recognize and cultivate their talents. Teachers involved with gifted students learn to stimulate creative, artistic, and scientific thinking, and they learn to help students understand themselves, develop good self-concepts, and value educational and career accomplishments. In short, teachers of the gifted become better teachers, and their skills benefit "regular" students as well. Society also reaps a profit. Realistically, it is only today's gifted and talented students who will become tomorrow's political leaders, medical researchers, artists, writers, innovative engineers, and business entrepreneurs. Indeed, it is difficult to propose that this essential talent be left to fend for itself—if it can—instead of being valued, identified, and cultivated. Tomorrow's promise is in today's schools, and it must not be ignored.

HISTORY OF GIFTEDNESS AND GIFTED EDUCATION

The history underlying today's interest in the education of the gifted and talented is not a long one. In fact, five events—four people and one Russian satellite—will bring us up to date.

Hereditary Genius: Sir Francis Galton

The English scientist Sir Francis Galton (1822–1911), a younger cousin of Charles Darwin, is credited with the earliest significant research and writing devoted to intelligence (or genius) and intelligence testing. Galton himself, incidentally, was reading at age 2½ and writing well at age 4. Lewis Terman, who will be person three on our history list, estimated Galton's IQ at 200, based on the tasks he could perform at particular ages (Terman, 1917). In 1838, at age 16, Galton began studying medicine at Birmingham General Hospital and later at King's College in London. In 1840, with a change in career plans, he switched to mathematics at Trinity College. With his proper training in algebra and trigonometry, Galton embarked on several adventurous trips to Africa, exploring some areas for the first time, and in 1854 earned the Royal Geographical Society's gold medal. Following his first book, *The Art of Travel,* and a second pioneering book on weather prediction, Galton turned in the 1860s to the study of intelligence.

Galton believed that intelligence was related to the keenness of one's sensory equipment; for example, vision, audition, smell, touch, and reaction time. His efforts to measure intelligence therefore involved such tests as those of visual and auditory acuity, tactile sensitivity, and reaction time. Having been highly impressed by cousin Charles's *Origin of the Species,* Galton reasoned that evolution would favor persons with keen senses—persons who could more easily detect food sources or sense approaching danger. Therefore, he concluded that one's sensory ability—that is, intelligence—is due to natural selection and heredity. The hereditary basis of intelligence seemed to be confirmed by his observations—reported in his most famous book *Hereditary Genius* (Galton, 1869)—that distinguished persons seemed to come from succeeding generations of distinguished families. Galton initially overlooked the fact that members of distinguished, aristocratic families also inherit a superior environment, wealth, privilege, and opportunity—incidentals that make it much easier to become distinguished.

Galton is also noted for conducting the first "twin research," estab-

---

INSET 1.1 AN ARGUMENT FOR EQUALITY

Kurt Vonnegut in *Harrison Bergeron* wrote a spoof on equality: "The year was 2081, and everybody was finally equal. They weren't only equal before God and the law, they were equal in every which way. Nobody was smarter than anybody else. No one was better looking than anyone else." [The reason for this enforced equality was that people who were outstanding in various ways were given handicaps. Those who could dance well had to wear sandbags on their feet; those who were good looking had to wear a mask. Intelligence?] "George, while his intelligence was way above normal, had a little metal handicap radio in his ear. He was required by law to wear it at all times. He was tuned to a government transmitter. Every 20 seconds or so, the transmitter would send out some noise to keep people like George from taking unfair advantage of their brains."

---

lishing a pattern for twentieth-century twin studies aimed at isolating genetic versus environmental (learned) components of intelligence. In its simplest form, the logic of these studies is that if intelligence is due mainly to heredity, the intelligence of identical twins (with identical genes) should be extremely similar, even if the twins are separated at birth and raised in different environments. In twentieth-century research, the comparative intelligence of identical twins reared together is compared with the intelligence of identical twins raised separately, fraternal twins raised together or separately, ordinary siblings raised together or separately, and many other combinations, including comparisons of IQ scores of adopted children with those of their foster and natural parents. While Galton's emphasis on the high heritability of intelligence is today shared by some (Jensen, 1969, 1974; Gage and Berliner, 1979), many other psychologists and educators argue that the primary determinants of intelligence are environment and learning. The debate continues.

Roots of Modern Intelligence Tests: Alfred Binet

While Galton's sensory acuity tests are the first recorded efforts to measure intelligence, modern intelligence tests have their roots in France, in the 1890s. Alfred Binet, aided by T. Simon, was hired by government officials in Paris to devise a test to identify which (dull) children would not benefit from regular classes and therefore would be placed in special classes to receive special training. Someone had perceptively noticed that teachers' judgments of student ability were biased by such traits as docility, neatness, and social skills. Some children were placed in schools for the retarded because they were too quiet, too aggressive, or had problems with speech, hearing, or vision. A direct test of intelligence was badly needed.

Binet tried a number of tests that failed. It seemed that normal students and dull students were not particularly different in (a) hand-squeezing strength, (b) hand speed in moving 50 cm (almost 20 in.), (c) the amount of pressure on the forehead that causes pain, (d) detecting differences in hand-held weights, or (e) reaction time to sounds or in naming colors. When he began measuring the ability to pay attention, memory, judgment, reasoning, and comprehension, he began to obtain results. The tests would separate children judged by teachers to differ in intelligence (Binet and Simon, 1905a, 1905b).

One of Binet's significant contributions was the notion of *mental age*— the concept that children grow in intelligence, and that any given child may be at the proper stage intellectually for his or her years, or else measurably ahead or behind. A related notion is that at any given age level, children who learn the most do so partly because of greater intelligence.

In 1890, fifteen years before the Binet tests were publicized, noted American psychologist James McKeen Cattell called for the development of tests that would measure mental ability (Stanley, 1978a); his request was at least partly responsible for the immediate favorable reception to Binet's tests in America. In 1910 Goddard described the use of Binet's methods to measure the intelligence of 400 "feebleminded" New Jersey children, and in 1911 summarized his evaluation of two thousand normal children. The transition from using the Binet tests with below-average children to employing them with normal and above-average children thus was complete and successful.

Lewis Terman: The Stanford-Binet Test, His Gifted Children Studies

Stanford psychologist Lewis Terman made two historically significant contributions to gifted education. First, following on the heels of Binet's work, Terman supervised the formal modification and Americanization of the Binet-Simon tests, producing in 1916 the progenitor of all American intelligence tests, the *Stanford-Binet Intelligence Scale*. The test was revised in 1937 and again in 1960. In 1972 new norms were published, based on a sample of 2,100 children, including black and Spanish-surnamed children. The test itself remained almost identical to the 1960 version.

Terman's second contribution was his identification and long study of 1,500 gifted children—800 boys and 700 girls. These people were, and still are, the most studied group of gifted individuals in the world. In the 1920s, Terman and Melita Oden (1925, 1947, 1951, 1959) administered the Stanford-Binet test to students initially identified by teachers as highly intelligent. The final sample consisted almost entirely of those who scored 140 or higher, the upper 1 percent. The ensuing field studies in 1927–1928, 1939–1940, and the late 1950s, interspersed with occasional mailings, traced the personal and professional activities of the subjects for over half a century. Terman died in 1956, but his work is being carried on (for example, R. R. Sears, 1977; P. S. Sears, 1979; P. S. Sears and Barbee, 1977).

Leta Hollingworth: "Nurturant Mother" of Gifted Education

According to Stanley (1978a), Galton was the grandfather of the gifted-child movement, Binet the midwife, Terman the father, and Columbia University's Leta Hollingworth the nurturant mother. Her pioneering contributions to gifted education consisted of personal efforts supporting gifted education and gifted students in the New York City area, until her death in 1939, and the publication of two books, *Gifted Children: Their Nature and Nurture* (Hollingworth, 1926) and *Children Above 180 IQ Stanford-Binet: Origin and Development* (Hollingworth, 1942). One noteworthy 1931 quote is: "It is the business of education to consider all forms of giftedness in pupils in reference to how unusual individuals may be trained for their own welfare and that of society at large" (Passow, 1981). Curiously, in his biography of Terman, Segoe (1975) could find no evidence of any contact between Hollingworth in New York and Terman in California (Segoe, 1975; Stanley, 1978a).

Sputnik: The Russians Are Gaining! The Russians Are Gaining!

Our last significant historical event to predate the 1970s is the launching in 1957 of the Russian satellite Sputnik. To fully appreciate the impact of this astronomical gadget on American politicians, educators, and indeed the American public, one must remember the cold-war thinking of the 1950s. Both the United States and the Soviet Union possessed large stores of nuclear bombs, and both countries feared that the irrational other would at any moment initiate the destruction of Earth in response to an imagined attack. A "hot line" from Washington to Moscow was installed, and thousands of Americans built bomb shelters.

To many, the launch of Sputnik was a glaring and shocking technological defeat—Russia's scientific minds had outperformed ours (Tannenbaum, 1979). Suddenly reports criticizing American education and, particularly, its ignoring of gifted children became very popular. For example, a 1950 Educational Policies Commission had noted that mentally superior children were being neglected, which would produce losses in the arts, sciences, and professions. In a book entitled *Educational Wastelands,* Bestor (1953) charged that "know-nothing educationists" had created schools that provided "meager intellectual nourishment or inspiration," particularly for bored gifted students. Wolfle (1954), Director of the Commission on Human Resources and Advanced Training, charged that America was failing to prepare enough men and women in the fields of science, health, engineering, and teaching. Worse yet, his statistics indicated that the shortages would increase—unless gifted students were encouraged to pursue professional training. Following the 1957 launch, more reports compared the quality and quantity of American versus Russian education, and especially the numbers of American versus Russian children being trained in defense-related professions. America lost hands down. A report by the First Official U.S. Education Mission to the USSR (1959), entitled *Soviet Commitment to Education,* claimed that the typical Russian high school graduate had completed ten years of math, five years of physics, four years of chemistry, one year of astronomy, five years of biology, and five years of a foreign language.

Tannenbaum (1979) referred to the aftermath of Sputnik as a "total talent mobilization." Academic coursework was telescoped (condensed) for bright students. College courses were offered in high school; foreign languages were taught in elementary schools. Public and private funds were earmarked for training in science and technology. Acceleration and ability grouping were used, and efforts were made to identify gifted and talented minority students. New math and science curricula were developed, most notably the School Mathematics Study Group (SMSG) math, Physical Science Study Committee (PSSC) physics, and Biological Science Curriculum Study (BSCS) biology. In high school there was a new awareness of and concern for high scholastic standards and career mindedness. The bright and talented students were expected to take the tough courses, to " . . . fulfill their potential, and submit their developed abilities for service to the nation" (Tannenbaum, 1979).

Unfortunately, both the scare of Sputnik and the keen interest in educating gifted and talented students wore off in about five years. The awareness and concern was rekindled in the mid-1970s, however, and it seems here to stay. The federal government and individual states are enacting legislation and allocating funds. Teachers and administrators nationwide are becoming committed to gifted education. Virtually all large school systems have initiated new programs. Many individual schools and even individual teachers, not waiting for formal district action, are initiating special services and training for gifted children. Droves of researchers are developing tests, evaluating programs, and publishing hundreds of articles in new journals. The ball is indeed rolling.

DEFINITIONS OF GIFTEDNESS

Defining what is meant by "gifted" and "talented" is an extremely important matter. It is also surprisingly complicated.

Most readers of this book already have a more-or-less clear notion of what a "gifted" student is. Certainly, the very bright and mature student who earns straight *A*'s, performs the lead role in the school play, is voted captain of the debate team, and earns a scholarship to State University merits the title of "gifted." We would also agree that the outstanding violin player, the highly talented artist, and the electronics whiz kid also show definite gifts and talents. If pressed on the issue, we might further concede that the popular person elected school president, the quarterback of the high school football team, and maybe even the teenager who does beautiful body-and-fender work also possess unique gifts and talents. Is the issue beginning to sound more complex?

The problem becomes even more complicated and difficult in relation to defining and identifying gifted students who are underachievers, economically disadvantaged, culturally different, learning disabled, or physically handicapped. These special populations will be discussed in later chapters. For now we should simply acknowledge that we typically overlook and do not expect to find, gifted and talented students in these groups.

Stankowski (1978) outlined five categories of definitions of "gifts" and "talents." First, *after-the-fact* definitions emphasize prominence in one of the professions as the criterion of giftedness. The "gifted" thus are those who have shown consistently outstanding achievements in a valuable sphere of human activity. Unfortunately, this approach largely restricts giftedness to accomplished adults.

Second, *IQ* definitions set a point on the IQ scale, and persons scoring above that point are classed as "gifted." Terman's Stanford-Binet cutoff of 140 is a classic example. The practice remains popular despite its glaring shortcomings of ignoring creative and artistic gifts and discriminating against culturally different and low socio-economic level students.

Third, *talent* definitions focus on students who are outstanding in art, music, math, science, or some other specific aesthetic or academic area.

[Incidentally, it is common to use the word *gifted* to describe the generally bright, "intellectually gifted" person, and the word *talented* to refer to persons with superior skills and abilities in just one or a few areas (art, music, math, etc.). It is also common to use the words *gifted* and *talented* interchangeably, as when we speak of a "gifted artist" or a "talented straight-*A* student." Some see talent and giftedness as a continuum, with giftedness at the upper end (Cox and Daniel, 1983a; Perrone and Pulvino, 1979).]

Fourth, *percentage* definitions set a fixed proportion of the school (or district) as "gifted." The particular percentage may be based on intelligence test scores, overall grade-point averages, or sometimes just grades in particular areas, especially math and science. The percentage figure may be a generous 15 to 25 percent or a more strict 1 to 5 percent. A particularly irksome—but frequently heard—comment is that "five percent of our children are gifted!" The fact is, gifts and talents are distributed according to a normal, bell-shaped curve. Any percentage cutoff point is completely a matter of choice. Interestingly, Reis and Renzulli (1982) compared the quality of projects produced by students in the top 5 percent on measures of intelligence and achievement with projects produced by students in the top 15 to 25 percent—and found absolutely no detectable difference. They argued against restricting programs to the top 3 to 5 percent.

Finally, *creativity* definitions stress the significance of superior creative abilities as a main criterion of giftedness. Typically, creativity is recognized as one of several types of gifts and talents. However, gifted-education leader John Gowan (1978, 1981) uniquely defined a "gifted" person as one who is high in verbal creativity, and a "talented" person as one who is high in nonverbal creativity (for example, the arts).

The tremendous importance of definitions of giftedness lies in the fact that the particular definition adopted by a school or district will determine who is selected for the special services and training of a gifted program, and who is excluded. Normally, identification policies and procedures are based directly on the particular definition adopted. For example, if a school or district defines "giftedness" as high intelligence, then the selection process might accordingly be based on IQ and/or achievement scores, perhaps supplemented by teacher nominations. The identification procedures themselves operationally define who is "in" and who is "out" of a given program. Further, the link between definition and identification is definitely problematic. For example, there are difficulties with the accuracy and validity of the tests and nominating procedures, and there is great danger of discriminating against such special populations as poor, minority, handicapped, underachieving, and female gifted students.

One's definition of giftedness is indeed important, yet delicate and complicated. There is no one theoretically based definition of gifted and talented that will fit all programs and circumstances. Defining gifted and talented is a central feature of every planned program, and a feature that must be reviewed with great care.

For now we will summarize three prominent definitions of giftedness: the U.S. Office of Education definition, Joseph Renzulli's three-part definition, and the multiple-talent definition of Calvin Taylor. These three definitions are presented here because they are widely known, accepted, appreciated, and frequently adopted in written plans for gifted programs. They should also be thought-provoking, since all three are inconsistent with each other.

The 1972 U.S.O.E. Definition

For many educators, the sun rises and sets with the 1972 U.S. Office of Education definition of gifted and talented (Marland, 1972). It is a multitalent approach and it is usually cited on page 1 of state plans for gifted education. It also appears in a great many written program plans prepared by individual districts or schools. It reads:

> Gifted and talented children are those identified by professionally qualified persons who by virtue of outstanding abilities are capable of high performance. These are children who require differentiated educational programs and services beyond those normally provided by the regular school program in order to realize their contribution to self and society.
>
> Children capable of high performance include those with demonstrated achievement and/or potential ability in any of the following areas:
>
> 1. General intellectual ability
> 2. Specific academic aptitude
> 3. Creative or productive thinking
> 4. Leadership ability
> 5. Visual and performing arts
> 6. Psychomotor ability

The appeal of the U.S.O.E. definition is that:

> It recognizes not only high general intelligence, but gifts in specific academic areas and in the arts. It further calls attention to creative, leadership, and psychomotor gifts and talents. As we will see in Chapter 4, many specific identification strategies are based on the categories of the U.S.O.E. definition.
>
> It recognizes that gifted and talented students require "differentiated educational programs and services beyond those normally provided," thus justifying the development of gifted programs.
>
> It recognizes the two fundamental aims of gifted programs: to help individual gifted and talented students develop their high potential, and to provide society with trained creative leaders and problem solvers.
>
> By including "demonstrated achievement and/or potential ability" it takes into consideration the underachieving student who may not be demonstrating giftedness in school.

In 1978 the U.S. Congress revised Marland's definition to read:

> (The gifted and talented are) " . . . children and, whenever applicable, youth who are identified at the pre-school, elementary, or secondary level as possessing demonstrated or potential abilities that give evidence of high performance capability in areas such as intellectual, creative, specific academic or leadership ability or in the performing and visual arts, and who by reason thereof require services or activities not ordinarily provided by the school." (U.S. Congress, Educational Amendment of 1978 [P.L. 95-561, IX (A)])

The main difference between the 1972 and 1978 statements is that psychomotor ability was excluded. The reason for this change is that artistic psychomotor talents (for example, dancing, mime) could be included under performing arts, and athletically gifted students are already very well provided for. Indeed, athletic programs may be seen as almost ideal gifted programs: Special teachers (coaches) are hired; expensive equipment and space are provided; training is partly individualized; students meet with others like themselves, who encourage and reward each other for doing their best; and students even travel to other schools to meet and compete with other talented individuals and teams. Not much was lost by dropping "psychomotor ability" from Congress's definition.

The Renzulli Three-Ring Model

Gifted-education leader Joseph Renzulli has itemized at least three shortcomings of the U.S.O.E. definition (Renzulli, 1978; Renzulli, Reis, and Smith, 1981). First, it ignores high motivation as an important trait of all gifted persons who have achieved recognition for their contributions to society. Second, the six categories are not parallel and independent; that is, *specific academic aptitudes* and *visual and performing arts* are performance areas to which one's *general intellectual ability, creativity, leadership,* or *psychomotor ability* are applied. Third, many educators misinterpret and misuse the U.S.O.E. definition; they may formally acknowledge the categories (even write them into the formal plan), but then continue to use high IQ or achievement scores for the actual selection procedures.

Renzulli's three-ring definition (Figure 1.1) is a cure for these ills. In well-documented statements, Renzulli (1978; Renzulli, Reis, and Smith, 1981) argues that gifted persons who truly make valuable contributions to society in all cases possess three critical traits: high creativity, high task commitment (motivation), and above-average (but not necessarily high) intel-

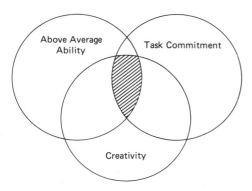

FIGURE 1.1 Renzulli's Three-ring Model of Giftedness. Gifted students are defined as those who are above average in intelligence (ability) and high in motivation (task commitment) and creativity. (Renzulli, 1978. Reprinted by permission.)

lectual ability. These characteristics are not only critical, but are seen as reasonably independent as well—requiring different sorts of tests, ratings, and so on, for their individual evaluation. If developers of gifted programs accept Renzulli's three-ring definition, they cannot escape measuring each of the three traits with potential program participants, and basing their selection judgments on *all three* of the characteristics. Strategies and instruments for assessing ability, creativity, and task commitment will be described in later chapters.

Overall, as with the U.S.O.E. definition, Renzulli's three-ring model is also widely accepted, particularly since it is an integral part of his high-impact *enrichment triad* and *revolving door* programming models. However, an important criticism of the Renzulli definition is that it omits underachieving children, students who may have plenty of ability and creativity but are lacking in task commitment. It seems an appropriate function of a gifted program to encourage task commitment among children with high ability but low motivation, not just exclude them.

Taylor's Multiple-Talent Totem Poles

Psychologist Calvin W. Taylor enjoys making the definition of gifted and talented as disturbing as possible. From Taylor's multiple-talent viewpoint, almost everyone is "gifted" or "talented." He may be right. It is a virtual certainty that you, the reader, have one or more special areas of skill, information, or interest—special strengths that most people do not have. Do you play an instrument well? Sing? Play a good game of chess? Tie flies? Speak fluent Spanish or Hebrew? Cook gourmet egg foo yong? Fix mufflers? Understand computers or the stock market? In an article entitled "How Many Types of Giftedness Can Your Program Tolerate?" Taylor described his famous totem poles (Figure 1.2). The idea is fairly straightforward: If we take the time to look, we will find that almost every student in a class is above average, if not outstanding, in some skill, ability, or knowledge area. Looking at Figure 1.2, if we use traditional academic ability (IQ, achievement) for identifying gifted students, Ann—who is at the top of the academic totem pole—is the natural choice for a gifted program. However, if creativity is also considered, Steve is the most outstanding. If we look at planning (organizing, designing) talents, Randy heads the top of the totem pole. For communicating (speaking, writing) Kathy is the most talented. How do we define gifted and talented? Who should be selected to participate in a gifted education program?

Clearly, Taylor does not so much define "gifts" and "talents" as raise our awareness that most students possess special skills and talents of some variety. There is, however, a serious problem in assuming that all children

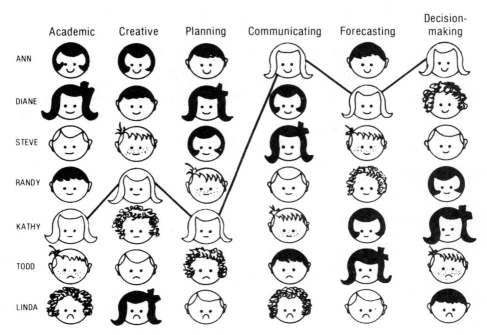

FIGURE 1.2 Taylor's (1978) Multiple Talent Totem Poles. The important point is that if you look at a large variety of gifts and talents, every child will be above average—perhaps even outstanding—in something. Who is gifted? Who is talented? Most every student? (Reprinted by permission.)

are gifted. If a G/T program tried to accommodate the unique strengths and talents of all or even most children, it actually would be an enrichment program for everyone, and would qualify only as a "watered-down" gifted program. Perhaps Taylor's broad definition of giftedness may be best viewed as an appropriate way to perceive, understand, and teach all children.

As an aside, the specific talents in Taylor's model have been used in some gifted programs as a curriculum guide (Eberle, 1974). That is, the program is partly organized around teaching academic content, creativity, planning skills, communication, forecasting, and decision making.

As a final comment on the definition challenge, we repeat that (1) there is no one final and agreed-upon definition of "gifted" and "talented," (2) the specific definition that a program accepts will determine the selection instruments and procedures, and (3) for any given program those instruments and decision criteria will actually define who is "gifted" and "talented," that is, who receives the special training and who does not.

DO SPECIAL PROGRAMS MAKE A DIFFERENCE?

As a final topic, we will consider whether or not differentiated educational programs truly make a difference in the lives of the participants. Realistically, not every program for gifted students is guaranteed to improve the educational or professional achievements of every child or adolescent who participates. It sometimes happens that a poorly run program will not provide the necessary training, motivation, or direction to enable gifted participants to later achieve at higher levels than gifted nonparticipants (Copley, 1961; Swing, 1973). Also, some gifted students may simply lack the intrinsic motivation necessary to pursue higher education or career achievements, despite their participation in a well-planned and otherwise "excellent" special program.

Often, however, gifted programs do make a difference in student achievements—a large and highly visible one. For example, Alexakos and Rothney (1967) compared the average GPAs, academic honors, and general scholarship of gifted high-school students who previously were enrolled in a special science program with the accomplishments of gifted students who were not enrolled. The enrolled children were hands-down winners in all three areas. Tremaine (1979) compared the achievements, accomplishments, and attitudes of gifted high-school graduates who had participated in special programs with those gifted graduates who had not. Compared with equally intelligent gifted nonparticipants, gifted students who had participated earned higher high-school GPAs, scored higher on the *Scholastic Aptitude Test* (54 points higher on SAT-Verbal, 80 points higher on SAT-Math), selected more challenging high-school courses, won three times as many college scholarships, more often planned to attend four-year colleges (71 percent versus 39 percent), showed better attitudes toward high school and their high-school teachers, and were more involved in high-school activities. The two groups did not differ in number of friends or quality of friendships, or in involvement in community activities. Concluded Tremaine (1979):

> The study provided no data to support the contention that gifted programs breed elitism, snobbery, indifference, conceit, or any other negative quality. On the contrary, . . . the study leads to the conclusion that gifted programs do indeed make a difference—and that difference makes program development vitally worthwhile.

As another line of evidence, more logical and intuitive than scientific, Gowan (1978) pointed out that virtually every outstanding professional athlete received special attention, equipment, training, and so on, as a youth. It appears to follow that the special cultivation of talent in other areas also should produce highly capable adult professionals in the arts, sciences, and business.

SUMMARY

Public awareness of gifted education is increasing dramatically. Nonetheless, many gifted students remain ignored, bored, or forced to satisfy their needs outside of school.

Some parents and educators argue that gifted programs are elitist and undemocratic, and that gifted students are not the ones in need of help. The counterargument is that gifted students also deserve a "special education" commensurate with their special needs.

Society also benefits: Tomorrow's leaders are in today's schools.

Historically, Sir Francis Galton is credited with the first significant research and writing on intelligence. He thought intelligence was related to keen senses, and so his "intelligence tests" evaluated visual and auditory acuity, reaction time, and other sensory skills. Influenced by cousin Charles Darwin, Galton concluded that intelligence was a product of natural selection and heredity. His book *Hereditary Genius* argues that genius runs in families. Galton conducted the first "twin studies" aimed at untangling genetic versus environmental components of intelligence.

Alfred Binet, invited by French officials to create a test to identify dull children, created the original prototype of the famous Stanford-Binet Intelligence Scale. He created the concept of mental age and the notion that a given child may be intellectually behind or ahead of his or her chronological age.

Lewis Terman Americanized the Binet tests, creating the Stanford-Binet scales. In the 1920s he used the Stanford-Binet to identify 1,500 gifted children—who have been tracked and studied ever since.

Over several decades prior to 1939 Leta Hollingworth worked on behalf of gifted students in the New York City area and wrote two books on gifted children and their needs.

The launching of Sputnik in 1957 triggered an American effort to improve education, particularly in the sciences and for gifted students. Unfortunately the enthusiasm disappeared after about five years.

In the mid-1970s a new and exciting gifted-education movement began, one which includes federal and state legislation, special funds, new programs, and very high interest and commitment by teachers, administrators, and educational researchers.

Defining "gifts and talents" is more complicated than simply pointing to high academic ability, artistic skill, or scientific talent. What about the often ignored gifts of underachievers? Minority and economically disadvantaged students? Learning disabled and physically handicapped students?

Definitions of giftedness are important because they determine the identification and selection of students for special programs. The U.S.O.E.,

Renzulli, and Taylor definitions are widely known and accepted, even though they are inconsistent with each other.

The 1972 U.S.O.E. definition is cited in many state plans and many individual written program plans. A multitalent definition, it includes six categories: (1) general intellectual ability, (2) specific academic aptitude, (3) creative or productive thinking, (4) leadership ability, (5) visual and performing arts, and (6) psychomotor ability. The U.S.O.E. statement cites the need for differentiated educational programs and cites the two basic goals of gifted education: to help individuals realize their potential and to provide society with high-level talent. The 1978 revision excludes psychomotor skills.

Renzulli and his colleagues noted that the U.S.O.E. definition ignores motivation, the six categories are not parallel, and educators often misuse the categories anyway. His own three-ring definition, based on traits of persons who truly contribute to society, includes above-average ability, high creativity, and high task commitment (motivation). The three traits require different types of assessment. This model excludes underachievers.

Taylor's multiple-talent totem pole model raises the possibility that virtually all students possess special gifts and talents, if we look carefully enough. Taylor's model has been used as a curriculum guide.

Finally, research studies have shown that participation of gifted students in special programs increases GPAs, SATs, academic honors, scholarships, and school attitudes. Gowan points out that all gifted, successful professional athletes received special early training, and that the same should apply to those in the arts, sciences, and business.

2

CHARACTERISTICS OF GIFTED STUDENTS

Understanding characteristics of gifted children and adolescents is important. If you are a teacher, familiarity with these traits, first of all, will help you recognize and identify gifted students in your classes. You will also become better able to understand them and their strengths, weaknesses, problems, and sometimes peculiar behavior. If you are a parent, a review of characteristics of gifted children should help you judge the degree of your child's giftedness, which is a natural and necessary first step before tackling the next problem of "What do I do now?" You also may discover, to your relief, that your unusual child is not the sole member of a new species.

It is true, of course, that children differ from each other not only in size, shape, and color, but in cognitive and language abilities, interests, learning styles, motivation and energy levels, personalities, mental health and self-concepts, habits and behavior, background, and any other characteristic that one cares to look at. Especially, they differ in their patterns of educational needs. Also, there are many types of gifts and talents; the traits of a particular talented artist may (or may not) be quite unlike the characteristics of a particular computer wizard. Payne, Halpin, Ellet, and Dale (1975), for example, found that both academically and artistically talented high-school students showed assertive and experimental traits, but the artists were more sensitive, self-sufficient, and casual. Walberg and others (1981), in reviewing childhood traits of over 200 historically eminent persons, identified some common traits (high intelligence, versatility, superior communication skills), but also found traits that were considerably different for different groups. For example, statesmen (Ben Franklin) were persuasive, popular, and economic minded; religious leaders (Martin Luther) were scholarly, ethical, and sensitive; generals (Simon Bolívar) were tall and motivated by external incentives; historians and essayists (Jean Jacques Rousseau) were persevering, intelligent, and had an absent father; poets and dramatists (Johann Wolfgang von Goethe) were neurotic, only children, and fatherless; and scientists (Isaac Newton) were single-minded, opportunistic, and had an absent mother.

The descriptions that follow, then, are "usual" characteristics, traits that have appeared and reappeared in studies of gifted children and adults. Therefore, they all will not and cannot apply to each and every gifted and talented child. Sometimes, one trait may be inconsistent with another in the lists, yet both are accurate. For example, while *confident* and *energetic* are frequent traits of the intellectually and creatively gifted, *withdrawn* and *alone* are also common among obviously different gifted children.

Overview

This chapter will begin with a look at the classic Terman research mentioned in Chapter 1, then turn to more recent studies and observations of the intellectual and affective traits of highly intelligent children. Following this, some recurrent personality and biographical characteristics of creative students of all ages will be reviewed. Finally, the chapter will examine two recent studies of the origins—environmental and hereditary—of precocity and extreme high talent. (Specific characteristics of gifted and talented minority, female, economically disadvantaged, underachieving, and handicapped students will be studied in later chapters.)

THE TERMAN STUDIES

Any discussion of characteristics of gifted children must begin with Terman's high-IQ gifted children (see, for example, Passow, 1981; Terman, 1981), labeled in gifted education circles as "Termites."

One of the most frequently cited findings of the Terman studies was the fact that these students were better adjusted and healthier—both physically and mentally—than average students. The myth of brilliant students being undersized, weak, unpopular, unattractive, disturbed, neurotic, one-sided in their abilities, or emotionally unstable was simply not true as a predominant trend. They not only were well adjusted in childhood, but in adulthood reported greater personal adjustment, emotional stability, and self-esteem, and were professionally successful and personally content (Karamessinis, 1980; Solano, 1976a, 1976b). Statistically, they showed a below-average incidence of suicide and mental illness.

Terman and Oden (1951) summarized the main characteristics of their gifted children as follows:

> The average member of our group is a slightly better physical specimen than the average child . . .
>
> For the fields of subject matter covered in our tests, the superiority of gifted over unselected children was greater in reading, language usage, arithmetical reasoning, science, literature and the arts. In arithmetical computation, spelling and factual information about history and civics, the superiority of the gifted was somewhat less marked . . .
>
> The interests of gifted children are many-sided and spontaneous, they learn to read easily and read more and better books than the average child. At the same time, they make numerous collections, cultivate many kinds of hobbies, and acquire far more knowledge of plays and games than the average child . . .
>
> As compared with unselected children, they are less inclined to boast or to overstate their knowledge; they are more trustworthy when under temptation to cheat; their character preferences and social attitudes are more wholesome, and they score higher in a test of emotional stability . . .
>
> The deviation of the gifted subjects from the generality is in the upward direction for nearly all traits. There is no law of compensation whereby the intellectual superiority of the gifted tends to be offset by inferiorities along nonintellectual lines.

The description of Terman's Termites presents them as almost perfect children. However, these were not your run-of-the-mill gifted children. While they were uniformly brilliant (IQ=140+ in almost all cases), there was a serious bias in their selection. The 1,500 children were selected from a larger group of children who were nominated by their teachers as "gifted," and we know that teachers are biased toward identifying as "gifted" those children who conform and who are well behaved, pleasant, attractive, and high achieving. Perhaps it should not be too surprising that Terman could describe their physical and mental health, along with their intellectual capability, in such glowing language. The conclusions would not necessarily apply, for example, to G/T students who are artistically or creatively gifted or who underachieve.

It is of amusing historic interest that two Nobel Prize winners, Luis Alvarez and William B. Shockley, were excluded from the Terman study because their IQ scores were below 140 (Hermann and Stanley, 1983).

INSET 2.1 STUDIES OF EMINENT PERSONALITIES: COX AND THE GOERTZELS

Catherine Cox (1926), a colleague of Lewis Terman, took an approach to understanding traits of gifted persons that was quite the reverse of her famous cohort. Instead of beginning with bright children and tracking their accomplishments, she began by identifying 282 eminent persons, and then examined their biographical and personal records in order to reach conclusions regarding their intellectual and personal traits. The findings related to intelligence are most enlightening. Cox estimated their IQ scores to range from 100 to 200, with an average of 159. However, many estimated IQs were rather modest: Thirteen IQ scores fell between 100 and 110, 30 between 110 and 120, and 30 between 120 and 130. Extraordinary innate brilliance helped, but was not essential. Cox concluded that individuals who achieve eminence are likely to (1) be born of intelligent parents and raised in advantaged circumstances, (2) show precocious childhood traits and behavior that indicate unusually superior intelligence, and significantly (3) be " . . . characterized not only by high intellectual traits, but also by persistence of motive and effort, confidence in their abilities, and great strength and force of character."

In two studies, the Goertzels (Goertzel and Goertzel, 1962; Goertzel, Goertzel, and Goertzel, 1978) reviewed the family background and personal lives of some 700 adults who had achieved eminence via highly creative achievements that made a strong impact on society. A composite picture, based on recurrent traits and behavior, runs as follows:

> The eminent man or woman is likely to be the firstborn or only child in a middle-class family. . . . In these families there are rows of books on shelves, and parental expectations are high for all children . . .
>
> Children who become eminent love learning but dislike school and school teachers who try to confine them to a curriculum not designed for individual needs. They respond well to being tutored or to being left alone, and they like to go to special schools such as those that train actors, dancers, musicians, and artists . . .
>
> . . . they are more self-directed, less motivated in wanting to please than are their peers or siblings. They need and manage to find periods of isolation when they have freedom to think, to read, to write, to experiment, to paint, to play an instrument, or to explore the countryside. Sometimes this freedom can be obtained only by real or feigned illnesses; a sympathetic parent may respond to the child's need to have long free periods of concentrated effort . . .
>
> They treasure their uniqueness and find it hard to be conforming, in dress, behavior, and other ways . . . (Goertzel, Goertzel, and Goertzel, 1978, pp. 336-38).

INTELLECTUAL TRAITS OF GIFTED CHILDREN

Precocious Language and Thought

The overriding trait—indeed, *the* definition—of very bright students is that they are developmentally advanced in language and thought. Their intelligence test performance matches that of older children. Their mental development, or *mental age* as Binet named it, simply outstrips both their chronological age and their physical development. For most of us, it is something of a shock to first meet and talk with a prepubescent child with the intellect of someone in their mid-teens.

The early development of verbal ability includes many specifics. The intellectually gifted child may learn to speak early, and the fluency improves rapidly. The high significance of early, rapidly improving speech is that, as Piaget (Piaget and Inhelder, 1969) tells us, a child will verbalize only what he or she can deal with conceptually. Therefore, the accelerated improvement in speech reflects not only a quickly growing vocabulary and knowledge base, but a rapidly improving conceptual and abstract-thinking ability as well.

Early Reading, Advanced Comprehension

Some gifted preschoolers not only talk and conceptualize at an advanced level, they may learn to read at age 4 or even 3. Some children teach themselves, and at a runaway pace. They might demand that mother or father point to each word as the parent reads books to the child; or the child may persistently ask, for example in a grocery store, "What does that say?" Some children learn to read traffic or street signs. Other gifted preschoolers learn to read in a more traditional way, with mother, father, or nursery-school teacher teaching the child to recognize letters, relate letters to sounds, recognize and pronounce words, and associate words with meanings.

Whether they learn spontaneously or are taught by family members, what is most dramatic is the ease and swiftness with which they learn. One gifted child known to one of the authors learned her complete alphabet at age 3 as her mother pointed to and pronounced the letters on the book covers of a set of encyclopedias. A usual sequence is for bright children to learn first a few letters or sounds, then a few words—and before long they are nimbly poring over early readers. Not all gifted children learn to read early or quickly—for example, Albert Einstein did not learn until he was 8—but many do.

The advanced language ability of the intellectually gifted child includes a superior comprehension skill. It is a time-tested principle of learning that what is comprehended and integrated into one's cognitive structures is also well remembered (Ausubel, 1978). Therefore, the intellectually gifted child usually acquires a large working vocabulary and a large store of information about many topics. Especially, the child may grasp complex and abstract concepts and relationships that are normally learned at an older age.

Logical Thinking

Compared with the average child, the thinking processes of the gifted child are quick and logical, two traits that can disturb some impatient parents and teachers. Combined with a natural curiosity and an urge to learn, the precocious child can be forever asking questions, wanting to know, and wanting to know "Why?" The bear-trap logic may not accept an abrupt "Because!" or any other incomplete or illogical response: "If we don't have enough money for a movie, how can daddy buy a new boat? Wasn't the boat $6,000?" In light of their swift and logical thinking, it is no surprise that "questioning ability," "a good understanding of cause-and-effect relationships," "convergent problem solving," and "persistence" (Cox, 1926; Franks and Dolan, 1982; Passow, 1981; Walberg and others, 1981) are frequently cited as traits of gifted children.

Early Writing, Math, Music, Art

In addition to the early reading and advanced comprehension and logical abilities, the intellectually gifted child may also begin writing at a precocious age. This talent will result from some combination of teaching by parents, older siblings, or preschool teachers, added to the child's strong drive and mental readiness to imitate and learn. For many gifted children, advanced mathematical, musical, and artistic abilities also appear early, paralleling the verbal and conceptual skills.

The mathematically precocious child may be counting by fives and tens and adding and subtracting double-digit numbers by kindergarten. If you ask the child how he or she arrived at an answer, the child may explain with surprisingly good reasoning his or her own special way of deducing or calculating a mathematical solution. For example, one such second-grade child concluded that "There certainly must be numbers below zero because temperatures can go below zero."

Incidentally, it is not unusual for the child's slower-developing motor ability to stand in the way of some accomplishments. For example, while some young gifted children may be able to manipulate complex calculations and ideas in their heads, or even read at a fifth-grade level, they may not be able to write numbers or letters or illustrate their ideas because of immature eye-hand coordination. A girl who can read about amoebas and paramecia may be unable to fit the slides into the microscope; a boy who understands the workings of a ukelele or clarinet may be unable to manipulate the strings or keys.

Motivation, Persistence, Advanced Interests

One of the single most recurrent traits of productive gifted students and eminent adults is high *motivation* (Horwitz, 1974; Renzulli, 1978; Treffinger, 1981; Walberg and others, 1981), sometimes labeled *persistence* (Fliegler and Bish, 1959; Franks and Dolan, 1982). Renzulli, for example, concluded that the main reason for some of Terman's students becoming successful and some not was differences in their levels of motivation. Albert (1975) also stressed that a crucial trait of the geniuses he studied—eminent scientists, musicians, artists, and psychologists—was the compulsion to be productive, the ability to work hard. Even with gifted nursery-school to second-grade children, Burk (1980) found that persistence was related to both achievement and personal adjustment.

Galton (1869) himself, in his book *Hereditary Genius*, noted that natural ability included both " . . . qualities of intellect and disposition, which urge and qualify a man to perform acts that lead to reputation. I do not mean capacity without zeal, nor zeal without capacity, nor even a combination of both of them, without an adequate power of doing a great deal of very laborious work." It would seem that Galton's "zeal" and his "power of doing . . . laborious work" both reduce to motivation, and Franks and Dolan (1982) seemed to agree. However, Freehill and McDonald (1981) argued that Galton's "zeal" is " . . . a special quality or drive transcending mere persistence or dogged hard work."

The high motivation and urge to learn found in many gifted children, combined with their curiosity and their advanced comprehension and logical abilities, frequently lead to surprisingly advanced interests. The nature and complexity of topics and projects tackled by enthusiastic gifted children seems unlimited. One elementary-school project in Manitowish Waters, Wisconsin, was an environmental impact study that led the State Highway Department to move a section of a proposed freeway.

AFFECTIVE CHARACTERISTICS

Low Anxiety and Depression, Better Self-Concepts

Affective characteristics include those relating to personality, self-concepts, self-esteem, attitudes, values, social skills, and moral thinking. We already noted that, on average, Terman's students were generally better adjusted both personally and socially, and were emotionally stable, less neurotic, and even more trustworthy than his unselected children. Indeed, as a general rule gifted and talented students are better adjusted, have better self-concepts, and lead comparatively happier lives (Bartell, 1983; Gallagher, 1959; Karamessinis, 1980; Lehman and Erdwins, 1981; Lytle and Campbell, 1979; Schauer, 1976). As stated by Milgram and Milgram (1976a), "Intellectual giftedness is an asset in coping with life's challenges and is associated with . . . favorable social and personal adjustment." However, as with any other population, among gifted and talented students—and partly because of their gifts—some will have social problems and some will be anxious and depressed (Berndt, Kaiser, and Van Aalst, 1982; Gensley, 1977; Ziv, 1977). According to Kester (1975), high levels of social ineptitude are not uncommon. As one might easily deduce, anxiety or depression reduces the academic achievement of gifted students (Dean, 1975; Milgram and Milgram, 1976a; Tetenbaum and Houtz, 1978).

Of 120 symptoms of childhood depression, Kovacs (1980) listed the five most common as mood changes (for example, sadness, irritability), sleep disturbances, sudden changes in appetite (loss of appetite or binge eating, known as *bulimia*), feelings of low self-esteem or worthlessness, and withdrawal. Some other symptoms of depression of which the teacher and parent should be aware include headaches, stomachaches, restlessness, fatigue, withdrawal, paranoia, delusions, and generally despairing mood (Bartell, 1983).

Using the *Tennessee Self-Concept Scale,* Colangelo and Kelly (1983) compared 57 gifted adolescents in grades 7, 8, and 9 with 181 regular students and with 27 students with special learning problems. For the overall scale, gifted students scored significantly higher than regular students in having a positive self-concept; and regular students in turn scored significantly higher than students with learning problems. As in several other studies, however (for example, Ross and Paker, 1980), the gifted students scored significantly higher on the "academic self" subscale. On the "social self" subscale of that instrument, Colangelo and Kelly found no significant differences among the three groups; the average social-self score of gifted students was about the same as that of other students.

High Moral Thinking, Empathy, and Perspective Taking

With many gifted children and adolescents, their high levels of comprehension, wide interests, eagerness to learn, and logical thinking lead to a number of intertwined affective consequences related to moral thinking. First, as a general trend gifted students are more sensitive to values and moral issues and they intuitively understand why certain behavior is "good" and other behavior is "bad." Piaget and Inhelder (1969) explain that developmentally advanced children are less egocentric; that is, they are able to view a situation from another person's point of view. Therefore, gifted students are more likely to acknowledge the rights of others (Perrone, Karshner, and Male, 1979) and to be sensitive to the feelings and expectations of others. Bright students therefore are less likely to steal from peers or to be abusive, and they are more likely to be fair and to empathize and sympathize with the feelings and problems of others.

Second, gifted children and youth are likely to develop, refine, and internalize a system of values and a keen sense of fair play and justice at a relatively early age. This internalized value system leads to consistency in behavior and attitudes (Perrone, Karshner, and Male, 1979). Therefore, the child not only is more likely to be fair, empathetic, and honest, he or she will evaluate others according to the same standards.

The student is also likely to develop an interest in social issues, particularly those in which his or her sense of reason and justice seems to be violated. Teachers or parents may find themselves in serious discussions with gifted children, trying to explain why adults litter the highways with beer bottles, why black children were murdered in Atlanta, why politicians cut benefits and programs for the elderly and poor, why the world seems bent on nuclear self-destruction, and why parents voted against enlarging the crowded school building.

As a caution, despite their high mental ability and high capacity for moral thought, some will turn to delinquency and crime, where their talents are immediately recognized and rewarded (status, money) by an antisocial peer group (Parker, 1979).

Kohlberg's Stages of Moral Development

Kohlberg (1969, 1974) described six stages of moral development, which divide into three main levels. In the *preconventional* level, behavior is guided only by outcomes—earning rewards or favors or avoiding punishments. At the *conventional* level, behavior is guided by conformity to stereotypes and by obedience to unchangeable rules and authority. This level includes the "good boy/good girl" syndrome. At the highest, *postconventional* level, right action is determined by agreed-upon and modifiable rights and standards (for example, as stated in the Constitution) and by personal conscience and self-chosen ethics. These ethics are based on universal principles of justice, equality of human rights, respect for individual differences, dignity, and the Golden Rule.

The main point is that many—but certainly not all—intellectually advanced gifted children think and function at a higher stage of moral development than their peers. As with language development, moral development is tied to intellectual development (Diessner, 1983). In some cases a gifted child may also function at a higher level than his or her parents or some teachers. This difference can lead to conflicts when, for example, parents or teachers insist that "rules are rules" (conventional level) while the gifted child may feel the rule is absurd and should be changed or ignored (a healthy postconventional level).

Independence, Self-Confidence, Internal Control

An important set of personality characteristics of the gifted child relates to his or her typically high level of self-confidence and independence. Such an attitude is a natural outgrowth of years of favorable comparisons with less-able peers; of glowing feedback and evaluations from parents, teachers, peers, and siblings; and from the child's clear history of success in school.

The concept of high *internal control* describes the confident children or adolescents who feel responsible for their successes and failures and who feel in control of their destinies (Milgram and Milgram, 1976a; Weiner, 1980). The child with high internal control is likely to use errors and failures constructively; he or she learns from mistakes. Importantly, the internally controlled child usually attributes failure to lack of effort, not lack of ability, and so a failure is a momentary setback that motivates the student to "try harder next time." In contrast, the externally controlled child is more likely to attribute success or failure to luck, chance, easy or difficult tasks, generous or unfair teachers, lack of sleep, a sick cat, and so on. The "external" child is also less likely to try harder after failure—since he or she does not accept responsibility for the outcome in the first place.

The generally higher levels of internal control and personal responsibility often lead gifted students to set high goals for themselves. When these goals are not met, the natural outcome is disappointment, frustration, and feelings of incompetence, stupidity, or ineptness. Parents and teachers are frequently mystified by displays of frustration and self-criticism by students who are obviously extraordinarily capable and talented. The frustration occurs not because the students are comparing their own performances with those of others, but with their own high expectations and standards.

Superior Humor

Whether it is a cognitive or affective characteristic, the superior sense of humor of so many gifted children and adults may appear in art, music, or creative writing, as well as in social interaction. Although humor is generally a positive trait and should usually not be considered "out of place" in school, in some cases it may be thoughtless, offensive, and in need of corrective feedback (for example, "Hey maggotface, whatja' get in Mr. Stupid's class?").

Two final comments: First, do not forget that, as explained at the outset of this chapter, each child is unique in his or her abilities, interests, per-

INSET 2.2 CHARACTERISTICS OF EFFECTIVE THINKERS: KARL ALBRECHT

Albrecht (1983; see also Albrecht, 1980) described ten traits of adult "effective thinkers," which basically amount to ten characteristics of intelligent, well-adjusted, and productive people. In the present context, these may be valuable in three ways. First, they may be viewed as traits of gifted students, traits that may aid in their identification. Second, the characteristics may be interpreted as valuable intellectual and affective goals for any G/T program. Lastly, the ideas may aid the reader in becoming a more effective thinker.

1. *Mental flexibility,* including a tolerance for ambiguity.
2. *Openness to information,* which is related to flexibility.
3. *Capacity to systematize knowledge,* so that it is structured, logical, and sequential.
4. *Capacity for abstract thought,* the ability to conceptualize.
5. *Fluency,* the ability to produce new combinations and patterns of ideas.
6. *Sense of humor,* which is part of psychological adjustment and positive thinking.
7. *Positive thinking,* which includes "input selection" to reduce depressing affect. (Albrecht suggested, only half in jest, that we not watch the evening TV news.)
8. *Intellectual courage,* which translates as high persistence and motivation.
9. *Resistance to enculturation,* that is, not forfeiting one's own values in favor of those of society. [Said Albrecht, one should continually engage one's "crap detector" (Albrecht, 1980; Postman, 1976), a device that enables one to decide what can and what cannot be believed (for example, in advertising and politics) and what is important and what is not.]
10. *Emotional resilience,* the skill of being happy, which results from a conscious decision by well-adjusted adults. (For this reason, says Albrecht, smart people typically are happier than dumb people.)

sonality, and educational needs. Second, a good educational program will seek to understand those differences and provide the best possible program for all students—gifted and "regular" alike (Treffinger, 1981).

CHARACTERISTICS OF THE CREATIVELY GIFTED

The student who is intellectually gifted may or may not be creatively gifted as well. While the relationship between intelligence and creativity is a long-standing issue, a contemporary view to which the authors subscribe is the *threshold* concept (MacKinnon, 1978). According to this view, over the wide range of intellectual ability, from retardation to genius, there is generally a positive correlation. The brighter children and adults tend to do more creative work and score higher on creativity tests. However, above a threshold IQ of about 120, the relationship drops to virtually nothing. Therefore, among most gifted students, creativity and intelligence may be quite independent of each other; the student with the comparatively modest 120 Stanford-Binet IQ may—or may not—show considerably more imagination and creative talent than the top scholar in the school.

It is important to distinguish between creativity and intelligence, especially in relation to selecting students for the special services of a gifted and talented program. For example, when asked to nominate gifted students many teachers will quickly select the conforming, prompt, neat, and dutiful "teacher pleasers" rather than the less conforming student who is high in creativity. Also, in many classes (for example, math or science courses in the middle school) the special talents of the creatively gifted may not be required. In such circumstances the creative student will be much less visible and less likely to be nominated as "gifted," compared with the intellectually gifted student who quickly grasps the complex ideas and who usually raises his or her hand first.

Ultimately, the achievements and contributions to society of highly creative students may surpass those of the brighter, conforming gradegetters (Renzulli, 1978; Renzulli, Reis, and Smith, 1981).

Creative Behavior

The first characteristic of creatively talented students is creative behavior itself. Creative students may bubble over with unusual, playful, perhaps "wild" ideas. Some creative children may entertain other students with stories or humor. In the classroom, when ideas are asked for, they usually have them. Virtually by definition creative students will be involved in creative activities both in and out of the classroom. Indeed, creative students will always have a history of creative projects, hobbies, and activities. For example, they might have collections of red tennis shoes, spider webs, or pictures of the Three Stooges. They may have made highly original valentines, race cars, new kinds of cakes and cookies, doll clothes, rockets, gardens, computer art, and so on. Many of their past and present hobbies and collections would be considered unusual.

Curiosity, Wide Interests, Question Asking

An especially strong and recurrent trait is *curiosity*, which may appear as a high interest in new topics and areas. Creative students may enjoy exploring attics, basements, abandoned buildings, museums, hobby stores, and libraries. They may take things apart to see what makes them tick. In high school or college they may select a surprising variety of "interesting" courses, causing problems for themselves with graduation requirements. They also like to learn new skills. For example, they may teach themselves calligraphy, learn to play a dozen musical instruments, or take up photography, creative writing, magic, painting, ballet, macrame, drama, Egyptology, astronomy, computers, or any other art, handicraft, music, or science activity.

Curiosity also relates to asking questions, sensing problems, and detecting gaps in information (Torrance, 1979). Creative students are often expert question askers, sometimes probing areas beyond the teacher's ability to answer. The teacher of creative and gifted students should be ready to steer the curiosity to encyclopedias, history books, and other appropriate resources or people.

Creative Abilities

Torrance (1962, 1979, 1980, 1984), Treffinger (1981), Smith (1966), Davis (1975, 1983a), Davis and Rimm (1979, 1982; Rimm and Davis, 1980) and others have itemized abilities, personality characteristics, and biographical traits that are recurrent in studies of creative students of all ages. The creative abilities topic will be more thoroughly explored in Chapter 10. For now, a sample of important creative abilities includes *ideational fluency*, the ability to produce many ideas; *flexibility*, the ability to take different approaches to a problem; *originality*, the tendency to be different, unique; *elaboration*, the ability to develop and embellish ideas; *sensitivity to problems* (described above as related to curiosity), the ability to detect problems, be aware of missing information, and ask pertinent questions; *visualization*, the ability to mentally picture and manipulate ideas; *metaphorical thinking*, the ability to transfer ideas and problem solutions from one situation to another; *evaluation*, the ability to assess the appropriateness of a problem solution; and *resisting premature closure*, the important ability to consider many solutions and not settle too quickly for the first plausible idea.

As with other characteristics of giftedness discussed in this chapter, these types of creative abilities may help the teacher or parent recognize and understand creativeness in their children.

Personality Traits

We already have seen that creative children are curious, have wide interests, and enjoy creative hobbies and activities. Creative people—at least from adolescence onward, when the word "creative" becomes meaningful—are typically quite conscious of their creative tendencies. On a rating scale, creative people will rate themselves as "high" in creativity.

Creative children and adolescents, as with intellectually gifted students, are usually quite self-confident and independent, and they are more willing than the average to take a creative risk. Innovative persons will dare to differ, stand out, make waves, break with tradition, and bend a few rules; in short, to think for themselves. Such confidence and risk taking also exposes them to criticism, embarrassment, and failure. Interestingly, Treffinger (1983) contended that highly creative people may appear to be risk takers, but truly are not. He argued that they typically are well organized and their innovative plans and zany products are carefully thought out, with possible problems, implications, and contingency plans already taken into account. Therefore, their "risk taking" and their chances of failure are considerably smaller than they appear to outsiders.

An unusually high energy level, spontaneity, adventurousness, and "sensation-seeking" tendency are also common among the highly creative (Davis, 1975, 1983a; Davis, Peterson, and Farley, 1974). There is often a remarkable eagerness to try new and exciting activities—for example, to be hypnotized, learn to ski or fly a plane, climb a mountain, sky dive, or explore a new city or country. Farley (1981) claimed that given a high "sensation-seeking" tendency, a high socio-economic status (SES) student usually will find outlets in creative activities while a low SES student is likely to vent the energy in exciting delinquency. Further, the delinquent low SES student represents a lost natural resource, since the energy might well have been channeled into creative outlets.

As in the description of the intellectually gifted, the creatively gifted student usually has a keen sense of humor and a childlike playfulness. The creative person is often willing to turn a problem upside down or backward, play with fanciful possibilities, and even climb right into the problem itself (Gordon, 1961). Townsend, Torrance, and Wu (1981) found significant correlations between measures of creative ability and the ability to make up humorous captions for cartoons (*Making Up Captions* test). It has been said that the creative adult is essentially a perpetual child; the tragedy is that most of us grow up (Fabun, 1968).

More serious traits of idealism and reflectiveness are also common. More than the average, creative teenagers and adults ponder their role and goals in life and the significance of their existence. Their idealism and individuality may surface in antiestablishment cynicism or in dropping out of high school or college.

Another creative trait is the characteristic preference for complexity and attraction to the mysterious. For example, Barron (1969, 1978) found that creative individuals, similar to good artists, preferred drawings on the *Barron-Welsh Revised Art Scale* (Welsh and Barron, 1963) that were asymmetrical, complex, and imbalanced. There is also an interesting tendency for the creative person to be a strong believer in spirits, extrasensory perception, flying saucers, and other psychic and mystic happenings (Davis, Peterson, and Farley, 1974); they also seem more likely to report having psychic experiences or paranormal capabilities.

Artistic and aesthetic interests are also stronger than average. While the creative person may or may not be an accomplished actor, artist, or writer, a considerable interest in art, literature, music, and theatre is common.

The authors' own research suggests that the characteristic of impulsiveness versus reflectiveness (Kagan, 1965) shows an interesting developmental change among creative persons. Creative elementary school children tend to be more reflective in their thinking, to be more careful and meticulous in their work and decisions. However, somewhere in adolescence there is frequently a transformation to impulsiveness—the confident and adventurous spontaneity of the creative adult appears.

So far, the creative personality seems nearly ideal. However, some characteristics of our independent, confident, curious, energetic, witty, and nonconforming creative students can cause more than a few headaches in the traditional classroom. Smith (1966) noted that creative children can be uncooperative, demanding, egocentric, capricious, too assertive, discourteous, indifferent to conventions (such as promptness or addressing teachers by their last names), stubborn, emotional, withdrawn, and resistant to teacher domination. Such traits require understanding and some patience; and in many cases some correction and/or rechanneling.

Biographical Traits

There are also biographical patterns that recur among creative children and adults. As we have seen, creative students and adults have a background of creative accomplishments, such as unusual hobbies and collections, artistic activities, theatrical involvement, scientific projects, writing, and composing. Such biographical facts are not highly surprising; however, they are very useful in identifying creative students.

Other biographical trends are more unexpected. Schaefer (1970), for example, found that creative high school students were more likely to have friends younger or older than themselves rather than the same age, and they were less interested in sports. The creative students also had histories of living in more than one state and may have traveled outside the United States. The creative students more often reported having an imaginary childhood playmate, a background trait that appears to be remarkably accurate in identifying creative children or adults. Girls who were good creative writers were more likely to own a cat.

THE ORIGINS OF HIGH TALENT AND EXTREME PRECOCITY

Heredity and environment, working together in some favorable combination, are obvious explanations for the origin of high talent. But this kind of glib answer, though basically accurate, tells us little. Recently, however, two scholars have sketched in some detail on just how "heredity" and "environment," especially the latter, guide the development of extremely high levels of gifts and talents.

Parental Support and Intense Individualized Instruction: Bloom

Benjamin Bloom (1981; Bloom and Sosniak, 1981) examined the home environment and the early training of exceptional, accomplished pianists, swimmers, and mathematicians, whose talents roughly represented artistic, motoric, and cognitive skill areas. Bloom discovered that the home environments and the "gifted" persons' parents were almost entirely responsible for nurturing the children's early interests and developing their skills to extraordinary levels.

Almost always, one or both parents had a strong interest in the particular talent and were themselves above average in the skill. In every case the parents strongly supported the children, encouraging and rewarding their interests, talents, and efforts. Importantly, the talented parent or parents served as role models, exemplifying the personality and life-style of the pianist, swimmer, or mathematician. In essence, the children could not resist exploring and participating in the particular talent area; it was expected and accepted as proper.

Initially, parents provided the necessary training and supervision of practice. However, at some point each child switched to a professional instructor and the partnership with parents became weaker. In many cases the degree of parent support was so strong that the family would uproot and move to another location to be nearer an outstanding teacher or better facilities.

Throughout the early years, all instruction was individualized and focused specifically on developing talent in the specialized area. Normally, the child or adolescent would spend four or five years with each teacher before moving to a more advanced instructor. Often, the single outstanding student would be the central concern of the devoted instructor. During this time the student's dedication to the talent area would grow very strong—which explains his or her willingness to spend approximately fifteen hours per week in lessons and practice. Importantly, these students who eventually achieved extremely high levels of proficiency learned to handle failures constructively. That is, failures were learning experiences used to pinpoint problems to be solved and new skills to be mastered. In contrast, according to Bloom, among "talent dropouts," failures led to feelings of inadequacy and quitting.

In the middle and later years there were many public performances (at least for the swimmers and pianists) that rewarded the learner's dedication. By this time the person's habits and motivations were well established and parental influence was diminished even more than when the child first transferred to an outside teacher.

Bloom (1981) contrasted the development of talent with traditional educational philosophy and methods. The four-point comparison is instructive. First, in the early years of home instruction, talent development is informal, exploratory, and similar to play; the school setting is traditionally serious, formal, and on a set schedule. Second (and most important), with talent development, instruction is totally individualized, with praise and rewards based completely on individualized objectives and standards. School learning, of course, is group oriented, usually with a minimum of individualized attention, and rewards, at least to some extent, are based on group achievements. Third, the purpose of school is to provide all students with a broad basic education. Students are expected to do well in all areas and overly strong specialization is not encouraged. Indeed, concentration in an area that a student enjoys and is proficient at may be actively discouraged in favor of a balanced educational program. In talent development, the students and their teachers are fully mobilized toward moving the learner to higher and higher levels of accomplishment in just one specialized area. Fourth, for many students (and not just a few parents), school learning is seen as devoid of meaning, something "to be suffered through." On the other hand, the purposes and meaning in talent development are quite clear, which inspires the necessary dedication and hard work.

Strykowski and Walberg (1983; see also Walberg and others, 1981) studied the psychological traits and childhood environments of eminent male writers, based on their biographies. Supporting Bloom's conclusions, they also found the home environment and parental support to be critical to the development of interest in writing. Interestingly, the support and clear positive expectations of the father seemed particularly important.

Precocity, Available Knowledge, and Coincidence: Feldman

While Bloom did not estimate the comparative significance of inborn versus acquired talent, his emphasis was clearly on the environmental and learning side of the scale. David Feldman (1979) credited both. Feldman reviewed the precocious talents and early achievements of such rare individuals as chess player Bobby Fisher, who became a grand master by age 15, and Wolfgang Amadeus Mozart, who composed mature works by age 10. In his research at Tufts University, Feldman has also been studying a few extremely gifted people—male chess players and music composers—all of whom were performing " . . . in his chosen field at the level of an adult professional before the age of 10." Basically, Feldman attributed such youthful accomplishments to an " . . . astonishing . . . concidence . . . of human and cultural factors interacting across a few moments of evolutionary time."

The human component in this coincidence is the rare precocious prodigies themselves, whom Feldman described as remarkably "preorganized," highly intelligent, and quite developmentally advanced. Said Feldman, it is not the level of achievement of these prodigies that is so remarkable, but the speed with which they achieved these levels. Importantly, however, such prodigious talent cannot develop by itself. The second component of the coincidence is the existence of a highly evolved field of knowledge that can be taught to the precocious child.

Bobby Fisher taught himself to play a fair game of chess by age 6, and from that time on he read hundreds of chess books. As with Bloom's talented people, he received intense formal instruction. Without the existence of this body of knowledge and its communication to Fisher, his talents would have been lost or, at best, rechanneled into another outlet. Mozart too, while clearly a gifted and precocious child, grew up in a home where music was composed, played, and continuously discussed and valued. Mozart thus received considerable personal instruction, based on an existing body of knowledge, plus extensive exposure to the values and lifestyles of musicians.

Based on the observations of his precocious chess players and musicians, Feldman itemized a few "striking" conclusions regarding the prodigies and their teachers. Note that most of the items duplicate Bloom's conclusions.

1. The children received superb instruction.
2. To some degree, the curriculum included a history of the field. For example, the chess masters reviewed world championship games of 150 years ago. All formal music instruction, of course, includes ever-increasing exposure to classical composers.
3. The children themselves showed a passionate commitment to their field and derived a strong sense of joy from their achievements.
4. The teachers were as dedicated to the field as their students.

SUMMARY

Identifying characteristics of gifted students is important because it helps teachers and parents recognize and understand gifted children. Even though all children differ in physical, intellectual, affective, and behavioral traits, some characteristics of gifted and talented students recur frequently in the research literature.

Terman's gifted children (Stanford-Binet IQs of 140+) were better adjusted as children and adults. Compared with other children, they were better achievers and learned more easily, had more hobbies, read more books, were more trustworthy, healthier, and even better "physical specimens." However, their selection was biased due to their initial nomination by teachers prior to testing.

Bright children are developmentally advanced in language and thought. Early, rapidly improving speech reflects a growing conceptual ability and knowledge base. Bright children may learn to read early, sometimes teaching themselves. Comprehension, retention, vocabulary, stored information, and logical abilities are also usually superior.

High curiosity, an urge to learn, and persistence will lead to inquisitiveness. Bright children also better understand cause-and-effect relationships.

The intellectually gifted child may learn to write early; mathematical, musical, or artistic gifts also may appear early. Interests may be relatively advanced.

Affective characteristics are those relating to personality, values, social skills, and moral thinking. Intellectually gifted students intuitively comprehend values and moral issues and are less egocentric, thus able to empathize with the rights, feelings, and problems of others. They are usually more honest and trustworthy, although some may be delinquent. Values and a sense of fairness and justice develop early, leading to consistency in attitudes and behavior and an interest in social issues.

Gifted children may reach Kohlberg's postconventional level of moral thinking, leading to conflicts with the conventional-level thinking of parents or teachers.

Feedback from others and a history of success leads to high self-confidence, independence, and internal control. Gifted students thus may set high goals, which sometimes produces paradoxical feelings of ineptness and incompetence.

Superior humor may sometimes be offensive.

Creativity and intelligence are different traits. Teachers often select conforming "teacher pleasers" for gifted programs, even though creative students may ultimately make greater contributions to society. Creative students often may be less visible.

Creative students bubble over with original ideas and engage in creative activities, including unusual hobbies and collections. They have wide interests and high curiosity, and enjoy learning new skills.

A sample of creative abilities includes ideational fluency, flexibility, originality, elaboration, sensitivity to problems, visualization, metaphorical thinking, evaluation, and resisting premature closure.

The creative personality includes high self-confidence, independence, risk taking, high energy, adventurousness, creativity consciousness, playfulness and humor, idealism, attraction to the complex and mysterious, and artistic and aesthetic interests. Treffinger argues that risk taking by creative persons is actually lower than it appears, due to good planning.

Creative elementary school children tend to be reflective; creative adults lean toward impulsiveness.

Some negative traits of creative children are stubbornness, uncooperativeness, egocentrism, discourteousness, indifference to conventions, and resistance to teacher domination.

A background of creative activities is an unsurprising biographical characteristic. Less expected ones include having younger or older friends, having an imaginary playmate, and much traveling.

Studying pianists, swimmers, and mathematicians, Bloom concluded that home and parental influences were critical to high levels of talent development. Parents supported the child and modeled the appropriate personality, values, and life-style. All instruction was individualized. Student (and teacher) motivation and dedication ran high. Rather than quitting, students benefited from failures. Compared with traditional schooling, talent development is informal, individualized, specialized, and more meaningful (Bloom).

Feldman reviewed the training and personal lives of such prodigies as Bobby Fisher and Mozart, along with a few contemporary young male musicians and chess players. He stressed the coincidence of human factors (the precocious child) and cultural factors (availability of communicable knowledge). Feldman noted that the curriculum included the history of the field; in agreement with Bloom, instruction was excellent, and both students and their teachers were highly dedicated.

3

PROGRAM PLANNING

Whether you are a teacher (future or present), administrator, parent of a gifted child, or someone else interested in the education of the gifted and talented, a familiarity with (1) components of G/T programs and (2) the attitudes of school board members and teachers is essential to understanding gifted education and planning successful programs.

TREFFINGER'S INDIVIDUALIZED PROGRAMMING PLANNING MODEL

Treffinger (1981) itemized the main global components of programming for the gifted in his *Individualized Programming Planning Model (IPPM)*. Planners of any program will attend to these six components—in either a knowledgeable and systematic way or else a haphazard, hit-or-miss fashion.

COMPONENT	KEY QUESTION(S)
1. Definition	What do we mean by giftedness?
2. Characteristics	What characteristics are associated with our definition?
3. Screening and Identification	How do we document that students display these characteristics?

COMPONENT *(continued)*	KEY QUESTION(S) *(continued)*
4. Instructional Planning	What is our plan for responding to the students' needs?
5. Implementation of Services	How will we carry out our Instructional Plan?
6. Evaluation and Modifications	How will we determine our success or the need for changes in our plans?

These topics comprise a substantial portion of this book and do not need to be outlined in detail at this point. Also, one component omitted in Treffinger's model of program planning is preparing a written statement of philosophy and goals. That is, a very first preliminary step in program planning includes (1) stating one's position on gifted education in general, (2) itemizing one's reasons for creating or supporting a given program, and (3) outlining the general and sometimes specific goals of the particular program.

WHO, WHAT, WHERE, WHEN, WHY QUESTIONS

As an embellishment on Treffinger's IPPM components (plus philosophy and goals), one can view program planning as a series of questions: Who? What? Where? When? and Why?

Who will the program be for? Which grades? Which students? How will "gifted" and "talented" be defined? How will the students be identified? Who will direct and coordinate the program?

What will we do? What sorts of grouping, acceleration, and enrichment opportunities should we provide? Which will produce the best results? Which will be the most cost-effective? What are our goals and objectives?

Where will we do all of this? In the regular classrooms? Special classes? A district resource room? A special school? A "school-within-a-school"? In the community?

When can the training take place? When the students finish regular assignments? On Wednesday afternoon? All day every day? Saturdays? Summers? After school?

When can the plan begin? Can we formulate timelines for completing the planning? For beginning the identification procedures? For initiating the instructional program?

Why are we doing this? Can we prepare a defensible statement of philosophy on gifted and talented? Rationale for our general and specific goals and objectives?

Overview

In this chapter we will itemize fifteen problem areas in program planning that relate to Treffinger's six components (plus philosophy and goals) or the above "who, what, where, when, and why" questions. These fifteen problem areas are not sequential in the one-at-a-time sense. Many will be dealt with simultaneously in planning a G/T program. In the last sections of the chapter, program planning and development will be viewed from the perspectives of members of the local school board and of other teachers. It may be enlightening to explore how gifted education program plans are seen from their particular viewpoints.

PROGRAM PLANNING: FIFTEEN AREAS

Some of the following problem and decision areas are major ones, dealing, for example, with whether or not there will be a program at all and, if so, the directions the program will take and the students who will be served. Other problem areas are lesser managerial or administrative matters necessary for smooth program operation. As an overview, the problem areas are listed in Table 3.1.

1. Needs Assessment

A *needs assessment* aims at determining the discrepancy between the current status of gifted education in the school or district and the desired status. The main question: Is there a need for a gifted program? The pres-

TABLE 3.1 Overview of Fifteen Areas in Program Planning

1. Needs Assessment
2. Preliminary Personal and Staff Education
3. Philosophy, Rationale, Goals, Objectives, and a Written Program Plan
4. Types of Gifts and Talents to be Provided for and Estimated Enrollment
5. Identification Methods and Specific Criteria
6. Specific Provisions for Identifying Female, Underachieving, Handicapped, Culturally Different, and Economically Disadvantaged Gifted Students
7. Staff Responsibilities and Assignments
8. Arranging Support Services
9. Acceleration, and Enrichment Plans
10. Organizational Administrative and Design
11. Transportation Needs
12. Community Resources: Professionals and Organizations
13. In-Service Workshops, Training, and Visits
14. Budgetary Needs and Allocations
15. Program Evaluation

ent discussion will also touch on (1) the "selling job" typically needed to persuade district administrators, members of the school board, and the other members of the school staff that a G/T program is needed and justifiable, and (2) the creation of a steering committee to start planning.

There are three excellent sources of information regarding school and district needs for a G/T program: parents of gifted and talented students, gifted students themselves, and teachers and administrators who have become "gifted conscious." First, many parents of gifted students are frustrated by and vocal about the lack of specific services for their children. The authors regularly receive phone calls and letters from exasperated parents who register these types of complaints: "My third-grade daughter has a Stanford-Binet IQ of 145, but the teacher says she can't help because the superintendent is opposed to special programs for the 'haves,' and current rules do not even permit skipping a grade." "My son obviously is gifted and does wonderful and creative things at home, but in school he has become bored and lazy, and I am afraid his talent and enthusiasm are going to waste."

In one recent survey of major needs for gifted children (Weiss and Gallagher, 1983), the need most strongly endorsed by parents of gifted children was for more programs. The second-place need was for public support. Incidentally, the impetus for most G/T programs has begun with vocal parents and parent groups (Erlich, 1982; Mitchell, 1981; Weiss and Gallagher, 1983).

Second, many upper elementary and older gifted students can explain their strong special interests. Their curiosity and high energy levels also may be visible. Would they like to learn to use a computer? Would they like a special Saturday science or drama class? Would they be able to handle math or social studies at higher grade levels? Would they like to spend time with a professional artist, executive, or medical researcher? Would they be interested in a three-week summer education program at State University? You bet they would.

Third, another confirmation of the need for G/T programming may come from teachers and administrators who attend conferences or take courses that address the needs and problems of gifted children. With their newly found awareness, they may take an enthusiastic leadership role in helping document district needs and initiating gifted programs.

The need for a G/T program may be documented formally or informally, briefly or extensively depending on the type and source of the documented evidence and the size and formality of the school district. For example, in a small school district, parents of gifted children may meet together to discuss their ideas and to petition the administration or school board. In some circumstances, such action alone may be sufficient to initiate gifted programming. However, it is usually not that easy. Even in a small district the petitions will need to be followed up by meetings with and phone calls to administrators and school board members. Such meetings and phone calls will be most effective if they involve three *p*'s—positiveness, perseverance, and patience. Sometimes those three may be difficult as parents watch their children's educational needs continue to be unmet. However, the fourth *p*—pushiness—will only antagonize.

If a school board or district administration prefers a more formal and objective documentation of needs, needs-assessment questionnaires may be distributed to parents, teachers, and/or students to quantify the extent of the community desire for gifted programs. Such a needs-assessment questionnaire should include two main components: (1) an indication of the perceptions of what needs to be provided in the community and (2) opinions regarding the extent to which current school programs are meeting these needs. Such a questionnaire can identify community perceptions of the need for differentiated educational services, preferred directions for the services, and the extent of community support. An example of a needs-assessment questionnaire appears in Table 3.2.

Gifted children and parents of gifted children are minorities in the community, so one cannot expect landslide majority support for such programs. Therefore, the criteria for deciding that programs are needed should only be "sufficient" support, not necessarily strong majority support.

After a need for special services is confirmed (formally or informally), a committee of teachers, administrators, and parents can meet to discuss possible directions for gifted programs. The fifteen problem areas may provide a few topics for discussion. Eventually, a formal steering committee will be organized, usually appointed (on request) by a district administrator or school principal, to make concrete plans with a definite timetable. In the elementary school, the steering committee might be composed of a district coordinator; teachers from the lower, middle, and upper grades; administrators at the school and district levels; one or two school board members; the school librarian and school psychologist or counselor; parents; and some gifted and talented students (Robinson, Davis, Fiedler, and Helman, 1982). It may also be helpful to have some gifted high-school students represented; they may be able to provide important insights into the kinds of challenges which, in their experience, have been effective, ineffective, or absent.

2. Preliminary Personal and Staff Education

The goal of building a gifted education program cannot wait for several teachers and some parents and administrators to take one or two college courses in gifted education. Teachers must educate themselves and each other in the essential basics—preferably before they all make some uninformed assumptions and mistakes.

TABLE 3.2 Needs-Assessment Questionnaire

Please rate the statements below in two ways. The first rating relates to the strength of a particular program as you see it in the school. The second rating refers to the way in which you think the program should be. Program need will be determined by subtracting Rating 1 from Rating 2. Programs that are presently weak but are determined to be important preferences will be set as first priorities.

Rate 1 if you STRONGLY DISAGREE with the statement.
Rate 2 if you DISAGREE SOMEWHAT with the statement.
Rate 3 if you are UNDECIDED.
Rate 4 if you AGREE SOMEWHAT with the statement.
Rate 5 if you STRONGLY AGREE with the statement.

		NOW	FUTURE
1.	In general, the needs of gifted children in the school district are being met.	1 2 3 4 5	1 2 3 4 5
2.	The attitude of most teachers toward the gifted child is positive and helpful.	1 2 3 4 5	1 2 3 4 5
3.	The program provides individualization of curriculum for gifted children.	1 2 3 4 5	1 2 3 4 5
4.	Special enrichment opportunities are provided for gifted children.	1 2 3 4 5	1 2 3 4 5
5.	Classes that teach creative and critical thinking are available.	1 2 3 4 5	1 2 3 4 5
6.	The school has appropriate guidelines for determining early entrance to kindergarten.	1 2 3 4 5	1 2 3 4 5
7.	The school has appropriate guidelines for determining subject or grade skipping	1 2 3 4 5	1 2 3 4 5
8.	The school provides for the needs of the underachieving gifted child.	1 2 3 4 5	1 2 3 4 5
9.	The special social-emotional needs of gifted children are being addressed.	1 2 3 4 5	1 2 3 4 5
10.	The special needs of the highly creative child are being met.	1 2 3 4 5	1 2 3 4 5
11.	The school provides for the needs of gifted and talented girls.	1 2 3 4 5	1 2 3 4 5
12.	The school provides for the needs of gifted and talented minority children.	1 2 3 4 5	1 2 3 4 5
13.	The school includes parents in the planning and guiding of gifted and talented children.	1 2 3 4 5	1 2 3 4 5
14.	Teacher-education opportunities in the area of gifted and talented are provided for the teaching staff.	1 2 3 4 5	1 2 3 4 5
15.	The administration supports education of the gifted and talented.	1 2 3 4 5	1 2 3 4 5

Part of a preliminary education will include becoming acquainted with the present status of gifted education in your school, district, city, and even state. One might ask such questions as:

1. What is being done at the present time?
2. Do other schools in the area have programs? What exactly are they doing?
3. What do school board members and the district superintendent think about special programs for the gifted?
4. Do existing district policies allow students to enter kindergarten early? Skip a grade? What screening procedures are in effect? What are the criteria?
5. Can high-school students take college courses in person or by correspondence?
6. Is there a written district policy? A state plan? A district or state gifted-and-talented coordinator who is available?
7. Are other teachers interested and supportive? Are they just being agreeable, or are some willing to assume responsibility for the work?
8. Are parents or parent groups becoming restless about their ignored children?
9. Importantly, what kinds of G/T services are needed?

Some of these questions can be answered with a few phone calls. Others will require lengthier exploration and thought.

People seriously interested in gifted education must acquaint themselves with any written district policies or position statements. They should read any state plan and learn about approved or pending state legislation on behalf of the gifted. Any *state legislation* will at the very least (1) define gifted and talented, (2) endorse the concept of differentiated educational experiences, and usually (3) allocate funds for developing and maintaining programs. (Eventually, one can ask the State G/T Director how to apply for the funds.) A *state plan,* which is formally accepted by the superintendent of the state board of education rather than the state legislature, will also define gifted and talented and endorse providing G/T services and programs. The state plan may further itemize specific objectives related to program development, and will usually itemize training services and resources that may be used to meet those objectives.

Many state and local educational organizations will sponsor one- or two-day conferences and workshops usually led by one or more experienced leaders in gifted education or related areas. For one- or two-hour workshops, chances are good that a nearby college or state education office can suggest speakers to address specific topics in gifted education.

National and state conferences are immensely informative, for example, those sponsored by the National Association for Gifted Children, the Council for Exceptional Children, the National/State Leadership Training Institute for Gifted/Talented, and by state parent groups and state educational associations. Speakers at national and state conferences will describe the workings of their programs, the pros and cons of their own identification, acceleration, and enrichment strategies, and how they coped with some of the same problems the reader will face. Several journals and magazines are also devoted to the education of gifted, talented, and creative stu-

---

INSET 3.1 BUILDING A GIFTED PROGRAM IS LIKE BUILDING A HOUSE

Pennsylvania elementary-school librarian Skip Sumpter and tri-county elementary coordinator George Schauer (1979) drew an instructive analogy between building a house and building a program for gifted-and-talented students. Their blueprint ran about as follows:

Just as a new house grows from a need for more space, a new G/T program grows from a need for more options for G/T students.

While the home builder must select a site, the program planner must decide where the program is to be conducted. In one building? In several? In none?

Both a new home and a G/T program will require attention to financing and funding. Grants from local industries and organizations (such as the Kiwanis Club) were recommended.

Complying with building codes suggests investigating legal obligations and implications of a gifted program.

Importantly, architects and other professionals will design a house. A G/T program that is built without consulting experts and authorities may be a shaky and amateur job; and the organized planning must precede construction.

A well-organized parent group forms a firm foundation.

The studding is seen as analogous to a competent staff of teachers, whose capabilities support the program.

Windows are critical, so that gifted students can see out of the school and the community can see in.

There must be a back door " . . . for creative students and underachievers to slip in without wiping their feet on the IQ-test doormat at the front."

Large, open, undefined living spaces suggest including plenty of flexibility in space, programming, and scheduling, adaptable to the needs of individual students.

An unfinished basement or attic, planned in advance for future expansion, suggests including expansion plans for the G/T program right from the outset.

Just as natural solar heating warms a house, a G/T program must provide a warm affective tone, a natural product of a good teacher.

Gifted students also should be placed in an "insulated" atmosphere conducive to learning and protected from low-level thinking or disruptive students.

It pays, conclude Sumpter and Schauer, to do the job right in the first place, not " . . . hack around with a half-completed job as many homeowners and school directors do."

When the home is completed, it is furnished with gifted students.

---

dents, especially the *Gifted Child Quarterly, G/C/T Magazine,* the *Roeper Review, Journal for the Education of the Gifted,* the *Journal of Creative Behavior,* and the *Creative Child and Adult Quarterly.*

A highly enlightening staff activity is visiting schools with successful programs. By speaking directly with involved teachers one will get an inside look at how plans are implemented and how problems are dealt with. One will also gain valuable insight into what works and what does not, tips that will help avoid common pitfalls.

3. Philosophy, Rationale, Goals, Objectives, and a Written Program Plan

A brief statement of philosophy and goals is essential because everyone (parents, teachers, administrators, the local school board) will want to know exactly what the program entails and why. The written philosophy and rationale should include the reasons for the program—a "position statement" explaining why the program is necessary—plus general and, if desired, specific program objectives. An excellent guide for preparing a statement of philosophy is Kaplan's (1974) *Providing Programs for the Gifted and Talented,* which supplies examples of rationale statements and program goals. Two other fine sources of ideas are the Fall 1979 issue of the *Gifted Child Quarterly* and Joyce Juntune's (1981) book *Successful Programs for the Gifted and Talented,* both of which include summaries of many gifted programs around the country. Most of the descriptions present a brief program philosophy and list general and specific program goals. Also, a state plan, if one exists, will undoubtedly include a statement of philosophy and objectives that could be modified to fit a specific program.

A sample of the possible contents of a philosophy and goals statement appears in Appendix 3.1 at the end of this chapter. Take the time to read it now. A one-page philosophy statement for a small Wisconsin City appears in Inset 3.2.

If a statement of philosophy and goals is expanded, it can serve as a written plan for a program. A written program should present sufficient detail to answer any question that anyone could possibly ask about a proposed program. The written plan is often built around:

1. A definition of gifts and talents. For example, the U.S.O.E. definition is often used.
2. Philosophy and goals. This section explains why a program is necessary. Itemizing the cognitive and affective goals can be as brief and general or as tedious and specific as one judges appropriate.
3. Screening and identification methods. This section describes the information used (test scores, grades, teacher nominations, teacher ratings, self-nominations, and so on), the specific cutoff scores, and how the various sources of information will be combined in making final selection decisions. The identification section should also comment on provisions for identifying culturally different, economically disadvantaged, and handicapped students. This information will be scrutinized by any state or federal funding agency reading your written plan.

INSET 3.2 A PHILOSOPHY OF GIFTED AND TALENTED EDUCATION

The Watertown, Wisconsin, Public School System is committed to an education program that recognizes individual student differences. Embodied in this commitment is a responsibility to talented and gifted students to help them maximize their high potential.

Gifted children differ from others in learning ability: they learn faster, have wider interests, remember more, and think with greater depth about what they learn. An education program can be designed that will more adequately meet the needs of the gifted student.

A program for gifted students should provide a comprehensively planned curriculum that utilizes within discipline and/or cross-disciplinary studies. These studies should allow for both vertical (acceleration) and horizontal (breadth and depth in a topic) movement that is educationally relevant. The program should stress higher-level thinking skills such as inquiring skills, problem solving, and creative thinking. In addition, development of self-direction, risk-taking, curiosity, imagination, and interpersonal relations should be emphasized. The program framework will allow for individual projects and peer-group interaction.

The long-range goals of this program are self-actualization for the gifted person and the development of a sense of responsibility to self, school, and society.

(Watertown, Wisconsin, School District, 1980. Reprinted by permission.)

4. Instructional programming strategies. This section outlines the curriculum model (if any) on which the program is built. Also included are the specific grouping, acceleration, and enrichment plans, along with the necessary organizational changes; subject areas of concentration and planned activities; the use of community resources; and so on.
5. Program evaluation and modification. This section outlines specific evaluation plans, both of the "formative" type, which provide continuous feedback regarding the ongoing methods and activities, and the final "summative," did-we-succeed type at the end of the unit, the semester, or most likely, the year.

Specific sections of the written plan may deal with any of the fifteen points described in Table 3.1 and in this chapter. Two good sources of ideas for your written plan are Kaplan (1974) and Sato, Birnbaum, and LoCicero (1974).

4. Types of Gifts and Talents to Provide for and Estimated Enrollment

The topics of *types of gifts and talents* and *definitions of giftedness* are intimately related, and both belong in any statement of philosophy or written plan. The problem of specifying types of gifts and talents to be accommodated is also intimately related to the identification problem—defining who will be "in" the program—and it relates closely to the proposed program plans. Some relevant questions and considerations are: Will the program serve only bright, intellectually gifted students? Or will a multidimensional definition of gifts and talents be used, providing special opportunities to students with specific academic talents, scientific talents, creative talents, communication (speaking, writing) talents, artistic and musical talents, and perhaps others? One high-school program with which the authors are familiar arranged special training for students especially talented in body-and-fender work.

As for size of the "gifted" population, the mathematics acceleration plan in Stanley's (1979) *Studies of Mathematically Precocious Youth* (*SMPY*) caters to students in the top one percent in math ability. In contrast, the Renzulli, Reis, and Smith (1981) Revolving Door Identification Model identifies about 25 percent of the school population, the "talent pool," who "revolve" in and out of a resource room to work on special projects. Both the Stanley and the Renzulli models are widely accepted and growing in popularity. A good size for a single "pullout" or other special class is about 12 to 15.

If grade-skipping, taking advanced classes, or some other acceleration strategy is to be part of the plan, then fixing a number of "in" students is not as sensible as setting criteria cutoff scores that qualify *any number* of students for the acceleration. For example, standardized achievement test scores, probably already on file, are one good basis for decision making. But here is a warning: Due to random score variability, a single cutoff score should never be rigidly used to exclude students who are close to the magic cutoff number. Selection should be flexible and include subjective judgments as well as test scores.

5. Identification Methods and Specific Criteria

Issues and methods related to identifying gifted and talented students are at least sufficiently complex to merit a chapter of their own—a highly condensed chapter at that (Chapter 4). For now, we will simply mention (or repeat) a few basic considerations.

1. Identification methods must be consistent with one's definition of gifted and talented students. It is common for a stated plan to endorse the U.S.O.E multiple-talent definition, but then use IQ scores for the selection procedure (Renzulli, Reis, and Smith, 1981). The identification methods will define exactly who is "gifted and talented" for any given program.

2. Identification methods must be coordinated with the type of program(s) one plans to implement. For example, intelligence test scores, reading and math abilities, and teacher nominations might be appropriate for selecting students for grade-skipping. Math ability would be critical for participation in an accelerated math program. If a program accommodates many types of gifts and talents, a variety of ability, achievement, motivation, and creativity tests, inventories, and nominations may be appropriate.

3. The identification methods must be defensible to the community. Parents will ask why one child was selected for a program while another (theirs) was not. Selection decisions must be clearly justifiable. Some identification methods include intelligence tests, standardized achievement tests (particularly reading and math), creativity tests and inventories; inventories assessing interests, hobbies, special needs, and past special opportunities; teacher ratings of various characteristics (for example, academic talent, abstract thinking, creativity, motivation, leadership, organizing ability, visual or performing art talents); peer ratings of various characteristics, parent ratings and inventories, and self ratings; and work samples and products (for example, in art, music, or science).

6. Specific Provisions for Identifying Female, Underachieving, Handicapped, Culturally Different, and Economically Disadvantaged Gifted Students

We mentioned earlier that not only males and females must be fairly represented, but also economically disadvantaged, minority, and handicapped gifted students. The problem is not that these students have no gifts and talents; it is that educators do not usually look to these populations for G/T students.

Gifted underachievers may be even less visible than gifted minority, economically disadvantaged, or handicapped students. For underachieving students, their lost talent development is a personal crisis for them and a lost natural resource for humankind. More than one underachieving gifted student has become motivated toward higher educational and career achievement by the specific attention of teachers in gifted programs and, in some cases, by individual and family therapy (Rimm, 1984).

7. Staff Responsibilities and Assignments

The question of "who is going to do what?" is simple enough; it is the answer that may be difficult. There is a large difference between the passive acceptance, or even hearty endorsement, of a new gifted program versus the willingness to roll up one's sleeves and do the work. It is an essential preliminary problem to decide just who will assume responsibility for what and when.

It is not unusual to include some accountability checks, for example, by setting deadlines for obtaining certain information, preparing reports, purchasing tests or materials, conferring with administrators, and so forth. Scheduled weekly or biweekly meetings have the effect of establishing accountability, that is, getting things done.

8. Arranging Support Services

A successful program for gifted and talented students will involve experts and professionals beyond the immediate teaching staff. The school psychologist, counselors, the district or state coordinator, and outside consultants will all play important roles.

If the school psychologist is not an expert in gifted education (some are, some are not), his or her main contribution will probably be the administration and interpretation of tests. Individual intelligence tests, mainly the Stanford-Binet and the WISC-R, require a trained administrator. The psychologist might also administer and interpret interest or personality inventories such as the *Edwards Interest Inventory* or the *Kuder Preference Record* to help secondary students better understand themselves, their possible career directions, and the educational preparation necessary for various career alternatives. The school psychologist might administer and interpret personality inventories or supervise the administration of group achievement or group intelligence tests. In addition, many school psychologists are able to work with underachieving gifted students and their parents, or with gifted students with different problems. It is advisable to encourage your school psychologist to educate himself or herself in the area of giftedness by attending conferences, reading relevant books and journals, and so on. Very few school psychologists have taken any formal coursework whatever in gifted education.

If a school psychologist does have expertise in the gifted area, he or she can be helpful with all aspects of program planning and implementation.

School counselors also may or may not have expertise in gifted education. If not, the elementary school counselor will be involved in helping students cope with academic difficulties and with personal problems. The counselor can also help educate parents of gifted children regarding the child's particular talents, academic strengths and weaknesses, and personal difficulties. Importantly, the counselor can help specify the parents' role in developing the capabilities of their gifted child. For example, the counselor can recommend participation in the school's gifted program (many parents are surprisingly reluctant) and can recommend valuable summer programs such as science, art, music, language, or computer camps and workshops. As with the school psychologist, it is important that counselors learn about the special needs of gifted children. Without such additional background, they may make some shortsighted and inappropriate recommendations, for example, by stressing social adjustment and conformity instead of achievement and uniqueness.

In both the junior and senior high schools, counselors serve an invaluable function in fostering self-understanding with gifted and talented students. The educational and career counseling services of the secondary-level counselor should help steer the gifted adolescent into an educational program that is challenging and suitable to the student's college and career needs. Again, a special knowledge of personal and career needs of gifted students is mandatory for guiding them appropriately.

Planning a gifted program frequently involves a series of consultants, for example, a state or district coordinator, a university instructor with relevant experience or knowledge, a professional G/T consultant or workshop leader, or an experienced teacher-coordinator from another location. These consultants can present workshops for the entire school staff, perhaps dealing with methods of identification, alternative instructional models and strategies, program evaluation methods, problems of gifted girls, or other topics in which they have expertise. Particularly, some might describe in colorful detail the workings and problems of their own successful program.

You may also work with consultants on a one-to-one basis, outlining strategies for:

Obtaining funds
Preparing written statements
Selecting goals and objectives
Designing relevant acceleration and enrichment activities
Selecting or creating nomination forms, rating forms, or questionnaires for identification
Insuring proper representation of different student groups
Designing program evaluation procedures
Selecting or creating instruments for program evaluation
Promoting good public relations

9. Acceleration and Enrichment Plans

Issues, details, and recommendations regarding acceleration (for example, grade-skipping, advanced classes) and enrichment (for example, resource room or Saturday programs) are elaborated in Chapters 5, 6, and 7. For now, we will simply emphasize that specific instructional plans must be designed to produce sensible, defensible, and valuable educational benefits. While this recommendation may sound obvious and trivial, as Renzulli and his colleagues (Renzulli and Smith, 1978; Renzulli, Reis, and Smith, 1981) have repeated, far too many programs entertain the children with fun-and-games time fillers and interest-getters, with little attention to worthwhile, theoretically based goals. For inspiration regarding valuable goals and activities, you may review the philosophy and goals ideas in Appendix 3.1. Some examples of high-level goals that guide specific acceleration and enrichment plans are:

High achievement; advanced academic skills and content
Complex, abstract, theoretical thinking
Creative, critical, evaluative thinking
Scientific research skills
Library research skills
Communication (speaking, writing) skills, including creative writing
Career-related content
College preparatory content
Self-awareness, affective, and humanistic principles

Each of the curriculum models outlined in Chapter 8 is based on these and other potentially valuable instructional outcomes. One or more of the models often serves as the basis for planning specific acceleration and enrichment activities.

10. Organizational and Administrative Design

Most G/T plans require some administrative reshuffling of the school organization and budget to staff the program; provide the necessary time, space, and facilities; and coordinate the G/T activities with the rest of the school schedule. If the program is district-wide or city-wide, the planning will take place partly, not entirely, at these higher levels. In addition, any program for gifted and talented students will require considerable record-keeping by those directly involved—the teacher or teacher-coordinator, although secretaries can carry some of the burden.

For example, acceleration plans as straightforward as grade-skipping or taking college or correspondence courses will require that new types of records be created and maintained, and that student progress be monitored. Also, clear arrangements will have to be made with the local college. (University registration staff have been known to become disagreeable when an unexpected troop of grinning 15-year-olds march in to register.) A more complicated acceleration plan such as telescoping (for example, condensing three years of math or science into two) will require not only a teacher, a classroom, and a time slot, but complete coordination with the rest of the school course offerings and organization, along with creating and keeping records of student participation and success.

Enrichment plans also require attention to organizational and administrative matters. A Wednesday pullout program will require at the very least a teacher-coordinator and a resource room, plus such miscellaneous supplies and equipment as resource books, workbooks, chemistry and biology supplies, calculators, microcomputers, typewriters, art supplies, perhaps a 35-mm camera and an 8-mm movie camera, and so forth. Other enrichment plans, such as Saturday classes, extra classes, field trips, and

mentoring programs will also require attention to organizational, administrative, and managerial matters of staff, space, scheduling, transportation,
materials, and record keeping.

If a plan is district-wide or city-wide, particularly when special schools
for the gifted and talented are created or Saturday or summer programs
are planned, the organizational and administrative planning is clearly more
involved. It is not unusual for metropolitan areas to have several full-time
G/T personnel in the central office to help plan and manage city-wide programs. However, regardless of the size and type of program, a local school
staff member must be designated as having administrative responsibility
for the G/T program in that school. Without a designated responsible person at whose desk the buck stops, even excellent programs will flounder
and disappear.

11. Transportation Needs

Transportation plans may be simple and relatively minor, but they
cannot be ignored. Transportation problems and costs must be considered
for students who attend special schools, take college courses, or travel to
schools with special resource-room programs. Transportation must also be
considered for field trips, mentoring programs, after-school projects and
clubs, summer programs, and Saturday programs.

12. Community Resources: Professionals and Organizations

Community resources, namely professional people and organizations,
will be invaluable in at least three types of instructional plans and programs
for the gifted: mentoring plans, enrichment-oriented field trips, and career education. Therefore, in planning a program at either the elementary
or secondary level, potentially valuable community resources should be reviewed and itemized.

Mentoring plans involve the placing of gifted students with a community professional for usually a few hours each week. The professional
might be an artist, architect, dancer, musician, engineer, executive, owner
of a business, university professor in any field, medical researcher, doctor,
lawyer, marine biologist, astronomer, and so on. There can be no substitute
for the values, attitudes, skills, job requirements, and knowledge of daily
routines and life-styles acquired by gifted students in such a personal educational experience.

While mentoring plans are used almost entirely at the secondary level,
using community resources for field trips and career education is useful
with any age group. Some possibilities for field trips are an art gallery,

museum, public aquarium, planetarium, newspaper office, research laboratory, hospital, university department or laboratory, computer center, police department, capitol building, federal court, manufacturing plant, and so forth. While many of these are exotic big-city attractions, others are available in smaller cities. Do not forget that all students—not just the gifted—may benefit from such experiences.

Using community resources for career education would involve small-group or even individual visits with professional persons, including guided tours of their organizations. To ensure an educational benefit, the concrete plans for such a trip must include specific questions to be answered. Follow-up activities can include discussions and/or the preparation of written or verbal reports on the experience.

13. In-Service Workshops, Training, and Visits

Part of the continuing education of teachers, administrators, and support staff should include a planned series of in-service workshops. These may be led by a state director of gifted programs, a district coordinator, a professional G/T consultant, or a staff member from a nearby college. Initially, the school staff should receive in-service education at the awareness level. The purposes of an introductory exposure are (1) to attempt to alter the attitudes of teachers who happen to believe that gifted children do not require special services and (2) to generally heighten the commitment of all teachers.

Next in order should be in-service training dealing with the identification of gifted children, and the teacher's role in this process. A good understanding of the selection tests, criteria, and weighting procedures—and the role of subjective judgment—may prevent some special problems later. For example, teachers should understand why Johnny, a highly creative "B" student, may be included in the program even if his tested IQ is not 135.

The choice of other topics will vary according to the direction of the G/T program. If acceleration strategies are planned, teachers must understand both the philosophical bases for selecting these strategies and the specific procedures for conducting the acceleration. If an enrichment resource program is used, all participating teachers should understand the curriculum of that program and how they can facilitate their own students' participation. They also must help resolve a traditional dilemma: the extent to which their students will be expected to make up missed work while in the resource room.

Regardless of the specific type of program, teachers will need in-service education dealing with methods for helping gifted and talented children in the regular classroom. Also, such topics as identifying and helping minority, female, handicapped and underachieving gifted students are appropriate in every school district. Finally, in-service training on the evaluation of gifted programs will help teachers to participate in the continued improvement of the gifted and regular school program.

An excellent source of inspiration for planning or improving a G/T program is visiting other successful programs. With their rapid growth in America, one probably will not need to travel very far to visit a number of functioning gifted-education programs.

It is best to visit several types of programs. These may include special schools for gifted and talented students of schools with resource-room or pullout programs, special classes, Saturday programs, mentoring plans, telescoping plans, or whatever else you might be considering for your own school. Do not be surprised if the visits help you decide what *not* to do. You can speak with teachers regarding such matters as:

> What they are doing and how they are doing it.
> Who the target students are and how they were identified.
> What the students are specifically supposed to get out of the program (goals and objectives).
> Their perceptions of the success of their plan.
> The difficulties they experienced and how they were resolved.
> The sorts of resistance they have encountered from other teachers, parents, or the community.

You also might speak with the gifted and talented students in various types of programs. How do they like school? Do they like the program? What are their problems? How could the program be improved?

14. Budgetary Needs and Allocations

Many programs operate on a shoestring, using part of the regular school budget to purchase special workbooks, calculators, art supplies, or other inexpensive items. It can be done. However, to plan a proper program one should consider expenses related to some or all of the following:

> A full-time or part-time teacher/coordinator—or several, in a larger district
> Physical facilities
> Texts and workbooks
> Special equipment and supplies
> Transportation costs
> Tests and inventories
> Secretarial services
> Office supplies
> Duplicating expenses
> Consultant and in-service training expenses

Travel to visit other programs

Travel to state and national conferences

Services of psychologists and counselors

Evaluation expenses (a consultant; purchasing or constructing tests, rating scales or questionnaires)

Budgetary matters must be considered at the time you are planning the various identification strategies, instructional program alternatives, and needed evaluation data. From the outset, one should be concerned with watching cost-benefits. Some programs clearly cost more than others, and priorities may need to be modified in light of the available dollars. However, with creative cost-cutting many goals can be achieved relatively economically, without a large loss in interest value or educational benefit.

Finally, a search for federal, state, or private funding surely will be worthwhile. Even though funding may be scarce for "a program for gifted and talented students," requesting funds for a specific category of persons or subject matter—such as handicapped or minority gifted, computer literacy, math and science, or arts and humanities—can improve one's chances for an award or grant. Local service organizations, medical and health organizations, or local businesses or industries may be willing to provide small amounts of designated funding. Usually, a newspaper story or other publicity can be arranged to reward such contributions. Note too that chances for a financial commitment by the school district will be improved if administrators recognize that funds from other sources also are forthcoming.

15. Program Evaluation

The evaluation of gifted programs is an important and complex topic which will be discussed in more detail in Chapter 17. For now, the reader should keep in mind that good evaluation information has a direct bearing on (1) the survival and continuation of the program, (2) the continuation or improvement of budgetary allocations, and (3) the modification and improvement of the program. Evaluation is indeed important, and should be part of the program planning from the beginning. Every aspect of the program—the staff, the materials, the identification procedures, the acceleration and enrichment activities, and each and every goal and objective—can be evaluated regarding its effectiveness in contributing to program success.

Evaluation is of two types—first, a *formative,* ongoing process aimed at continuous modification and improvement of the program; second, a *summative,* final assessment of the overall success of the program. Both are necessary. Evaluation can be aimed at determining how well students' needs and goals were met; evaluation also is sometimes directed at assessing how well the program plan was carried out.

Comment

Gifted education leader Dorothy Sisk (1980) noted that educators are beginning to realize that, to survive, a gifted program cannot be perceived as serving just a handful of "elite" children. Rather, the gifted program should be integrated with the total effort to meet the needs of each individual child. In states where this integration is successful, there is usually good support for gifted education. Treffinger (1981, 1983) voiced the identical viewpoint in emphasizing *blending* the gifted program with the regular school programs and activities. Meeting the needs of gifted students, says Treffinger, should be embedded in the effort to meet the needs of all students—not detached from it. We should be oriented toward responding to needs, not excluding students. In agreement with some critics of gifted education, Treffinger rightfully concedes that many things are being done in a special setting for a small group of select students that truly should be done for all students in any classroom.

Mosley (1982) also itemized some timely recommendations " . . . which might determine whether or not the program will last one year or several." The suggestions are facetiously put into the form of "Suggestions to Ensure the Brevity of Your Gifted Program."

1. Make sure that the program always is "fun." Entertaining students is a high priority.
2. Talk about the program continuously; other teachers love to hear about your innovative program, your challenging students, and your field trips. Try also to tell parents of average children about the marvelous qualities of gifted students.
3. Try to interrupt the regular school day as much as possible, and on a regular basis. Other teachers enjoy this.
4. Emphasize that you are a "loner" and that your program is "different." You must separate yourself from the rest of the school system.
5. Avoid reading literature in the gifted education area. Because each program is different, you will learn nothing from the experiences of others.
6. Be sure to ignore professional adults in the community. They have little to offer.
7. Avoid using parents in the program. They sometimes are demanding and will only confuse matters.
8. If the program is challenged, it is easiest to concede that the program is of borderline relevance. If a response is necessary, try to use jargon and clichés, such as "high taxonomic levels," "Marland's U.S.O.E definition," and "Renzulli's three-ring identification model."
9. Try to get widespread publicity for expensive activities such as field trips, so that everyone will know that the program is adequately funded.

THE VIEW FROM THE SCHOOL BOARD

The main function of the district school board is to set the policy governing school administration and programs. The board thus is largely responsible for deciding whether a school district does or does not provide a specific program for gifted and talented children. Since board members are either elected directly by the community or appointed by elected officials, they are accountable to the public. Whether or not school board members support providing educational services for the gifted therefore may be a political question (for example, "What will my constituency think?") as well as an educational issue. Furthermore, the scope of a gifted program—the number of grades and children served and the diversity of program alternatives and activities—will be affected by the support and funding by school board members.

Programs for gifted and talented students, by definition, are directed at a minority of children and adolescents. Therefore, teachers and parents must convince board members that even though gifted children are a minority, their educational needs are genuine and they must be served as part of a comprehensive educational program. How can educators and parents encourage board members to maintain a quality gifted program in a school district? The following are some suggestions for fostering support:

Keep board members educated and aware.   Before board members voted for that gifted program, parents probably attended meetings and, in a positive way, showed interest in gifted education. When the G/T program is in place, that communication process must continue. Teachers or coordinators may make yearly presentations on program progress. If an oral presentation is not feasible, a short written report is helpful. Brevity is critical, since board members often are overwhelmed with reports.

Keep board members involved.   One or two board members should be included on each district or school G/T steering committee. Board members can be invited to in-service meetings, parent meetings, or student performances and shows. They also may be invited to speak at local or state parent meetings or other educational meetings.

Help board members to be accountable.   For board members to justify continued support and funding for gifted programs, they absolutely must be assured that the program is being evaluated and that the evaluation indicates that the program is achieving its objectives. Educators therefore must keep board members informed of the effectiveness and accomplishments of the G/T program.

Encourage boards to have a written policy.   Board policy is a formalization of philosophy and should be incorporated into a formal policy manual. The written policy becomes the basis by which the school administration and teaching staff can justify decisions favorable to gifted education. An example of a written school board policy is shown in Inset 3.3.

INSET 3.3 A SAMPLE SCHOOL BOARD POLICY

The Board of Education and professional staff members are dedicated to developing a comprehensive program for the identification and education of the gifted and talented child. Empathy and understanding are of paramount importance for all personnel having contact with such a child, and are basic to achievement of the district goals.

The gifted and talented child is an individual who, by virtue of outstanding abilities, is capable of high performance. This child possesses demonstrated or potential intellectual or specific academic abilities, leadership capabilities, creativity, or talent in the performing or visual arts. This child may need educational services beyond those being provided by the regular school program in order to realize his/her potential.

To provide a comprehensive program for the gifted and talented child, the Board recognizes that:

1. Early identification of the gifted and talented child is necessary to maximize the opportunities for the child's own self-realization. This shall be accomplished through the application of several criteria.
2. The educational program should provide for continuity and overlap among the elementary, junior high, and high school levels. The program should specify long-range goals for the district, with major emphasis on differentiated curriculum and programming.
3. The objectives of the educational program shall be to meet the gifted and talented child's needs, whether they be intellectual, social, physical, or emotional.
4. Active parental involvement is viewed as an integral and crucial ingredient of a quality gifted and talented program. Every effort should be made to foster parental involvement in all aspects of their child's educational program.
5. Qualified instructional and administrative personnel with appropriate knowledge, training, and experience are required to implement an effective program of education for the gifted and talented.
6. The achievement of a quality gifted and talented educational program demands the presence of a competent ancillary support staff, particularly for the early identification of the gifted or talented child.
7. The administration of the gifted and talented program shall provide leadership and coordination in developing and maintaining a comprehensive district K–12 program.
8. The placement and progress of the gifted or talented child will be continually evaluated and documented, with periodic progress reports issued to the parents of the child.

Be patient, but not too patient. Board members need time to gather support and plan resources for a comprehensive gifted program. Furthermore, they logically must view the gifted program in relation to the total needs of the district. At the same time, however, parents and educators must not permit board members to forget or indefinitely postpone the needs of gifted children, regardless of the stresses of educational problems and too-small budgets.

Remember that all board members should be encouraged to support gifted education. On any school board there always will be a variety of viewpoints on gifted education. Some members will be active supporters, and it may be tempting to believe that they alone can keep programs going. It is necessary, however, to also focus one's attention on those less-willing potential supporters, those who require further convincing. Note their doubts and questions and make a special effort to personally give them the information they need to convince them that gifted education truly is legitimate, important, and a widespread national movement. Even if they cannot be converted into strong supporters, the strength of their opposition might at least be reduced. In the long run, even a small victory may help a gifted program survive.

Help board members be answerable to their public. Board members will be asked by constituents why they support gifted education. They will also be presented with reasons why they should not help gifted students. In raising their awareness of the needs of the gifted, give them the information they will require to justify to their constituents the existence of special programs for the gifted. The issues they will need to debate may not always seem reasonable, but they nonetheless must be prepared with answers. Some issues to which board members often must respond are included in Inset 3.4.

INSET 3.4 SOME QUESTIONS SCHOOL BOARD MEMBERS MUST ANSWER

1. *Isn't gifted education elitist?*
RESPONSE: Gifted education only provides appropriate education for children who need a special challenge. These children come from all neighborhoods and economic backgrounds. Children from poor families often need G/T education the most because their families frequently cannot afford enrichment opportunities for them. Also, difficult financial circumstances and backgrounds sometimes prevent parents from having higher expectations for their children. If we are to keep our country a place where people can achieve regardless of their economic background, gifted education can help us. It provides a special challenge to all very bright and talented children, regardless of their cultural or economic background.

2. *We have special programs for the low-ability child and the high-ability child—but what about the average child?*

RESPONSE: Most educational programs are geared to the needs of the average child. In a real sense, most money is now spent on the average child. We agree that the average child should never be short-changed in the educational process, but neither should the gifted child.

3. *Aren't all children really gifted, so don't we need to provide for all their gifts?*

RESPONSE: In a sense, yes, all children certainly do have special gifts and talents. Some may play basketball well; some sew well; others have marvelous personal charm. The purpose of a gifted program is to provide for students' academic and creative needs not met by the regular educational program. For example, a star basketball player already has the team; the sewer has an opportunity to do excellent work in home economics courses. However, the young creative writer or poet rarely has a writing class to challenge and focus his/her skill; nor is the mathematics whiz provided with advanced or accelerated math. These students may be bored, and their talents are not challenged or strengthened. When we find special gifts and talents, we must provide opportunities to develop them.

4. *Why should we spend more money for kids who will make it anyway?*

RESPONSE: While many gifted kids will "make it anyway," it is nonetheless unfair to hold them back and make them succeed in spite of the system. More importantly, many gifted children do not "make it anyway." Their lost talent is both a personal tragedy for them and a loss to society. Studies of high school dropouts have found that between 9 and 20 percent are in the gifted IQ range—certainly many more than one would expect based on their ability, and certainly a waste.

Schools often turn off gifted children because they do not provide appropriate challenges. Further, when children become bored they sometimes use their creative energy and their giftedness in inappropriate, antisocial, and even destructive ways. They need special help and guidance.

5. *Can we afford to pay for more special education?*

RESPONSE: Gifted programs can be very inexpensive, compared to all other kinds of special education. Also, we save money in the long run by investing small amounts to help make school more meaningful. This small investment helps insure us against larger problems that can be more costly—for example, bored, apathetic, or even antisocial students, to say nothing of lost talent development.

6. *What do the rest of the kids get out of it?*

RESPONSE: Teachers who become involved in gifted education learn to stimulate creative development, to use questions effectively, to foster good self-concepts and humanistic attitudes, to individualize instruction, and other valuable concepts and skills. Much of this can be—and is—applied in the regular classroom. They become better teachers, and this benefits other children as well.

Also, when there are gifted programs in a school, it becomes apparent to all that excellence is rewarded and valued. When excellence is valued more children become motivated to achieve, and we sometimes discover giftedness where we might not have expected to find it. For example, if there has been peer pressure not to achieve, some students will hide their abilities and talents. Gifted programs encourage these children to achieve too. So while providing for the special needs of gifted children, we also encourage hard work and excellence in our schools for all children.

Support school board members who support gifted education. When school board members visibly endorse a program, they need to know there is a public "out there" supporting them. Be vocal in expressing your appreciation to board members who assist with the education you believe in. You can also help them in their campaigns, both formally and informally (for example, by telling your friends what a fine job you believe they are doing). Keeping supporters of gifted education in office will help them to provide appropriate educational opportunities in your community.

PERSPECTIVES OF OTHER TEACHERS

Not all teachers agree that gifted students truly need special services. In fact, some are downright antagonistic. However, with time and exposure some indifferent teachers come to understand the issues and concerns and will become more receptive to gifted programming. Others will never change, and progifted teachers simply will have to work around them.

What are their concerns? Some will have the same reservations expressed to school board members (see Inset 3.4); others will express different problems. For example:

Some teachers will object to their brightest students leaving their classes; they will miss the contributions these students make.

Some will argue that they already are challenging the gifted child in the classroom (sometimes they are; more often they are not).

Some will complain that the gifted program requires additional work, and they already are overworked.

Some believe that the gifted child is somehow "getting out of" required work, and will individually penalize those children by requiring makeup work or even "busy work."

If they teach a section of gifted students, some teachers will penalize them by grading on a normal curve, ignoring the fact that the students were preselected. A few might delight in awarding gifted children *C*'s and *D*'s to somehow prove the students are *not* gifted.

Some negative teachers may subtly attempt to sabotage the gifted program.

There is no secret psychological strategy to elicit the cooperation and support of every teacher. One should, however, be ready for antigifted attacks and not take them personally. If one remains positive there is a better chance of gaining converts and allies. For example, you can listen to their arguments and try to explain the unmet needs of gifted children. Negative teachers can be encouraged to take a course in gifted education or to attend a conference with you. Lend them this book. Make the assumption that they *do* care about all children and that, with a better understanding of the issues, they may develop a sincere concern for gifted children as a mistreated minority.

Fortunately, in most school districts there will be more allies than enemies. There will be many teachers who enthusiastically support the program and contribute time and ideas. There will be many who enjoy the new challenge of gifted education and the excitement of seeing new enthusiasm in energetic and talented children. Without these supporters, being a teacher of the gifted would be lonely indeed.

SUMMARY

Understanding the components of a gifted education program is essential for planning a successful one. Treffinger's Individualized Programming Planning Model includes the six components of definition, characteristics, screening and identification, instructional planning, implementation of services, and evaluation and modifications. And one can view program planning as a series of who, what, where, when and why questions.

Fifteen problem areas in program planning are summarized as follows.

1. A needs assessment aims at determining the need for a G/T program in the school or district. Three information sources are parents, gifted students, and teachers and administrators who are "gifted conscious." The need must be documented, formally or informally, and communicated to school board members and administrators.

Because gifted students are a minority, only "sufficient" (not majority) support should be needed to establish a clear need for G/T services.

A steering committee for planning a program may consist of teachers, parents, administrators, school board members, and perhaps the librarian, school psychologist, counselor, and gifted high school students.

2. Preliminary personal and staff education is necessary to proceed with informed planning. A first step is determining the present status of gifted education in the area. An acquaintance with state plans and state legislation, and the attitudes of board members, administrators, and fellow teachers will be important. Courses, books, workshops and conferences, G/T magazines and journals, and visits to other programs will help clarify many issues and problems.

3. A written statement of philosophy and rationale should explain the reasons for, and the goals and objectives of, a program.

An expanded statement can serve as a written program plan, which should answer virtually any question about the program. Along with philosophy and goals, it includes a definition of gifts and talents, a description of who the program is for, identification methods and criteria, plans for identifying female, underachieving, culturally different, economically disadvantaged, and handicapped students, acceleration and enrichment alternatives, and evaluation plans.

4. The types of gifts and talents to be accommodated must be specified. This matter is related to (1) one's definition of giftedness and (2)

specific identification methods. The estimated enrollment must be planned. For acceleration plans, achievement and/or ability cutoff scores are more sensible than fixing numbers.

5. Identification methods and criteria must be consistent with one's definition of giftedness and coordinated with the type of program being planned. Tests and inventories plus ratings and nominations by teachers, peers, parents, and the students themselves may be included. The methods must be defensible, yet both objective and subjective.

6. Identification methods must include plans for locating gifted female, culturally different, economically disadvantaged, underachieving, and handicapped students.

7. Staff responsibilities and accountability checks (such as monthly meetings or reports) must be planned.

8. Support staff and services should include the school psychologist, school counselor, and consultants.

9. Program plans should include both acceleration and enrichment alternatives. There are many specifics to select from. They should aim at defensible goals and objectives, namely, the development of high-level skills and knowledge.

10. Any plan will require attention to the organizational and administrative design, including space allocations, record keeping, modifications to the budget, and much more. Much planning usually is at the district level.

11. Transportation needs cannot be ignored.

12. Community resources exist for enriching field trips, mentorships, or career education; they include professional persons plus local business, industry, art, university, and other organizations and institutions.

13. In-service workshops begin with general "awareness" information and proceed to the identification of the gifted or talented child and then other matters. Visits to several differing types of programs can be very informative.

14. Budgetary needs and cost-effectiveness must be considered from the outset. Some programs operate on almost nothing; others pay for teacher-coordinators plus plenty of materials and equipment. Federal, state, or private funds often can be obtained.

15. Program evaluation is important for survival and expansion. Every component of the program can be evaluated. Formative evaluations are continuous ones aimed at modification and improvement. Summative evaluations at the end of the year evaluate overall success.

Sisk and Treffinger argue that gifted programming should be integrated with an effort to meet the educational needs of all students, that is, blended with the regular program. Many G/T activities are indeed good for all students.

School board members must be convinced that G/T students have important unmet needs. Some suggestions for fostering support include:

Keeping board members educated regarding the gifted, and aware of program activities.

Keeping board members involved—for example, on school G/T steering committees.

Helping board members be accountable by assuring them that the program is meeting its objectives.

Focusing attention on nonsupportive board members in order to elicit support or at least reduce antagonism.

Helping board members justify their support of the program to their constituents.

Supporting board members who support G/T education.

For various reasons, many teachers may not support a G/T program in a given school. One should attempt to alter their attitudes in a more positive and helpful direction—for example, by encouraging them to take a course or otherwise become better acquainted with gifted education.

Typically, there are more supportive teachers than antagonistic ones.

APPENDIX 3.1 IDEAS FOR STATEMENTS OF PHILOSOPHY, RATIONALE, AND OBJECTIVES

To provide gifted and talented students with an educational environment that will provide the greatest possible development of their abilities, thus enabling them to realize their contributions to self and society.

"The gifted and talented represent a group of students whose learning style and thinking dimensions demand experiences which are outside the educational mainstream . . . (we need) an education commensurate with each child's ability to learn" (Kaplan, 1974).

To provide programs designed to help meet the psychological, social, educational, and career needs of gifted and talented students.

To assist students in becoming individuals who are able to take self-initiated action and accept responsibility for that action, and who are capable of intelligent choice, independent learning, and problem solving.

(Our program will include) " . . . administrative procedures and instructional strategies which afford intellectual acquisition, thinking practice, and self-understanding" (Kaplan, 1974).

To meet the special needs of minority gifted children.

To develop a functional procedure for identifying gifted and talented students in the school in order that they may express and develop their gifts or talents.

To provide a program that will stimulate individual interests and develop individual abilities in academic and/or talent areas.

To provide the superior learner with new and highly challenging learning experiences that are not ordinarily included in the regular classroom curriculum.

At the conclusion of their elementary school experience, students will demonstrate competency in basic skills at least equal to that of other elementary schools in the district, even though they are exposed to numerous areas of instruction not commonly found in traditional elementary school programs.

To provide opportunities that will develop self-awareness, personal strengths, and social responsibilities beyond those in the regular school program.

To provide gifted children with the opportunity to explore personal interests through independent study and community involvement.

To foster high-level thinking and self-development processes, resulting in a more complete, productive individual who is challenged by the school environment.

To provide a learning atmosphere that will enable the gifted child to develop his/her potential and exceptional abilities, particularly in the areas of decision making, planning, performing, reasoning, creating, and communicating.

To provide experiences that develop the higher operations of analyzing, synthesizing, divergent production, and evaluation.

To provide activities and experiences that will stimulate critical thinking, comprehension, competency, and creativity.

To enable those students desiring to do so to prepare for advanced placement.

To prescribe particular curricula to meet individual needs.

To encourage cross-discipline exploration.

To include strong components of basic skills, career awareness, sex-equity, and multiethnic experiences.

To develop an ability to transfer information to humanistic goals.

To develop intrinsic motivation.

To provide experiences that guide a student toward independence.

To provide gifted and talented students with a positive self-concept.

To foster awareness of self and others.

Many parents and other community leaders will be involved in the learning process.

To develop problem-solving abilities and creative thinking skills; develop research skills; strengthen individual interests; develop independent study skills; exercise communication skills in the humanities (visual, oral, and written); receive intellectual stimulation from contact with other highly motivated students; expand their learning activities to include resources available in the entire community area.

"The good of any program for the gifted should be to provide meaningful experiences in the most efficient and effective way in order to maximize learning and individual development and to minimize boredom, confusion, and frustration" (Fox, 1979).

IDENTIFYING GIFTED
AND TALENTED STUDENTS

There are probably as many different strategies and policies for identifying gifted and talented students as there are programs. For example, some programs use a single ability score, most often a WISC-R or Stanford-Binet IQ, as the sole selection criterion. At least one state requires that all children who score 120 or above on an individually administered intelligence test must receive differentiated educational experiences—a position that intrinsically favors an IQ identification criterion. In Stanley's (1977, 1979) Studies of Mathematically Precocious Youth (SMPY) acceleration program, the selection of mathematically precocious seventh-grade students similarly is based on a cutoff score of 640 on the *Scholastic Aptitude Test—Mathematics* (SAT-M).

Other programs take a more multidimensional approach, for example, basing identification methods upon some combination of the five components of the U.S.O.E. definition (general intellectual ability, specific academic talent, creativity, leadership, or talent in the visual or performing arts). Measures of student motivation sometimes are added to the list. Also, as we will see later in this chapter, the *Kranz Talent Identification Instrument* (KTII; Kranz, 1981) assesses ten categories of gifts and talents, including most of the U.S.O.E. list. It can be seen that if these various types of abilities, gifts, and talents are combined with the many possible measures of each—student tests, grades, and questionnaires; teacher questionnaires and nominations; parent questionnaires and ratings; peer evaluations; plus evaluations of products or performances—the number of permutations and combinations will boggle even a gifted mind.

Overview

In this chapter we will first review some issues that frequently complicate the significant—and often delicate—matter of selecting participants in a gifted education program. An awareness of these issues should help the program developer design procedures that are as reasonable, fair, accurate, and appropriate to the program goals as possible. We will then turn to descriptions of specific identification strategies and instruments. For each strategy, its unique uses and advantages will be reviewed, along with its unique faults and problems. We will also offer suggestions as to proper usage and interpretation.

ISSUES AND PROBLEMS

Test Reliability and Validity

No test, rating scale, or questionnaire will have perfect *reliability* or *validity*. Reliability refers to the accuracy or consistency of a test and is quantified with a reliability coefficient that may range from .00 to 1.00. As a general guideline to evaluating reliability (and validity) coefficients:

.00 to .20 is low.
.20 to .40 is moderately low.
.40 to .60 is fair.
.60 to .80 is good.
.80 to 1.00 is excellent.

Reliability. The reader will encounter four types of reliability in perusing test manuals and research literature—and one should remain aware of each in considering any tests, inventories, rating scales, or other strategies. First, *internal consistency* reliability reflects the degree to which each test item or question is measuring the same trait, for example, intelligence, creativity, mathematics ability, leadership, or self-esteem. The most common internal reliability coefficient is a correlation between students' scores on even-numbered items and scores on odd-numbered items (split-half method). Second, with *test-retest* reliability, the same test is administered to the same group of students with an intervening time interval, usually a matter of weeks, sometimes months. This reliability coefficient is the correlation of the first set of scores with the second set of scores. Third, *equivalent-forms* reliability involves the administration of two different forms of the same test to the same students during the same administration period. The reliability coefficient is the correlation between scores on "Form A" and scores on "Form B." Fourth, when rating scales are used, *inter-rater* reliability will refer to the agreement, say, between two teachers in rating characteristics of creativity, leadership, and so on. Inter-rater reliability can be low if one teacher sees abilities or traits that another does not.

Poorly designed test items, questions, or rating scales will lower any reliability coefficient—the accuracy of the scores—and therefore should lower the confidence you have in decisions based on those scores. Whenever identification procedures and tests are considered, one of the first concerns should be their reliability. Another first concern should be validity.

Validity.   The extent to which a test truly measures what it is supposed to measure is a gauge of its *validity*. For example, a spelling test is clearly a valid measure of the ability to spell those words. The same test may or may not be a valid measure of spelling ability in general. Also, a test may be reliable—consistently and accurately measuring something—but it may or may not be valid for its intended purpose. Alvino, McDonnel, and Richert (1981) itemized a number of "blatant misuses" of tests that. illustrate this problem—for example, using creativity tests to identify intellectual ability, and vice versa.

There are three conceptually different kinds of validity (American Psychological Association, 1974): *criterion-related validity, content validity,* and *construct validity. Criterion-related validity* refers to the ability of a test to predict performance on some other relevant criterion measure. For example, a creativity test has criterion-related validity if it accurately measures how creatively students perform in their art, science, or creative writing activities. There are two types of criterion-related validity. We speak of *concurrent validity* when both measures—the test and the criterion—are obtained at about the same time. *Predictive validity* refers to the use of test scores to predict some future performance.

Content validity refers to how well the test content represents the content of the material or the skills being assessed. For example, a test of only long-division skills would not be a content-valid measure of mathematical ability in general. Similarly, as Passow (1981) noted, " . . . standardized tests of language and cognition do not help identify a potential poet in the elementary school." That is, intelligence tests have no content validity for identifying poetic ability.

Many psychological traits or abilities, such as intelligence, motivation, anxiety, self-esteem, or creativity, are referred to as *constructs,* even "hypothetical" constructs. Tests designed to measure these traits or abilities have *construct validity* to the extent that they truly evaluate these constructs. This is not easy, since the constructs themselves—obscure rascals that they are— defy direct measurement. According to Gronlund (1977), about the best one can do in construct validation is to make predictions that would be consistent with the assumptions underlying a test, and then see if the data agree with the predictions. Discussions of construct validity thus will describe relationships of high test scores to other evidence of the trait.

Finally, psychologists and others also speak of "face validity," the degree to which a test simply "looks like" it should measure what it is intended to measure. Sometimes face validity will be the only information one has to go on.

When considering tests, questionnaires, rating scales, and nomination procedures for use in identifying gifted and talented students, one always must examine both the reliability and the validity of the tests or procedures. Reliability and validity coefficients, and the research behind them, most often are reported in test manuals and in research articles. The value and usefulness of the instruments or procedures are tied very closely to their degree of reliability and validity. Furthermore, because all identification tests and methods will have less than ideal reliability and validity, reliance on a *single* instrument will cause far too many gifted children to be overlooked (Sisk, 1980). A multidimensional definition of giftedness and multidimensional criteria should be used, both objective and subjective, with plenty of flexibility to accommodate imperfect selection procedures and atypical gifted children and adolescents.

Biases in Ratings and Nominations

As noted earlier, there is a natural and understandable tendency for teachers to favor students who are cooperative, smiling, and anxious to please, who do their work well, neatly, and on time, and who absolutely never talk back. While "teacher pleasers" (Taylor, 1978) are a pleasure to work with, they may or may not be the most gifted and talented students in the class. However, they have a high likelihood of being perceived by teachers as "gifted," and of being nominated for participation in special programs. If teachers rate students on specific qualities such as academic talent, leadership, motivation, or sometimes even creativity, teacher pleasers again are likely to be selected. The extremely bright or the creative, curious, and questioning students, who may be stubborn, rule-breaking, egotistical, or otherwise high in nuisance value, may not be the teachers' favorites, but they sometimes are the most gifted.

Disadvantaged and Minority Students

The identification of gifted and talented minority, economically disadvantaged, and culturally different students is an especially sensitive problem, and one that deserves more than lip service (Sisk, 1980). Too often administrators claim they have "none of those children in our school." Teachers, too, are guilty of this oversight. LeRose (1977), for example, reported, "Martin Jenkins, who has conducted more studies of high IQ Black children than any one else, has commented on how frequently children with IQ's above 150 have not been spotted as outstanding by their teachers."

Culturally different learners do tend to score, on the average, about one standard deviation (15 points) lower than middle-class students on standardized intelligence tests. We repeat, "on the average." Many minority children will score extremely high in both verbal and nonverbal measures of intelligence. Nonetheless, if IQ testing is part of the selection battery, there is frequently a built-in bias against minority and economically disadvantaged children. And if your school population includes minority and culturally different students (for example, Black, Chicano, Native American, Native Hawaiian, Vietnamese, immigrant), it simply will not be acceptable to produce an all-white list of children of middle-class professional people. The authors encountered one G/T program composed entirely of white students, even though the school population was 40 percent black.

Issues related to minority and culturally different students will be explored in more detail in Chapter 11, along with suggestions for identification and programming. For now, we will emphasize that a multidimensional approach to identification is essential for identifying gifted and talented minority students—a procedure that looks beyond IQ scores. LeRose (1977) noted that using " . . . the IQ as the sole criterion for identification of giftedness has never been the practice of thoughtful educators." The quota system is one frequently used solution to the problem of ensuring racial, sexual, geographical, or economic balance in G/T programs (Hersberger and Asher, 1980; LeRose, 1978).

Often we overlook gifted students among the ranks of physically or psychologically disabled (for example, learning disabled) students. Do not be shocked when ten-year-old Joe Smith, whose dyslexia prevents him from reading or writing normally, is nominated as an intellectually or artistically gifted child. Albert Einstein, Thomas Edison, Nelson Rockefeller, and other "slow learners" have had the same problems.

Regarding girls, we should be aware in our identification activities that, while times are indeed changing, cultural and social influences and perhaps parental "overprotectiveness" (Lois Hoffman, 1972) still may produce girls who are more dependent, more conforming, less motivated and aggressive, and less success-oriented than boys.

IDENTIFICATION METHODS

Intelligence Tests

Virtually every G/T program is interested in intellectual giftedness. The bottom-line instruments for confirming suspected brilliance are individual intelligence tests, particularly the *Wechsler Intelligence Scales for Children–Revised* (WISC–R) and the *Revised Stanford-Binet Intelligence*

Scales. Every school psychologist is qualified to administer and interpret either of these. If you have a university in your area with a graduate clinical or school psychology program, it is likely that competent graduate students might practice administering one of these tests free of charge.

Stanford-Binet tests.

The Stanford-Binet produces one IQ score, based on a variety of verbal and nonverbal subtests (for example, memory, verbal reasoning, mathematical reasoning, vocabulary). The examiner also will record relevant behavior during the test—for example, attention, activity level, self-confidence, persistence, reactions to a challenge, anxiety, coping with failure, and others. An advantage of administering the Stanford-Binet to verbally gifted children is that it has virtually no ceiling for elementary children. This means that very bright children cannot "top out"; they can continue to be challenged by test items that are at the Superior Adult Level. Although a true deviation IQ score, based on the normal (bell) curve, cannot be calculated for these children, the old formula for arriving at IQ (mental age ÷ chronological age × 100) can be used to assess these profoundly gifted children.

WISC-R.

Many school psychologists, however, prefer the WISC-R because it produces both a *Verbal* IQ score and a *Performance* (nonverbal) IQ score, along with the combined *Full-Scale* IQ score. Therefore, a student with spatial or mechanical gifts is more likely to be identified. The WISC-R also has an advantage over the Binet in terms of reduced time for administration. Further, the "scatter," or differences between subtest scores, reveals to the trained psychologist some important information about learning styles and strengths and weaknesses. A disadvantage of the WISC-R is that very gifted children may score at the top of the scale on three or four, or more, of the 10 subtests. That is, it is not difficult enough to discriminate among extremely intelligent children. This is not a serious weakness; the "ceiling" is sufficiently high to enable one to conclude that such a high-scoring child should be placed in a gifted program.

Group intelligence tests.

IQ scores from group intelligence tests are useful for identifying gifted students because they continue to be routinely administered in many school systems, and so scores may be in the office file. Some of the better-known group intelligence tests are the *Cognitive Abilities Test,* the *SRA Primary Mental Abilities Tests,* the *Henmon-Nelson Test of Mental Ability,* the *Otis-Lennon Mental Ability Test,* and the *Kuhlman-Anderson Intelligence Tests.* However, despite their comparatively low cost and convenient group administration, consider these shortcomings: Group tests tend to be less reliable and less valid than individual tests. Also, children who are not motivated will produce lower IQ scores than their informally observed ability would indicate. Group tests are mainly verbal and are highly correlated with actual school achievement; therefore, they are biased against children who are nonverbally gifted (or who speak a subcultural dialect). Because most group tests were designed to discriminate in the midsection of the bell curve, they tend to be unreliable at high IQ levels; a few chance errors may substantially lower a bright student's IQ score. Speed is an important factor in group tests, since all are timed. This is not true of individual intelligence tests.

In view of these problems, one well may question the value of group intelligence tests. However, children who score high on these tests virtually always will be capable and certainly should be included in a G/T program. If used with other indicators of giftedness, group intelligence tests become an efficient indicator of some children who need the challenge of a high-level school program.

A big plus for intelligence tests, group or individual, is that they may identify underachieving students: students whose grades and classroom performance give no hint of the students' true—and unused—potential. In the negative column, if undue weight is given to intelligence test scores, students with other legitimate gifts and talents will be missed—particularly creative students, but also students with gifts in one special academic or aesthetic area, such as art, music, computers, mathematics, or even dinosaurs.

As an incidental note on IQ scores, the highly publicized "Pygmalion" expectancy research by Rosenthal and Jacobson (1968), and many others since (for a review, see Cooper, 1979; Davis, 1983b), demonstrated that teachers frequently are strongly biased by IQ scores. In effect, IQ numbers tend to permanently brand students as bright, average, or stupid—often to the student's detriment. As a self-fulfilling prophecy, many teachers expect and get more from students with high IQ scores; they expect and get less from students with low IQ scores. The expectations are communicated to students, and students' self-concepts and self-expectations are shaped by this feedback. Teachers also do a better job if they think the class is filled with bright kids. According to one story, a teacher did a marvelous job with a class of students with scores between 110 and 150—until she discovered these were locker numbers.

Achievement Tests

Specific academic talent is an important category of giftedness. An excellent indicator of academic talent is standardized achievement tests, such as the *Iowa Tests of Basic Skills,* the *Stanford Achievement Tests,* the *Metropolitan Achievement Tests,* the *SRA Achievement Series,* the *California Test of Basic Skills,* and the *Sequential Tests of Educational Progess* (STEP). Other good indicators of specific academic talent are teacher-made achievement tests and course grades.

Standardized tests produce scores based upon national norms (for example, grade-equivalent, percentile, or stanine scores). Consider this advantage. A teacher in an upper-middle-class neighborhood may be accustomed to very bright students who learn quickly. He or she may not realize that—compared with national norms—there are a half-dozen or more highly gifted students in the class who should be participating in the district's G/T program. On the other hand, a teacher accustomed to working with slow learners may feel that a particular student is gifted when, relative to a national comparison, the student is just slightly above average. With this broader perspective, the teacher may or may not wish to recommend that the student receive the differentiated educational services reserved for truly gifted students.

Two important problems should be considered relative to standardized achievement test scores. The first concerns the *grade-equivalent* score. "Grade equivalent" refers to the average score earned by children at a particular grade level on a particular test—not to the grade level at which a specific gifted child can function well in the classroom. Experienced teachers, administrators, and psychologists, as well as parents, make the faulty assumption that if a gifted fourth-grade child performs at the eighth-grade level on, say, a math achievement test, he or she could be moved into an eighth-grade classroom and perform successfully. Not so. While certainly a good math student, this child probably lacks many skills of the average eighth grader. The score is misleading and should only be used as an indication that the child needs special challenge. Further diagnostic testing would be used to determine the child's specific mathematics skills and skill levels.

The second problem relates to the *low ceiling* score of most typical achievement tests. That is, for gifted children most achievement tests are not sufficiently difficult to measure their high ability and skill levels; they "top out." One solution is to give gifted children higher-level achievement tests, but few schools use this alternative or deal with this special problem at all. The result is that a considerable number of children will score above the ninety-fifth percentile or at the ceiling grade equivalent level (for example, eighth grade, eighth month for fourth graders). It is thus incorrectly assumed that all of these children are equally talented and need a similar skill program. Actually, after diagnostic testing with more difficult tests, a wide range of skill levels will be found among these children. One example of this problem comes from Stanley's (1979) SMPY program in which seventh and eighth graders who are selected to take the SAT-M must have performed above the 95th percentile on a group achievement test. The SAT-M scores for this group of "similar" children will vary between 200 and 800 on this more difficult test.

Teacher Nominations

Teacher nominations may be very informal (for example, "Say, we're starting a new gifted program, be thinking about one or two kids you want in it!"). On the other hand, the procedure may involve the formal use of rating forms or checklists to be objectively scored. Teacher nomination of gifted children is one of the most widespread methods, yet one of the most troublesome. According to Martinson (1974), Gear (1976), Stanley (1974), and Fox (1981c), teacher nominations are less valid than IQ scores, achievement scores, parent nominations, or peer nominations. Rimm and Davis (1976), for example, found an inter-rater reliability coefficient of only .18 for teacher ratings of creativity. Some reliability and validity difficulties can be overcome by training teachers to rate and identify G/T candidates (Kranz, 1981). It also is recommended that teachers get to know students well before nominating them—for example, by waiting until October or November.

One structured nomination form used by a major metropolitan school district appears in Appendix 4.1 at the end of this chapter. Many more are available in Martinson (1974), Clasen and Robinson (1978), and Renzulli, Reis, and Smith (1981). The *Kranz Talent Identification Instrument* (Kranz, 1981), also a structured teacher nomination strategy, is described later in this chapter. Also, a teacher, school, or school district may develop its own teacher nomination forms.

Creativity Tests

In some classes and with some creativity-conscious teachers, it may be easily apparent which students are highly creative and which are not. Creativity tests can be used to confirm a teacher's suspicions about the creativeness of one or more students. The tests also may be used to identify creative students whose unique talents are not visible in many classrooms.

It is important to emphasize that creativity tests are not perfect. Especially, scores from a single creativity test might be quite misleading, either showing an average student to be highly creative, or a creative student to be highly average. Criterion-related validity coefficients of published creativity tests (remember criterion-related validity?) typically range from about .25 to .40, sometimes lower and occasionally higher. The figures are not spectacular, but then creativity is a complex ability that can take innumerable forms; it is impossible to measure creativity exactly. The authors have repeatedly emphasized that data from creativity tests—including their own—must be combined with other information to make valid decisions regarding creativeness (Rimm and Davis, 1976). Using two criteria of creativeness is recommended (Davis, 1975). Thus if a given student scores high on both, one can be reasonably certain that the student is indeed creative. For example, a student who scores high on a creativity test and is rated as highly creative by one or more teachers is virtually certain to be a bona fide creative person. Similarly, a student who scores high on two different types of creativity tests is likely to be categorized correctly. Similarly, two high (or two low) creativity ratings by two different teachers will probably also be accurate.

Teachers who have opportunity to observe creative ideas and products may be asked to rate students' creativeness. For example, art teachers or teachers who supervise original science projects, creative writing, or drama activities are in a good position to identify creative talent.

As for creativity tests themselves, there are two main categories: divergent thinking tests and inventories that assess personality and biographical traits (Davis, 1983a). Divergent thinking tests require students to list all the ideas they can for an open-ended problem, such as listing unusual uses for a brick, listing outcomes of an unlikely event ("What would happen if . . ."), or asking as many questions as possible about an object or event. Such tests are scored at least for ideational fluency (the number of ideas produced) and originality (uniqueness of the ideas). The *Torrance Tests of Creative Thinking* (Torrance, 1966) are the most widely used divergent-thinking tests (see Inset 4.1). They include verbal and nonverbal (figural) subtests, and are scored for *fluency, flexibility* (number of different categories of ideas or approaches to the problem), *originality,* and, with the figural tests, *elaboration* (number of additional details and embellishments). Other divergent thinking batteries are the Guilford (1967, 1977) tests, the Wallach and Kogan (1965) tests, and the Getzels and Jackson (1962) tests. In view of their extensive development and evaluation, and the availability of standard administration and scoring procedures, the Torrance Tests are the recommended divergent thinking battery. In the negative column, the administration and scoring of any divergent thinking test are very time-consuming.

As for inventories that assess personality and biographical information, the authors—without bias or prejudice—recommend their own *PRIDE, GIFT, GIFFI I* and *GIFFI II* instruments (Rimm and Davis, 1983). There is a stereotype of personality traits and biographical characteristics that appears again and again in studies of creative people of all ages. As described in Chapter 2, some personality traits are independence, self-confidence, curiosity, playfulness, humor, risk taking, adventurousness, attraction to the complex and mysterious, and interests in ideas, art, and other aesthetic activities. Not surprisingly, some dependable biographical traits are: a history of creative activities, hobbies and inventions and, more subtly, having had an imaginary playmate.

PRIDE (Preschool and Primary Interest Descriptor; Rimm, 1982) is a preschool/kindergarten inventory that parents fill out. *GIFT (Group Inventory for Finding (Creative) Talent)* consists of yes-no items in lower-, middle-, and upper-elementary school forms. *GIFFI I* and *II (Group Inventory for Finding Interests)* are in a rating scale form designed for junior and senior high school students, respectively.

The GIFT and GIFFI instruments have been validated in the United States, Israel, Australia, Spain, Taiwan, Canada, and France. They have surprised the authors with their consistently high reliabilities and very

INSET 4.1 TORRANCE TESTS OF CREATIVE THINKING

The *Torrance Tests of Creative Thinking* (Torrance, 1966) measure creative abilities of *fluency* (number of ideas), *flexibility* (number of different types or categories of ideas), *originality* (uniqueness), and *elaboration* (number of embellishments). Exercises similar to Torrance's subtests are presented below. Spend a few minutes on each one. Are you fluent? Flexible? Original? Are you high in elaboration?

Directions: Make a meaningful picture out of each of the nonsense forms below. Try to be original. Give each one a name.

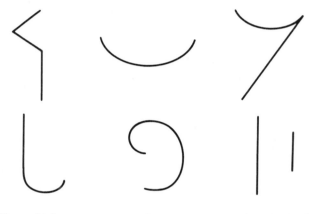

Directions: List as many unusual uses as you can for discarded rubber tires.

_____   _____

_____   _____

_____   _____

_____   _____

_____   _____

_____   _____

_____   _____

_____   _____

_____   _____

good validity coefficients. They seem to work well with middle-class, disadvantaged, foreign, domestic, learning disabled, gifted, and even normal students. PRIDE is new, but preliminary results are consistent with its predecessors, despite the young preschool and kindergarten age of the children.

An added advantage of GIFT, GIFFI, and PRIDE is the dimension scores. These subscale scores can be used to help understand and guide gifted children, as well as for identification purposes. For example, an apparently creative child may produce a somewhat lower total score because of a low Independence subscale score. This could alert a teacher to the student's dependence or to peer pressures, either of which could have an adverse effect on creativity.

Parent Nominations

No one knows children and adolescents better than their own parents. For example, only the parents will know a child spoke in sentences at age two, taught him- or herself to read at age four, and drew the solar system, composed melodies, produced creative art, and asked about reasons for the Middle-East strife at age five. Unfortunately, parent nominations are not used as often as they should be. Martinson (1974) recommends that in a child's early school years, parents may be asked to provide information regarding advanced knowledge and abilities. A one-page form may simply state that the teacher is interested in planning appropriate educational experiences for the child, and would the parent please provide information pertaining to:

1. The child's special interests and hobbies
2. Recent books he or she has enjoyed or read
3. Special interests other than reading
4. Unusual accomplishments, past or present
5. Special talents
6. Special opportunities the child has had
7. Preferred activities when alone
8. Relationships with others
9. Special problems and/or needs

Another nomination rating form, developed by Tongue and Sperling (1976), appears in Appendix 4.2. This form evaluates precocious cognitive development (items 1–5, 9, 20), creativity (items 6, 8, 10–13), leadership (item 14), motor coordination (item 16), energy and persistence (items 7, 15, 19), and other characteristics of gifted and creative children. Using descriptions of gifted and talented students presented in Chapter 2, a teacher or G/T coordinator could tailor-make an even more suitable parent nomination inventory.

Two cautions are in order. First, some parents may not know their children well. For example, very busy or highly career-minded parents may not or cannot follow all of the adventures and creations of their gifted child. Other parents, particularly nonintellectually oriented ones, may not understand their own child's giftedness. Second, some parents overestimate their child's talents. In some neighborhoods it seems that every parent is convinced they have at least one gifted child; some assume that all of their children are intellectual or artistic geniuses. Their attitude seems to be that "because they are my children, they must be superior."

Peer Nominations

Peers are extraordinarily good at nominating gifted and talented students, and may be especially useful in identifying gifted minority and culturally different children (Cox and Daniel, 1983a). They know who's who. Year after year they watch Freddy finish his work first, get all the problems right, answer all the teacher's questions correctly, volunteer to go to the board every time, and understand the most confusing issues. One simple approach is to ask a handful of individual students, "Who's the smartest kid in the class?" or "Who's the best reader in the class?"

A more structured, but very brief, peer nomination form appears in Appendix 4.3. The reader will deduce that this form essentially asks students to nominate which of their classmates is the brightest (items 1, 3), the most creative (items 2, 5), and the strongest leader (item 4).

Self-Nominations

Some students have strong artistic, creative, or other interests and talents, and they may want to participate in a special program—but nobody asks them. Teachers may be unaware of the talent, creativity, and high motivation. A self-nomination form used in Charlottesville, Virginia, simply asks students, "Check the area(s) in which you think you have special abilities or talents, and tell why you think you have special abilities or talents in these areas." The ten areas were general intellectual ability, math, science, social studies, language arts, reading, art, music, drama, dance, creativity, and leadership, areas based upon the U.S.O.E. definition. Self-nomination is especially recommended at the junior and senior high school levels, where peer pressures may cause youths to mask their special talents.

Product Evaluations

A good index of academic, artistic, creative, or scientific talent is simply the quality of work the student has done or is doing. Art teachers are in a unique position to evaluate artistic talent and creativity. Other teachers also may have an opportunity to evaluate the quality of students' poetry, science projects, electronic or computer projects, dramatic talent, photography, unusual hobbies, and so on. Such information—"face valid" reflections of gifts and talents—should be very useful in the overall identification process.

Usually, product evaluations are quite informal; the product may obviously reflect high creativity, science ability, writing skill, analysis or synthesis talent, and so on. However, if a more structured and objective product rating form is desired, Appendix 4.4 presents a form developed and used by the State of Michigan Education Department. It is helpful to use more than one rater, since teacher variation (inter-rater reliability) in judgments of creative products needs to be considered. A method for establishing inter-rater reliability is described in Chapter 17.

Rating Scales

We already have seen several rating scales in conjunction with the teacher-, parent-, peer-, and self-nomination procedures and product evaluations. Renzulli and Hartman (1981; Renzulli, 1983) developed their *Scale for Rating Behavioral Characteristics of Superior Students* which provides a structured and quantifiable method for evaluating characteristics of intellectual ability, creativity, motivation, and leadership (see Appendix 4.5). While the scales can provide useful information, some teachers have found the scales to be time-consuming and unwieldy. A teachers' committee could consider abridging the scales. Even in briefer form, they would be more useful than an unstructured teacher nomination.

The Renzulli and Hartman motivation and leadership rating scales, incidentally, are unique in that usable, published tests of motivation and leadership are scarce to nonexistent. Rimm is developing a motivation inventory patterned after the GIFT and GIFFI inventories.

KRANZ TALENT IDENTIFICATION INSTRUMENT

The *Kranz Talent Identification Instrument* (KTII; Kranz, 1981) is an update of Bella "Bea" Kranz's very successful *Multidimensional Screening Device* (MDSD). A core assumption of the KTII is that (1) teachers are not good at identifying gifted children, but (2) they can be trained. The KTII involves training teachers to rate all children in their classes on ten different talent dimensions, some of which are rather unusual. A frequent outcome—if not the main purpose—of the training is to raise teachers' awareness of the multidimensionality of their students. As Fiedler (1982) said, "It forces teachers to walk all the way around the kids and look at them from different perspectives." An anonymous testimonial similarly claimed, "This instrument proved invaluable for (teacher) attitude development and awareness."

Significantly, and uniquely, the KTII specifically aims at identifying gifted and talented children from among students who are underachievers, minority members, or poor, or whose parents are immigrants or blue-collar workers who are not education oriented.

According to Kranz, the KTII procedure involves three main steps: (1) in-service training of the teachers, using in part a videotape starring Bea Kranz, in order to acquaint teachers with the ten talents and the rating procedure; (2) the actual rating of every student; and (3) the final selections by a separate screening committee, based upon the ratings and other student data. "Other student data" usually will include information from the *KTII Peer Nomination Forms,* the *KTII Parent Questionnaire,* and the *KTII Pupil Questionnaire,* an interest inventory.

The ten KTII talents are:

1. Visual arts talent
2. Performing arts talent
3. Creative talent
4. One-sided talent
5. Academic talent
6. Leadership and organizing talent
7. Psychomotor talent
8. Spatial and abstract thinking talent
9. Underachievement talent
10. Hidden talent

The KTII videotape and the KTII manual explain each of the talents and how they are recognized. The manual also suggests specific classroom activities and exercises that enable a teacher to observe and evaluate each type of talent.

Most of the talents need not be defined here; in fact, they almost duplicate the categories of the U.S.O.E. definition. However, (4) "one-sided talent," (9) "underachievement talent," and (19) "hidden talent" require a brief comment. One-sided talent refers to the energetic student who has maintained a long-term involvement with—and is an expert on—one particular hobby or interest. It might be photography, red-tailed hawks, the Beatles, or in Kranz's favorite example, salamanders. No matter what the topic of the class lesson or discussion—math, history, geography, spelling, social studies, or weather—the Salamander Kid can twist it into something relevant to salamanders.

Underachievement talent is not, as the name seems to suggest, a highly polished excellence in performing below one's ability. It simply refers to underachieving, the combination of high ability with low academic performance.

The most interesting of the Kranz talents is hidden talent, which comes in many forms. Primarily, it is the unusual ability to cope with school problems, despite significant home difficulties. The difficulties may include poverty, a different ethnic background, home tension and stress (as with drinking parents), caring for younger children and preparing meals because both mother and father must work (latchkey children), or else managing a dairy herd of 15 cows—morning and night—because father is incapacitated or absent. One of Kranz's examples of hidden talent was a 12-year-old boy who often accompanied his father to taverns, took the car keys when father got drunk, and then drove them both home. The hidden talent student may show " . . . fantastic oral ability, poetry-writing talent, or dramatic story-telling ability; the ability to think in two languages (English at school, native language at home); music and art talent; or an unusual depth of understanding" (Kranz, 1981).

An awareness of all ten talent areas should indeed alter teachers' perceptions of their students.

Kranz recommends some specific rating methods that might well be applied to any student-rating procedures. (1) She recommends "rating vertically," that is, rating each student in the class on one particular talent before proceeding to the next talent. (2) With the KTII, a 7-point scale is used. With the exception of academic talent (talent 5), Kranz recommends awarding only one 7 for each of the talents for each class, although there many be many 6's, 5's, 4's, and so on. (3) Rate students after January, when you know them. (4) Do not rate them in subject matter areas; the ten scales are intended to be content free. Grades and achievement test scores will provide plenty of information on specific academic talents.

Kranz (1981) notes that some talent combinations frequently occur in clusters. The same students might score high in visual arts, creativity, one-sided, and underachievement talent. Another group might score high in academic, performing arts, psychomotor, and leadership talent. However, you will never see the same student rated high in academic talent and underachievement talent.

As for the screening committee itself, Kranz recommends a group consisting of the principal, librarian, art teacher, music teacher, and G/T teacher. The screening committee gathers information about every child, including the ten KTII ratings, parent and peer nominations, the student interest questionnaire, and any other academic, ability, or creativity information. The information may be conveniently summarized on the KTII Public Composite Form for easier review. If questions arise concerning ratings needing clarification, such as a 7 in underachievement accompanied by a 7 in creativity, the teacher may ask for details. However, the screening committee, not individual teachers, will make the final decision.

THE REVOLVING DOOR IDENTIFICATION MODEL: RENZULLI

We noted in Chapter 3 that in Renzulli's *Revolving Door Identification Model* (RDIM; Reis and Renzulli, 1982; Renzulli, Reis, and Smith, 1981), about 25 percent of the school population is placed in a talent pool. These students revolve into a resource room to work on individual projects, then revolve out when the project is finished. Students are identified for the talent pool according to Renzulli's three-ring definition of giftedness described in Chapter 1. That is, a truly gifted student—one who is likely to make significant creative contributions to society—is one who possesses high creativity, high motivation, and above-average intelligence. Unlike the either-or strategy of the U.S.O.E. or other multiple-talent approaches, in which students high in any of the several abilities or talents will be selected, the Renzulli definition requires each selected student to possess all three characteristics. While this seems restrictive, selection is flexibly based on " . . . any objective and/or subjective knowledge about a child that can be gathered and recorded for purposes of making decisions about entrance into a Talent Pool" (Renzulli, Reis, and Smith, 1981, p. 7).

Renzulli and his colleagues specifically listed the following information sources to identify creativity, motivation, and ability: test scores, product evaluations, teacher ratings, peer ratings, self-ratings, and parent ratings, along with anecdotal records, observational reports, unstructured self-expressions, and classroom performances. Student interests and preferred learning styles (for example, group versus independent) are used both for identification and for individualized programming. Informal "action information," described as " . . . the type of dynamic interactions that take place when a student becomes 'turned on' about a particular topic, area of study, issue, event, or form of creative expression," is used by teachers to recommend specific motivated students for individual work in the resource room.

POLITICAL PROBLEMS IN IDENTIFICATION

In the real world of schools, identification of giftedness is surrounded by political and personal problems that go beyond reliability and validity. Teachers and administrators must be prepared for some controversies that surround identification. The criticisms one can expect will include everything from "Why isn't my child in the program?" to "Don't you dare identify my child as gifted," and anything in between. School board members may complain that teachers' children appear to be favored; teachers may note that offspring of administrators and board members are being selected. Some will call the selection process discriminatory and elitist; others will say it favors disadvantaged children.

Final Comment

The identification procedure is clearly a crucial part of any G/T program. We have emphasized that the identification procedures themselves operationally define exactly who is gifted and talented for any particular program. Further, the strategies described in this chapter do not alwa$_{\gamma}$ agree, that is, they will not identify the same students as "gifted" or "talented." Therefore, it is important that identification be related not only to one's definition of giftedness, but to the purpose and goals of the program.

As a reminder, gifts and talents extend beyond high intelligence, although academic ability is a highly important consideration. The U.S.O.E. definition, Taylor's Totem Poles, and the *Kranz Talent Identification Instrument* all emphasize the multidimensionality of gifts and talents. Using objective scores tempered by flexibility, reasonableness, and a real concern for children is necessary and defensible. Do not permit a low test score or a teacher/child conflict to eliminate an obviously gifted child from a challenge he or she needs.

SUMMARY

There are many identification strategies, based upon either one— usually IQ—or preferably many alternative criteria.

Reliability and validity of tests, rating scales, questionnaires, and identification procedures in general are a key concern. The four types of reliability are internal consistency, test-retest, equivalent forms, and inter-rater.

Criterion-related validity may be concurrent or predictive. Content validity refers to the degree to which the test content adequately represents the information or skills being assessed. Construct validity is the degree to which (unseen) psychological constructs are validly measured. Face validity is the degree to which the test appears to measure what it is supposed to.

The value of tests is tied to their reliability and validity. The flexible use of objective and subjective multidimensional criteria is recommended.

Teachers are biased toward identifying "teacher pleasers"—cooperative, neat, and punctual students—as gifted, perhaps missing creative, artistic, or extremely bright students. Going beyond IQ scores, a multidimensional approach to identifying gifted minority students is recommended; perhaps using a quota system to guarantee representation. Special attention also must be paid to identifying gifted girls, and learning-disabled and physically handicapped students.

The Stanford-Binet and WISC-R individual intelligence tests are recommended. The Binet has a very high ceiling; the WISC-R produces both Verbal and Performance (and Full Scale) IQ scores. Group intelligence tests are useful, but suffer from lower reliability and validity, low ceilings, and high verbal content. Any intelligence test will help identify gifted underachievers.

The Pygmalion research showed that IQ scores bias teachers' perceptions and (self-fulfilling) expectations of students.

Achievement tests are good indicators of specific academic talent. However, they usually have relatively low ceilings and they may not discriminate among gifted students who "top out." Grade equivalent scores do not mean that the student belongs in the grade indicated in the score. Teacher nominations are widely used, yet among the least reliable and valid.

Creativity tests may identify creative talent that is otherwise not visible. Because "creativity" is so complex, tests can have only moderate validity coefficients. Therefore, two indices of creativity are recommended for accurate identification. Two main types of creativity tests are divergent-thinking tests and personality/biographical inventories.

Parents know their children well and may provide valid information for identification. Peers are notoriously good at identifying classmates who are bright, creative, good readers, and good at math. Self-nominations also are recommended.

Product evaluations can be informal or conducted with structured evaluation forms.

The unique Renzulli-Hartman rating scales may be used to rate intellectual ability, creativity, motivation, and leadership.

Kranz's KTII evaluates ten talents, excluding specific academic talent. The procedure emphasizes training teachers to evaluate accurately. The KTII uniquely evaluates gifts and talents among underachieving, minority, poor, immigrant, or blue-collar children. Most notable are her "one-sided" and "hidden" talent categories.

Renzulli's Revolving Door Identification Model selects talent pool members according to Renzulli's three-ring definition of giftedness: high creativity, high motivation, and above-average ability. Many sources of information are used to select students for the talent pool. "Action information" is used to select specific students for work in the resource room.

Be aware of political problems, which range from charges of elitism and discrimination to accusations of favoring disadvantaged children and the children of teachers and administrators.

Identification procedures must be related to one's definition of giftedness and to the goals of the program. A multidimensional definition of gifts and talents is stressed; that is, a reduced emphasis on a strict IQ selection criterion. Criteria must be defensible, yet objective criteria should be modified by subjective concern for children.

APPENDIX 4.1 CANDIDATE NOMINATION FORM

Each of the five columns has a space provided at the top in which to print the FULL NAME of each of the five students with whom you work who would most nearly fit the U.S.O.E. definition of gifted and talented.

Place a "1" beneath the name of the student you rank first in each respective area. Place a "2" beneath the name of the student you rank second in each respective area. Continue by placing a "3," "4," and "5" under the names of those students you rank third, fourth, and fifth, respectively.

EXAMPLE

	Jon	Fred	Janice	Nancy	Miguel
Ability to analyze	5	2	1	4	3

In the box above, Janice was ranked first in Ability to analyze, Fred second, Miguel third, Nancy fourth, and Jon fifth.

Total each column. NOTE: The lowest total represents the top ranked student.

Ability to analyze					
Ability to generate ideas					
Acceptance of change					
Communication					
Cooperation					
Creativity					
Curiosity					
General knowledge					
Imagination					
Industriousness					
Intelligence					
Leadership					
Organization					
Physical ability					
Problem solving					
Reading					
Responsibility					
Self-concept					
Self-direction					
Sense of humor					
Sensitivity toward others					
TOTAL					

Starting with the lowest total score, enter the name and the total points for each of the five students on the lines below.

Candidate's Name	Total Score	Sex M F	Grade	Native American	Black	Asian	Spanish Surname	White	Other

School _____   Date _____

Teacher's signature _____   Principal's signature _____

APPENDIX 4.2 SAMPLE PARENT NOMINATION FORM AT THE EARLY CHILDHOOD LEVEL

Name of Student _____ Age _____

Address _____ School_____ Grade ___

Parent's Name _____

Instructions: In relationship to the typical child in your neighborhood, please circle a number for each item which best describes your child: 5—has this trait to a high degree; 4—has this trait more than the typical child; 3—compares with the typical child; 2—has this trait less than the typical child; 1—lacks this trait.

1. Has advanced vocabulary, expresses himself or herself well   5 4 3 2 1

2. Thinks quickly   5 4 3 2 1

3. Recalls facts easily   5 4 3 2 1

4. Wants to know how things work   5 4 3 2 1

5. Is reading (before he/she started kindergarten)   5 4 3 2 1

6. Puts unrelated ideas together in new and different ways   5 4 3 2 1

7. Becomes bored easily   5 4 3 2 1

8. Asks reasons why — questions almost everything   5 4 3 2 1

9. Likes "grown-up" things and to be with older people   5 4 3 2 1

10. Has a great deal of curiosity   5 4 3 2 1

11. Is adventurous   5 4 3 2 1

12. Has a good sense of humor   5 4 3 2 1

13. Is impulsive, acts before he/she thinks   5 4 3 2 1

14. Tends to dominate others if given the chance   5 4 3 2 1

15. Is persistent, sticks to a task   5 4 3 2 1

16. Has good physical coordination and body control   5 4 3 2 1

17. Is independent and self-sufficient in looking after himself/herself   5 4 3 2 1

18. Is aware of his/her surroundings and what is going on around him/her   5 4 3 2 1

19. Has a long attention span   5 4 3 2 1

20. Wanted to do things for himself/herself early — example: dressing and feeding himself/herself   5 4 3 2 1

APPENDIX 4.3 WHO KNOWS WHO'S WHO? PEER NOMINATION FORM

The Milwaukee Public School System created a structured peer nomination form which seems to ask: Who has a lot of information (1) Who does school work quickly and easily (2) Who is creative (3 and 5) Who is a leader (4).

You simply tally up who has the most votes in each category. A student who is outstanding in *all* categories is a good prospect for your gifted program.

Directions to Teacher

Read the following statements to your class:

1. "Each of you has been asked to assist in an information gathering survey for the Milwaukee Public Schools."
2. "Please take out a sheet of paper and a pencil."
3. "Number your paper from 1 to 5."
4. "Please answer each question that I will read with the *complete* name of one student in our class."
5. "Pick someone whom you think is the best choice and not just your friends."
6. "You can pick the same person for more than one question if you think that person is your best choice."

Questions

1. If a person from outer space wanted someone in your class to tell him about different things on earth, who do you think could tell the most?
2. What student in class can complete his or her work and still have time to take part in other activities?
3. Who says things in class that are most original, things that you never thought of before?
4. If kids didn't have to go to school, what student in your class could talk you into going?
5. Who do you think might invent or make something that no one ever made before? (This is the person you might ask to help you write a poem or play, or help you make something for a school science fair.)

APPENDIX 4.4 INSTRUMENT FOR RATING THE EXCELLENCE OF PROJECTS SUBMITTED BY STUDENTS

1. Briefly describe the product.

2. To what extent does the product represent an in-depth or superior handling of the subject?

5	4	3	2	1
To a great extent		Somewhat		To a limited extent

3. To what extent is this product of a "quality-level" beyond what one might expect of a student of this age?

5	4	3	2	1
To a great extent		Somewhat		To a limited extent

4. To what extent does the product indicate close attention to detail?

5	4	3	2	1
To a great extent		Somewhat		To a limited extent

5. To what extent is the central idea/ conception of the product beyond what a student of this age might undertake?

5	4	3	2	1
To a great extent		Somewhat		To a limited extent

6. To what extent is the product of overall excellence?

5	4	3	2	1
To a great extent		Somewhat		To a limited extent

7. List some of the criteria you used in evaluating the excellence of this product.

APPENDIX 4.5 THE RENZULLI-HARTMAN SCALE FOR RATING BEHAVIORAL CHARACTERISTICS OF SUPERIOR STUDENTS

Name_____ Date_____

School_____ Grade_____ Age_____
                                                          Yrs.   Mos.
Teacher or person completing this form_____

How long have you known this child? _____months

DIRECTIONS: These scales are designed to obtain teacher estimates of a student's characteristics in the areas of learning, motivation, creativity, and leadership. The items are derived from the research literature dealing with characteristics of gifted and creative persons. It should be pointed out that a considerable amount of individual differences can be found within this population; therefore, the profiles are likely to vary a great deal. Each item in the scales should be considered separately and should reflect the degree to which you have observed the presence or absence of each characteristic. Since the four dimensions of the instrument represent relatively different sets of behaviors, the scores obtained from the separate scales should not be summed to yield a total score. Please read the statements carefully and place an X in the appropriate place according to the following scale of values.

1. If you have seldom or never observed this characteristic
2. If you have observed this characteristic occasionally
3. If you have observed this characteristic to a considerable degree
4. If you have observed this characteristic almost all of the time

Space has been provided following each item for your comments.

SCORING: Separate scores for each of the four dimensions may be obtained as follows:

Add the total number of X's in each column to obtain the "Column Total."
Multiply the Column Total by the "Weight" for each column to obtain the "Weighted Column Total."
Sum the Weighted Column Totals across to obtain the "Score" for each dimension of the scale.
Enter the Scores below.

               Learning Characteristics   _____
            Motivational Characteristics   _____
               Creativity Characteristics   _____
               Leadership Characteristics   _____

(Reprinted by permission.)

APPENDIX 4.5 (Continued)

PART I: LEARNING CHARACTERISTICS

	1*	2	3	4

1. Has unusually advanced vocabulary for age
    or grade level; uses terms in a meaningful
    way; has verbal behavior characterized by
    "richness" of expression, elaboration, and
    fluency.

2. Possesses a large storehouse of information
    about a variety of topics (beyond the usual
    interests of youngsters his or her age).

3. Has quick mastery and recall of factual
    information.

4. Has rapid insight into cause-effect
    relationships; tries to discover the how
    and why of things; asks many provocative
    questions (as distinct from information
    or factual questions); wants to know
    what makes things (or people) "tick."

5. Has a ready grasp of underlying principles
    and can quickly make valid generalizations
    about events, people, or things; looks for
    similarities and differences in events,
    people, and things.

6. Is a keen and alert observer; usually
    "sees more" or "gets more" out of a
    story, film, etc., than others.

7. Reads a great deal on his or her own; usually
    prefers adult-level books; does not avoid
    difficult material; may show a preference for
    biography, autobiography, encyclopedias, and
    atlases.

8. Tries to understand complicated material by
    separating it into its respective parts;
    reasons things out for himself or herself;
    sees logical and common sense answers.

Column Total

Weight	1	2	3	4

Weighted Column Total

TOTAL

* 1—Seldom or never
  2—Occasionally
  3—Considerably
  4—Almost always

APPENDIX 4.5 (Continued)

PART II: MOTIVATIONAL CHARACTERISTICS

	1	2	3	4
1. Becomes absorbed and truly involved in certain topics or problems; is persistent in seeking task completion. (It is sometimes difficult to get him or her to move on to another topic.)				
2. Is easily bored with routine tasks.				
3. Needs little external motivation to follow through in work that initially excites him or her.				
4. Strives toward perfection; is self-critical; is not easily satisfied with his or her own speed or products.				
5. Prefers to work independently; requires little direction from teachers.				
6. Is interested in many "adult" problems such as religion, politics, sex, race — more than usual for age level.				
7. Often is self-assertive (sometimes even aggressive); stubborn in his or her beliefs.				
8. Likes to organize and bring structure to things, people, and situations.				
9. Is quite concerned with right and wrong, good and bad; often evaluates and passes judgment on events, people, and things.				
Column Total				
Weight	1	2	3	4
Weighted Column Total				
TOTAL				

APPENDIX 4.5   *(Continued)*

PART III: CREATIVITY CHARACTERISTICS

	1	2	3	4

1. Displays a great deal of curiosity about many things; is constantly asking questions about anything and everything.

2. Generates a large number of ideas or solutions to problems and questions; often offers unusual ("way out"), unique, clever responses.

3. Is uninhibited in expressing opinion; is sometimes radical and spirited in disagreement; is tenacious.

4. Is a high risk taker; is adventurous and speculative.

5. Displays a good deal of intellectual playfulness; fantasizes; imagines ("I wonder what would happen if ..."); manipulates ideas (i.e., changes, elaborates upon them); is often concerned with adapting, improving, and modifying institutions, objects, and systems.

6. Displays a keen sense of humor and sees humor in situations that may not appear to be humorous to others.

7. Is unusually aware of his or her impulses and more open to the irrational in himself or herself (freer expression of feminine interest for boys, greater than usual amount of independence for girls); shows emotional sensitivity.

8. Is sensitive to beauty; attends to aesthetic characteristics of things.

9. Is nonconforming; accepts disorder; is not interested in details; is individualistic; does not fear being different.

10. Criticizes constructively; is unwilling to accept authoritarian pronouncements without critical examination.

	1	2	3	4
Column Total				
Weight	1	2	3	4
Weighted Column Total				
TOTAL				

APPENDIX 4.5 (Continued)

PART IV: LEADERSHIP CHARACTERISTICS

	1	2	3	4
1. Carries responsibility well; can be counted on to do what he or she has promised and usually does it well.				
2. Is self-confident with children his or her own age as well as adults; seems comfortable when asked to show his or her work to the class.				
3. Seems to be well-liked by classmates.				
4. Is cooperative with teacher and classmates; tends to avoid bickering and is generally easy to get along with.				
5. Can express himself or herself well; has good verbal facility and is usually well understood.				
6. Adapts readily to new situations; is flexible in thought and action and does not seem disturbed when the normal routine is changed.				
7. Seems to enjoy being around other people; is sociable and prefers not to be alone.				
8. Tends to dominate others when they are around; generally directs the activity in which he or she is involved.				
9. Participates in most social activities connected with the school; can be counted on to be there if anyone is.				
10. Excels in athletic activities; is well-coordinated and enjoys all sorts of athletic games.				
Column Total				
Weight	1	2	3	4
Weighted Column Total				
TOTAL				

5

ACCELERATION

Feldhusen and Wyman (1980) thoughtfully itemized the central needs of gifted and talented children and adolescents in twelve points:

1. A maximum level of achievement in basic skills and concepts.
2. Learning activities at an appropriate level and pace.
3. Experience in creative thinking and problem solving.
4. The development of convergent-thinking abilities, particularly in logical deduction and convergent problem solving.
5. The strengthening of mental imagery, imagination, and spatial abilities.
6. The development of self-awareness and the acceptance of students' own capabilities, interests, and needs.
7. Stimulation to pursue higher-level goals and aspirations (perhaps via models, standards, or even "pressure").
8. Exposure to a variety of fields of study, including the arts, the professions, and various occupations.
9. The development of independence, self-direction, and discipline in learning.
10. Experience in relating intellectually, artistically, and affectively with other gifted, talented, and creative students.
11. A large fund of information about diverse topics.
12. Access to and stimulation of reading.

There are many types of programs and services designed to fit these needs while accommodating the level of interest, commitment, and resources of the particular school or district. Programs may differ in (1) the categories of students served, (2) the general curriculum model(s) followed, (3) specific enrichment curricula content and program goals, (4) acceleration plans, (5) grouping and organizational arrangements, (6) instructional or delivery strategy used, (7) community professionals and resources involved, and (8) program level (national, state, district, school, or classroom; Fox, 1979).

Overview

Entire books have been written about programming models, methods, and curricula; for example, Maker (1982), Juntune (1981), and Clasen, Robinson, Clasen, and Libster (1981). We are allowing four chapters for an overview of some major programming alternatives. Dividing programming into five topics, this chapter will summarize advantages, disadvantages, and recommendations associated with several frequently used acceleration strategies. Special attention will be given to the highly successful *Talent Search* programs, which include *Studies of Mathematically Precocious Youth* (SMPY), plus SMPY's more recent verbal offspring such as the *Project for the Study of Academic Precocity* (PSAP). Chapter 6 will focus on grouping methods, along with some basics of educational and career counseling. Chapter 7 will review enrichment options, and Chapter 8 will summarize some main curriculum models. These five categories overlap—for example, grouping may be for the purpose of acceleration, enrichment, or counseling, and a particular curriculum model may be designed to provide specific types of enrichment activities. Nonetheless, the present five-part approach—acceleration, grouping, counseling, enrichment, and curriculum models—should help clarify what can be done in successful programs, and provide ideas for how to do it.

ACCELERATION VERSUS ENRICHMENT

Before beginning, one issue deserves space: the traditional controversy regarding the merits of acceleration versus enrichment (see for example Daurio, 1979; Passow, 1958, 1981). For example, acceleration advocate Julian Stanley (1978b; Benbow and Stanley, 1983a, 1983b; Stanley and Benbow, 1983) argued that " . . . most of the supplemental educational procedures called 'enrichment' and given overly glamorous titles are, even at best, potentially dangerous if not accompanied or followed by acceleration . . . in subject matter and/or grade." On the surface, the distinction between acceleration and enrichment seems simple enough—

acceleration implies moving faster through academic content, while enrichment implies richer and more varied content. Looking more closely, however, the clear distinction has very fuzzy edges.

Acceleration, according to Fox (1979), means " . . . the adjustment of learning time to meet the individual capabilities of the students . . . leading to higher levels of abstraction, more creative thinking, and more difficult content." *Grade skipping,* for example, is a traditional acceleration method. At a 1981 "Great Debate," Van Tassel-Baska (1981b; "For Acceleration") argued that " . . . acceleration implies no more than allowing students to move at a rate with which they are comfortable and can excel, rather than holding them back to conform to a 'speed limit' set by the average learner. As for enrichment," she continued, "the term has no meaning for the gifted unless it is inextricably linked to good acceleration practices . . . "

Speaking for the opposition, Frost (1981; "For Enrichment") pointed out that enrichment " . . . implies a supplementation of the depth, breadth, or intensity of content and process as appropriate to the students' abilities and needs . . . [and is the prevailing practice because] . . . of the diversity in meeting student needs." One example of enrichment is the popular Wednesday or Thursday afternoon pullout or resource-room plan in which ten to fifteen elementary school students meet with a G/T teacher/coordinator for special exercises, activities, and individual projects. Fox (1979) noted that enrichment may be " . . . defined as the provision of learning experiences that develop higher processes of thinking and creativity in a subject area."

Defining Acceleration and Enrichment

According to these various descriptions, then, both acceleration and enrichment accommodate the high abilities and individual needs of gifted students, and both lead to depth, breadth, and the development of creativity and other high-level thinking skills. There are indeed G/T programs and activities in which the definitions of acceleration and enrichment seem overlapping and ambiguous. For example, is a special math, computer, or foreign language class in the elementary school considered "enrichment" or "acceleration"? And what of a similar course taught in high school?

There is a convenient rule-of-thumb definition that permits a reasonably clear distinction between acceleration plans versus enrichment plans: Any strategy that results in advanced placement or credit may be titled *acceleration*; strategies which supplement or go beyond standard grade-level work, but do not result in advanced placement or credit (that is, anything else) may be called *enrichment.* Thus the special foreign language or math class taught in elementary or junior high school, or a special drama or photography class taught in high school, that does not result in advanced credit or standing would be enrichment. If a junior or senior high school course or curriculum plan leads to early high school graduation or advanced standing in college, it is acceleration.

The recommendation of Fox (1979), Treffinger (1981), and others—with which we totally agree—is that both enrichment and acceleration are necessary. A well-rounded, coherent G/T program will implement plans for both types of services. Gifted students should be permitted to work at their own rapid pace, accelerating through and out of primary and second-ary schools. They also should have opportunities for greater variety in con-tent, greater depth, and the development of affective, creative, scientific, and other high-level skills, that is, enrichment. In addition, they should re-ceive educational and career counseling to help them understand them-selves and make their best educational decisions.

ACCELERATION STRATEGIES

Early Admission to Kindergarten or First Grade

Early admission to either kindergarten or first grade is an accelera-tion strategy relatively easy to administer and well supported by research. While the studies have varied in their criteria for selecting students and in their methods for evaluating success, the conclusions nonetheless have con-sistently favored early admission (Birch, 1954; Cutts and Mosely, 1957; Hobson, 1948; Reynolds, Birch, and Tuseth, 1976). Early-entering gifted children who are carefully selected for readiness perform schoolwork bet-ter and have been found to be at least as well adjusted as nonaccelerated gifted control groups.

Despite these research conclusions, teachers and administrators rarely favor admitting gifted youngsters early. This paradox becomes clearer with a closer comparison of the research findings with the typical teacher's experience.

Each of the successful early admission projects was based on a care-fully organized and administered screening program. For example, in the Birch (1954) study in Pittsburgh, 29 girls and 12 boys were selected from almost 400 applicants for early admission to first grade. Admission criteria included IQ scores above 130, superior reading readiness, superior social and emotional maturity, good health, and normal height and weight. In-formation about the first-grade population of the particular child's school also was considered.

On the other hand, teachers' negative experiences usually stem from children who were too immature to function well in their classes. The prob-lem is that these children typically have not been carefully screened. Imma-turity is certainly a disadvantage for an average child or even for a child with only slightly above-average ability. After several experiences with such children, teachers may incorrectly conclude that early entrance causes too many academic, personal, and social problems.

How can a school district resolve the differences between the results of multiple research projects and the typical teaching staff impressions? An early admission policy that gives careful consideration to the following variables is likely to select gifted children who will be successful despite their younger age.

Intellectual precocity.   An individual intelligence test score of 130 or more is recommended for early admission.

Eye-hand coordination.   Tests of eye-hand coordination should suggest at least average perceptual-motor skill, since problems in this area may put unnecessary stress on the early entrant who must participate in cutting, pasting, drawing, writing, and so on.

Reading readiness.   Reading is the skill most critical to early school success. Test scores should show clear readiness to read. Many gifted children are able to read prior to school entrance.

Social and emotional maturity.   Observations of the child in a preschool environment or by a psychologist will be important in determining likely school social adjustment.

Health.   A child who has a history of good health is more likely to attend school regularly and concentrate on classwork. Frequent health problems combined with a young age may put too much stress on even a very gifted child.

Sex.   Although each child must be considered individually, males do mature later than females and physical maturity is an important consideration. For this reason, it is not unusual or necessarily unfair for girls to be favored for early entrance.

School of entrance.   The average IQ in some schools may be 120 or 125, while in others the average may be 100 or less. Thus an early-entering child's intellectual ability should be considered relative to the school population. If the school has many very bright children, its regular fare is likely to provide adequate challenge. The gifted child therefore may do just as well by waiting to enter with same-age children.

Family values.   The child who is permitted to enter school early needs the support of a family that values education and academic achievement. For example, if success in team sports is an important family goal, there is a high risk of stress for the undersized accelerated boy. Hobson (1948) found that 550 early admitted youth compared favorably to nonaccelerates in general high school extracurricular activities; however, in a ten-year review of underage gifted boys he found only two who were outstanding in contact sports.

In sum, early entrance to kindergarten or first grade is definitely recommended for gifted children who are carefully screened according to the above criteria. If parents are considering early kindergarten admission for their precocious child, teachers and principals might recommend that they enroll the child in a quality nursery school. The nursery school will be helpful in providing parents and educators an opportunity to observe the child's social and cognitive adjustment in a school setting. Of course, the experience also will foster further skill development and will acquaint the child with some social and academic classroom routines.

Grade-skipping

Grade-skipping is the traditional method of accelerating precocious elementary school students. It requires no special materials or facilities, no G/T coordinator, not even a G/T program. In fact, it is extraordinarily cost-effective in moving the gifted or talented child through and out of the school system ahead of schedule. Grade-skipping may be initiated by parents who are aware that their child is one or two years ahead of the rest of the class and is bored with school and impatient with his or her peers, or by a teacher who makes the same observation. Grade-skipping or "double promotion" usually takes place in the lowest elementary grades, but sometimes in advanced grades. Some gifted children skip two or three grades (occasionally more) and enter college at age 15 or 16. Some parents become frustrated and agitated if their district does not permit grade-skipping; and many districts do not.

There are at least two major concerns regarding grade-skipping. The first is the problem of missing critical basic skills. Many teachers feel that if a child is not taught an important math or reading skill, he or she will be at a great disadvantage in later grades. They frequently predict that the child (1) will not be able to maintain good grades, (2) will see him or herself as less capable, and therefore (3) will lose school motivation. It is true that some skills are absolutely critical to the learning of later skills, and their absence could place stress on the student. However, many gifted students have acquired knowledge and skills far ahead of their grade levels, learned either independently or from an interested parent or older sibling. That is, the "missing skills" may not be missing at all. As a precaution, a series of diagnostic tests for the grade to be skipped can identify missing skills, and the motivated gifted child typically can learn these quickly, either working independently or with the help of interested adults.

The second problem, social adjustment to peers, is even more common. The concern here comes mainly from parents and teachers familiar with a gifted child who skipped a grade and experienced social problems or maladjustment. Once again we find a conflict between research conclusions and what many teachers, administrators, and parents claim. The current research-based consensus is that in most cases gifted students are quite comfortable with their *intellectual* peers—older students—and suffer no noticeable maladjustment or neuroses (for example, Daurio, 1979; Fox, 1979; Reynolds, 1960; Stanley, 1979; Witty, 1965). Terman and Oden (1947) found that children with IQs of 135 and above (mostly 140+) who had been accelerated one or two years made better adjustments than gifted students who were not accelerated.

The apparent contradiction may come from some faulty assumptions and interpretations, for example:

1. Many persons look back to their adolescence as being a difficult time for social adjustment; persons who have been accelerated may incorrectly blame these problems on their acceleration. Persons who were not accelerated might blame their problems on other factors. For example, in an interesting self-analysis of "social life and adjustment" by a person who entered college early, Richard J. Cohn (1980) observed that accelerated students determine their own adjustment, and " . . . people who have little or no social life (in college) at age 17 or 18 would probably have the same problems if they were older. . . . Some people adjust, but some don't."

2. Although many studies concluded that gifted children are better socially adjusted than typical students, other studies have found that for children with very high intelligence social adjustment is indeed a most difficult task (Hollingworth, 1942; Terman and Oden, 1947). Since these children are the ones most likely to be skipping grades, their social problems, actually related to their extremely high intelligence, may mistakenly be attributed to acceleration.

3. When outsiders observe a school child who is noticeably smaller or younger than average, based on appearance alone they may infer that the child certainly must be having social problems, even though testimony from the child him- or herself does not indicate any special problems.

To reduce the risk of problems related to grade-skipping the authors recommend the following guidelines, some of which duplicate the above recommendations for early admission to kindergarten or first grade:

1. To skip an entire grade, a child should have an individually tested IQ score of 135 or higher.

2. Regardless of ability, only one grade should be skipped at a time. After the child has had several years for adjustment, there may be reason to consider skipping another grade.

3. Skill gaps should be diagnosed so that the child can be assisted in acquiring any missing basic skills.

4. A supportive teacher, counselor, and/or group of gifted peers should be available to help the child with social problems related to grade-skipping.

5. Parent value systems need to be considered. Especially if families place more emphasis on athletics than academics, grade-skipping may put considerable pressure on the student who may not be big enough to compete.

6. An appraisal of the child's present intellectual and social adjustment should be considered in the decisionmaking. If the child is not making a good social adjustment in the present grade, grade-skipping cannot be assumed to improve that adjustment; and continued poor adjustment in the higher grade should not necessarily be attributed to the grade-skipping. Grade-skipping is not a cure-all, and a given child may require further guidance regardless of the grade-skipping decision.

7. Every grade-skipping decision needs to be made separately. Physical maturity, height, general emotional stability, motivation, and ability to handle challenge all should be part of the decisionmaking. Centrally important is the gifted child's need for intellectual stimulation.

Finally, teachers and parents too often conclude that it is simply easier to avoid making a decision that favors grade-skipping. Administratively, and in view of general inertia, they are of course correct. However, teachers and parents should recognize that keeping a highly precocious child in an unstimulating environment is also making a decision—one that communicates to the gifted child that he or she is not expected to perform up to his or her capability. That decision, says most research, is more intellectually and sometimes even socially harmful to the gifted child than the decision to skip grades. Boredom, restlessness, frustration, and disruptiveness can be replaced by enhanced motivation, improved self-concepts, and improved study habits and productivity (Bartkovich and Mezynski, 1981; Hall, 1982; Karnes & Chauvin, 1982a, 1982b; Tobin, 1979).

Subject-skipping

Grade-skipping is sometimes called "full acceleration," and subject-skipping therefore is "partial acceleration." Subject-skipping involves taking classes or studying particular subjects with students in higher grades. It is especially appropriate in sequential types of subject matters, particularly reading, math, and languages, but possible in other subjects as well. Subject-skipping therefore is appropriate for the student with special skills and talents primarily in a single area. The acceleration may begin in the elementary school and continue through high school.

Subject-skipping has important advantages and only one major disadvantage. On the positive side, it permits the child to be intellectually challenged in a specific area of strength while he or she continues to develop appropriate grade-level skills in other areas. It also permits the child to remain with chronologically similar peers to whom he or she already may be socially adjusted. The disadvantage of subject-skipping is the problem of continuity. Too often a particular school or teacher may be willing to accelerate a student in a single subject, such as math, but makes no overall organizational plan for continuous progress. Therefore, the child who masters three years of math in just one may suddenly discover that he or she must repeat two of them. Such repetition is likely to be more boring and damaging than moving the child through the material more slowly in the first place. However, if continuous accelerated coursework can be planned for the child, subject acceleration is an ideal approach for children with high abilities in specific areas.

Early Admission to Junior or Senior High School

This particular acceleration alternative seems not to be popular. However, for some students, the best grade to be skipped is the one just before junior or senior high school, that is, grade five or six, or grade eight or nine. From an academic perspective, the student may be ready and anxious for advanced work in the specialized and departmentalized junior or senior high school. Socially, it may be an opportune time to accelerate, since new friendships inevitably develop when students from several elementary or junior high schools meet for the first time in the new school setting.

Credit by Examination

In the junior or senior high school, one cost-free mechanism for justifiable subject-skipping is credit by examination. For example, if a talented mathematics or language student feels he or she already has acquired the content of a semester course, perhaps through home study or foreign travel, the student should be allowed to "test out" of the course and, if mastery is demonstrated, receive academic credit. In addition to preventing repetition and boredom, allowing credit by examination will encourage gifted students to accept challenges, set goals, and work toward them.

As a precaution in using this option, the student should be provided with an outline of the material to be included in the test. This gives the student a fair opportunity to appraise his or her own skills and to concentrate study on those not yet mastered. Failure experienced on tests due to lack of adequate preparation, or else miscommunication about the test content, is likely to be an unpleasant experience for both the student and the school staff involved.

College credit, which permits advanced placement when the student enters college, also may be earned through examination, as in the *Advanced Placement* (AP) program described below or in the *College Level Examination Program* (CLEP; see for example, Karnes and Chauvin, 1982a). Unlike the AP program, CLEP does not offer courses, just examinations. Examinations for college credit are available in science, math, English (composition and literature), social sciences, business, computer science, nursing, education, psychology, and foreign languages. Most of the exams are 90 minute multiple-choice tests. A person is limited to four of these tests in one day (not many ask for more). A failed exam may be repeated after six months. The examinations are given at selected centers in the third week of every month (excluding December and February). Special administrations at more convenient locations may be requested by persons living more than 150 miles from the nearest center. The cost at the time of this writing is an exceedingly generous $22 for the first test and $18 for additional tests taken within one month. Before registering, one should check to determine if the college of one's choice will accept CLEP credits, because not all do. For additional information, write to College Board, Box 1824, Princeton, NJ, 08541.

College Courses in High School

Several approaches may be used for giving students the opportunity to take college courses while still in high school. With a dual enrollment program, a student may be excused from high school for part of the day to take one or more courses on the college campus. The earned college credits may be used at the particular college to place the student in advanced standing when he or she actually is admitted; alternatively, the credits normally can be transferred to another college of the student's choice. Importantly, the courses also should be credited toward high school graduation requirements so that the student is not burdened—punished—with twice the amount of coursework.

If a sufficient number of capable high school students wish to take a particular college course, it is possible for a college professor to come to the high school to teach the course for college credit. The students will need to pay college tuition.

A highly desirable alternative, the *Advanced Placement* (AP) program, like CLEP, is conducted by the College Board. The AP program consists of college-level courses and examinations for high school students. The courses may take the form of an honors class or a strong regular class taught by a teacher following an Advanced Placement outline, or via independent study, perhaps with a tutor. Current offerings include three courses in physics, two courses each in calculus, English, Spanish, German, French, music, and studio arts, and one course in American history, European history, biology, chemistry, and art history. The courses require a full year to complete, primarily because all exams are given each spring in the third week of May.

Any student may take the exams, whether or not he or she has formally participated in an AP course. The AP program thus allows credit by examination. Presently, about 650 of America's 3,000+ colleges accept AP credits. As for cost effectiveness, an entire year of college credit may be earned for about $42 per exam, " . . . at a savings ranging from $2,000 to $8,000" (Karnes & Chauvin, 1982a). The brochure *Guide to the Advanced Placement Program* is available free from College Board Publications Orders, Box 2815, Princeton, NJ, 08541. Additional information about AP programs is available from the College Board offices whose addresses are listed at the end of this chapter.

Generally, the factor most critical to the success of permitting—indeed, encouraging—high school students to accept the challenge of earning college credits is high school administrative flexibility.

Correspondence Courses

If a college is not accessible, and perhaps AP courses or independent study are not feasible, every major university offers correspondence courses at least at the college freshman and sophomore levels. Correspondence courses thus present valuable opportunities for the talented student who lives in a rural area or a small city or town. Correspondence courses carry full college credit. They are written by a professor and are taught by a college professor, instructor, or a qualified graduate student. Courses are available in a variety of areas, for example, college math, algebra, or statistics, or introductory psychology, educational psychology, sociology, economics, anthropology, astronomy, history, foreign languages, and others. The courses may be taken in the summer, as a form of independent study, or as a form of enrichment in conjunction with a regular high school program. Typically, courses requiring student-teacher interaction or laboratories are not taught by mail—for example, biology, physics, or chemistry.

If the reader plans to encourage a student to take a correspondence course, it is important to realize that a considerable amount of self-motivation and independence is needed to successfully complete such a course. Students are more likely to be successful if several of them are working on the same course, thus permitting mutual support, stimulation, and assistance. It is also helpful if a high school faculty member can serve as an advisor for the students in case they need help in understanding or interpreting the material or solving practice problems.

Telescoped Programs

Telescoping means, for example, collapsing three academic years' work into two, or four years of high school into three. In the junior high school, if enough talented young mathematicians are available for special classes a normal three-year math and algebra sequence might be taught at an accelerated pace in two years. It is less common, but the same telescoping can be used with other subjects, for example, by condensing three years of junior high school science into two years.

In high school, telescoping four years' work into three is almost entirely a counseling problem, assuming that district policies will permit such acceleration. The energetic and capable student, with the assistance of his or her counselor, simply cuts down on the "study hall" classes and schedules four years of high school requirements into a more compact and busier three. If three years is unrealistic for a student, a three-and-a-half year program still would permit a capable student to begin college a semester early.

Early Admission to College

Sometimes this plan is called "early high school graduation" (Kaplan, 1974). Either way, with or without a deliberate telescoping plan many gifted and talented high school students are permitted to enter college early on a full-time basis (Fox, 1983; Karnes and Chauvin, 1982a, 1982b). In some cases high school requirements are met early, as in telescoping plans. In other cases high school requirements are flexibly waived and a qualified student simply enters college full-time without meeting all of the usual graduation requirements. With the latter plan, in view of college entrance requirements one must be sure that the particular college admissions office is agreeable to such short-cutting before plans reach an advanced stage. Some college admissions offices are not wildly enthusiastic about early entrants.

Early graduation is an excellent way for a mature gifted student to accelerate his or her education, which is likely to extend through many years of graduate work. Said early graduate R. J. Cohn (1980), it is a good strategy " . . . for people who feel they've outgrown school socially and emotionally, as well as for those who are bored academically. Many people with whom I've spoken have felt their senior year of high school could have been better spent." Unfortunately, although the authors feel that school policies should support such initiative, many high school teachers and administrators discourage early graduation and early college admission. Also, high school students who attempt this approach may feel pressure to remain in high school in the form of missing opportunities for scholarships and honors and, of course, missing the social and extracurricular activities.

The early graduate should be prepared to trade some of these opportunities for the challenge of early college entrance.

TALENT SEARCH: STUDY OF MATHEMATICALLY PRECOCIOUS YOUTH

The best-known example of accelerating bright secondary students into college-level work is the highly successful *Talent Search* programs, which began at Johns Hopkins University in 1971 as Julian Stanley's *Studies of Mathematically Precocious Youth* (SMPY; Benbow and Stanley, 1983b; Stanley, 1977, 1979, 1982b; Stanley and George, 1980; see also Bartkovich and Mezynski, 1981; S. J. Cohn, 1983a; George, 1976, 1979a, 1979b; Tobin, 1979). The purpose of SMPY has been to locate students with extraordinarily high mathematics talent and help them develop their gift. In an Annual Mathematics Talent Search, primarily seventh-grade students are selected on the basis of very high Scholastic Aptitude Test–Mathematics (SAT-M) scores, usually above 640, about the top one percent, but currently 700 (S. J. Cohn, 1983a). In its early years the students took summer or Saturday mathematics classes, usually taught by a college professor at Johns Hopkins. According to Stanley (1982a), by working 5 to 6 hours per day, these students in three weeks can master one to two years of high school algebra and geometry. Said Stanley, many of them learn more effectively in three weeks than in a full academic year—they are working, not sleeping. By eighth grade, they are ready for calculus.

High school SMPY participants are encouraged to pursue any of a "smorgasbord" of acceleration options (Stanley, 1977, 1979, 1982a; Stanley and Benbow, 1983): (1) They may attend college part-time, earning credit for advanced placement; (2) they may earn college credit by examination in the Advanced Placement program; (3) they may skip a grade, particularly the one at the end of junior high school; (4) they may complete two or more years of mathematics in one year; (5) they may enter college early, either by early high school graduation or " . . . simply by leaving high school before completing the last grade(s) . . . " (Stanley, 1979). In every case, Talent Search students receive individual counseling regarding the educational alternatives that might be appropriate for them to pursue.

A few selected and unbiased testimonials by Stanley (1979) may be of interest: "The boredom and frustration of even the average-scoring (SMPY) contestants when incarcerated in a year-long algebra class is difficult to appreciate. Often, highly able youths themselves are not aware of the extent of their slowdown, because it has been their lot from kindergarten onward. . . . Often, they take off like rockets intellectually when allowed to do so. . . . It is clear that a large reservoir of virtually untapped mathematical reasoning ability exists all around the region . . . "

In recent years, the program has been extended in two ways: (1) It extends to verbal academic areas, with selection based upon the verbal portion of the SAT (SAT-V), and (2) it is virtually a national program, if not an international one.

In 1979 at Johns Hopkins University the Office of Talent Identification and Development was created, now named the Center for the Advancement of Academically Talented Youths (CTY). SMPY still conducts a search, now nationally, for students who score 700 or higher on the SAT-M before age 13 (seventh or eighth grade); CTY searches for students who score 630 or higher on the SAT-V prior to age 13. As of 1983, all fifty states, five Canadian provinces, and Hamburg, West Germany, have participated in Talent Search activities, which have included an estimated 70,000 to 90,000 students (S. J. Cohn, 1983a). Talent searches are sponsored by a number of universities, including Arizona State University, University of Denver, Duke University, Northwestern University, and, of course, Johns Hopkins University. The College Board has taken an interest in Talent Search and warns test-site administrators that students who are younger than usual will be taking the SAT.

Sanford J. Cohn's (1983a, 1983b) *Project for the Study of Academic Precocity* (PSAP) at Arizona State University is a good example of how a worthy Talent Search program can be conducted. Over 12,200 young people took part in the "1983 Western States and Canadian Provinces Talent Search." This summer program offered fourteen "rigorous academically-oriented classes" plus three Advanced Placement (AP) classes: geology, computer science (Fortran, Pascal, microcomputers), speech and debate, advanced language and composition (AP), expository writing, vocabulary development, Latin, Latin and Greek, calculus (AP), "fast mathematics," survey of social sciences, chemistry (AP), economics, mythology, and laboratory science. Admission to each class was based upon minimum SAT scores plus a fee. For example, Computer Science-Fortran required an SAT-M score of 450 and a combined SAT-M and SAT-V score of 850, along with $190 plus books.

In addition, PSAP offers four counseling workshops and five classes for 8- to 11-year olds (math, writing, Spanish, science, classics). The counseling workshops cover educational planning, communication skills, study skills, and career exploration.

Interestingly, PSAP flexibly accommodates the needs of students who are younger or older than the standard seventh- or eighth-grader. We noted that the 1983 program offered five classes for students age 8 to 11. For others, based upon ten hours of testing, Individualized Education Programs (IEPs) are developed based upon a detailed profile of the students' assessed abilities and skills.

Clearly, there is good reason the Talent Search acceleration programs, such as Cohn's PSAP, have been highly successful and have been enthusiastically received.

SUMMARY

Gifted students must develop in the areas of basic skills, creative and convergent problem solving, self-awareness, self-direction, general information, and career information, along with acquiring high-level aspirations and experience in relating to other G/T students.

G/T programs vary in students served, acceleration, grouping and enrichment plans, resources involved, program level, and other dimensions.

Acceleration, which speeds up learning time to match student capabilities, is defined as programming that results in advanced placement or credit; *enrichment,* which adds depth and breadth, is anything else. Both accommodate the high abilities and individual needs of gifted students. Educators have debated the merits of each. However, both are required in any well-rounded program.

With early admission to kindergarten or first grade, students are most likely to succeed if they are carefully screened. They should be intellectually precocious (recommended IQ = 130+), at least average in motor coordination, and possess adequate reading readiness, social/emotional maturity, and good health. Girls often are more mature. If a particular school already caters to very bright students, early admission may be unnecessary. Family values should emphasize academic achievement.

Grade-skipping is a good alternative. The problem of missing some essential basic skills can be solved via diagnostic tests and remedial work, if necessary. Research shows that social adjustment is usually not a problem. Acceleration is sometimes blamed for normal adolescent personal or social problems. Maladjustment due to extremely high IQ also is sometimes blamed on grade-skipping. Grade-skipping may be most successful if the student shows an IQ score of 135+, if one grade is skipped at a time, if support from a teacher, counselor, or gifted peer is available, and if intellectual and social adjustment is considered in the decision.

Subject-skipping permits the child to remain with age-mates while being challenged in a particular area of strength. Continuity with later grades probably is the only shortcoming, and one which can be provided for.

Early admission to junior or senior high school is a socially opportune time to skip a grade. The student may well be ready for the more specialized course content.

Credit by examination encourages G/T students to accept challenges and saves repetition and boredom. To be fair, an outline of the material to be covered on the test should be provided. College credit by examination may be earned in the AP program or the CLEP. Both are highly cost effective.

In a dual enrollment program, students take college courses while still in high school. Credits from college courses taken in high school should count toward high school graduation. In the AP program, students take college courses in an honors class, a fast regular class, or as independent study. With or without taking the AP courses, students may earn college credit by scoring sufficiently high in the May AP examinations.

Correspondence courses require considerable self-direction. It is therefore desirable for a group of students to take the same course and for a high school teacher or counselor to monitor progress and perhaps assist.

Telescoping involves condensing a two- or three-year course, or high school program, into fewer years.

Early college admission, or early high school graduation, is strongly recommended, despite the problem of forfeiting honors or scholarships that require attendance for the full four years. Many good students are socially and academically ready.

Stanley's Johns Hopkins University SMPY program has been remarkably successful in identifying and assisting young students, typically seventh graders, who show extraordinary math talent, that is, who score above 640 on the SAT-M. They take special summer or Saturday math classes, covering one or two years' work in a few weeks. They also may attend college part-time, earn college credit by examination, skip a grade, telescope two or more high school years of math into one, or enter college early.

In recent years SMPY has expanded into the national Talent Search program, and includes verbal as well as mathematical precocity as measured by the SAT-Verbal test.

Sanford Cohn's PSAP program at Arizona State University involves a rich assortment of summer courses and counseling, with admission based upon SAT-M and SAT-V scores. The program also accommodates younger students, with classes for 8- to 11-year-olds and IEPs for others.

COLLEGE BOARD OFFICES

New York Office:
888 Seventh Ave.
New York, NY 10019
(212) 582-6210

Middle States Regional Office:
Suite 1418
1700 Market St.
Philadelphia, PA 19103
(215) 567-6555

Midwestern Regional Office:
1 American Plaza
Evanston, IL 60201
(312) 866-1700

New England Regional Office:
470 Totten Pond Rd.
Waltham, MA 02154
(617) 890-9150

Southern Regional Office:
Suite 200
17 Executive Park Dr., NE
Atlanta, GA 30329
(404) 636-9465

Southwestern Regional Office:
Suite 922
211 E. Seventh St.
Austin, TX 78701
(512) 472-0231

Denver Office:
Suite 23
2142 South High St.
Denver, CO 80210
(303) 777-4434

Western Regional Office:
800 Welch Rd.
Palo Alto, CA 94304
(415) 321-5211

6

GROUPING AND COUNSELING

Grouping students of like ability has an interesting history in American education. Ability grouping or "tracking" was common prior to about 1969–1970. The altruistic rationale was that faster-learning students with higher intelligence and achievement scores should be grouped together so they could receive the greater breadth and depth that their abilities permitted. Less able students should be allowed to move at a slower pace and not be forced into frustrating competition with brighter children. On the other hand, such grouping tends to permanently brand students as either bright or stupid. As we mentioned in Chapter 4, psychologists Rosenthal and Jacobson's (1968) book *Pygmalion in the Classroom* launched a stormy "I-knew-it-all-the-time" reaction in American intellectual and educational circles. Although their work has been soundly criticized (for example, Elashoff and Snow, 1971), they essentially demonstrated that IQ scores bias teachers' expectations of students. In a self-fulfilling prophecy, teachers expect less and get less from children labeled as "slow learners" or "low-IQ" students. Publicity was widespread, and ability grouping and routine IQ testing—both of which influence teacher expectations—were scrapped in district after district (see Brophy, 1982; Cooper, 1979; or Davis, 1983b, for reviews).

With the resurgence of interest in gifted-and-talented programming that arose in the 1970s, however, some forms of grouping have become acceptable, even recommended.

Grouping is "providing various organizational structures of either long or short duration whereby students of like ability can work together" (Robinson, Davis, Fiedler, and Helman, 1982). These may include:

Full-time homogeneous classes:
      Magnet schools
      Special schools for the gifted
      Private schools
      School-within-a-school plans
      Special G/T classes in the elementary school

Full-time heterogeneous classes:
      Combined grades in a regular class
      High-ability cluster groups of gifted students placed with "regular" students
      Mainstreaming in the regular class

Part-time or temporary groups:
      Pullout programs
      Resource-room plans
      Special classes
      Activity clubs
      Honors programs
      Special or accelerated classes in the secondary school.

There are indeed many grouping plans, most of which will require a formal reorganization of the school's staff, space, and material resources. Many plans (for example, magnet schools) will require some degree of reorganization of the school system of the entire city or district.

Overview

In this chapter we will take a closer look at grouping options categorized under full-time homogeneous grouping, full-time heterogeneous grouping, and part-time or temporary grouping. Then we will turn to that important and often neglected component of gifted education: counseling. Too many gifted students feel alone or that they are "freakish outcasts"; many receive precious little of the educational, career, and/or personal guidance they may desperately need (Delisle, 1982).

FULL-TIME HOMOGENEOUS GROUPING

Magnet Schools

Several large cities have sought to accommodate the needs of not only gifted and talented high school students, but "regular" students seeking special training in a trade or skill. A clear purpose is to make school relevant to realistic student goals, particularly for potential dropouts who view school as "prison," rather than a path to economic and social success. Note that gifted students, as well as low-ability students, too often become frustrated and drop out. Boston, Cincinnati, Houston, Winston-Salem, Milwaukee, and St. Louis, for example, are experimenting with magnet high schools (Cox and Daniel, 1983b). New York City has used such specialty schools for many years. All of these offer specialized training in, say, the arts, math and science, business, or trade skills. A school also may be designated as a "superior abilities school" with a curriculum planned around students with those abilities. Students are bused in from all corners of the city or district to attend the high school that suits their educational and career interests. In some cases, they are placed in career-related part-time jobs so they may earn money and gain valuable experience while attending school. Such programs are indeed relevant, and they do meet students needs. They also are known to reduce the dropout rate.

Special Schools for the Gifted

Creating special schools for the gifted typically is a big-city alternative. An entire elementary or secondary school may be designated for gifted and talented youngsters. In all cases the curriculum will include both traditional academic content—based upon district guidelines and requirements—plus special enriched and accelerated training in whatever personal development, artistic, or scientific areas the school chooses to emphasize.

At the elementary level, one example of a special school is the Golda Meir School in Milwaukee. Students are selected from the entire district based upon the U.S.O.E. criteria (general ability, specific academic aptitude, creativity, leadership, or visual or performing art talent), as reflected in test scores, grades, and teacher, parent, and peer nominations (Pfeil, 1978). A quota system is used to balance the school composition for sex, race, and representation from all school districts in the Milwaukee system. Because this is an elementary school, subject matter acceleration is limited so that students will not be advanced beyond grade level in particular subjects when they enter the regular junior high school.

Enrichment opportunities, however, are diverse and exciting. They include foreign language training; piano, violin, viola, and general music lessons; drama lessons from members of the Milwaukee Repertory Company; the creation of a school newspaper, aided by Milwaukee Journal reporters; field trips to Milwaukee's civic, financial, and cultural centers (between about 12 and 30 trips per student per year); "MACS Packs" (math-arts-crafts-science) which offer daily student projects; and "Lunch Bunch" involvement in games, films, reading, or just visiting. There is a Classics Club which reads above-grade level books, an Advanced Science Club, a school chorus, a Student Senate, and sometimes an infant-care class featuring a real infant—typically a student's younger brother or sister. Enthusiasm of staff and students runs extremely high. This model plan continually hosts many visitors.

An example of a special school at the secondary level, the Alabama School of Fine Arts in Birmingham offers a six-year curriculum (grades 7–12) of general academic studies (history, social studies, English, general sciences, math, and foreign languages) plus career-oriented preprofessional training in creative writing, dance, drama, music, or the visual arts. Identification and admission are based upon the student's previous academic history, an evaluation of his or her artistic training and background, an audition or other talent evaluation by a "jury board," and an interview designed to " . . . determine the degree of potential ability, the seriousness of purpose and the maturity of the student" (Juntune, 1981).

Private Schools

In recent years James Coleman (1981), author of the famous Coleman Report, has received considerable publicity for his research-based conclusion that achievement runs higher in private schools than in public schools. The glitch in his conclusion, obviously, is that only privileged students can attend the schools, and so achievement would be expected to be higher. Whatever the reasons for the higher achievement, Stanley (1982a) also recommended private schools as one avenue for an accelerated education.

Some private schools cater especially to gifted and talented students. In Hillsborough, California, for example, the Nueva Learning Center is designed " . . . to provide high potential students (age 4–12 years) with opportunities for developing living skills, attitudes, and knowledge which are rarely available to them through normal learning channels . . . to stimulate curiosity, encourage participation, and generate interest" (Juntune, 1981). There is training in six *R*'s (reading, writing, arithmetic, rights, respect, and responsibility), piano, ballet, math, science, and more unusual topics such as organic gardening, aviation, karate, and cross-country skiing. Responsibility, awareness, and confidence are prime goals. Student selection is based upon standardized testing (for example, the WISC-R) and interviews. Roughly following the U.S.O.E. definition, "high potential" at the Nueva Learning Center means exceptional intellectual ability, and/or high creativity, and/or special and unusual talent in some specific area (art, science, math, leadership, or physical prowess).

School-within-a-School

Similar to special regular classes for G/T students (section follows), an entire school may be organized around a school-within-a-school concept. Here, gifted and talented students from around the district attend a particular school that also accommodates "regular" students. For part of the day, G/T students attend special classes taught by special teachers. They mix with the rest of the students for nonacademic subjects (for example, physical education, study hall, manual arts, home economics) and for sports and social events.

Special Classes

Special classes for gifted and talented students may take several forms. First, at the elementary level all gifted students within a particular grade level, age, or age range, may be assigned to a special class. In addition to covering prescribed grade-level objectives—and usually extending beyond them—a variety of enrichment, personal development, and skill development experiences are planned. These may include exercising higher-thinking skills, such as creativity, analysis, synthesis, evaluation, and critical thinking, values training and other personal development activities, library and research skills, foreign language training, exposure to classic literature, typing, computer work, and others.

There are pros and cons to separating G/T elementary students into special classes. In the plus column, the students naturally benefit academically and personally from a curriculum that matches their abilities, and which tells them they have special talents. Importantly, they need to meet and interact with students like themselves, students who will accept, encourage, and challenge them. In the negative column, they may resist being physically and psychologically separated from regular students, and perhaps labeled as "gifties" or "brains." Other students may resent their special status and may cause them to feel socially uncomfortable.

In the typical secondary school, there already are available a variety of college preparatory classes to challenge the abilities of gifted and talented students, for example, in chemistry, physics, calculus, art, journalism, and drama. Special classes beyond these also may be created, for example, courses in college algebra, organic chemistry, advanced physics, advanced botany, creative writing, photography, or whatever else students need and the school budget will allow. If some of these can be taught in accord with Advanced Placement program guidelines they may lead to college credit, as described in Chapter 5. Budget and staffing are critical considerations, since special classes may be considered "frills."

FULL-TIME HETEROGENEOUS GROUPING

Multi-Age Classrooms

Frequently, a school will combine grades—say, a group of fourth-graders with a group of fifth-graders. In many cases this arrangement is an administrative convenience—the school has too many fourth and fifth graders to fit them into existing classes, but not enough to justify *two* additional classes. Therefore, "good" fourth-grade students usually are selected who might benefit from learning and interacting with children who are one chronological year older. Probably a minimal form of acceleration, it is effective only if the fourth-grade students are not required to repeat similar learning experiences the following year.

Some entire elementary schools are organized according to a multi-age plan. These grouping strategies usually are not designed specifically as G/T programs. However, they lend themselves nicely to the type of individualization and cluster grouping which does accommodate G/T children. For example, Klausmeier's *Individually Guided Education-Multi-Unit School* (IGE-MUS) plan (Klausmeier and Goodwin, 1975; Klausmeier, Quilling, Sorenson, Way, and Glasrud, 1971) eliminates the traditional concept of age-graded, lock-step, self-contained classrooms. Briefly, a 600-student elementary school is divided into four units of about 150 students each; for example, with students ages 4–6, 6–9, 8–10, and 10–12. Each unit is composed of a unit leader, two or three staff teachers, a first-year teacher, an intern, an instructional aide, and an instructional secretary. There is instruction with large groups, for example, a movie or demonstration for the 150 students, class-sized groups, small groups, and individuals.

The plan centers upon individualized instruction, which permits capable students to accelerate through the regular curriculum at a comfortable pace, skipping content they already know. Reading, math, and science materials have been specially written for IGE-MUS schools. The IGE plan also accommodates early entry of preschool students into school, and cluster grouping of G/T students for special assignments and projects. According to Klausmeier, IGE schools facilitate the analysis of individual learning problems, the development of creative and problem-solving skills, and the development of aesthetic potential of students (Klausmeier and Goodwin, 1975). Elman and Elman (1983) described how flexible, multi-age grouping in a laboratory school easily permitted groups of fast students to tackle more advanced material, particularly in reading and math.

Cluster Groups

There are several variations and interpretations of "cluster groups." To some, "cluster grouping" means placing G/T students together in a special class, either in the elementary school or the secondary school. Others speak of "cluster grouping" students in accelerated classes or honors classes. To still others, "cluster grouping" means putting a selected group of, say, 5 or 10 gifted students together in one regular class, along with 15 or 20 other students. We will review the latter form of cluster grouping in this section.

A cluster group of G/T students in a regular class engages in a variety of enrichment activities either individually or in small groups. For example, they might "contract" for independent learning activities such as a library research report, an independent research project, or the mastery of an advanced math, computer, science, or language-learning assignment. Alternatively, groups of three to twelve students sharing similar interests and abilities might work on a particular problem or project for a mutually agreed-upon period of time. The teacher, who normally has received some in-service training or taken coursework in gifted education, also might involve the students in exercises and activities aimed at strengthening creative and research skills or other types of high-level thinking abilities.

Kaplan (1974) itemized a number of "necessities" and "checkpoints" in planning a cluster group G/T program:

1. Developing criteria for selecting students.
2. Defining the qualifications of, and the selection process for, the teachers.
3. Clarifying the teachers' responsibilities and activities.
4. Planning the differentiated experiences for the cluster of gifted students.
5. Planning for support services and special resources, for example, counselors or computers.

The individual teacher will need to organize individual and small-group meetings, help students plan contracts and projects, organize field trips, and plan other educational exercises and experiences. Kaplan (1974) recommended that, with cluster grouping, the gifted students should have an opportunity to share their unique learning experiences with the total class, thus reducing their isolation. Also, the staff must be certain that the special activities and experiences stimulate—not penalize—students in the gifted cluster. For example, if "special learning experiences" amount to piling on more work, the students may prefer *not* to be gifted.

As an example of a cluster group plan, Project Lift of Marion, Massachusetts, places groups of five fourth-, fifth-, and sixth-grade G/T students in selected regular classes (Juntune, 1981). Students are identified according to the Renzulli three-ring model: those who show creativity, task-commitment, and academic excellence. The goal of the program is to develop higher-level thinking skills as defined in Bloom's taxonomy: application, analysis, synthesis, and evaluation. Teachers *compact* the regular curriculum so that time is available for enrichment activities, including training in creative and critical thinking and the development of research skills via independent research projects.

In Lawrence, Kansas, a district-wide secondary G/T program (grades 7–12) uses cluster grouping as one of sixteen alternative programming options (Juntune, 1981). In addition to almost every other enrichment and acceleration plan described in this book (special classes, credit by examination, correspondence courses, college courses, independent projects, mentor plans, and so on), gifted students are clustered in regular classes. The standard curriculum is compacted, permitting in-depth explorations of special topics, the development of individual projects, and increased involvement with higher thinking skills (for example, creativity, evaluation, critical thinking, and the scientific method, which are applied to the regular class content).

Mainstreaming

If a school or district has no formal G/T program, many teachers use their own ingenuity to provide special differentiated and enriched learning experiences to eager, fast-learning, creative (and perhaps bored) students. Such "mainstreaming" is very often a default plan. As Treffinger (1981) pointed out, we do not mainstream gifted and talented students into a regular classroom; they already are there and will continue to be there into the foreseeable future. Even if a school already has in place a pullout or resource-room program (described later in this chapter), gifted students will spend most of the school day in the regular classroom. As Treffinger (1982) has observed, children "do not save their unique characteristics and needs for the block of time that is set aside for the gifted program; their needs and characteristics are with them all day long every day."

D. R. Clasen (1982) itemized a number of alternatives available to the individual teacher in schools " . . . where there is minimum involvement in programming for the gifted. . . . " Specifically:

1. A student may be individually accelerated, perhaps by reading or working ahead or through the use of advanced or supplementary texts and workbooks.
2. The curriculum may otherwise be modified to permit greater depth, more complexity, or higher levels of abstraction.
3. Enrichment activities may be planned that build on or challenge the student's special skills and abilities, for example, in creative writing, photography, or computer programming.

4. Academic and perhaps career advising may be appropriate, for example, helping students understand their special capabilities and the training necessary for them to realize their full potential.

Looking specifically at helping bright math students in the regular classroom, Tucker (1982) recommended the use of (1) puzzles; (2) mental arithmetic games; (3) projects and applications—for example, computing vacation expenses or plotting data and making inferences; (4) enrichment units, which include strengthening already learned skills and learning new material; and (5) reading, particularly about mathematicians.

Hazel Feldhusen (1981) described how she accommodated gifted children in her regular classroom primarily by using teacher-developed learning centers and by individualizing instruction. For example, her classroom includes a *library center* used for individual reading or study. It is filled with commercial reading-skill materials and educational games, and includes one rocker for comfort and a typewriter for creative writing. A *math center* includes math kits, math games, a calculator (and calculator activities), and a microcomputer. Math folders or "modules" for individualized math instruction were created by cutting up math books. Said Feldhusen, "When a child finishes a module and has it corrected, he or she then gets the next module from the cabinet." A microcomputer presents fun games, logic games, math challenges, and spelling lessons.

An *art center* presents a new art project each week. A *science center* is supplied with two to five activities coordinated with each science lesson. The science center includes a record player, tape player, and film-strip viewer. The school library houses a *Learning Resource Center* that contains tapes and activities in math and language arts, all aimed at developing high thinking skills. Students also use the library for research, for selecting reading, and for learning library skills.

At the heart of Feldhusen's system is the *Learning Agreement* (Figure 6.1). The chart specifies daily and weekly optional activities, plus activities that are required "musts." A self-discipline approach is used, which allows total freedom of movement and considerable decision-making regarding their self-paced learning activities. According to Feldhusen, they " . . . develop independence, self-direction, and discipline in their learning tasks."

Not every dedicated, gifted-conscious teacher who is stuck with gifted kids and no program is expected to develop a showpiece mainstreaming plan such as Hazel Feldhusen's. However, her innovations suggest many ideas and alternatives for mainstreaming the gifted.

The Palo Alto School System (California) deliberately elected to mainstream their gifted elementary students rather than create special classes or pullout programs. Reasons cited were (1) they have so many of them (about 20 percent either meet criteria or "act gifted" [!]), and (2) they felt it best for G/T students to learn, play, and solve problems with students of all

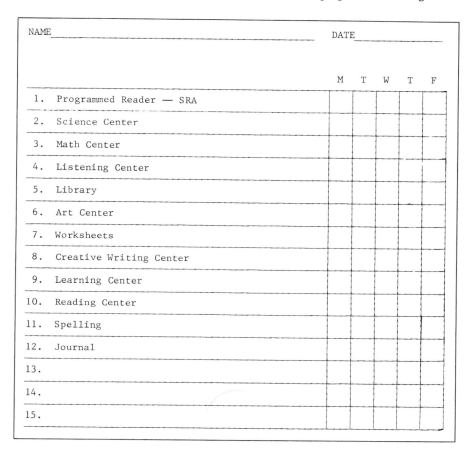

NAME			DATE			
	M	T	W	T	F	
1. Programmed Reader — SRA						
2. Science Center						
3. Math Center						
4. Listening Center						
5. Library						
6. Art Center						
7. Worksheets						
8. Creative Writing Center						
9. Learning Center						
10. Reading Center						
11. Spelling						
12. Journal						
13.						
14.						
15.						

FIGURE 6.1 Learning Agreement. (Reprinted by permission from H. Feldhusen, "Teaching Gifted, Creative, and Talented Students in an Individualized Classroom," *Gifted Child Quarterly* (1981), *25*, 108–111.)

backgrounds and ability levels. "Enrichment is found in our literature, math, science, and social studies programs, most of which were developed by the district" (Juntune, 1981).

To offer two notes on mainstreaming: First, some teachers—in concert with counselors, parents, and students themselves—use *Individualized Education Programs* (IEPs) to structure the independent work of mainstreamed gifted students (just as IEPs are used to plan the education for retarded, learning disabled, or handicapped students; see Inset 6.1)

Second, Treffinger (1982) stressed that "Gifted education is becoming more concerned with meeting [all] students' needs and less concerned with developing a rationale for selecting or excluding students from various programs or activities." Treffinger itemized no less than 60 sugges-

---

INSET 6.1 USING INDIVIDUALIZED EDUCATION PROGRAMS (IEPS) WITH GIFTED AND TALENTED STUDENTS

The reader probably is aware that Public Law 94-142, the "mainstreaming law," mandated the use of an *Individualized Education Program* (IEP) for each student classified as handicapped. IEPs also serve that other variety of exceptional student, the gifted and talented, particularly when they too are mainstreamed in the regular classroom. For handicapped students, IEPs are prepared jointly " . . . by a qualified school official, by the child's teacher and parents or guardian, and if possible by the child himself . . . " Consultants such as a psychologist, reading specialist, speech pathologist, social worker, guidance counselor, curriculum specialist, or doctor are also involved in the planning. Similar personnel can help plan IEPs for G/T students.

The IEP serves as a guide for managing the testing, placement, instruction, and procedural safeguards that each student needs (National Advisory Committee on the Handicapped, 1976; Torres, 1977). For gifted students, the IEP will include:

1. Present levels of performance, as determined by intelligence tests, achievement tests, rating scales, and informal observations and reports by teachers, parents, school psychologists, or others.
2. Annual goals, which include short-term instructional goals. These goals will dictate most of the instructional methods, learning activities, and individual projects for each student required under item 3.
3. Specific educational services to be provided, based on the needs of the individual student. These will include special teaching strategies, special equipment, individual projects and assignments, field trips, and others.
4. The extent to which the student will participate in the regular program versus special G/T classes and activities.
5. A projected date for initiation and the anticipated duration of the services.
6. Evaluation procedures and appropriate objective criteria, which may result in a review and revision of the IEP.
7. A schedule for determining whether the objectives are being achieved.

---

tions for providing better instruction for gifted and talented students in the regular classroom. Some representative examples are:

> Using pretests or mastery tests to permit students to "test out" of material they already know.
>
> Using individualized learning packets, programmed learning, learning modules, learning centers, and minicourses, particularly in the basics.
>
> Allowing uninterrupted time every day for individual or small-group projects.
>
> Incorporating creative-thinking techniques into subject areas.
>
> Helping students to learn the meaning of such higher-level thinking processes as *analysis, synthesis,* and *evaluation,* and to plan independent projects around these processes.

Bringing in guest speakers to describe their careers or unusual hobbies.
Using cross-age and peer tutoring.

Helping students to understand their own strengths, interests, learning styles, and preferences, and to become sensitive to those of others.

Exploring many points of view about contemporary topics and allowing opportunity to analyze and evaluate evidence and conflicting ideas and opinions.

Helping set personal and academic goals.

As a final caution, do not permit a mainstreaming program to become camouflage for offering no program at all. If gifted and talented children are not truly involved in differentiated curriculum within their regular classrooms, one cannot say that the school is providing for their needs.

PART-TIME AND TEMPORARY GROUPING

Pullout Programs

The old standby in programming for gifted and talented students is the pullout program. With minor variations, elementary students (but sometimes secondary) are usually pulled out of their regular classes two to three hours per week to participate in special enrichment activities guided by a G/T teacher or district teacher/coordinator. Often, one G/T coordinator serves an entire district by conducting a pullout class in a different school each afternoon. The meeting place often is called a *resource room*, since it is supposed to provide special reading material and equipment resources. As with other special classes and cluster grouping, pullout activities focus on creative development, higher thinking skills, personal development and values clarification, and independent projects which may involve virtually any sort of endeavor—art, craft, math, history, writing, science, computers, and so on.

Before describing some pullout programs, we should mention that many knowledgeable educators oppose this strategy. Friction frequently develops when teachers are saddled with the dilemma of permitting students to miss important content, or else forcing them to make up missed work—thus punishing them for their G/T participation (Reis, 1983). In one Wisconsin district in the authors' experience, many teachers opposed a G/T pullout program for this reason; their policy was to require that all missed work be made up. Other schools adopt the opposite strategy: Under the assumption that G/T kids can afford to miss some regular content, they are not held responsible for missed work.

Elman and Elman (1983) further noted that pullout programs (1) require the expense of an additional teacher and specialized materials and (2) involve the student for only a fraction of the school week. Moreover, (3) the regular teacher may feel undermined and resent the implication that he or she is not providing adequate instruction for gifted and talented students. Finally, (4) selecting specific students for special privileges can be detrimental to student social relationships. That is, students may or may not be comfortable being visibly separated from their classmates and classified as "different." Another often-voiced criticism (for example, Renzulli and Smith, 1978) is that such plans frequently result in too much "fun and games" and too little valuable, theory-based training; solid reasons are needed for every activity.

More positively, the pullout program is a popular and often successful means of bringing G/T students together for social and intellectual support, and for the special differentiated and enriched training they deserve. When it has a well-planned, challenging, and integrated curriculum, this program can offer gifted children good opportunities for developing high-level skills. The authors have observed some very successful and effective pullout programs.

In Livonia, Michigan, as an example, public-school students in grades 3 to 6 meet twice weekly for a half-day session (Juntune, 1981). The students are ferried to the Enrichment Center from around the district by enthusiastic parents. Many individual learning modules are available, introducing students to such topics as impressionist painters and computers. The plan also aims at creative development and at helping students understand their special abilities and potential.

A quite different sort of pullout program, *QUEST* ("Questioning, Understanding, Expanding, Searching, Thinking"—Kansas State Plan for Special Education) identifies G/T elementary students with a healthy variety of ability and achievement tests, rating scales, and nominations (Juntune, 1981). Individualized Education Programs are prepared for each student, based upon the student's abilities and needs. Students meet with a member of a teaching team, either individually or in a small group, from one to three hours per week. The focus of the individualized work is on (1) affective training, (2) creativity, and (3) independent studies and self-directed learning.

Resource Programs and Resource Rooms

As with "cluster groups," in G/T education the phrases "resource program" and "resource room" are used rather freely. A resource room is just that, a room with special resources that " . . . provide a learning environment specifically tailored to the needs and objectives for educating the gifted and talented" (Kaplan, 1974; see Inset 6.2). Since pullout students are sent to a resource room, pullout programs are sometimes called *resource programs* or *resource-room programs*. A special class for gifted students (discussed later) might also be held in a resource room and similarly earn the

INSET 6.2 RESOURCE ROOM RESOURCES

Cecile Frey (1980) itemized materials she has found to be "absolutely essential" to the decent operation of an elementary school resource room:

A good unabridged dictionary
A copy of *Roget's Thesaurus*
Bartlett's Familiar Quotations
A biographical dictionary (Webster)
A complete atlas

In the "nice but not essential" category she recommended:

The People's Almanac
Isaac Asimov's *Biographical Encyclopedia of Science and Technology*
Mathematics Illustrated Dictionary
World Almanac and Book of Facts
Any decent grammar book
The Encyclopedia of Ignorance

As for a set of encyclopedias, Frey said, "I must answer that question with a resounding 'No!' " The reason: Students rely too heavily on them and, anyway, they are (1) expensive and (2) available in the school library. However, if funds are available, and only for limited use, she recommends *The World Book* and the *Encyclopedia Britannica's Micropedia and Macropedia*.

The resource room also should subscribe to:

Art and Man
Literary Cavalcade
Time or *Newsweek*
Science Digest
National Geographic World
New York Times

label *resource program.* Kaplan (1974) further noted that a resource room may be used (1) for the development and dissemination of materials to be used by teachers and students in other settings, and (2) as a center for teacher in-service training and parent education.

To contrast it with pullout programs, the present meaning of resource program is a district-wide pullout or magnet-type plan in which students with special needs are transported to specially equipped and taught resource rooms or enrichment centers for one or two sessions per week (see Inset 6.3).

INSET 6.3 A COMMUNITY RESOURCE CENTER

The Manchester (Connecticut) Community Resource Center was designed to allow community professionals, business persons, and educators to share their expertise with local school children, both gifted and "regular" (Plese, 1982). The Center was designed for a small, limited-budget community; it is managed, in fact, by a single part-time volunteer. The Center basically assists teachers in locating and scheduling resource persons and programs for exploratory types of enrichment experiences. Students thus are exposed to new topic areas with the goal of stimulating interest and encouraging further study in an independent or small-group project.

A key component of the plan is the resource file, a cataloged list of community persons willing to speak to a youthful audience. Ideas for resource persons were found " . . . with the guidance of blue and yellow page directories (and a list of talented friends) . . . " (Plese, 1982). While newspaper ads, direct mailings, college interdepartment mail, and other assorted recruitment methods were tried, a full 85 percent of the resource persons were recruited via a personal phone call. Something worth remembering.

Even in this small community the "general file topics" included 200 specific entries, for example: architecture, banking and finance, business and careers, communications, cultures, engineering, environment, foreign languages, health and safety, history, hobbies, horticulture, insurance, law, the military, politics and government, real estate, science, social studies and social science, theatre, travel, women, and "miscellaneous." Some specific presenters included a hypnotist, a poet, a UFO specialist, and an Arabic translator. In some cases the presentation would result in a follow-up field trip to the work location of the speaker. Directories listing the resources were placed not just in school secretaries' files, but in school libraries and teachers' lounges.

The mechanics of arranging a presentation were reasonably straightforward. Teachers would phone in information regarding the topic desired, three possible dates and times, and the age and size of the class. The Center Coordinator would contact a resource person who would agree to a certain time and would specify what AV aids might be needed and what advance preparation by students (if any) is desirable.

The Resource Center has been valuable for all Manchester students. However, according to Plese (1982), it has been especially valuable to G/T programs that emphasize broad, exploratory academic and career exposure and contact with creative and productive community experts.

Additional details regarding speaker guidelines, request-confirmation forms, evaluation procedures, teachers' responsibilities, and the always necessary thank-you notes are available from Plese (1982) and the Minneapolis Public Schools.[1]

---

[1]"How to Initiate and Administer a Community Resource Volunteer Program" (1971)—Minneapolis Public Schools, 807 N.E. Broadway, Minneapolis, MN 55413.

One prototypic resource program is the South Windsor (Connecticut) *Project Talent* (SWEPT; Juntune, 1981). G/T students in grades 4, 5, and 6 from four schools spend one morning and one afternoon per week in a resource room. The specific morning and afternoon combination depends upon which of three units the particular student selects to explore—for instance, geology, the future, or art history—topics not ordinarily covered in elementary school. In the first phase teachers lead students through general explorations of particular topics, plus group-training experiences (for example, development of creative thinking skills, and library and scientific skills). In the second, independent-study phase " . . . each student selects an issue-oriented topic and investigates it in depth." With experience, students are permitted increased freedom. A sixth-grade student, for example, might proceed directly into a research study without participating in the teacher-led phase of the resource program.

In Ankeny, Iowa, the *Ankeny Gifted and Talented Education* (AGATE) program uses city buses to transport K–9 students to a junior high school equipped with AV equipment, books, magazines, a science lab, a language corner, games, plants, a piano, and miscellaneous materials for independent projects. The enrichment curriculum has included such activities as astronomy, including building a telescope; rocketry, with student-made—and launched—rockets; film animation; journalism, resulting in a newspaper; foreign languages; American Sign Language; art; literature; theatre; photography; oceanography; and more (Juntune, 1981). Students alternate mornings and afternoons, and days of the week, to avoid missing the same activities in the same classes.

Part-Time Special Classes

Special classes (discussed under "Full-Time Homogeneous Grouping") may also be offered as part-time options. For example, in *Project Horizon* (Seattle, Washington) elementary school G/T students are placed in specialized self-contained classes for 50–70 percent of the school day. Their differentiated experiences include independent projects, accelerated subjects, and small-group enrichment activities, all of which aim at developing creative and other high-level thinking skills. In junior high school, special Horizon classes stimulate abstract thinking within the prescribed curriculum content; they also cover advanced content and allow self-directed research projects.

Another variation on part-time or temporary special classes, the *Wheaton-Warrenville District Talented and Gifted Program* includes magnet-type, district-wide special classes for junior and senior high school G/T students. For example, a junior high school offers bused-in students an accelerated math class. One high school offers a specially designed Key Seminar and another a Humanities class; both classes are cross-subject, and both focus on developing high-level thinking skills.

We might note that honors programs often are made up of one or more part-time special classes, for example, a course in Comprehensive Law at Chelmsford High School in North Chelmsford, Massachusetts. Here, participants are high-achieving English and social studies students interested in law careers.

Of course, no limit exists to the variety of courses that might be created as options for bright, creative, and energetic elementary or secondary students.

Special Interest Groups and Clubs

Most secondary schools have these. The message here is that G/T-conscious teachers can assume the leadership necessary for organizing these enriching activities for interested students. There are drama clubs, German clubs, French clubs, computer clubs, chess clubs, math clubs, and so forth. The teacher-leader can organize meetings, competitions, research projects, field trips, and meetings with community experts, and can provide career information and guidance. One also can organize mini-courses, taught either by teachers or community experts, dealing with areas such as music writing, computer programming, jewelry making, or any other academic, career, or hobby topic. Clubs and courses may meet before or after school or on Saturdays. Activities may include work with equipment not normally available; for example, a high school laboratory might be borrowed for an elementarty school physics class.

COUNSELING

In addition to plans for acceleration, grouping, and enrichment, a gifted and talented program for students of any age should include a counseling component. Indeed, Delisle (1982) noted that according to a longitudinal follow-up study of one thousand Project TALENT students, the single " . . . most blatant curricular omission made in secondary schools is career guidance. Students bemoan the fact that they either have not been counseled, or have not been counseled well." Perrone and Pulvino (1979) similarly noted that while efforts to identify gifted children have been made since the turn of the century, efforts to *guide* them did not begin until the 1950s.

There are three traditional, and logical, areas of counseling concern: (1) students' personal concerns and adjustment, plus the interrelated components of (2) educational and (3) career counseling. Zaffrann and Colangelo (1979) caution us that a good counseling program should be a *coherent* plan—one which includes goals and objectives, a rationale, methodologies geared to the objectives, and a means of evaluation. It should not consist of sporadic, hit-or-miss services aimed at testing, place-ment, referral, and occasional counseling sessions. As another caution, Sanborn (1979a) further noted that, in their case-by-case experience " . . . gifted and talented students differ from each other in more ways than they resemble each other . . . and counseling services require highly indi-vidualized contacts and interpretations."

One of the main purposes of counseling is to discover unique patterns of student characteristics—abilities, interests, values, and motives—and then to help students relate these characteristics to educational, career, and life-style opportunities (Sanborn, 1979a, 1979b, 1979c). A related use of these patterns of characteristics is to help teachers develop appropriate ed-ucational experiences.

Personal and Social Needs

Because regular classes group students according to chronological age, not mental age, G/T students often find themselves in situations which meet neither their social nor their intellectual needs. Therefore many ex-perience feelings of isolation and social frustration, and they may develop poor social skills from their inability to find "true peers" with similar abili-ties, interests, and needs. Sanborn (1979a) noted that G/T youngsters may become "social outcasts" in an egalitarian, democratic-minded society. They may be discriminated against by intimidated age-mates, students who do not appreciate peers who are more adult in their abilities and interests, who are labeled *gifted,* and who learn and excel with little apparent effort. Due in large part to their social isolation, Herr and Watanabe (1979) con-cluded that many gifted children have an identity crisis regarding who and what they are, and who and what they should become.

The total pattern may easily produce social maladjustment. Said Witty and Grotberg (1970), gifted and talented students may experience an imbalance between intellectual and special ability growth, on one hand, and development in the social and emotional areas, on the other.

Parents may not understand their child's gifts and talents; they may not know how to respond to talented children nor how to nurture the gifts (Exum, 1983; Sanborn, 1979b). Some parents may ignore, disbelieve, re-sent, or be intimated by any apparent intellectual superiority. Others will fear for the normalcy, social adjustment, or happiness of their child (Dettman and Colangelo, 1980).

In rural and economically disadvantaged areas the lack of adult models—successful, gifted adults who understand an can empathize with G/T students—adds to problems of isolation and identity. Exum (1983) rec-ommended family counseling for gifted black students, addressing such parental concerns as loss of authority over the gifted child, the student's possible loss of respect for family and culture, the student's emotional stability, and the student's ability to interact normally with other people. Exum warned that students deliberately may underachieve to return a family disrupted by giftedness to a more comfortable homeostasis. As a general principle, " . . . the involvement of parents in the education of their gifted child can be a significant positive force" (Dettman and Colangelo, 1980).

Pulvino, Colangelo, and Zaffrann (1976) used "personal essay writing" as a means for clarifying problems, feelings, and perceptions of individual gifted students. One favorite topic, for example, is "My Place in the Future." Many gifted high school students are quite good at writing, yet may be uncomfortable talking with a counselor. Thus they may be asked to write about important personal, social, educational, or career problems, and their feelings and perceptions about those problems. The essays provide unique information for counselors to use in personal interviews and guidance.

As a solution to problems of social isolation and lack of academic stimulation, Zaffrann and Colangelo (1979) recommended bringing gifted students together, as in the grouping strategies cited earlier. Because they are experiencing many of the same problems, gifted peers offer strong understanding and social and academic support for each other. If no organized groups currently exist, a counselor may informally bring small groups together. One school district used lunch period as an opportunity for informal discussions; the weekly "sandwich seminars" allowed gifted students to discuss with each other and with a counselor such topics as peer pressure and academic challenge. While social sanctions may prevent boys from showing creativity, or girls from showing high intelligence, in groups gifted and talented peers can help each other understand their talents and recognize that it is fine—indeed, fortunate—to be different and to be bright.

Educational and Career Counseling

In the educational and career counseling of gifted and talented students, two recurring problems are: (1) multipotentiality and (2) expectations (Delisle, 1982).

Multipotentiality. The dilemma of multipotentiality has been described as an "embarrassment of riches" (Zaffrann and Colangelo, 1979). While some G/T students show abilities and interests in one concentrated area, the majority possess capabilities in a number of areas. Often it is extremely difficult for them to make just one or two choices from among the many possibilities. French (1959), for example, found that more high-ability students scored above the seventieth percentile in three or more areas on the *Kuder Preference Record,* an inventory that identifies different spheres of career interest. In a case known to the authors, a gifted student was confused by her results on the *Differential Aptitude Career Test*—she had scored above the ninety-fifth percentile in eight out of nine possible career areas. Such results hardly provide clear future direction.

Sanborn (1979b), using the personal-essay-writing strategy mentioned earlier, reproduced the following concerns of a twelfth-grade male: "Nothing is so simple for me that I can do a perfect job without effort, but nothing is so hard that I cannot do it. This is why it is so difficult to decide my place in the future." From a female: "There are so many things I'd like to do and be, and I'd like to try them all; where to start is the problem. . . . I'd like to be a physical therapist, a foreign correspondent, a psychiatrist, an anthropologist, a linguist, a folk singer, an espionage agent, and a social worker."

To further complicate the multipotentiality problem, teachers and professors who discover an unusually talented student will enthusiastically encourage the student to specialize in their particular area. One extraordinarily capable student known to the authors took college courses in philosophy and computer science while in high school. Both college professors noted her excellence and invited her to major in these subjects. Once she was attending college full-time, professors in literature and science also discovered her talent and encouraged her to choose those areas for her college major.

The multipotentiality matter is made difficult if students are unaware of the diverse possibilities before them, are unclear about the implications of their high talent, or do not understand how to pursue career goals (Herr and Watanabe, 1979). The counseling challenge is to help students understand their abilities and interests, and identify and rank career possibilities. Some interests should be categorized as real career possibilities, others as likely avocational pursuits.

It is critical that a gifted student consider vocations that have potential for extensive *growth*. Too often students are attracted to careers that whet their immediate interests. Counselors should acquaint students with the kinds of careers that will be sufficiently open-ended to permit students to be continually challenged and to grow.

Expectations. The second problem, *expectations*, has many facets. First of all, career selection is seen by gifted students as highly significant—it will be their future identity, their means of self-expression, and their philosophy of life. Career selection is also the source of many conflicts, pressures, and dilemmas. For example, some parents, keenly aware of their child's high ability, may expect great things—the highest test scores and grades, academic awards, enrollment in a prestigious university, and entrance into a status profession (Zaffrann and Colangelo, 1979). Other parents may ignore their child's special abilities and talents and expect him or her to enter the family business or work on the farm, with little or no support for the essential college education.

Career expectations may be limited by socioeconomic status. It is therefore especially important that counselors help gifted students from economically deprived homes to aspire beyond the life-style familiar to them. In guiding these students, counselors must be innovative in searching out scholarship assistance which can make such career aspirations realistically possible. In one case, a guidance counselor helped a gifted high school student from an economically disadvantaged family discover enough scholarship aid to support her entire college education. Prior to the counselor's help, this student did not expect to have enough money to even begin college. Needless to say, this guidance counselor made a dramatic impact on the girl's life.

Expectations can cause other conflicts. Parents and relatives—and even gifted students themselves—may expect high academic and career accomplishments. However, the student may actually prefer to spend his or her life in a totally different fashion. From a high school girl's essay: "I'd like to move to England and live in the fog with a house by the sea [and] I'd like to write books. . . . my future probably will be much different. I'll go to college for four years and major in something like math. Then I'll teach high school for awhile and get married and have a bunch of kids. . . . I'm saying to myself that this is what you should do with your life, and if I keep saying it maybe I'll start believing it."

Final Comment

Counseling activities should be designed to assist gifted students in self-discovery—understanding themselves, their problems and their abilities, motives, interests, and values. In educational and career counseling, G/T students need help in relating their interests and abilities to specific career alternatives, and in understanding the requirements, training, lifestyles, advantages, and disadvantages of various careers. Field trips, mentor programs, and work-study programs often are helpful. Gifted and talented students also need to understand the commitment in time and finances, and the necessity for "deferred rewards," which are required for high levels of professional training. Many will need help arranging resources necessary to make extended education possible.

Further, some students will have special problems. For example, many female students may need to be convinced that a professional career and a family are not necessarily incompatible. Other students may need to understand that responsibility, effort, and following social rules are closely tied to career and life success.

Information from counseling and guidance evaluations can help teachers and other school staff understand gifted students and their abilities, problems, and educational and career needs. Despite their gifts, many students need help with study skills—note-taking, summarizing, studying for exams, reviewing, and test taking. Perrone and Pulvino (1979) recommended that counselors become sensitive to cognitive-thinking preferences: for example, holistic versus analytic, convergent versus divergent thinking, and left-brain versus right-brain learning and thinking patterns. There are tests and evaluations to aid the counselor in understanding student abilities and interests; for example, ability tests; achievement tests; interest inventories; reading tests; personality tests; cognitive styles tests; creativity tests; work samples; observations by teachers, parents, and community leaders; and more (Pulvino, Colangelo, and Zaffrann, 1976).

While G/T students may indeed "make it on their own," systematic counseling and guidance will make the task much less painful and more sensible. It also will help those gifted and talented students who will not "make it on their own."

SUMMARY

Once made unpopular by the Rosenthal and Jacobson expectancy research, grouping has reemerged as a viable G/T programming strategy. Options include full-time homogeneous grouping, full-time heterogeneous grouping (that is, G/T students combined with regular students), and part-time or temporary grouping.

There are many types of full-time homogeneous grouping. With magnet high schools, students of various ability levels are bused to the particular school that accommodates their needs and educational/career interests. Special schools, either elementary or secondary, are devoted solely to programs that accelerate and enrich the education of gifted students. Some specialize, for example, in the fine arts. Private schools usually produce higher average achievement levels than public schools. Some private schools are totally designed for gifted and talented students. With the school-within-a-school plan, G/T students attend special classes for part of the day and mix with regular students for other (usually less academic) classes. Special classes for G/T students may be created in the elementary school or the junior or senior high school.

There are also various full-time heterogeneous grouping options: With multi-age classrooms two grades may be combined, allowing bright younger students to learn with students at the next higher grade. Some entire schools, such as those organized under the Individually Guided Education–Multi-Unit School plan, are designed for flexible, individualized learning.

Cluster grouping, as used in this chapter, involves placing a group of five or ten gifted students in the same regular class for special assignments (for example, via contracting), independent projects and field trips. The regular curriculum may be compacted to allow time for enrichment activities.

Mainstreaming is planning special learning experiences and projects in the regular classroom. H. Feldhusen's model mainstreaming classroom included learning centers for art, science, reading, and creative writing, and for individualized math. In Palo Alto, so many students were gifted that mainstreaming was adopted as the single district plan.

Part-time and temporary grouping options include the following: Pullout programs, the most common elementary G/T plan, involve sending gifted students to a resource room for one or two afternoons per week for enrichment and personal development activities. One recurrent problem is dealing with missed work. Other disadvantages: The program may be expensive; it will serve students for only part of the week; teachers may feel undermined; and social relationships may be damaged.

A resource program, as used in this chapter, is a district-wide "pullout" plan in which students travel to a resource room once or twice per week for special learning activities and projects.

Special classes may be used on a part-time as well as a full-time basis. Students may attend special elementary classes for part of the day; secondary students may be bused to a district-wide special class in, say, the humanities or accelerated math. Honors programs use part-time special classes.

Special interest groups and clubs are a good outlet for students whose enthusiasm and ability exceeds the regularly offered coursework. Teachers will need to assume some organizational leadership.

Counseling is an important component of any G/T program. It may deal with personal/social concerns or educational and career decisions. Counseling should involve a coherent plan, not sporadic hit-or-miss services. The main purpose of counseling is to help students discover abilities and interests and then relate these to educational, career, and life-style opportunities.

Counseling can also help with personal and social needs. G/T students may become social outcasts, leading to identity crises. Parents may disbelieve, resent, fear, or not understand their child's gifts and talents. Family counseling can help. Personal essay writing helps counselors identify problems. Bringing gifted students together can result in academic and social support.

Educational and career counseling deals with problems such as multipotentiality. Students should be helped to rank career possibilities, favoring those open-ended ones that allow continued challenge and growth.

"Expectations" involves many subproblems. Parents may place too much achievement pressure on their children; or conversely expect them to remain in the family business or farm. Career expectations may be depressed by SES level. Counselors should help raise aspirations of gifted low-SES students, and help them locate college resources. Moreover, career expectations of parents and others may not coincide with a student's true desires; the student actually may prefer a different life-style.

Gifted students need assistance in self-discovery and guidance in educational and career planning. They should be helped to understand "deferred rewards" and good study habits. Females may need convincing that career and family are compatible. Gifted students do not always "make it on their own."

7

ENRICHMENT

SELECTING WORTHWHILE ENRICHMENT ACTIVITIES

All enrichment activities should be planned and designed with "higher order" objectives in mind. In addition to accelerated and advanced content, Sato and Johnson (1978) listed the following as suitable differentiated curricula for the gifted:

1. High content complexity, which permits some student control over the direction and rate of learning, and which requires higher-level thinking (analyzing, synthesizing, creating, evaluating).
2. Content beyond the prescribed curriculum, emphasizing new disciplines and interrelatedness of disciplines.
3. Student-selected content, allowing student interests and needs to determine what will be learned.
4. Working with abstract ideas, theories, and concepts, requiring reflective, creative, and critical thinking.
5. Working with non-grade-level resources; that is, materials, equipment, and information other than books and beyond the designated grade-level.

Kaplan (1974) similarly produced a list of "what enrichment is" and "what enrichment is not." In a modified form, enrichment:

1. Extends and/or replaces traditional learning experiences; it does not just provide more work.
2. Is productive thinking (goal-oriented creative thinking); not reproductive thinking (learning correct answers).
3. Is complex thinking; not just harder work.
4. Is learning concepts and generalizations; not just learning names, places, facts, and figures.
5. Is applying learning; not just regurgitating it.
6. Is associating and interrelating learning with other areas; it is not "separate entity learning."
7. Is based on student needs and readiness; not grade-level appropriateness.
8. Is learning to seek problems; not answer teacher-posed questions.
9. Is learning to critically evaluate; not blindly accept.
10. Is learning things as they should be or as they could be; not learning things only as they are.

In Chapter 5 we presented Feldhusen and Wyman's (1980) twelve-point list of basic needs. A teacher-coordinator who keeps the Sato-Johnson, Kaplan, and Feldhusen-Wyman guidelines in mind will select activities that are based in theory and aimed at worthwhile high-level learning and thinking.

Overview

We noted in Chapter 5 that topics within our five-part classification—acceleration, grouping, counseling, enrichment, and curriculum models—would overlap. For example, many forms of enrichment require grouping; and curriculum models are used primarily to suggest and guide enrichment. Two forms of enrichment, training in creative thinking and in affective development, are sufficiently important that Chapters 9, 10, and 11 are devoted entirely to them.

In this chapter we review a variety of enrichment strategies, all of which amount to delivery methods for achieving process and content goals. Process goals include developing such skills as creative thinking and problem solving, critical thinking, scientific thinking, and others (see Inset 7.1). The content is the subject matter, projects, and activities within which the processes are developed.

Enrichment strategies will include:

1. Independent study and independent projects
2. Learning centers
3. Field trips
4. Saturday programs
5. Summer programs
6. Mentors and mentorships

INSET 7.1 PROCESS GOALS FOR ENRICHMENT ACTIVITIES

There are innumerable activities, topics, projects, and learning experiences that a teacher-coordinator might use for individual and group enrichment. However, any such planning and selection should aim at achieving worthwhile goals. With sound goal-oriented planning, the students' time and the district's resources can lead to improvements in academic knowledge and skills and the strengthening of high-level cognitive processes. One should consider many alternatives before finalizing an instructional plan. A cheaper and less troublesome option could be the most interesting and productive.

The following list includes important processes—specific thinking skills—that can be developed within many different content areas.

Working with theories	Abstract thinking
Creative thinking	Critical thinking
Discovery, inquiry skills	Problem solving
Independent thinking	Problem finding
Generalizing	Problem defining
Futuristic thinking	Decision making
Application	Analysis
Synthesis	Evaluation
Leadership	Planning
Scientific skills	Organizing
Listening	Reading
Writing, outlining	Library skills
Moral/ethical thinking	Humanitarian attitudes
Self-concept development	Achievement motivation
Interrelating subject areas	Mnemonic memory strategies

As for content suggestions, virtually any university catalog or encyclopedia will suggest many interesting topics (from aeronautics, art, astronomy, and Aztecs to parapsychology, Rome, sociology, the stock market, TV production, and weaving) which can serve as the vehicle for developing process skills.

---

7. Future Problem Solving competition
8. The Olympics of the Mind program

INDEPENDENT STUDY AND RESEARCH PROJECTS

We noted in Chapter 6 that independent study and research projects are a common mainstreaming approach. Independent activity also takes place within most enrichment strategies from our list, and within many of the acceleration and grouping strategies of Chapters 5 and 6. For bright and energetic students, the possibilities for independent study and independent projects are without limit. Students may work on projects relating to library research, scientific research, art, drama, journalism, photography, and so on. They may work alone, in pairs, or in small groups.

Library Research Projects

A library research project must be based on strong student interest and should be student-selected. Although potential topics are endless, some students will have difficulty selecting a topic and getting started. A brainstorming approach is one way to identify interesting possibilities. It may be best to pose a specific problem or challenge, although the nature of the initial problem may change as the project develops. For example, some questions might be "Why and how were pyramids built?" "What are the relationships between Greek and Roman gods?" "What is the evidence for Indian migration from Asia?" "What led to the Civil War; what were the crucial battles; and what were the postwar social effects?" and so on.

In addition to the library, this type of research also might involve trips to a natural history museum, an art gallery or research laboratory, and visits with or phone calls to relevant university faculty or other community (or national) experts. Students in one Wisconsin gifted program telephoned the National Aeronautics and Space Administration in Cape Canaveral to obtain answers about space and rockets.

With any independent project, it is important that a *product* be produced and that the product or performance be presented to an appropriate *audience*, either students in the class or outside groups (Renzulli, 1977). A library research project could include more than a neatly typed report: It might include a student-made movie or a narrated slide show; a demonstration of some activity or skill (for example, sand painting, musket loading); a table-top demonstration (rolling 30-ton stone blocks, dinosaur models); a news report on the progress of a specific battle or the happenings at the local tar pit; a mini-play about mythological or historical characters; a classroom or school newspaper; a newspaper column describing recent activities in the Spanish Inquisition; an ESP test for the class; and so on.

While selecting an appropriate audience is an important component of the project, occasionally there are some special problems. Most of the time any class—G/T or otherwise—will serve as a suitable audience. However, reports by some unusually bright students may be too sophisticated; a peer audience may be unable to comprehend the material. Such a student may need to prepare two reports—one simple enough for the peers to understand, and a second full-blown one to be shared with an expert. Here are two case studies of this problem:

Eric prepared a complex discussion of space travel for his sixth-grade class. His research, organization, and scientific terminology were of his usual high quality. However, his classmates greeted his enthusiastic report with boredom and teasing because of the incomprehensibility of the material. Although Eric easily could have prepared a much simpler report, it would not have allowed him an honest demonstration of what he had learned and figured out. Paradoxically, the sophisticated and, to him, exciting report alienated him from his peer group. He said that sometimes he just really wished he could be in a school where he could challenge himself yet continue to be accepted by friends. Said Eric, "Kids think I'm weird!"

Jean, a high school sophomore, prepared an English term paper on amniocentesis, the procedure that tests for prenatal defects. Her teacher made two grammatical corrections and awarded her the usual *A+*. In an effort to further reinforce Jean's high-quality work, the English teacher passed the report on to the biology teacher. Unfortunately, the biology teacher knew very little about the topic and apologized for his own lack of information. Jean's extensive research had been exciting to her, but it would have been much more meaningful if she could have shared her thinking and discoveries with someone knowledgeable in the field. Jean thought she had expressed her findings in simple enough terms. However, students and teachers apparently were threatened by her vocabulary and depth of thinking, and did not feel sufficiently confident to even discuss the topic with her.

Scientific Research Projects

Possibilities for scientific research are innumerable, but scientific studies will be limited by available equipment and resources. A few phone calls, however, could determine if, say, chemistry labs in the local college might be available to supervised junior high school students who promise to behave themselves.

Many elementary and junior high schools organize science fairs in which each student in the science classes creates a small scientific demonstration. Ribbons are awarded to the most elaborate, well-done, or technically competent projects. Parents visit the school and try to understand each exhibit. Projects by G/T students usually are outstanding, and their effort and ingenuity is reinforced with ribbons and usually peer admiration.

With any type of research project, the teacher's main role is "the guide on the side." With elementary or secondary students, the teacher-coordinator directs the budding scientist to appropriate library or human resources for background information, helps the student formulate the problem and plan the research, aids in locating equipment and other resources and tools, and gives other advice and assistance when needed and appropriate.

Other Independent Projects

In addition to library and scientific research projects, individual art or handicraft projects may include drawing, painting, sculpture, silk-screen, lettering, printing, batik, pottery, ceramics, photography, weaving, or other media. Students interested in theatre and drama can research how plays are written and then write, direct, and perform in their own.

A student newspaper is an especially good independent project for a small group of students. Creating a newspaper involves interviewing people and writing stories, taking photographs, planning and designing the paper, and arranging for its printing. Students in one Wisconsin elementary school who interviewed and photographed elderly people in a retirement home, learned first-hand about local and state history, and about unusual hobbies and skills (quilting, candle-making, tatting, blacksmithing, and so on). Of no small importance, their appreciation and respect for the elderly increased dramatically from the experience.

LEARNING CENTERS

Learning centers were mentioned earlier in conjunction with Hazel Feldhusen's (1981) mainstreaming approach to programming. There are teacher-made learning centers; there also are commercial learning centers. The focus may be upon independent language learning, science projects and experiments, mathematics puzzles and activities, social-studies knowledge and concepts, creative writing, arts and crafts, and even music appreciation. Students—gifted and others—may self-select centers and activities, or teachers and students together may plan valuable and interesting learning center goals. Learning centers may be located in the regular classroom, someone else's classroom, the building resource room, or the district G/T resource room.[1]

The teacher should always be certain that learning center time is well spent; that is, learning center activities should meet some of the goals and purposes of enrichment itemized at the beginning of this chapter and in Inset 7.1. Learning centers can also offer time for unsupervised fooling around.

FIELD TRIPS

The profitable use of field trips requires little explanation. Field trips can be used as an exploratory activity, aimed at acquainting students with cultural or scientific areas or with career possibilities. Field trips can also be a

[1] "Learning center" sometimes is used to mean "resource center," an entire room in a school or district set aside for pullout types of learning experiences.

source of information for students' independent projects. An entire class (even an entire school) might visit a natural history museum, a manufacturing plant, an art gallery, planetarium, and so on. Alternatively, a small group of interested students might visit the kitchen of a local Greek restaurant, where they talk with the owner and the head chef—and also usually eat. Some carefully written requests might earn them a tour of a major newspaper, a research laboratory, or a film-processing plant, or perhaps seats at a symphony rehearsal.

Field trips are most beneficial if students have specific problems to solve, questions to answer, or post-tour projects or presentations to prepare. As Friedman and Master (1980) observed, streaking to the gift shop and cafeteria to buy postcards and potato chips is not the main intent of the trip. Needless to say, such major cities as Boston, New York, Washington, Chicago, and San Francisco offer richer opportunities than Rock Springs, Wyoming, or Grand Forks, North Dakota. For an important trip, however, parents typically are willing to supply bus fare. District school buses usually may be used at minimal cost.

Friedman and Master emphasized that in planning a successful field trip one must evaluate the materials and exhibits and the ability of the guide/educator to communicate effectively with the group. An outline of the program/tour should be planned in advance by the teacher and guide/educator. During the tour the guide should not just "lecture at" students, despite his or her strong temptation to impart knowledge of the beloved subject; rather, students should be allowed to touch, respond, and question. During the tour, teacher and guide should work together to stimulate learning, with both partners commenting, contributing, and remaining open to spontaneous twists and turns in the children's interests. Students should be encouraged to discuss and evaluate during the program.

So far, the reader might correctly conclude that field trips are no different for gifted students than for typical students. Indeed, all students, regardless of ability, should have enrichment opportunities, including visits to places of artistic, historic, and scientific interest. However, if the gifted child's field trip is to be part of a differentiated curriculum, the preparation for the trip, the tasks of the visit, and the resulting reports or projects should be tied to higher-level thinking skills. Thus when field trips are to be enrichment for all children, gifted children will certainly benefit from them. However, if they are designed as part of a gifted program, they should be much more than just a passively interesting visit.

SATURDAY PROGRAMS

Saturday programs present the delightful advantage of permitting gifted students to meet and work with each other away from the stresses and problems of daily school requirements. Saturday programs normally take the form of a noncredit mini-class, covering one or a few topics and taught by volunteer teachers, college faculty, or community experts (who often are parents of gifted children).

One model Saturday program is Feldhusen's *Super Saturday* plan sponsored by Purdue University (Feldhusen and Sokol, 1982; Feldhusen and Wyman, 1980; Gregory, 1982). Feldhusen and Wyman noted that their Saturday program meets *cognitive* needs of gifted and talented youth by providing opportunities for the development of basic thinking skills and the acquisition of a broad store of knowledge. *Affective-social* needs, specifically, motivation and an appropriate self-concept, are met via associating " . . . with intellectual and artistic peers and through identification with adult models of creatively successful individuals." *Generative* needs—needs to be producers of new ideas and products—grow out of involvement in independent investigations and creative activities.

Super Saturday offers many courses at different age levels. All courses engage students in active inquiry and/or hands-on experiences, and all are designed to foster the development of high-level thinking skills. In the spring of 1982 no less than 27 courses were available. Some examples: *Creative Thinking, Mime,* and *Exploring Space* for kindergarten and lower elementary grade children; *Art, French,* and *Probability and Statistics* for intermediate elementary grade students; *TV Production, Computers,* and *Native American Cuture* for upper elementary students; and *Economics, Electrical Engineering,* and *Computers* for junior and senior high school students. Gregory (1982) described a studio arts class which was divided into four sections for four age groups. The course, taught in the Purdue Art Department by undergraduate Art Education majors, included animation filmmaking, drawing, painting, calligraphy, life-size soft sculpture, murals, and puppetry. Exceptionally able students in seventh grade or above could earn college credit in some courses, such as Psychology, French, English Composition, and Political Science.

As for the details and mechanics of the operation, parents provide transportation—from fourteen counties around Lafayette, Indiana. Parents also pay minimal registration fees and, for some courses, materials charges. Teachers are university faculty and students, public school teachers, and others in the greater Lafayette community. They must be good teachers and show energy, enthusiasm, and an interest in teaching gifted kids. Students are selected using fairly generous criteria, for example, IQ scores above 115, *or* grades in the top 10 percent, *or* evidence of artistic talents, *or*, for preschoolers, parents' statements regarding talents and abilities. The program is " . . . designed to be inclusive rather than exclusive . . . " (Feldhusen and Sokol, 1982).

To maintain high quality, classes are observed (unannounceed) by supervisors. Also, students are evaluated according to such criteria as degree of cooperation, achievement of high-level thinking skills, understanding and mastery of information, and the quality of performances, products, and projects. Importantly, parents, teachers, and students are asked about their likes and dislikes regarding Super Saturday. While there are naturally bugs and problems, the program generally has been a smashing success and an exemplary model for other program planners.

More informal approaches have been used by many communities for exciting Saturday and Sunday programs. For example, instead of a regularly planned weekly program, members of parent/educator groups will sponsor an occasional fun-filled and challenging day for their own children. No identification criteria are needed for admission, which permits interested siblings to join in. As a bonus for parents and teachers, a speaker can be invited to discuss issues of concern to parents and teachers of gifted children. Since the entire family often is involved, all emerge from the day with an exciting sense of family challenge and learning.

SUMMER PROGRAMS

Most cities offer summer programs for all students. Obviously, these may be capitalized upon by the teacher, parent, or counselor seeking enrichment opportunities for energetic and able children. In addition, teachers can organize or teach specific classes for gifted children.

University Sponsored Programs

Many summer programs are designed specifically for gifted, talented, and creative children and adolescents. Especially notworthy are the national *Talent Search* programs noted earlier, such as SMPY and CTY at Johns Hopkins University, PSAP at Arizona State University, the *Midwest Talent Search* at Northwestern University, the *Summer Residential Program for Verbally and Mathematically Precocious Youth* at Duke University, and related Talent Search programs at the University of Denver, Earlham College, and elsewhere. With Talent Search, junior high school students who achieve high scores on the SAT-Mathematics and/or SAT-Verbal tests are invited to take accelerated math and other advanced courses on the college campus. However, in view of the restrictiveness of the Talent Search programs, it is fortunate that there are other college-based programs with more lenient entrance requirements and, sometimes, lower costs.

Purdue University offers a *Super Summer Program,* modeled after their successful Super Saturday plan, and three residential summer programs that attract gifted students from throughout the midwest. The *Star* program is for gifted seventh- and eighth-grade students capable of taking highly accelerated courses in math, science, and humanities. The *Purdue Academic Leadership Seminars* (PALS) are for ninth- and tenth-grade students selected on the basis of both leadership and achievement, as recommended by teachers and counselors. PALS participants also are offered courses in math, science, and humanities. The *Purdue College Credit Program* is for ninth- through twelfth-grade students who are selected via recommendations from their schools. In the summer of 1983, these students had the opportunity to earn college credit in university courses in psychology, English composition, history, the solar system, or computers. For all summer programs, 30 to 40 scholarships are available for qualified students with economic need. By way of evaluation, Feldhusen noted that " . . . the students made incredible academic gains" in both content mastery and school attitudes (Van Tassel-Baska, 1983).

Various *College for Kids* and *University for Youth* plans are similar to the Purdue program in offering high-level summer enrichment for gifted and talented students. For example, at the University of Wisconsin–Parkside (Kenosha, Wisconsin) a College for Kids plan was initiated in 1979 for children in kindergarten through fourth grade (Robinson, 1981). The purposes of this plan were, first, to provide quality enrichment experiences for gifted students and, second, to train elementary teachers to be more effective with gifted children in their regular classrooms.

With this program a parent/teacher committee was created to handle most of the preliminary conceptual planning. In addition, a paid, full-time university coordinator (starting in January) helped locate a few hundred gifted children and lots of teachers and university faculty; scheduled classrooms, laboratories, and studios; plus coped with mechanical problems of registration, scheduling, equipment, supplies, budget, and so on. The program was to last for three weeks, five half-days per week. Fees were set at a modest $30 per child.

Students were selected by sending registration brochures to parents of all students in the area already identified as "gifted" and participating in area G/T programs. Said Robinson, "The university did not want to debate with parents or teachers at registration about whether or not a given child was gifted." The response to the mailing was overwhelming—confirming the need for this type of program—and some students had to be denied participation due to limited space.

Interestingly, course topics were selected by the students themselves. The parent/teacher committee held a brainstorming session with the kindergarten to fourth-grade G/T children at one school. The problem: What courses would be best for a summer enrichment program? After narrowing an extensive list, and meeting a strict qualification of not conflicting with the regular curriculum, nine winners were oceanography, chemistry, astronomy, entomology, drama, photography, animation/cartooning, art, and ancient life. On the registration form, children and parents indicated their first, second, and third choices for courses. Depending upon schedule conflicts, children were assigned to two courses, with a strong effort to put everyone into their first choice.

Teachers were recruited from area school districts and were enrolled in a four-credit practicum. Their major jobs were to (1) meet the children and march them to their classes, and (2) assist the faculty in teaching or in any other way. During the week prior to the students' arrival, teachers were acquainted with concepts relating to teaching gifted and talented students, particularly within the Renzulli (1977) Enrichment Triad Model (Chapter 8).

In accord with the triad model, most children became involved in independent or small-group projects resulting in "real" products. For example, the Ancient Life class placed a time capsule in a new building; the Drama class produced, directed, and performed a play for parents and guests; and the Cartooning/Animation class produced two comic books and a 20-minute animated film.

The University of Wisconsin, Madison campus, began offering a three-week program for gifted elementary school children also titled *College for Kids*. This program, however, differed substantially from the Parkside plan (Clasen, 1982). Particularly, the Madison strategy was not to emphasize content. Rather, the goals were to (1) help students understand and value their own abilities and talents by bringing them into contact with other gifted students and—especially—with successful adult models; (2) have students observe, learn, and practice processes of creative thinking, problem solving, and inquiry; and (3) help students grasp the interrelatedness and interdependencies of various scientific and artistic disciplines.

A complete roll-call of students and staff included 250 children entering grades 3–6 (who, as at Parkside, had been identified by area schools as gifted), a university planner/coordinator employed full-time for the spring semester, 27 elementary school teachers, and no less than 81 university faculty. The teachers registered for a four-week graduate seminar, taught by the university planner/coordinator, which began one week before the three-week "college." Later, the seminar met every morning before the children arrived. The seminar focused on strategies (and their theoretical bases) for teaching processes of inquiry, critical thinking, creativity, problem solving, problem finding, concept learning, listening, and others.

Following the morning seminar, each teacher met with his or her "family," a group of 10 to 12 children, both before and after the classes and demonstrations conducted by university faculty. The main purpose of the family meetings " . . . was to help students integrate their experiences both cognitively and affectively" (Clasen, 1982). They discussed their experiences and practiced relevant processes and skills. For example, they brainstormed solutions to some problems. They also learned to use some creative-thinking techniques.

The first week of the "college" presented a smorgasbord of exploratory, awareness-raising experiences in a variety of disciplines. There were special demonstrations and presentations in chemistry, animal sciences, genetics, cryogenics, lyric theatre, astronomy, and meteorology, plus visits to a campus nuclear reactor, biodynamics lab, computer center, and educational TV station. Such enrichment does indeed extend beyond the regular elementary curriculum. Following the *pot pourri*, children elected to continue in one of four interest areas: visual and performing arts, biological sciences, physical sciences, or social sciences.

The last two weeks involved a series of lengthier, "family-size" encounters: 1½ to 2 hours per day for three days, sometimes longer, with one faculty member. The students' activities included creating their own lasers, experimenting with holography, using an electron microscope, exploring French language, culture, and cuisine, writing and performing a mini-operetta, producing a TV commercial, writing and producing a radio show, and publishing a newspaper on College for Kids. They dealt not only with issues such as pesticides and natural resources, but more abstract ones such as nuclear power, world hunger, and cloning.

Overall, the plan appeared to work very well, based upon evaluations and feedback from students, teachers, university faculty, and parents.

Variations on the two University of Wisconsin programs are also regularly offered by other campuses and other colleges around the country. While the specific classes and age ranges may vary, each provides a challenging summer program for gifted children, a training opportunity for teachers, and a very different teaching experience for college professors.

Music, Art, Language, and Computer Camps

College and universities traditionally have sponsored summer clinics or camps in music, art, and drama, and many now are offering computer camps, too. Others sponsor foreign language camps where students eat, sleep, swim, canoe—and communicate—in Spanish, French, German, or Russian. An especially good example is the *International Language Village* sponsored by Concordia College in Moorhead, Minnesota.

Although virtually none of these camps and institutes identify themselves as "programs for the gifted," for all practical purposes they do provide a gifted program in a specific area. Students are attracted to the camp because of their talent and interest in that area. They are expected to put many hours of dedicated effort into acquiring knowledge and skills. In addition, gifted students receive stimulation and support from other students who are equally enthusiastic and talented in the same ability. For students with few peers who share their special talents, such camps are refreshing ways to meet like-minded friends. Friendships born there often continue for years through correspondence and visits. Summer camps thus can do much to enhance social confidence and self-esteem in gifted children who may feel alone in their own schools.

As a final note on summer programs, they need not be highly involved and sophisticated. Simpler plans involve arranging for classes to be taught and teachers to teach them, identification methods and criteria (if any), plus publicity and registration details. Classes may include math, science, art, music, theatre, crafts, space, computers, and so on. Juntune (1981) presents brief descriptions of several successful summer programs for gifted and talented students.

MENTORS AND MENTORSHIPS

The concept of mentoring is hardly new. In ancient Greece Mentor himself tutored Telemachus, son of Odysseus. Socrates was mentor to Plato, Plato to Aristotle, and Aristotle to Alexander the Great (Cox and Daniel, 1983b). With contemporary mentorships, experts are usually recruited to work with and teach students on a one-to-one basis. Mentorships, normally a form of career education, typically are used with secondary students. While the usual pattern is for students to visit the mentor at work, mentors also may be invited to make presentations at the school. Also, a series of mentors may be used in short-term exploratory fashion, to acquaint one or a group of students with various career opportunities and the necessary preparation.

The typical mentorship includes an extended relationship between a community professional and a single student over a period of months. The student may be called a protégé, intern, apprentice, or assistant. The student visits the mentor at the job site on a scheduled basis to learn first-hand and in detail the activities, responsibilities, problems, worries, and, importantly, life-style associated with the particular business, art, or profession. A hands-on education, students work and usually identify with their mentors. Noted Cox and Daniel (1983b), "Mentorship presumes a commitment on the part of student and mentor and has as its goal the shaping of the student's life outlook." As even more dramatically described by DeMott (1981), one goal of a successful mentorship is to facilitate " . . . that extraordinary inner experience in which the human creature is suddenly seized with the realization—inexplicable, incontestable—that this is what I want. This is how life could be lived!" Boston (1976) described the mentorship as a transformation, the realization of the learner's potential, with a joint motivation to learn, to believe in each other's potential, and to develop a unique relationship. Frequently, mentorship experiences in the real world have a maturing effect on students such that some " . . . find it difficult to fit into the high school environment and social life . . . " (Cox and Daniel, 1983b).

In some cases a formal work-study plan is developed for which the student is paid for working while learning. Students normally receive high school credit for the mentorship experience. Mattson (1983) pointed out that gifted students themselves often possess a high level of expertise—perhaps acquired at the knee of a mentor/professional—which qualifies them to serve as mentors who may tutor peers or younger students.

The variety of potential mentorships and potential mentors literally is endless; the *Yellow Pages* will supply one short list. At Millville High School (New Jersey), mentorships " . . . have included matches with professionals in such areas as veterinary medicine, architecture, advertising, law, art, music, teaching [!], marine biology, psychology, optometry, medicine and journalism" (Juntune, 1981). Said Mattson (1983), in creating a mentor pool planners should use their imaginations and give careful consideration to all individuals in the community and even in the broader region.

Describing mentors as " . . . devoted men and women lighting intellectual sparks and setting the passion for learning aflame" (J. Epstein, 1981), Mattson itemized characteristics of good mentors that are intended to help a teacher or steering committee assemble a mentor pool. The list admittedly is idealistic in the sense that no mortal will possess all of the traits. However, the list can serve as a guide that will sensitize the teacher or committee to good "spark lighters" when they appear. The ideal mentor should possess expertise in his or her specialized field, of course. The mentor also should be high in personal integrity and have a strong interest in teaching young people. He or she should possess enthusiasm and optimism, and an "anticipation of tomorrow." Also important are tact, flexibility, and humor, all of which contribute to a desirable "acceptance of foolishness and errors." Tolerance and patience contribute to a safe, experimentally oriented environment; agility, creativity, and the ability to bring the protégé to higher levels of thinking and problem solving also are valuable. Good mentors should provide opportunities for students to use their gifts and abilities, to use their imaginations, and to see their own possibilities.

Students too should possess certain traits that enable them to maximally benefit from a mentorship. In describing qualifications of students interested in an executive assistant program or a creative and performing arts mentorship, Cox and Daniel (1983b) recommended that students be in the upper 20 percent of their class, have excellent communication and computational skills, and demonstrate leadership, initiative, maturity, dependability, and creativity.

In planning a mentorship program, Cox and Daniel detailed many helpful guidelines. Some of the more salient recommendations were:

1. Select a coordinator who has access to an administrator at the decision-making level.
2. Specify the purpose of the mentorship and the role of the students.
3. Elicit the support of the district superintendent, the school board, and community leaders.
4. Prepare written criteria for student selection based upon multiple indices, not just one.
5. Develop a clear, defensible academic credit policy. If high school credit is given, the work experience should relate directly to the course for which the credit is received.
6. Try to achieve the best mentor/student match possible. Mentors should be creative producers who will not treat the students as "go-fers."
7. Orientation seminars should be planned to acquaint students with the professional and business environments in which they will work.
8. Students should be prepared for the mentorship with related course work prior to the experience.
9. Students should be helped to develop individual goals.
10. Mentors should be asked to help evaluate each student's work.
11. The program must meet the academic needs of students. Students should be assigned required reading; they also should keep journals in which they analyze their activities and experiences.

FUTURE PROBLEM SOLVING

The fast-growing *Future Problem Solving* (FPS) program is an enrichment activity that can take place in a pullout, resource center, special class, or Saturday program, or with gifted students who are mainstreamed or clustered in the regular classroom. If the troops are good, they will travel to a state Future Problem Solving Bowl or even to the National Future Problem Solving Bowl, now held annually at Coe College, Cedar Rapids, Iowa. FPS was begun in 1975 by E. Paul Torrance at the University of Georgia (Crabbe, 1979, 1982; Torrance and Torrance, 1978; Torrance, Williams, Torrance, and Horng, 1978). It soon grew into a statewide Georgia plan, then a national program, and by 1982 included 100,000 children from all over the United States and ten foreign countries. They must be doing something right.

According to FPS director Anne Crabbe (1982) the objectives of the program are to help gifted children:

1. Become more aware of the future in order to deal with it actively, with feelings of optimism and the attitude that they can effect changes.
2. Become more creative; learning to go beyond the logical and obvious.
3. Develop and increase communication skills, including speaking and writing persuasively, clearly, and accurately.
4. Develop such teamwork skills as listening, respecting, understanding, and compromising.

5. Learn to use a problem-solving model and integrate it into their daily lives.
6. Develop research skills, learning how to gather information, where to go, and who to contact.

For the National FPS Bowl, the year-long program begins with the registration of each four-student team in one of three grade-level divisions (4–6, 7–9, 10–12). The teams are sent three practice problems that they solve by using this brainstorming-based four-step model:

1. Identify and state the underlying problem.
2. Generate many alternatives, with wild and crazy solutions encouraged and evaluation postponed.
3. Evaluate alternative solutions.
4. Select the best solution.

The teams' solutions are sent to trained evaluators who review, rate, and constructively comment on them. Based on their solutions to the third practice problem, teams are invited to the National Problem Solving Bowl.

Interestingly, it is the FPS students themselves who select and vote on the problems to be used the following year. For the 1979–1980 competition, the three problems dealt with underwater colonization, space exploration, and the increasing population of elderly people. The 1981–1982 problems were more social: child abuse, paranormal mental powers, and drug use/abuse (Crabbe, 1982).

In addition to the problem-solving component, FPS Bowls include both a *solution selling* competition and a *scenario-writing* competition. With solution selling, teams develop a five-minute presentation in which they try to convince the audience that their solution is clearly superior. While the content is serious, the presentation itself usually is a semiamusing commercial. In scenario writing, students are asked to predict the outcomes and consequences of their solutions to one (or more) of the practice problems in relation to a short period of time in the future.

The structure of FPS does indeed strengthen skills and talents listed in the above six goals. All components of the activity require creative problem solving—not just listing ideas, but defining the problem and evaluating the ideas as well. Communication skills are developed in several ways. First, in the group situation students must explain ideas clearly and persuasively to teammates. Second, in the process of writing their solutions accurately, clearly, and completely for the evaluators who score the ideas, the students themselves develop keen interests in grammar and spelling. Third, the solution selling component also demands concise organization of ideas, and a few minutes of convincing oration. Finally, the scenario-writing component further strengthens communication skills, along with creativity and futuristic thinking.

The intrinsic nature of the FPS teams requires teamwork and

cooperation—listening, respecting, understanding, and compromising (Crabbe, 1982). Ineffective teams have been known to engage in shouting matches and even name-calling. Research skills in FPS primarily are of the information-gathering variety. Team members learn to track down books and journals, contact experts, and sometimes visit agencies and institutions. Sometimes an entire class will join the information search to help their team, thus producing improvements in problem solving, teamwork, and research work for everyone.

Torrance and Torrance (1978) reported a few student testimonials on the benefits of FPS. A fifth-grade girl reported, "I learned to cooperate, to share ideas, to produce creative and clever ideas, to be excited, to learn and to work." A female high school junior stated, "I was starting to be more open and daring in my thoughts. . . . By becoming more aware of myself, and my mind, and my capabilities, I know now that I have a lot of self-potential and that I should use it to achieve whatever goals I set for myself." Information on FPS is available from Future Problem Solving, Coe College, Cedar Rapids, Iowa 52402.

OLYMPICS OF THE MIND

Like Future Problem Solving, *Olympics of the Mind* (OM) is a nationally organized program. At this writing, it operates in about 1,500 schools in 27 states, plus Washington, D.C., and Ontario, Canada. In January 1982 it was featured on Bill Moyers' PBS series *Creativity,* and has been recommended to the U.S. Congress as an "exemplary program" for gifted students. OM also has been reviewed in *Psychology Today, Omni,* the *New York Times,* and other periodicals.

The key assumption of its founders, Ted Gourley and Sam Micklus, is that the mind can be trained and strengthened through exercise with mental games just as the body is trained with physical exercise (Gourley, 1981). OM thus was designed to combine " . . . the excitement of athletic competition with fun-filled mental gymnastics for youngsters" (Olympics of the Mind Association, 1983). It focuses on creative problem solving, which leads to diligence, hard work, fun, and the " . . . thrill of constructively seeing their imaginations at work."

There presently are three age classifications, grades K–5, 6–8, and 9–12. While teams usually are organized through schools, they can be organized through community organizations such as 4H Clubs, Scout Troops, and others. Following the athletic competition model (Gourley, 1981), students in a given school "try out for the team" with practice creative-thinking problems. Faculty coaches explain the nature of the "elimination trials," the games, rules of competition, and the criteria for team selection and for judging events. The team will have seven members;

in formal competitions, only five can be "on the playing field." While losing probably is not much fun, even those who do not make the team receive practice and coaching in creative problem solving.

A "member" is one school, which registers with the OM Association for a fee (in 1983, of $65). Participation in regional and state OM competitions usually will require another small fee to cover phone, postage, and duplicating expenses. The member must also purchase the book *Problems, Problems, Problems* (Micklus and Gourley, 1982; $10.95), which discusses creativity and presents about 65 creative problems.

The OM Association provides each member with long-term problems in advance of competition. Teams thus have time to prepare their own creative solutions to the problems. Design specifications and monetary limits are clearly indicated. Here are a few examples of 1984 long-term problems used in preliminary and "World Finals" competition:

Mousemobile Relays, divisions II (6–8) and III (9–12). Each team will design five vehicles that use a mousetrap as its power source. The five vehicles will compete in a relay race with the five vehicles of other teams. Scores are based upon speed and accuracy. Accuracy will be determined by the ability of each vehicle to stay within its boundaries and break a balloon after crossing the finish line. Time limit: 10 minutes.

Moby Dick, divisions I, II, and III. As a drama, each team recreates Chapter 136 of *Moby Dick*, "On the Rachel," which takes place in Captain Gardiner's stateroom. Ishmael is discussing part of the legend of Moby Dick with the captain; some officers and/or crew may be included. As the meeting takes place, slides will be projected on a screen illustrating the discussion. During the meeting Captain Gardiner gives Ishmael a box found from the sunken *Pequod*. Ishmael opens the box to display its artistic contents: a sculpture of a whale, a drawing/painting of a whaling scene, and an article of scrimshaw (carved ivory). The team is to write the script and prepare the playbill and any background or props. Time limit: 12 minutes.

Strategy Structure, divisions I, II, and III. Each team will design a structure using ⅛ by ⅛ by 36 in. strips of balsa wood. It must be between 8 and 8½ in. high and must weigh 18 grams or less (⅝ oz). Only glue may be used; straight pins, nails, and so on are allowed only during construction. The team will place weights on the structure. A section of the structure must be removed after each 25 pounds is added, continuing until the structure is broken or time expires. Time limit: 12 minutes.

The competitions also include short-term problems. Teams will not know the nature of these problems until a judge reads a problem to them on the spot. Some examples: "With one minute to think and two minutes to respond, name as many birds as you can"; "With one minute to think and two minutes to respond, name as many different kinds of springs as you can and what they are good for." For the latter problem, an on-its-toes team will include oases, leaps, and Colorado Springs.

For further information, contact Olympics of the Mind Association, Inc., P.O. Box 27, Glassboro, N.J. 08028.

SUMMARY

Worthwhile enrichment has high content complexity (for example, ideas, theories, abstract concepts) that requires high-level thinking, creating, evaluating, and critical thinking, and stresses interrelatedness of disciplines. Good enrichment extends or replaces traditional coursework; is productive rather than reproductive; is based on needs and readinesses, not age; and deals with things as they could or should be.

Enrichment strategies are delivery methods for achieving process and content goals. Library research projects, extending perhaps to museum or laboratory visits, aim at answering specific questions. For independent science projects, the teacher plays a supportive, guiding role. Generally, independent projects may be in any area—art, theatre, journalism, and so on.

Commercial- or teacher-made learning centers can teach languages, science, math, computers, social studies, creative writing, music appreciation, and others. Field trips are good experiences for regular and gifted students. The teacher and the guide/educator should discuss and preplan any tour. Students should be allowed to touch and question, not just be lectured at.

Feldhusen's Super Saturday is a model Saturday enrichment program which results in cognitive, affective, and "generative" benefits. Members of parent/educator groups also may organize one-time Saturday programs, with activities for gifted and talented children and a speaker for adults. Regular city summer programs may be capitalized upon by parents, teachers, or counselors seeking summer enrichment activities. The SMPY, CTY, and related Talent Search programs offer mathematical and other accelerated and enrichment classes for extremely precocious students, mainly in the junior high school.

Summer programs, such as the Purdue Super Summer and summer residential programs or the University of Wisconsin College for Kids, require plenty of planning in order to recruit participants and teaching staff, and to organize the course offerings, activities, space, facilities, selection, and registration procedures, and more. Students may help choose the curriculum. The programs provide marvelous opportunities for learning advanced content and subject matter skills, and for developing process skills. The programs help increase self-understanding and self-appreciation. Teachers also receive valuable training in such programs.

Music, art, language, and computer summer camps also are excellent, *de facto* gifted programs that teach high-level content and thinking skills. The self-confidence and peer support is invaluable for many psychologically isolated gifted students. Simple Saturday classes can be informally arranged.

Mentor programs usually involve extended on-the-job, one-to-one interaction with a community professional. Students and mentors typically develop a unique relationship. Students learn professional activities and problems, and the life-styles of mentors. Many students experience rapid maturation and attitude transformation. Work-study plans are one type of mentorship. The ideal mentor is interested in teaching and is high in integrity, enthusiasm, flexibility, humor, patience, agility, creativity, and the ability to stimulate high-level thinking and problem solving.

Cox and Daniel recommended that students suitable for mentorships should be in the upper 20 percent academically and be high in communication skill, leadership, maturity, dependability, and creativity. Planning mentorships requires clarification of the purposes of the mentorship, the role of the student, student selection criteria, the academic credit policy, optimal student/mentor matches, student goals, evaluation of the student's work, and others.

The nationally organized Future Problem Solving program, created by Paul Torrance, helps children become future-oriented and strengthens creative thinking, problem solving, communication skills, research, and teamwork skills. Problems are solved following a four-step model. The National FPS Bowls include scenario writing and solution-selling competitions. Overall, it has been a fast-growing and highly successful program.

Olympics of the Mind also is a national program, and a successful one. OM assumes that the mind, like the muscles, can be strengthened with exercise. It follows an athletic model, with students trying out for school teams and competitions guided by strict rules. There are long-term problems, worked on during the year, and short-term problems, which are sprung on students at the local, district, regional, state, and "World Finals" competitions.

8

CURRICULUM MODELS

As mentioned in earlier chapters, curriculum models help provide a theoretical framework within which specific enrichment activities may be planned. Now any theory performs several functions: It will (1) simplify a complex phenomenon, (2) allow explanation and prediction, (3) provide a "language" and a point of view, and, importantly, (4) provide prescriptive guidance (Davis, 1983b). Therefore, the models described in this chapter should:

1. Help clarify and simplify important components of gifted education, characteristics of gifted children and their higher-level needs, or the content of a worthwhile educational program.
2. Explain why particular recommended activities are useful and predict benefits to students.
3. Supply a point of view and a set of related concepts regarding the purpose of gifted education or the nature of gifted students.
4. Make specific recommendations and prescriptions for activities, providing theory-based direction and structure to program planning.

Overview

This chapter will briefly summarize nine curriculum models, all of which have provided justifiable bases for planning differentiated experiences for G/T students (see Inset 8.1). In most cases—but not all—the mod-

INSET 8.1 A SUMMARY OF PRINCIPLES FOR A DIFFERENTIATED CURRICULUM FOR THE GIFTED AND TALENTED

In earlier chapters, we reviewed three lists of principles for selecting appropriate enrichment and acceleration programming strategies. Another list comes from the National/State Leadership Training Institute, which has itemized the following principles designed to guide the selection of suitable curriculum for G/T students. The list overlaps yet complements the previous ones. The recommendations are the product of considerable experience and thought.

1. Present content that is related to broad-based issues, themes, and problems.
2. Integrate multiple disciplines into the area of study.
3. Present comprehensive, related, and mutually reinforcing experiences within an area of study.
4. Allow for the in-depth learning of a self-selected topic within the area of study.
5. Develop independent or self-directed study skills.
6. Develop productive, complex, abstract, and/or higher-level thinking skills.
7. Focus on open-ended tasks.
8. Develop research skills and methods.
9. Integrate basic skills and higher-level thinking skills into the curriculum.
10. Encourage the development of products that challenge existing ideas and produce "new" ideas.
11. Encourage the development of products that use new techniques, materials, and forms.
12. Encourage the development of self-understanding, that is, recognizing and using one's abilities, becoming self-directed, and appreciating likenesses and differences between oneself and others.
13. Evaluate student outcomes by using appropriate and specific criteria through self-appraisal, criterion-referenced and/or standardized instruments.

els and their prescriptions are quite consistent and complementary, permitting a teacher-coordinator to draw ideas from two or more curriculum models simultaneously. Some models, such as the *Revolving Door Identification Model* (Renzulli, Reis, and Smith, 1981) provide extensive details regarding program philosophy, identification, evaluation, and the specifics of carrying out the entire plan. Other models propose more general suggestions as to worthwhile skill development goals and activities, leaving it to the teacher-coordinator to fill in the specifics. These are the nine models:

1. The Enrichment Triad Model (Renzulli, 1977)
2. The Revolving Door Identification Model (Renzulli, Reis, and Smith, 1981)
3. Feldhusen's Three-Stage Enrichment Model (Feldhusen and Kolloff, 1978, 1981)

4. The Guilford/Meeker Structure of Intellect Model (Guilford, 1967, 1977; Meeker, 1969)
5. Bloom's Taxonomy of Educational Objectives (Bloom, Englehart, Furst, Hill, and Krathwohl, 1956)
6. Treffinger's (1975) model for increasing self-directedness
7. The Williams (1970) model for developing "thinking and feeling processes"
8. The Taylor (1978) Multiple-Talent Totem Pole Model
9. The U.S.O.E. definition as a curriculum guide

THE ENRICHMENT TRIAD MODEL

One of the best known enrichment plans is the *Enrichment Triad Model* originated by Joseph Renzulli (1977). The plan may be implemented with students of any age and in a variety of grouping arrangements. As an overview (see Figure 8.1), the three sequential but qualitatively different steps include: Type I enrichment, general exploratory activities designed to acquaint the student with a variety of topics and interest areas; Type II

FIGURE 8.1   Renzulli's Enrichment Triad Model.

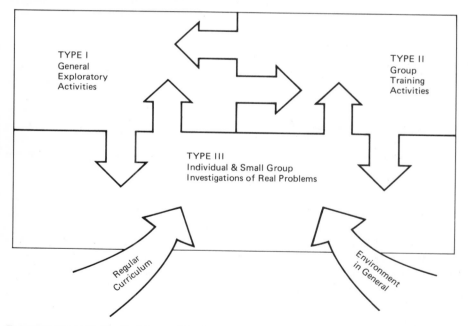

From J. S. Renzulli, *The Enrichment Triad Model: A Guide for Developing Defensible Programs for the Gifted and Talented.* Mansfield Center, Conn.: Creative Learning Press, 1977. Reprinted by permission.

enrichment, group training activities dealing with the development of "thinking and feeling" processes—for example, creativity and research skills; and Type III enrichment, the investigation of real problems " . . . that are similar in nature to those pursued by authentic researchers or artists in particular fields" (Renzulli, 1977). Importantly, Type I and II activities are considered valuable for—and should be used with—all students. Type III activities, however, are felt to require the special creativity, ability, and energy of truly gifted students.

Type I Enrichment

Type I enrichment—general exploratory activities—is intended to expose students to a wide variety of topics and inspire ideas for later Type III independent projects. Students should understand that they are to explore these interest areas purposefully, with a view toward identifying ideas for further study. Some students already will have longstanding interests or hobbies which are well suited for Type III projects (photography, drama, calligraphy, and so on). In these cases, Type I activities serve mainly to expose the student to new topic areas. Problems arise when a student cannot find an area he or she is enthusiastic about. Since the main thrust of the program is to involve gifted students in Type III activities, such students may need to be counseled out of the program. However, every effort should first be made to encourage an interest.

Resource centers should be well stocked with books, magazines, and other media dealing with a large number of topics. Appendix 8.1 at the end of this chapter lists well over a hundred possibilities, some of which are categories (for example, languages). Topics, discussed in group settings or studied individually by students, typically are selected jointly by teachers and students.

Another good exploratory activity is field experiences in which gifted and talented students meet dynamic people involved in creative and problem-solving endeavors—artists, actors, engineers, museum and art gallery curators, TV show directors, business leaders, restaurant owners, and so on. This type of "field trip" goes beyond just visiting an art gallery or planetarium or taking a guided tour through the Schlitz Brewery. The purpose is not to "look at"—Renzulli's "museum experience"—but to *become involved with* professionals and their activities.

The design of Type I exploratory activities will require effort and ingenuity by participating teachers. Renzulli (1977), in fact, recommends brainstorming sessions aimed at such problems as: "What are some topics (issues, events, authors, periods in history, modes of communication, etc.) to which we can expose students that ordinarily are not encountered in the regular program?" Or "How can we give an Interest Development Center the magnetic power to draw children's attention?"

Type II Enrichment

The purpose of Type II enrichment—group training activities—is to strengthen "thinking and feeling" processes. These are skills, abilities, attitudes, and strategies intended to enable all students to cope more effectively with a variety of problems in different life areas. Many of the skills are important for the advanced independent work (Type III enrichment) of G/T students.

Some affective concerns, all of which are elaborated upon in Chapter 9, are:

Values clarification.   Helping students understand their own and others' values, and helping them develop positive, constructive, and success-oriented values.

Awareness training.   Increasing students' awareness of others' problems, handicaps, feelings, perceptions, and points of view.

Self-concept development.   Fostering positive self-images and constructive, achievement-oriented expectations for the future.

Internal evaluation.   Helping students understand that they are responsible for their own successes and failures, and that they are in charge of their destinies.

Motivation.   Helping students understand that achievement and personal success stem from effort.

Valuing education.   Fostering the notion that education is the route to career success and personal fulfillment.

Some activities and processes aimed at developing skills and attitudes related to creative thinking are:

Awareness of the importance of creative thinking and creative people.
Understanding steps and processes in creative thinking.
Practice with creative-thinking techniques, such as brainstorming, metaphorical thinking, and others (Chapter 11).

Other cognitive processes and skills are based upon Bloom's taxonomy of cognitive objectives: application, analysis, synthesis, and evaluation. Still more process skills include classification, comparison, interpretation, critical thinking, problem solving, discovery, inquiry, and reflective thinking; plus such practical considerations as library skills, research skills (including equipment operation), report writing, and so on.

Renzulli recommends that the process activities be related to students' interests and topic areas. For example, within her pet area of photography, Cheryl Shutterbug might do creative, analytic, comparative, evaluative, or metaphorical activities. However, such content relevancy will not always be possible or particularly important (for example, in many awareness, sensitivity, creative-dramatics, or reflective-thinking exercises).

Incidentally, many gifted programs focus exclusively on the previously mentioned kinds of process activities. In their article entitled "Developing Defensible Programs for the Gifted and Talented," Renzulli and Smith (1978) warn that too strong an emphasis on process activities definitely is not defensible, which brings us to Type III enrichment.

Type III Enrichment

With Type III enrichment activities, the gifted young person becomes an actual researcher investigating a real problem. Renzulli emphasizes that students should act as *producers* of knowledge, not merely consumers of information. More concretely, they should not simply be asked to consult more encyclopedias, textbooks, or other already-summarized sources and then write a report. They should not summarize the conclusions of other people; they should use raw data as their main information source, from which they draw their own conclusions.

Most of the topics itemized in Appendix 8.1 could stimulate ideas and problems researchable by talented youngsters even in the elementary school. For example, student Robin Finch, keenly interested in birds, could ask all sorts of questions about the local feathered friends—their eating, sleeping, nesting, migration, molting, walking and flying habits, and their natural enemies, preferred habitats, roles in ecological niches, and so on. The student should play an active part in formulating the problem, designing the research methods, and planning the final product. The teacher, as the "guide on the side," helps with clarifying the problem, designing the research and locating materials and equipment, and recommends information sources or community experts.

Outlets for Creations

It is important for students to have audiences for their Type III products. Grown-up artists, scientists, and other professionals do not keep their work to themselves. Indeed, a good part of their motivation and satisfaction derives from at least a limited amount of publicity and public awareness of their accomplishments (Renzulli, Reis, and Smith, 1981). Gifted students also are product-oriented; they wish to hold up their accomplishments and to inform and perhaps influence a particular audience.

Renzulli (1977) suggested that local organizations such as historical societies or science or dramatic groups might be suitable audiences. Also, children's magazines and newspapers routinely publish children's writings and research summaries. Further, there may be children's art shows or science fairs that could be good outlets for the children's or adolescents' products. If such shows are not available, an energetic G/T teacher-coordinator could think about starting some. Local newspapers also like a human-interest story, and good publicity will not hurt any G/T program. Of course, as we noted in Chapter 7, the student's own class is a ready audience for products and reports that are not highly specialized or sophisticated.

THE REVOLVING DOOR IDENTIFICATION MODEL

Renzulli, Reis, and Smith (1981; see also Delisle and Renzulli, 1982; Reis and Renzulli, 1982) combined Renzulli's three-ring identification model, Enrichment Triad Model, and many other concepts into their *Revolving Door Identification Model* (RDIM). According to one reviewer, "The RDIM probably will be recognized as one of the most significant and revolutionary contributions to gifted education to date. This book is absolutely must reading for anyone who wishes to feel literate in the education of gifted and talented children and adolescents" (Davis, 1981b). Another reviewer, notably less impressed, among other points concluded that, "The RDIM is totally conceptualized around a pull-out model of program organization. Consequently, it is built on the least sound grouping approach used to serve the gifted. . . . The RDIM may be innovative, but it falls short of providing a theoretical base for current practice" (Van Tassel-Baska, 1981).

The Revolving Door Identification Model actually is more than an identification model—it is a complete programming guide. It includes an identification philosophy and methods, a clear programming plan, and program evaluation procedures. The basic and unique thrust of the RDIM lies in the definition of who is "in" and who is "out" of a school's gifted education program. With the traditional or "absolutist" approach, about 5 percent or so of the school's population is selected in the fall for participation. The selection procedure ends, the names are etched in granite, the students begin participating in the acceleration or enrichment activities, and teachers stop concerning themselves with identifying gifted students until the fall of next year. With the RDIM, about 25 percent of the students are selected for a *talent pool.* All students in the talent pool receive special services—Type I and Type II enrichment activities, educational and career counseling, and perhaps acceleration.

In order for students in the talent pool to work on a Type III independent project, however, all teachers all year must remain alert for students who show " . . . signs of interest, creativity, task commitment, and expressions of advanced ability" (Renzulli, Reis, and Smith, 1981). Note that these traits correspond to Renzulli's three-ring definition of true giftedness: high creativity, high task commitment (motivation), and above-average ability. When such a student surfaces and wishes to work on a project, the teacher sends a "light bulb"—an Action Information Message—to the resource-room teacher. If there is an available slot, the resource teacher meets with the regular teacher and then with the student to decide if the project is a worthwhile one that cannot be completed in the regular classroom. If accepted, the student is *revolved* into the resource room until the project is completed (a few days, weeks, or even months later), and then revolves out again to make room for another person. Experience with the RDIM shows that about 50 to 60 percent of the students in the talent pool actually work on at least one independent Type III project in the resource room each year.

One commendable feature of the RDIM is that no student is permanently barred from participation. Any student who shows creativity and high interest in an independent project can be nominated by a teacher, which may result in that student working in the resource room on his or her project and then becoming a bona fide member of the talent pool. In practice, many non-talent-pool students become aware of the RDIM opportunities, wish to become involved, design an independent project, and are permitted to carry it out. "The door revolves, but is not slammed shut on anyone" (Davis, 1981b). Combined with the 25-percent identification figure, such a policy should prevent complaints by irate parents whose children otherwise would be firmly "out" of a program.

The RDIM has undergone several preliminary tests and many problems have been debugged. The book *Revolving Door Identification Model* (Renzulli, Reis, and Smith, 1981) presents plenty of step-by-step explanations and examples, sometimes with case histories. For example, the three-ring identification philosophy, process, and useful instruments are described in detail. There also are forms for nearly everything—nomination forms, management plans, "light bulbs," class-survey sheets, parent questionnaires, student questionnaires, teacher questionnaires, revolving-in letters (used to inform parents of their child's participation), revolving-out letters (informing parents that the project is complete), and others. Interestingly, many of the forms serve as a system of staff accountability checks, motivating everyone to do their job.

Renzulli, Reis, and Smith (1981) describe many implementation and operating problems, along with their solutions. Their last chapter is composed entirely of questions and answers related to philosophical and political difficulties a coordinator may encounter. For example, "Won't we reduce the quality of our program if we include a full 25 percent of the students?" (No, while it does open the program to more students, only a limited number are handled at a given time in the resource room.) "What should parents do if their child has an intense interest that is only evidenced in the home?" (Both parents and students should be aware that they can initiate an Action Information Message [light bulb].) And many more.

FELDHUSEN'S THREE-STAGE ENRICHMENT MODEL

Feldhusen's *three-stage enrichment model* centers upon three types of instructional activities aimed at three levels of skill development. While teaching for creative development clearly is central, the training also aims at strengthening convergent problem solving, research skills, and, importantly, independent learning. While the three types of instructional activities may be used intermittently throughout a G/T program, " . . . there should be increasing emphasis on the higher levels" (Feldhusen and Kolloff, 1981).

Stage 1 focuses upon the development of *basic divergent and convergent thinking abilities*. The corresponding instructional activities include relatively short-term, teacher-led exercises, mainly in creative thinking but also in logical and critical thinking. Some creativity exercises are, for example, listing unusual uses for trash bags, thinking of improvements for a bicycle, predicting outcomes of unlikely events (What would happen if there were no television or no McDonald's?), or " . . . designing a vehicle of the future using anything you might find in a junkyard" (Kolloff and Feldhusen, 1981). Such exercises are assumed to develop such creative abilities as ideational fluency, originality, flexibility, and elaboration, along with other relevant abilities and attitudes.

Stage 2 of the model requires *more complex creative and problem-solving activities* that (1) may extend over a longer period of time and, importantly, (2) require less teacher direction and more student initiative. Some suggested examples were learning and practicing creative-thinking techniques, such as brainstorming and the *synectics* methods (Chapter 11); working through a systematic problem-solving model (for example, defining the problem, listing ideas, evaluating ideas, implementing the solution); and working through the detective mysteries of the *Productive Thinking Program* (Covington, Crutchfield, Olton, and Davies, 1972).

Stage 3 activities aim at strengthening *independent learning abilities*. Said Feldhusen and Kolloff (1981), "Stage 3 projects should involve gifted youngsters in challenging efforts to define and clarify a problem, ambitious data gathering from books and other resources, interpretation of findings, and the development of creative ways of communicating results . . . . Stage 3 activities help students learn to use library resources other than the encyclopedia, plan toward a goal, and develop methods of presenting their ideas to others in forms other than a written report." Some examples of Stage 3 projects are:

Writing haiku

Writing short stories

Writing and producing a short play

Writing and videotaping TV commercial skits

Researching a report on local air pollution

Investigating alternate waste disposal systems (students in one Purdue G/T program presented the results to the Lafayette City Council)

Researching backgrounds of community leaders and presenting the stories on local radio

Photographing historical homes and preparing a show with the pictures

In attempting to master concepts such as Renzulli's Enrichment Triad Model and Feldhusen's three-stage enrichment model, it is helpful to match them side by side and point out similarities and differences; Feldhusen and Kolloff (1981) have done this. Renzulli's Type I enrichment (exploratory activities) has no counterpart in Feldhusen's model. Renzulli's Type II enrichment, the development of thinking and feeling processes, is similar to Feldhusen's Stage 1 activities, the development of basic (mainly creative) skills. Renzulli's Type III enrichment, while similar to Feldhusen's Stage 3, calls for " . . . quite dramatically high independent project and inquiry activities" (Feldhusen and Kolloff, 1981). Feldhusen's less ambitious Stage 3 stresses independent study with a focus on reading, gathering information, interpreting the material, and creatively presenting the results.

Feldhusen's more modest Stage 3 activities, in comparison with Renzulli Type III enrichment, are related to Feldhusen's more generous definition of "gifted and talented": students with achievement levels in the sixtieth to eightieth percentile and IQs between 110 and 140. Higher-ability students, argue Feldhusen and Kolloff, might well be accelerated in grade-skipping or early admission programs, college courses in high school, or SMPY (Stanley, 1979) types of advanced programs.

The Feldhusen model aims at social and affective goals, as well as cognitive ones. Gifted students work with peers of similar ability—peers who understand and appreciate special talent. This social contact and support helps gifted students view themselves as effective, competent, and creative independent learners.

THE GUILFORD/MEEKER STRUCTURE OF INTELLECT MODEL

Mary Meeker (1969, 1981a, 1981b, 1981c) criticizes modern education for its "antiquated learning theories" (that is, Pavlov/Skinner behavior modification) and, especially, for its absence of a theory of human learning abilities. Said Meeker, " . . . it takes certain intellectual abilities in order to learn." A theory of learning abilities, she argues, could and should form the base of an educational training program that prepares teachers to (1) diagnose needs of individual students and (2) prescribe appropriate learning activities. Indeed, "Curriculum should be based on abilities to learn rather than on subject matter" (Meeker, 1981a); and—as she elaborates— "Basic to the academic skill 'basics' are foundational intellectual abilities which, if lacking or undeveloped in a student (no matter how high the IQ), will prevent the youngster from being a successful learner . . . " (Meeker, 1981b). The identification of these abilities, their assessment, and the prescription of remedial skill-building activities is the highlight of Meeker's work.

Meeker just happens to have a theory of intellectual abilities in mind. Since 1962 she has used the Guilford (1967, 1977, 1979b, 1981) *Structure of Intellect* (SOI) model to guide diagnosis and prescription. In a non-modest appraisal, she observes that "The SOI concept is the most fundamental (technological, educational) advance in the past 200 years." Navarre (1983) apparently agrees: " . . . an SOI assessment of the student in the gifted classroom (or any classroom) provides the teacher with information he/she cannot afford to neglect."

What is this structure of intellect model? Guilford (1967, 1977, 1981) created a three-dimensional cube—a theory of intelligence—which was intended to describe everything one could do with one's intellect. Figure 8.2 presents the SOI cube and its three dimensions of *contents, products,* and *operations.* Our limited space will not permit a complete description of the SOI model. Briefly, each of the 120 cells of the model is interpreted to be a unique cognitive ability—an approach that stands in sharp contrast with the single IQ score of the Stanford-Binet test or the two IQ scores of the WISC-R. Joy Paul Guilford has invested about three decades creating tests that measure each one of those 120 abilities.

As an example, the darkened slab of the model in Figure 8.2 includes the operations of *divergent production.* Somewhere in that slab will be a cell identified as the "divergent production (operation) of symbolic (content) units (product)," or just *DSU.* Some tests of DSU—or *Word Fluency*—ask the examinee to list words with the first and last letters specified (for example, R_____M); list words which include one, two, or three specified letters; or list words which rhyme with a specified word (for example, *roam*). Two tests of divergent production of semantic relations (*DMR* or *Associational Fluency*) ask the person to (1) list as many words as he or she can that are similar in meaning to each given word, or (2) list words that are opposite in meaning. The tests Guilford developed to measure the 24 divergent production abilities (6 products × 4 contents) are published as tests of creativity. See Guilford (1967, 1977) for descriptions of the many, many other specific SOI tests.

Now, with 120 SOI abilities it seems logical that some are more critical for learning, or readiness to learn, than others. Meeker's *Structure of Intellect-Learning Abilities* (SOI-LA) test measures 24 of Guilford's abilities

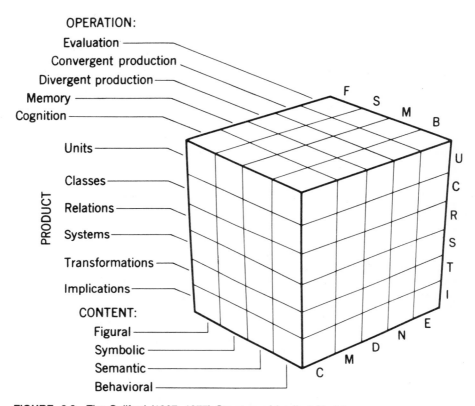

FIGURE 8.2 The Guilford (1967, 1977) Structure of Intellect Model.
From J. P. Guilford, The Nature of Human Intelligence (New York: McGraw-Hill, 1967). Reprinted with permission.

having a critical bearing on school learning, particularly in reading, math, writing, and creativity. Abilities (nonverbal) necessary for cognitive readiness to read (not actual reading) include:

> *CFU,* Cognition for Figural Units, or Visual Closure
> *EFU,* Evaluation of Figural Units, or Visual Discrimination
> *CFC,* Cognition of Figural Classes, or Visual Conceptualization
> *EFC,* Evaluation of Figural Classes, or Judgment of Figural Similarities
> *MSU-v,* Memory for Semantic Units–Visual, or Visual Attending
> *MSS-v,* Memory for Semantic Systems–Visual, or Visual Sequencing

Abilities necessary for actual reading include:

> *CMU,* Cognition of Semantic Units, or Vocabulary of Math and Verbal Concepts
> *CMR,* Cognition of Semantic Relations, or Comprehension of Verbal Relations

CMS, Cognition of Semantic Systems, or Ability to Comprehend Extended Verbal Information

MFU, Memory for Figural Units, or Visual Memory for Details

NST, Convergent Production of Semantic Transformations, or Symbol Pattern Discrimination

For success in arithmetic these abilities must be developed:

MSU-a, Memory for Semantic Units–Auditory, or Auditory Attending

MSS-a, Memory for Semantic Systems–Auditory, or Auditory Sequencing

CSS, Cognition of Symbolic Systems, or Comprehension of Numerical Progressions

ESS, Evaluation of Symbolic Systems, or Judgment of Correctness of Numeric Facts

NSS, Convergent Production of Symbolic Systems, or Application of Math Facts

ESC, Evaluation of Symbolic Classes, or Judgment of Arithmetic Similarities

Contrasted with success in arithmetic, these abilities are necessary for success in mathematics:

CFS, Cognition of Figural Systems, or Constancy of Objects in Space

CFT, Cognition of Figural Transformations, or Spatial Conservation

MSI, Memory for Symbolic Implications, or Inferential Memory

CSR, Cognition of Symbolic Relations, or Comprehension of Abstract Relations

NSI, Convergent Production of Symbolic Implications, or Formal Reasoning (logic)

The authors realize that the reader cannot possibly recall a fraction of these names and descriptions. The important point is to note the flavor of the detailed analysis of the specific cognitive abilities that may underlie "reading," "arithmetic," or "mathematics," an analysis uniquely made possible by the SOI model and the SOI-LA test. Said Pennsylvania G/T Supervisor Bruce Gurcsik (1981) of the SOI-LA:

A clear advantage to SOI diagnostic-prescriptive programming is that teachers have access to data which will guide them in effective identification of a gifted child's learning abilities, strengths and weaknesses. This information may suggest that staff concentrate on a specific ability rather than generalizing about work which may or may not be appropriate. This additional perspective can be of great benefit when teaching low achieving gifted children. The SOI data may show that the child is gifted but does not plan or organize well for success in school work.

Normally we do not speak (or even think) of "teaching intelligence." Indeed, Meeker notes that resistance to her approach is based partly upon the traditional notion that to a large extent intelligence and IQ scores are fixed and unmodifiable. Nonetheless, her SOI curriculum strategy is based exactly upon the premise that children can and should be trained " . . . in those learning abilities that comprise intelligence" (Meeker, 1981c). In the words of Kester (1982), "The concept from which all the SOI curricula derives states that it is possible to teach people to think."

A SOI profile, based upon the SOI-LA test or SOI scores derived from the WISC-R, Stanford-Binet, or other individual intelligence test items (see Meeker, 1969), summarizes an individual's "pattern of intelligence." This pattern or profile serves to diagnose weaknesses that are remediated via individual and group tasks in five workbooks, one each for *cognition, memory, convergent production, divergent production,* and *evaluation* (Meeker, 1976). For example, brainstorming and other ideational tasks would be used for students weak in divergent production skills. Critical-thinking activities are used to strengthen both cognition and evaluation operations. After a teacher (or parent) becomes comfortable with the SOI model and the recommended tasks, he or she will be able to select other instructional materials that provide training beyond the exercises in the workbooks.

Gurcsik (1981) itemized the benefits of the SOI approach for preparing Individualized Education Programs for gifted students:

IEP conferences are concise and meaningful.
The IEP document is brief.
Student abilities are easily recognized.
Disabling weaknesses are identified and remediated.
Strengths are accurately stressed.
Source Book activities are easily incorporated into the curriculum.
Students may be compared to other pupils.
Personal profiles can be developed to evaluate individuals.
Programming decisions are justified based on appropriate data.

Meeker's SOI approach presents a different perspective on the conceptualization and identification of gifted and talented students, both majority and minority. Meeker (1981c) argued that Anglo children, even before they enter school, have the cognitive abilities necessary for learning—namely, those itemized earlier. However, minority children from non-English-speaking, low-education, low-income families often do not. Therefore, with identification based upon IQ tests, minority children often are excluded from participation in gifted programs. Within the multifaceted SOI theory, however, Meeker finds that non-Anglos—Native American, Hispanic American, and Black students—score higher on different SOI abilities than Anglo children. Selection for program participation may be based upon these high, measured abilities.

Navarre (1983) itemized several uses for the SOI approach in gifted education. In addition to providing guidance for preparing IEPs and identifying gifted minority children, she suggested that the SOI-LA test itself could be used as subject matter for a junior or senior high school unit on intelligence. The students could take the test, score it, prepare their own profiles, and diagnose strengths and weaknesses. (Because such an activity could have a long-lasting impact, good or bad, the present authors would recommend caution with this activity. It should not be used without interpretive guidance by a counselor.) The SOI-LA also can be the basis of career education/exploration for students. The SOI Institute has available a computer program that identifies ten careers and ten vocations that "best fit" different profiles of SOI-LA abilities.

BLOOM'S TAXONOMY OF EDUCATIONAL OBJECTIVES

When educators speak of "high-level thinking skills" or "high-level objectives" they are referring explicitly or implicitly to the top end of "Bloom's taxonomy," more formally titled the *Taxonomy of Educational Objectives: Cognitive Domain* (Bloom, 1974; Bloom, Engelhart, Furst, Hill, and Krathwohl, 1956; Furst, 1981). Bloom's taxonomy has had an international impact on education by drawing attention to the difference between "low-level" academic knowledge, which is commonly taught, and "higher-level" thinking skills—which everyone suddenly seemed to realize were rarely taught. The taxonomy serves as a guide for the preparation of instructional objectives; it therefore helps dictate teaching strategies and learning experiences.

The six main levels of the taxonomy describe progressively higher levels of cognitive activity, from dealing with facts, figures, definitions, and rules at the *knowledge* and *comprehension* levels to expecting students to *apply, analyze, synthesize,* or *evaluate* that information at higher levels. Table 8.1 lists the six main levels of the taxonomy, along with examples of student activities associated with each level.

The reader will recall the continuous reference to "high-level thinking skills" as appropriate objectives for any program for gifted and talented students. While the knowledge and comprehension levels naturally are necessary for all students, teachers of gifted students, especially, will want students to *apply* rules, principles, or theories; *analyze* components, relationships, hypotheses, patterns, and causes and effects; *synthesize* parts into creative solutions, plans, theories, generalizations, designs, and compositions; and *evaluate* the accuracy, value, efficiency, or utility of alternate ideas or courses of action (see, for example, Royer, 1982).

We have already mentioned that many types of learning experiences, particularly independent projects, foster the development of high-level thinking skills. As a general rule, with any particular project students will

TABLE 8.1 Taxonomy of Educational Objectives: Cognitive Domain

Category	Examples
Knowledge	Defining terminology, symbols Recalling facts, names, examples, rules, categories Recognizing trends, causes, relationships Acquiring principles, procedures, implications, theories
Comprehension	Rephrasing definitions Illustrating meanings Interpreting relationships Drawing conclusions Demonstrating methods Inferring implications Predicting consequences
Application	Applying principles, rules, theories Organizing procedures, conclusions, effects Choosing situations, methods Restructuring processes, generalizations, phenomena
Analysis	Recognizing assumptions, patterns Deducing conclusions, hypotheses, points of view Analyzing relationships, themes, evidence, causes and effects Contrasting ideas, parts, arguments
Synthesis	Producing products, compositions Proposing objectives, means, solutions Designing plans, operations Organizing taxonomies, concepts, schemes, theories Deriving relationships, abstractions, generalizations
Evaluation	Judging accuracy, consistency, reliability Assessing errors, fallacies, predictions, means and ends Considering efficiency, utility, standards Contrasting alternatives, courses of action

From Metfessel, Michael, and Kirsner. Instrumentation of Bloom's and Krathwohl's taxonomies for the writing of educational objectives. *Psychology in the Schools* (1969), *6*, 227–310. Reprinted by permission.

progress from learning activities at the knowledge level to activities at higher levels. For example, virtually any independent or small-group research project, from creating a school newspaper or designing a terrarium to photography or physics research, will require the acquisition and comprehension of necessary information, and then various types of applications, analyses, syntheses, and evaluations. The latter four activities need not occur in a specified order, although a final evaluation tends to be last.

As another general rule, some gifted-oriented educators use the two pyramids in Figure 8.3 to point out the different emphasis which should be placed upon different taxonomic levels for regular students versus gifted and talented students (for example, Murphy, 1980). Thus the objectives and instructional focus for regular students might primarily emphasize

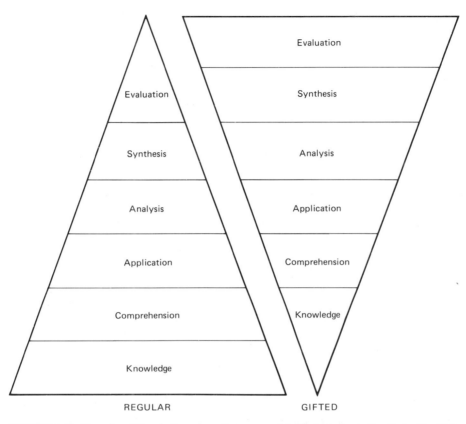

FIGURE 8.3 Based on Bloom's taxonomy, these pyramids illustrate the notion that with gifted students, more time should be invested on higher-level activities and objectives, compared with the reverse for regular students.

knowledge and comprehension, with less attention to higher-level skills. Gifted students, who grasp information and relationships rapidly, should invest more time and effort at the higher levels. The inverted pyramid is misleading in suggesting that evaluation should receive the absolutely largest proportion of emphasis, but you get the idea.

As an important and frequent use of Bloom's taxonomy, it serves as a good guide for questioning techniques (see Inset 8.2).

Finally, many teachers teach the taxonomy itself to students, acquainting them with different levels of learning and skill development. As shown in Inset 8.3, fifth-grader Monica Blanton (1982) understands the taxonomy very well.

INSET 8.2 BLOOM'S TAXONOMY AS A GUIDE TO CLASSROOM QUESTIONING

Sanders' (1966) book, *Classroom Questions: What Kinds,* describes how teachers can use questioning strategies to strengthen learning and skill development at all of Bloom's taxonomic levels: knowledge, comprehension, application, analysis, synthesis, and evaluation.

Knowledge questions require students to recognize or recall facts, definitions, generalizations, main points, points of view, and central issues. Some facts and definitions are ends in themselves, possessed by all literate members of a culture. Others serve as building blocks for further learning and thinking. As for which knowledge to emphasize, Sanders recommends that the teacher ask him- or herself, "What facts deserve emphasis?" and "What facts are necessary for further learning?" Examples of knowledge questions: *What is meant by "satellite"? What is the effect of the Gulf Stream upon winter weather in south Florida?*

Comprehension questions usually require students to translate information into another form (by paraphrasing or writing outlines or summaries, drawing diagrams or pictures, or making models, maps, or charts) or to interpret relationships or compare ideas. Examples: *What is the relationship between a satellite and its planet? Can you draw it? Explain in your own words the effect of the gulf stream upon southeastern coastal areas.*

Application questions require students to use knowledge, principles, generalizations and skills to solve problems. For example: *How would scientists place a satellite in orbit? In view of the effects of the gulf stream on Florida weather, how might you explain the relatively mild winters on the west coast of Oregon and Washington?*

Analysis questions can include examinations of statements and semantic meanings, interrelationships of parts, and so on. For example: *What factors could cause a satellite to crash? If you wished to become a citrus fruit grower, what geographical and weather factors would you have to consider?*

Synthesis questions can elicit creative thinking, the derivation of relationships, the formation of hypotheses, or the planning of a research project. *How would the many moons of Jupiter affect each other? How could we grow oranges in Minnesota?*

Evaluation questions implicitly or explicitly require students to establish standards or values, and then match an object or idea against those standards. Evaluation questions may require students to assess the quality of something, consider controversial or hypothetical issues, or evaluate alternate courses of action. Examples: *Is it a good idea to put so many satellites in orbit? What about the cost? Should the government help pay for orange crops lost from freezing? Why or why not?*

Asking questions is an ancient and honorable form of teaching, reviewing, and ensuring learning. With care and planning, questions can be used to teach both lower- and higher-level learning objectives.

INSET 8.3 BLOOM'S TAXONOMY REVISITED

I like your magazine very much. I read about "Bloom's Taxonomy on Bloom's Taxonomy." I am one of Alice Krueger's fifth grade students at Offerle Middle School.

I'm sending in questions on *Mrs. Frisby and the Rats of NIMH* to put in *G/C/T*. I would appreciate it if you did.

Yours truly,
Monica Blanton

Mrs. Frisby and the Rats of NIMH

Knowledge—Name Mrs. Frisby's four children in order of age.

Comprehension—Restate Mrs. Frisby's first talk with Brutus the time in the rosebush.

Application—Illustrate Mrs. Frisby flying on Jeremy's back going over the river.

Analysis—Break down Mrs. Frisby's big problem and see how many little problems you can find.

Synthesis—Write a new ending to the story pretending Timothy had died.

Evaluation—Pick three animals of those six that were mentioned in the story. Try to find a new name you think would be better than the one in the book. Tell why you think your names would be better.

Source: *G/C/T* (Sept.-Oct. 1982), 22. Reprinted by permission.

Whatever the form of enrichment or acceleration activities, attention to all levels of Bloom's taxonomy (particularly the higher levels of *application, analysis, synthesis,* and *evaluation*) will help ensure that the activities are not just "busy work" or time-fillers.

TREFFINGER'S MODEL FOR INCREASING SELF-DIRECTEDNESS

It would seem self-evident that children, throughout their educational lives, are told what, when, how, and where to learn. Further, their learning almost always is evaluated by others. They cannot be expected to suddenly become efficient, self-initiated, and self-directed learners with little or no experience or training. Even though gifted children typically are more independent and self-directed than others, many still require help in developing the skills and attitudes necessary for independent study or research.

Donald Treffinger (1975, 1978; Treffinger and Barton, 1979; Treffinger and Perez, 1980) developed a seemingly logical four-step plan for teaching increasing degrees of independent, self-initiated learning. (1)

In the initial teacher-directed step (*command style*), the teacher prescribes the activities for the entire class or for individual students. The working time, location, end product, and evaluation criteria also are teacher determined. (2) In the first self-directed step (*task style*), the teacher creates learning activities or project alternatives (for example, learning centers) from which students make a selection. (3) In the second self-directed step (*peer-partner style*), students assume a more active role, participating in decisions about their learning activities, goals, and evaluation. The teacher " . . . involves the pupils in creating choices and options concerning what will be learned" (Treffinger, 1975). For example, the teacher discusses with the class topics or projects for individual or group work. (4) Finally, in the *self-directed style* students are able to create the choices, make the selection, and carry out the activity—in a self-selected location over a self-selected period of time. The student also evaluates his or her own progress. Of course, the teacher is available to assist.

Students naturally differ in their abilities and experience in directing their own work. Therefore, the teacher must determine the level of self-directedness for which a student is ready. Treffinger (1975) provides checklists designed to help identify the level of help a given student requires. For example, a student would be ready for the fourth stage of self-directedness activity if (1) the student can evaluate progress mainly without teacher advice, and (2) the student can identify strengths and weaknesses in his or her own work or products using the same criteria others would use.

As some general recommendations for fostering self-directedness, Treffinger (1978) suggested:

1. Do not smother self-direction by doing things for children that they can do (or can learn to do) for themselves.
2. Develop an attitude of openness and support for self-directed learning.
3. Emphasize the interrelatedness and continuity of knowledge to help students synthesize and relate various topics and problems.
4. Provide training in problem solving and skills of inquiry and independent research; that is, help students learn to diagnose needs, develop a plan, locate resources, carry out appropriate activities, evaluate and present the results.
5. Treat difficult situations at school or home as opportunities for independent problem solving, not as problems requiring the unilateral wisdom of an adult.

THE WILLIAMS MODEL FOR DEVELOPING THINKING AND FEELING PROCESSES

Frank Williams (1970, 1982) developed a curriculum model that originally was intended to help teachers enrich educational programs for all students. While not designed specifically for G/T students, it is widely used in gifted programs for three good reasons. First, its content, methods and goals make good sense. Second, it is a relatively complete system: It includes teaching strategies across important content areas that are designed to produce specific student outcomes that can be evaluated with Williams' assessment instruments. In addition to his book, *Classroom Ideas for Encouraging Thinking and Feeling* (Williams, 1970), Williams also provides a kit that includes booklets, tapes, in-service training materials, and other practical items, such as needs-assessment forms and forms for recording student progress (Williams, 1972). Third, and of no small significance, the Williams model is comparatively easy to implement because of his hundreds of detailed learning activities and projects.

The Williams approach is summarized in a cube (Figure 8.4) reminiscent of the Guilford/Meeker SOI cube. Based on three dimensions, they may be described as *content, process,* and *strategy* (Williams, 1979). Dimension 1 is *Curriculum (Subject Matter Content),* with the six levels of art, music, science, social studies, arithmetic, and language. Dimension 2 is *Teacher Behavior (Strategies or Modes of Teaching)* and includes 18 activities and skills (defined in Table 8.2) that teachers may use to teach skills in any of the 6 content areas.

Dimension 3—containing the "thinking and feeling processes" for which Williams is famous—is called *Pupil Behaviors.* Its eight levels include the four *Cognitive (Intellective)* processes of fluency, flexibility, originality, and elaboration, plus the four *Affective (Feeling)* processes of curiosity (will-

FIGURE 8.4   The Williams Model.

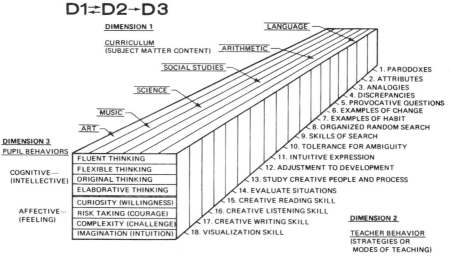

A Model for Implementing Cognitive-Affective
Behaviors in the Classroom

From F. Williams, "Classroom Ideas for Encouraging Thinking and Feeling." (Buffalo, N.Y.: D.O.K. Publishers, Inc.).

TABLE 8.2 Classification of Williams' Strategies Across Renzulli-type Activities

TYPE I ACTIVITIES: EXPLORATION STRATEGIES

Paradoxes	Self-contradictory statements or observations
Attributes	Inherent properties, traits or characteristics
Analogies	Similarities or situations of likeness
Discrepancies	Unknown elements or missing links
Provocative Questions	Inquiries bringing forth exploration or discovery
Examples of Change	Exploring the dynamics of things by alterations, modifications or substitutions
Examples of Habit	Sensing rigidity and habit-bound thinking

TYPE II ACTIVITIES: TRAINING STRATEGIES

Organized Random Search	Organized structure randomly leading to a production
Skills of Search	Skills of historical, descriptive, or experimental search
Study Creative People-Process	Analyze traits and study processes of eminent people
Evaluate Situations	Setting criteria, deciding, critical thinking
Creative Reading Skill	Idea generation through reading
Creative Listening Skill	Idea generation through listening
Creative Writing Skill	Self expression through writing
Visualization Skill	Expressing ideas in visual form

TYPE III ACTIVITIES: PRODUCTION STRATEGIES

Tolerance for Ambiguity	Tolerating open-ended situations without forcing closure
Intuitive Expression	Sensing inward hunches and expressing emotional feelings
Adjustment to Development	Developing from rather than adjusting to experiences or situations
Evaluate Situations	Deciding upon solutions and productions by consequences and implications
Creative Writing Skill	Self-expression through written production
Visualization Skill	Expressing ideas in visual form

Frank Williams, "Williams' Strategies to Orchestrate Renzulli's Triad," *G/C/T* (Sept.-Oct. 1979), 2–6, 10. Reprinted by permission.

ingness), risk taking (courage), complexity (challenge), and imagination (intuition). The "D Formula" in Figure 8.4 indicates that curriculum content (D1) interacts with teaching strategies (D2) to produce the pupil behaviors (D3).

Now with 6 subject matters, 18 teaching activities, and 8 thinking and feeling processes, there are a total of 864 (6 × 18 × 8) combinations of classroom activities. Williams (1970) outlines no less than 387 activities and tasks designed (1) for a specific subject matter, (2) using one of the teaching methods, and (3) intended to strengthen one of the thinking or feeling skills. Some of the learning activities are considered appropriate for several cells in the Figure 8.4 model.

For convenience, two tables in Williams's book list the ideas and activities first by process and then by subject.

The Williams Model and the Enrichment Triad Model

We mentioned earlier that G/T programming methods and strategies may be combined. Williams (1979) himself outlined how the Renzulli Enrichment Triad Model may be combined with his own curriculum model. Indeed, the two seem to complement each other very well. Said Williams, "One is a guide for what should be done, the other a multi-strategy approach for how to get it done. The Renzulli model provides direction, the Williams model yields results." The latter claim may not be an entirely unbiased one.

The reader may recall that the Renzulli Type I (exploratory) and Type II (group training) enrichment activities are considered appropriate for all students. Also the Williams activities originally were designed for all students. With just a little pencil work, Williams's 18 teaching strategies can be rearranged into Renzulli Types I and II activities good for all students, plus some Type III strategies judged by Williams to be appropriate for gifted, talented, and creative students. It's all in Table 8.2. See Williams (1979) for specific examples of Renzulli/Williams Types I, II, and III activities.

THE TAYLOR MULTIPLE-TALENT TOTEM POLE MODEL

In Chapter 1 we reviewed Taylor's (1978) *Multiple Talent Totem Poles* as a definition of giftedness, one that argues that if you look at enough talents, virtually everyone will be at least above average (if not outstanding) in something. His six totem pole talents, *academic ability, creativity, planning, communicating, forecasting,* and *decision making* (see Figure 1.2, Chapter 1), may be used as the basis for curriculum planning. That is, one would design activities and exercises aimed at strengthening each of the six talent areas.

Eberle (1974) designed a "flip book" that explains how the teacher can prepare learning activities and questioning strategies for each of Taylor's talent areas. For example: *Communication* focuses upon teaching the communicator to (1) express him- or herself clearly and effectively in spoken, written, or artistic forms; (2) develop ideas fully and completely; (3) observe clues and analyze feelings; (4) show respect for individuality; (5) avoid being too personal or offensive; and (6) receive and understand information effectively. The teacher can have students "Summarize the story . . . ," "Give an explanation for . . . ," "Describe your feelings about . . . ," "Have your painting express joy . . . ," "Show how . . . ," "Explain why . . . ," and "Draw a map showing . . . ."

Planning (and organizing) strategies aim to teach students to (1) identify desired goals and outcomes; (2) understand the need for a step-by-step procedure; (3) get needed information and materials; (4) generally formulate, design, arrange, and visualize methods or procedures; and (5) schedule time for work and play. The teacher can have students "Develop a plan for . . . ," "Prepare a budget for . . . ," "Develop a timetable for . . . ," and so on.

Forecasting (and predicting) activities try to teach students to (1) clearly perceive cause and effects; (2) view situations objectively, (3) anticipate effects and outcomes; (4) reorganize past knowledge and experience; and (5) be socially aware and sensitive to actions that would affect a situation. The teacher thus can ask students, "Foretell the outcome of a story," "Tell what you think _____ will be like in 20 years," and "Tell what would happen if . . . ."

The teaching of *decision making* (and evaluation) revolved around teaching students to (1) weigh consequences; (2) remain emotionally neutral; (3) withhold early judgment; (4) consider more than one course of action; (5) apply evaluative criteria; (6) make a decision, defend it, and act accordingly; and others. Some exercises would include asking students to "Examine all possibilities . . . ," "Appraise the situation . . . ," "Make a choice and justify your selection," "Support your decision . . . ," "Select the best . . . ," and "You be the judge, rule on the situation, and explain why."

THE U.S.O.E. DEFINITION AS A CURRICULUM GUIDE

Normally, the six-part U.S. Office of Education statement is used to define "gifted and talented" and to guide identification procedures. However, some have used the six categories as a type of curriculum guide. This somewhat general approach leaves the reader with the task of figuring out how to implement it; some categories will be easier than others. As you might guess, learning activities are planned in each of the general areas of (1) general intellectual ability, (2) specific academic talent, (3) creative thinking, (4) leadership, (5) visual and performing arts, and perhaps (6) psychomotor ability. We wish you the best of luck.

Final Comment

There is no single "best" program. The thoughtful program planner should consider all of the models in this chapter—along with acceleration, enrichment, grouping, counseling, career education, creativity training, critical thinking, affective development, and other possibilities. Select what seems to best meet the needs of the students in your particular district or school. There are many alternatives; aim for the best combination for the particular situation.

SUMMARY

Curriculum models clarify, explain, supply a theoretical point of view, and make specific recommendations regarding programming and other gifted-education components. Some of the nine models in the chapter make specific procedural recommendations; others make general suggestions.

The Renzulli Enrichment Triad Model includes enrichment Types I, II, and III. Type I enrichment—general exploratory activities—is intended to expose students to a variety of topics. Type II enrichment—group-training activities—tries to teach creative, critical, analytic, and evaluative thinking; good self-concepts, values and motivation; and library and research skills. Type III enrichment consists of individual and small-group investigations of real problems. Types I and II are recommended for all students, but Type III is primarily appropriate for G/T students only.

The Revolving Door Identification Model is a complete programming guide. A talent pool consists of about 25 percent of the school population. All talent pool students receive Types I and II enrichment. Motivated talent-pool students (and sometimes others) revolve into a resource room to work on projects.

Feldhusen's three-stage enrichment model focuses mainly on fostering creative thinking, but also on research and independent-learning skills and positive self-concepts. Stage 1 involves short-term teacher-led exercises in creative critical and logical thinking. Stage 2 requires more complex thinking, such as learning creative thinking techniques. Stage 3 activities focus on independent learning by challenging students to define a problem, gather data (from books or other resources), interpret, and creatively report the findings.

The Renzulli and Feldhusen approaches share some useful similarities. For example, Renzulli Type II enrichment resembles Feldhusen's Stage 1 exercises. Renzulli's Type III enrichment, however, involves "dramatically" higher-level thinking and activities than Feldhusen's Stage 3 activities.

The Guilford Structure of Intellect Model is a theory of intelligence based upon 120 combinations of 5 operations, 6 products, and 4 contents. Meeker uses 24 abilities from the Guilford SOI model to guide the diagnosis and remediation of specific learning abilities, particularly those related to reading, mathematics, writing, and creativity. The abilities are measured by the SOI-Learning Abilities test or by scores derived from the Binet, WISC-R, or other individual intelligence test. The SOI approach also may be used for guiding the creation of Individualized Education Programs, for identifying gifted minority and disadvantaged students, as subject matter for a secondary school unit on intelligence, or as the basis of career exploration.

Bloom's taxonomy of cognitive objectives draws attention to higher-level types of learning and thus guides the selection of learning activities and classroom questioning techniques. The taxonomy includes knowledge, comprehension, application, analysis, synthesis, and evaluation. Gifted students are assumed to need progressively more higher-level learning; regular students are assumed to require more lower-level learning.

Treffinger outlined four steps in increasing self-directedness. (1) The "command style" is totally teacher directed; (2) in the "task style" students select from among teacher-prepared activities; (3) the "peer-partner" style includes more student decisions about learning goals, activities, and evaluation; (4) in the "self-directed style" students create the choices, make the selections, and choose the location and the amount of working time. Some general recommendations for fostering self-directedness included encouraging self-directedness, providing training in problem solving and inquiry, and using home problems as an opportunity for independent problem solving.

The Williams model includes 864 classroom activities suggested by all combinations of subject-matter content (6 types), teaching strategies (18 types), and the 8 thinking and feeling processes themselves. Williams explains how his 18 teaching strategies may be classified according to the 3 categories of the Enrichment Triad Model.

The Taylor Multiple-Talent Totem Pole Model suggests that learning activities focus upon developing academic ability, creativity, planning/organizing, communicating, forcasting/predicting, and decision making/evaluating.

Similarly, the U.S.O.E. definition of gifts and talents suggests the general G/T curriculum categories of general intellectual ability, specific academic talent, creative thinking, leadership, visual and performing arts, and perhaps psychomotor ability.

There is no "best" G/T program. Each must be designed to meet the needs of particular gifted students.

APPENDIX 8.1 POSSIBLE TOPICS FOR ENRICHMENT ACTIVITIES

VISUAL ARTS, PERFORMING ARTS

Drawing
Sculpture (clay, metal, other)
Designing (virtually anything; toys, vehicles, machines, etc.)
Art in various cultures
Rug hooking
Jewelry making
Macrame
Calligraphy
Filmmaking (animation, drama)
Cartooning
Architecture
Pottery
Candle making
Music history
Folk music
Folk stories, legends
Acting techniques
Costume design
Improvisational theatre
Voice and diction
TV production
Dance (many varieties)
Dance notation
Dance history
Painting

Puppet making
Soft sculpture
Printmaking
Weaving
Art history
Art appreciation
Silk screening
Batik
Leather craft
Photography, cameras
Slide-show making
Political satire
Clothes design
Ceramics
Music lessons
Music composition
Harmony
Dramatic literature
History of theatre
Mime
Shakespeare
Dramatic production
Musical theatre
Creative dramatics
Set design, lighting

MATH, SCIENCE, COMPUTERS

Math
Astronomy
Space travel
Marine biology

Microbiology
Electricity, electronics
Physiology
Horticulture

Archaeology
Aquarium planning
Prehistoric animals
Energy (solar, geothermal, tidal, wind, etc.)
Physics
Animal behavior
Optometry
Aeronautics
Rocketry
Computer programming
Computer repair
Cartography
Ichthyology

Genetics
Botany
Holography
Agriculture
Meteorology
Ornithology
Geology
Mineralogy
Nuclear energy
Engineering
Ecology
Medicine
Brain science

LITERATURE, WRITING, COMMUNICATION

Short story writing
Poetry writing
Playwriting
Linguistics
Mysteries
Journalism
Sportswriting
Poetry appreciation
Literature appreciation (e.g., Junior Great Books)

Mythology
Public speaking
Speed reading
Broadcasting
Advertising
Word processing
Typing

SOCIAL SCIENCES, CULTURE, LANGUAGE

Psychology
Anthropology
Political science
Crime, criminology
Ancient Egypt
Ancient Greece
Aztecs, Mayas, Incas
Ancient China
Ancient Rome
Prehistory cultures
Contemporary cultures
Genealogy
Contemporary languages

Linguistics
Philosophy
Folklore
Sociology
Government
Overpopulation
Drug abuse
Career education
Future thinking
Parapsychology
Occult
History (U.S., Russian, etc.)
Problems of the elderly

BUSINESS, ECONOMICS

Accounting	Stock market
Operating a small business	Finance
Economics (models, theories)	Transportation, trucking

MISCELLANEOUS

Magic	Chess
Bridge	Karate
History of football	And so on

9

AFFECTIVE LEARNING, CRITICAL THINKING, AND LEADERSHIP

Overview

This chapter focuses on three important goals of programs for G/T students: affective learning, critical thinking, and leadership. All considered process goals, they would fall into Renzulli's Type II enrichment category, the development of thinking and feeling capabilities. *Affective learning* is a broad category that includes students' self-concepts, self-esteem, moral thinking, attitudes, values, personal adjustment, social adjustment, self-motivated learning, and such interrelated humanistic matters as self-actualization and a democratic concern for the welfare of others. That is, "... those talents anciently thought virtuous" (Getzels and Dillon, 1973). This chapter will examine the nature of affective learning, especially the self-concept, and review how positive values and good self-concepts may be taught.

Critical thinking is closely tied to the evaluation level of Bloom's taxonomy in the obvious sense that both require the weighing of evidence, but it implies an even stronger scrutiny of, for example, the qualifications and biases of a speaker (for example, a salesperson or politician) on an issue. Critical thinking is related to affective learning in that both are rooted in values, emotions, feelings, and beliefs (Budmen, 1967). Although training materials and clear strategies for teaching critical thinking are scarce, this chapter will review some possibilities.

With *leadership*, as well, few clear definitions and concrete training strategies exist. Leadership relates to affective learning in that leadership, in part, involves a sensitivity to the feelings and attitudes of others. Indeed, as noted by Fantini (1981), the promotion of humane, caring values is of particular importance in gifted education because G/T students are such likely candidates for future leadership roles. This chapter will attempt to define leaders and leadership and recommend some relevant teaching methods.

AFFECTIVE LEARNING

In our early discussion of characteristics of gifted and talented children we noted that, compared with the average, G/T students are better able to understand moral issues and more likely to comprehend other people's problems and viewpoints. They are also more likely to be honest, truthful, and ethical. If they are moderate-to-high achievers, they are also likely to have good self-concepts, high self-esteem, and reasonably high levels of achievement needs. Nonetheless, just as we try to strengthen the cognitive skills of students who already are cognitively superior, we also can help affectively superior students to better understand themselves and their values, to be more empathic towards others, and to generally acquire high-level values, ethics, achievement needs, and humanistic attitudes. Also, some gifted students do go astray morally and legally, and many drop out of high school and college. They forfeit both their full development and self-actualization and their potential contributions to society.

Affective education is an important matter. As Fantini (1981) noted,

" . . . the creation of a humane, caring society is, in fact, the most fundamental of all the basics—the bedrock if you will . . . [and there should be] . . . an integration of the cognitive with the affective—a combination of intellectualizing about caring values and genuinely feeling them through performance in action settings."

Ashley Montagu (1980) expressed the opinion that the single most important goal of schools is to help children develop into warm and loving human beings. Tan-Willman and Gutteridge (1981), in studying the relationship between creativity and moral thinking in gifted adolescents, emphasized that we should " . . . ensure that this particular giftedness will be applied not only effectively but also constructively and humanely. . . ." Humanist Arthur Combs (1975) said it all: "We can live with a bad reader; a bigot is a danger to everyone."

The following five subsections will examine, first, the nature of the self-concept—how it is formed and how its protection can lead to subtle defensive behaviors. The next will look briefly at how the classic Kohlberg (1974) stages in moral development can serve as guide for teaching moral and ethical thinking. The remaining sections review curriculum content and strategies for imparting constructive attitudes, awarenesses, values, and humanistic thinking; qualities of a humanistic teacher; and the teaching of achievement motivation.

The Self-Concept

Feelings of personal competence and self-esteem are closely tied to experiences of success. For adults, there are many types of success experience that can strengthen feelings of adequacy and self-esteem—for example, job or career success, or success as a parent or church member, as a home decorator or union member, and so on. For children, however, the school setting looms very large: Feedback from schoolwork and the teacher is extremely important in telling each child whether he or she is a capable, competent, and worthwhile little person. The following are some dynamics of self-concept development:

1. Developing a healthy self-concept in school is a goal in itself. Moreover, because a student who feels capable and confident will be more motivated and will have higher academic and career aspirations, promoting good self-concepts also is a means of stimulating higher school achievement (Bloom, 1977; Davis, 1983b).

2. There are many facets of the self. A person may perceive an academic self, a social self, an emotional self, and a physical self (Jordon, 1981). Gifted students sometimes have better academic selves than social selves (Ross and Parker, 1980).

3. The self-concept is organized, relatively stable, and evaluative. The evaluative component (self-esteem) relates to mental health; a person may or may not like his or her self-concept. According to Carl Rogers (1949), mentally healthy people see their actual selves as similar to their ideal selves.

Regarding self-esteem of gifted students, research results are mixed. Milgram and Milgram (1976b) found that gifted students did indeed have better self-concepts than regular students. However, other researchers have found that compared with nongifted students, a large proportion of gifted students are low in self-esteem. Kanoy, Johnson, and Kanoy (1980), Whitmore (1980), and Terman and Oden (1951) confirmed that underachieving gifted students and adults have predictably worse self-concepts and lower self-esteem than high achieving gifted persons.

4. The *mirror theory* of self-concept development assumes that the self-concept is created via assessments ("reflections") from others.

5. The *self-accepting* student understands him- or herself and therefore is aware of strengths and weaknesses. This student values himself despite the weaknesses. The *self-rejecting* student considers him- or herself of little worth, and may have other symptoms of maladjustment (Shepard, 1979).

6. Academic failure implies low worth as a person and prevents students from maintaining feelings of competence. Failure after great effort is especially devastating to feelings of competence (Covington and Omelich, 1981).

7. Excuses and rationalizations, constructed to explain why the effort did not produce success, will protect the self-concept.

8. Self-esteem and pride are greatest when the student succeeds at a difficult task; the success is attributed to both high ability and high effort (Covington and Omelich, 1981).

9. Most critically, feelings of self-esteem and self-worth are a highly treasured commodity. All students are strongly motivated to protect their feelings of self-esteem.

Most often, the gifted student succeeds. The person's history of success inspires confidence in his or her abilities, a sense of responsibility for his or her actions, and feelings of control over his or her environment. When failure occurs, it typically is attributed to lack of effort, not lack of ability. Failures therefore may be used constructively to evaluate shortcomings and prepare for next time. "The person has temporarily fallen short of a goal, and has not fallen short as a person" (Covington and Beery, 1976).

Many students, however, are motivated not by strong needs to succeed, but by strong needs to avoid failure. And when failure threatens, any of several defense mechanisms may be used to ward off threats to the self-esteem.

One is *deliberate underachieving*: There will be no humiliation or destroyed self-esteem due to poor performance if the student does not really try. Teachers or parents may think the child is unmotivated. Actually, the person is highly motivated—to protect his or her self-esteem. If the fear-of-failure student *accidentally* scores high on a test or paper there is a bonus. Doing well without trying is clear evidence of extra-high ability, thus reinforcing the underachievement pattern. In college, defensive underachieving produces the "gentleman's *C*" syndrome. An effortless *C* maintains the illusion of intellectual superiority without testing the scholar's actual abilities.

Defensive goal-setting can take several forms. A student may set a goal too high—for example, at the *A* + level—because it is no disgrace to fall short of such an impossibly high goal. Vice versa, the goal may be set too low. A low goal guarantees success, but it is a trivial and meaningless one. A student also can set goals with a wide distance between the highest expected success and the lowest acceptable achievement level—for example, "I'll get something between a *D+* and an *A*." Such a wide "confirming interval" makes success an absolute cinch (Birney, Burdick, and Teevan, 1969).

We already noted that excuses can protect the delicate ego of a failure-oriented student. Failures are attributed to external causes, not internal ones. Such students may blame anything and everything; for example, "The test was unfair," "My cat chewed up my assignment," or "I wasn't feeling well this morning." Ironically, these students may not accept credit for successes either, since success implies the ability and obligation for continued quality work.

The case history of Dan, a real-life underachiever unable to take credit for success, is instructive. Dan had been a consistent *C* student when he came to the author, Rimm, for underachievement counseling. After one quarter, his achievement had improved sufficiently to earn him a place on the honor roll. When the counselor asked Dan how he felt about his achievement, he replied, "I like it, but I guess I was just lucky." He had even thanked his English teacher for "giving" him an *A*. The counselor pointed out to Dan that he had both improved his study habits and increased the time he spent learning. He finally acknowledged, hesitantly, that there probably was some relationship between his new efforts and the improved grades.

One recommended solution to these self-defeating, self-perpetuating defense mechanisms is individualized instruction (Covington and Beery, 1976). By engaging fear-of-failure students in independent-learning assignments and projects, success is redefined in terms of meeting and exceeding one's own standards, not publicly competing with others for scarce classroom rewards and recognition. According to Covington and Beery, when students are not forced to compete they will set reachable, realistic goals, and these provide both the best challenge and the best conditions for a satisfying success.

Alschuler (1973) described a competitive—and boring—fifth-grade math class. Each day, yesterday's homework was reviewed, new material explained, and more homework assigned. The result was success for some, but defensive failure avoidance for others. Alschuler's successful solution, based on individualized learning, rewarded both academic performance and realistic goal setting:

1. Students worked at their own pace, chapter-by-chapter. When ready, they took a mastery test after each chapter.
2. They were rewarded with play money (!) according to the number of problems completed correctly.
3. Importantly, they were required to estimate the percentage of problems they expected to get correct, with "dollars" subtracted for setting goals too low or too high.

Note the important elements:

Goals were realistic and challenging.
Objectives and the route to the objectives were clear.
Success depended on effort.
The "work" included an element of play, which is a very nice intrinsic motivation.

With any type of individualized study, for gifted or regular students, some training in self-initiated, self-directed learning may be necessary. The Treffinger model in Chapter 8 outlined a four-stage model of self-directed learning plus some good general guidelines.

Moral Development: The Kohlberg Model

Based upon research with the same group of 75 boys over a period of twelve years, Lawrence Kohlberg (1974, 1976) developed a model of moral thinking that has proven very valuable for (1) understanding sequential stages in moral development and (2) suggesting how to teach for moral thinking. The model was briefly summarized in Chapter 2, in conjunction with characteristics of gifted and talented students. The following is a slightly more detailed explication.

Kohlberg's six stages of moral development are divided into three main levels, each containing two stages. According to Kohlberg, they are true invariant stages: (1) They occur one at a time; (2) every person proceeds through the stages in the same order; (3) movement is always forward, never backward; and (4) stages are never skipped. While some academics have debated the possibility of backward movement, the stages nonetheless are enlightening.

In both stages of the *Preconventional* level (ages 0–9) the orientation is toward the physical consequences of an action, regardless of any higher level notions of "right" or "wrong." Thus in Stage 1 obedience and good behavior are valued because they avoid punishments. This "might makes right" stage is characteristic of preschool children. In Stage 2 "right" action is that which produces rewards and satisfies one's needs or the needs of others—who will reciprocate ("You scratch my back, I'll scratch yours").

In the *Conventional* level (ages 9–15), behavior is heavily influenced by conformity pressures, strict stereotypes, social conventions and expectations, and rules and laws. Thus in Kohlberg's Stage 3 "good behavior" is that which pleases others or avoids disapproval, producing the "good boy–good girl" orientation. There is much conformity here. In Stage 4 right action is based upon rules and authority, "doing one's duty," and respecting the system. Laws are to be obeyed, not revised. This leads to the "law and order" syndrome. Many adults, including teachers, do not rise above Conventional moral thinking.

The highly desirable *Postconventional* level includes the acceptance of universal and personal moral principles (for example, "Do unto others . . .") that are valid apart from authority. In Stage 5 right action is defined by general rights and standards which have been examined and agreed upon. Personal values and opinions present the possibility of rationally changing these rights and standards. For the chosen few, Stage 6 includes self-chosen principles and ethics based upon such universal principles and rights as justice, equality, and respect for individual differences.

Kohlberg (1974) found that children and adolescents comprehend all stages up to their own, and understand only one additional stage. Importantly, they *preferred* this next stage. A child often moves to the next stage when he or she is confronted with the appealing views of peers who are in this next stage.

In one study of 233 gifted students ages 9 to 15, using Rest's (1972) *Defining Issues Test* (DIT) as a measure of moral thinking, Karnes and Brown (1981) found that the tendency to make Postconventional responses was positively correlated with age, as it should be, and also with verbal intelligence test scores. The higher the verbal comprehension, the higher the level of moral thinking. There were no sex differences, although males scored slightly higher (14.4 versus 13.3) than females. Karnes and Brown noted that "The progression . . . across ages in this group suggests that gifted students may reach Level III (Postconventional) moral reasoning during their secondary education years. Most people never reach this level of moral reasoning; the estimated 10–15 percent who reach this level typically do so in adulthood."

To keep matters interesting, Tan-Willman and Gutteridge (1981) administered the DIT to gifted and regular adolescents, ages 16 and 17, and found different results. Gifted girls scored significantly higher than gifted boys. Also, they reviewed literature arguing that moral development should be tied to intellectual development, leading to the expectation that their gifted kids should have scored substantially higher than the average students. However, although their G/T students' DIT scores were *slightly* higher than those of nongifted, "they are functioning predominantly on the Conventional level of moral judgment just like their age group in the general population. . . ." Importantly, Tan-Willman and Gutteridge concluded that " . . . the subjects' ability to reason morally is an area that needs serious and immediate attention. . . ."

As for teaching for moral development, Kohlberg suggests that a teacher might expose children to concepts just *one step higher* than their current stage, and encourage them to think at this more mature stage. Children also may be given opportunities to think about moral matters by role-playing someone who has been treated rudely, cheated, or, for example, who must put their suffering pet to sleep. A related strategy is to let children practice making moral decisions that require high-level moral thinking. Kohlberg has prepared filmstrips portraying moral dilemmas that children discuss and try to resolve.

High school English teacher Joan Weber (1981) used moral dilemmas from literature to encourage higher-level moral thinking. For example, *Old Man Warner* by Dorothy Canfield describes a 93-year-old obstinate man who, despite family pressure, refuses to move in with relatives or even move closer to town. Weber asks her class, "What should the man do? Why? Would it make a difference if he lived in a big city? If he were physically ill? If he were a woman and not a man?" Literature is a rich source of personal problems and conflicts centering on moral issues and values. And don't forget young children: Was Goldilocks guilty of burglary and vandalism? Was Jack irresponsible in trading a cow for three magic beans? What about stealing the hen that laid golden eggs and then killing the giant by cutting down the beanstalk?

Especially for gifted students, Kohlberg's six stages themselves might be good curriculum content for helping students understand moral thinking (Davis, 1983b).

An Affective, Humanistic Curriculum: Fantini

Fantini (1981) itemized a number of suggestions for creating an affective, humanistic curriculum for children. For example:

1. Emphasize the desirability of "caring" values and behaviors as they relate to the self, to others, and to nature and the environment. Specifics might relate to clarifying values and ethics and understanding ecology, principles of health and hygiene, and related topics.
2. Students can read about and discuss difficulties of the handicapped and the elderly.
3. Students can learn about people, both common and famous, whose behavior demonstrates humanistic, caring values.
4. High school students can become involved in community service programs, working in day-care centers, hospitals, or nursing homes or other centers for the elderly. These assignments may be voluntary or mandated as a graduation requirement. They may receive course credit or recognition on their school records.
    Young children can make gifts for the elderly or the hospitalized, or perform plays or skits for the sick, elderly or handicapped.
5. There are many walk-a-thons, swim-a-thons, and so forth, aimed at raising research funds for cancer, multiple sclerosis, heart disease, and other charitable causes. Students can participate in these.
6. Students can review social issues, for example, relating to refugees seeking asylum in America, political prisoners, military actions, migrant workers, and so on, from the perspective of humaneness.
7. To increase awareness of the environment, ecology and conservation students can participate in recycling drives and similar activities.

8. Importantly, while the above are "good for all children," Fantini recommended that gifted children can initiate, plan, implement, and evaluate such social action projects, perhaps as Renzulli Type III enrichment.

Materials and Strategies for Encouraging Affective Growth

Values clarification strategies are effective in helping gifted students explore their beliefs and feelings. As put by noted psychoanalyst Lawrence Kubie, "The child's fifth freedom is the right to know what he feels . . . and [to] put into words all the hidden things that go on inside . . . [and to end] . . . the conspiracy of silence" (Newburg, 1977). Affective education leaders Simon, Howe, and Kirschenbaum (1972) present no less than 79 values clarification strategies. One of the authors' favorites, which can be modified and revised for any student population, includes a list of attitudes and behaviors (see Table 9.1). The question is asked, "Are you someone who . . . ?" and the student checks yes (A), maybe (B), or no (C)—requiring

TABLE 9.1 Are You Someone Who . . . ?

(A=yes, B=maybe, C=no)

A	B	C	Are you someone who:
			1. Likes to break the curve on an exam?
			2. Likes to stay up all night when friends visit?
			3. Will stop the car to look at a sunset?
			4. Puts things off?
			5. Will publicly show affection for another person?
			6. Will do it yourself when you feel something needs doing?
			7. Will order a new dish in a restaurant?
			8. Could accept your own sexual impotence?
			9. Could be satisfied without a college degree?
			10. Could be part of a mercy killing?
			11. Is afraid alone in the dark in a strange place?
			12. Is willing to participate in a T-group?
			13. Eats when you are worried?
			14. Can receive a gift easily?
			15. Would steal apples from an orchard?
			16. Is apt to judge someone by his or her appearance?
			17. Would let your child drink or smoke pot?
			18. Watches television soap operas?
			19. Could kill in self-defense?
			20. Needs to be alone?

From Sidney Simon* and Sara Massey, "Values clarification," *Educational Leadership*, May, 1973. Reprinted with permission of the Association for Supervision and Curriculum Development. Copyright © 1973 by the Association for Supervision and Curriculum Development. All rights reserved.

*For information about current Values Realization materials and a schedule of nation-wide training workshops, contact Sidney Simon, Old Mountain Rd., Hadley, MA 01035.

the student to decide on the spot what he or she *strongly favors,* is *neutral toward,* or is *opposed to.* Discussion follows, of course.

The traits in Table 9.1 list only a few of the hundreds of possibilities. Simon and Massey (1973) suggested that students will have a rousing time brainstorming other lists of behaviors, which could include such items as "Blushes at a compliment," "Talks loudly when nervous," "Cheats on unfair tests," "Gambles on parking tickets," and so on. Adolescents will be intrigued by listing personal traits, and then responding "yes," "maybe," or "no" to the question, "I am looking for someone who is . . . ." Other values clarification strategies include writing letters to newspapers expressing views on issues, or classifying yourself as a "Cadillac" person or a "Ford Pinto" person and then discussing reasons why.

The *Magic Circle* technique helps children learn " . . . why people are sometimes happy or unhappy, how to feel good about themselves, and how to get along with others" (Lefkowitz, 1975). Seven to twelve children in a circle—few enough to maintain everyone's attention—voluntarily respond to "Today's Topic," such as "I felt good when . . . ," "I felt bad when . . . ," "I made someone else feel good when . . . ," or "Something I can do (or wish I could do) is . . . ." The teacher encourages learning and understanding with follow-up questions such as "Who can tell me why Dizzy Jones felt good on the roller coaster?" or "Why was he proud of himself?" See Lefkowitz (1975) for additional information.

In his *Good Person Book* (Davis, 1984; see also Davis, 1983b), Davis summarizes eight general teaching strategies designed to (1) stimulate creative thinking while (2) increasing understanding and awareness of specific issues and values. For example, with the *brainstorming* approach students are asked to "Think of all the ways you can to show friendliness in the classroom," "List all of the rights of teachers (students, family, store owners) that you can," "List all the ways you can think of to help your neighbors." Or with reverse brainstorming, "Think of all the ways you can to hurt other people's feelings," "Think of all the ways you can to show disrespect to your teachers (fellow students, family, school custodians, the elderly, and so forth)."

The *empathy* strategy requires students to imagine themselves in another role, for example: "What would it be like to be a very old person? You live in a small apartment, and you have no family and very little money. How do you feel? You want to go to the store, but you are very weak and slow, and you would have to walk through a bunch of rowdy teenagers on the sidewalk. You have heard them call you names; one lady had her purse snatched. How do you feel? What can you do? One month your social security check is missing from the mailbox and you cannot pay the rent or buy groceries. How do you feel? What can you do?"

With the *metaphorical thinking* approach students make imaginative comparisons. For example, "How is a cheating student like a broken-down automobile?" "How is a messy person like an out-of-tune piano?" "How is a good person like a good pizza?" "How is conserving school supplies like a squirrel burying acorns?"

With the *mental visualization* method the class relaxes and shuts their eyes while the teacher leads them through an episode eliciting feelings, attitudes, values, empathy, and so on. For example: "Imagine you are 25 years old. (pause) You worked for three years to pay for a shiny new red Corvette. (pause) One morning you find the battery and tires have been stolen. (pause) A dent is kicked in the door. (pause) The outside mirrors and window wipers are bent up. (pause) The window is broken and paint poured on the seat. (pause) Do you think this is funny? (pause) You wonder why someone, probably teenagers, did this to you. (pause) You cannot afford to have it fixed; it will have to stay this way for a few months. (pause) How do you feel. (and so on)." Discussion follows.

The *What would happen if . . . ?* strategy is very flexible. For example: What would happen if everybody always cheated everybody else? If everyone were a shoplifter? If your school building were vandalized once a week? If everyone always told lies? If nobody kept their promises? If nobody ever returned things they borrowed? If everyone chucked their MacDonalds wrappers and cups out the car window?

The *questioning* strategy is basically a class discussion approach to teaching value concepts: What is rudeness? What is responsibility? Why is it good to be a responsible person? Why is it good to wear clean clothes and take a bath regularly? What happens if we don't? Why should we care about other people? What is a "needy" person? Why should we try to help such people? What is a good person?

The *problem solving* method involves identifying a problem (such as wasting classroom materials), and having students consider each step:

> What is the problem and why is it a problem?
> What are some solutions?
> What are the consequences of each solution?
> Which idea(s) would work best?

Finally, with *role playing* the teacher sets simple scenes and asks students to play roles that involve empathy, expression of feelings, and an understanding of values. For example, one person can be a student caught writing on a freshly painted wall, one can be the custodian who painted the wall, one can be the principal, and one a parent. Students can trade roles and work in small or large groups. Follow-up discussions will help ensure that participants understand the issues, other people's feelings, and proper values and behavior.

The Humanistic Teacher

A teacher who has internalized humanistic values will be better able to communicate these values to students, both in direct teaching and by serving as a good role model. Pine and Boy (1977) listed characteristics of such a humanistic teacher. While the teacher who fully meets all of these criteria may not exist, we all might view these traits as ideals toward which we should work. The self-actualized, humanistic teacher:

1. Thinks well of him- or herself; he or she has a good self-concept.
2. Is honest and genuine; there is no conflict between the real inner person and the role-playing outer person.
3. Likes and accepts others.
4. Is a forward-growing person, continually in the process of "becoming" by learning, exploring, and changing.
5. Lives by humanistic values; is honestly concerned with the welfare of fellow humans and the improvement of human society.
6. Is sensitive and responsive to the needs and feelings of others.
7. Is creative, adventurous, risk-taking, willing to try something new, and secure enough to learn from the inevitable mistakes.
8. Has confidence in his or her feelings, intuition, decisions, and reaction.
9. Is open to the viewpoints of others, to new information and experiences, and to his or her own inner feelings.
10. Exercises control over his or her life and environment; initiates needed changes.
11. Is responsive, vibrant, and spontaneous, and tries to live optimistically and energetically.

Achievement Motivation: McClelland

David McClelland (1965, 1976) itemized several principles aimed at reducing students' *fear of failure* orientation and strengthening their *need to achieve*:

1. Instruction should explain the concept of achievement motivation and its importance for success in school and in one's eventual career.
2. The instruction must realistically convince the learner that, given his or her adequate abilities and talents and the values and realities of society, he or she can and should acquire success-oriented attitudes.
3. The instruction must elicit commitment to specific realistic and worthwhile goals.
4. The instructional atmosphere must support the confidence and individuality of the person.

In essence, these points encourage students to think as achievement-oriented individuals do, to accept moderate risks, to set realistic and achievable goals, and to feel confident that he or she can achieve these goals. An achievement orientation is not inconsistent with humanistic attitudes; we want gifted and talented students—indeed, all students—to acquire both.

CRITICAL THINKING

The improvement of critical thinking skills has been a classic educational objective, particularly with teachers of speech, English, and social studies—and currently in gifted education. However, critical thinking has been somewhat a "weather concept": Everyone talks about it, but few are sure what to do about it. For example, over twenty years ago Willis and his colleagues in the Educational Policies Commission of the National Education Association argued that critical thinking is " . . . the purpose which runs through and strengthens all other educational purposes . . . " and that the critical understanding of basic values and environmental forces that shape our lives is central to persons in a free society. However, they did not know how to train critical thinking with guaranteed success. The situation has not changed much. In 1981 Weinstein and Laufman observed, "Little has been done to design programs of study that would develop, with reasonable assurance, the ability of students to make valid inferences leading to logical conclusions [and that] even gifted students . . . are seldom taught skills essential for critical reasoning."

One problem is with defining critical thinking, which is a logical first step to teaching it. Critical thinking has been taken to mean carping criticism ("Whatta' piece a' garbage that is!"), wholesale skepticism, thoughtful contemplation, analytic thinking (including the analysis of propaganda), problem solving, Bloom's evaluation level of thinking, "careful thinking," "clear thinking," logical thinking (especially!), independent thinking, and the abilities to recognize assumptions, implications and inconsistencies. While it is an intrinsically complex topic, this section will try to clarify critical thinking and offer suggestions for its teaching. The discussion is based on two main definitions: critical thinking as *evaluating* and as *problem solving*.

Critical Thinking as Evaluating

Ronald R. Allen and his colleagues (Allen, Kauffeld, and O'Brien, 1968; Allen and Rott, 1969) reviewed definitions of critical thinking (see previous paragraph), itemized precise critical-thinking objectives, and created four programmed workbooks for training critical thinking. With a view toward itemizing concepts and skills that may be taught to students, Allen et al. defined critical thinking as " . . . an act of evaluation based upon previously accepted standards." The definition emphasizes a logical examination of information and the avoidance of judgments based only on emotion (Ennis, 1962; Hyrum, 1957; Russel, 1960). Such a definition seems to accommodate critical thinking in virtually any area, including—of critical importance to teachers—everyday thought and ordinary discourse. Indeed, Allen's goal was to prepare materials that help teachers encourage critical thinking in relation to ideas and implicit assumptions in such everyday media as comic strips (for example, the "far right" *Orphan Annie* and the continually sexist *Beetle Bailey*), movies, advertising and sales pitches, political messages, and television shows.

Some of Allen's specific critical abilities to be taught were:

1. The ability to appraise a speaker's testimony ("a statement issued by a source") in terms of the source's ability to observe. Specifically, was the source physically present? Or did he or she have access to valid information?

2. The ability to appraise testimony in terms of the source's competence to observe. Is he or she capable of making the particular observation or judgments? ("That car was going 62.5 miles per hour!") Was the source under stress at the time of the observation? Does the source have weak eyes or poor hearing?

3. The ability to evaluate the particular biases of a source. That is, does the source have something to gain by making the statement (for example, salespersons, politicians, athletes selling *Crunchie Wunchies*)?

4. The ability to appraise the source's qualifications—training or experience—necessary to make an informed statement. Does the source have the necessary medical, legal, educational, psychological, etc., training or experience?

5. The ability to appraise whether the source is consistent with him- or herself. Do present statements agree with previous statements? If not, should we question the credibility of the source?

6. The ability to appraise whether the source is consistent with other sources. If not, the source's statements should be questioned.

7. The ability to appraise whether the source's information is the most recent available. Will a 1935 map of Europe be accurate? Will a 1950 encyclopedia—prior to moon landings—be a good source for information about the moon?

8. The ability to differentiate between primary—firsthand—and secondary sources. Is the source merely reporting something someone else told him or her? If so, it is less credible.

9. The ability to identify a statement that functions as a claim. For example, "Our basketball team is going to win!"

10. The ability to identify statements used to justify claims, for example, "Our team is going to win because the other players are only four feet tall!"

11. The ability to identify arguments based on testimony, for example, "Mr. Jones is a lawyer; my dad told me so."

12. The ability to identify arguments based on reasoning, for example, "Mr. Jones is a lawyer; he spends a lot of time defending clients at the court house."

Other principles emphasizing critical thinking and reasoning involve:

Evaluating inferences
Evaluating reasons given for a claim
Checking the reliability and adequacy of information
Identifying unstated assumptions
Following logically valid lines of reasoning
Detecting missing parts of an argument
Discerning the relevance of objections
Recognizing appropriate conclusions

In his *Cornell Project on Critical Thinking,* Ennis (1962, 1964) developed an extended definition that included a number of *aspects* of critical thinking which, like the Allen approach, also seem to stress evaluation based upon previously accepted standards. As with Allen's abilities, we might easily view Ennis's aspects as critical thinking skills to be strengthened:

1. Judging whether there is ambiguity in a line of reasoning
2. Judging whether certain statements contradict each other
3. Judging whether a conclusion necessarily follows
4. Judging whether a statement is specific enough
5. Judging whether a statement is actually the application of a certain principle
6. Judging whether an observation statement is reliable
7. Judging whether an inductive conclusion is warranted
8. Judging whether the problem has been identified
9. Judging whether something is an assumption
10. Judging whether a definition is adequate
11. Judging whether a statement made by an alleged authority is acceptable

Such "aspects" do indeed constitute what many experts mean by critical thinking (Allen and Rott, 1969).

Recently, programs for teaching philosophy to children have been claiming statistically significant results in improving reading, interpersonal relations, ethical understanding—and reasoning and critical thinking (Lipman, 1976, 1981; Lipman, Sharp, and Oscanyan, 1980; Weinstein and Laufman, 1981). As with the above two approaches, learning to evaluate is central. With the materials developed by the *Institute for the Advancement of Philosophy for Children* (Lipman, 1976; Weinstein and Laufman, 1981), beginning in fifth grade, students learn about logical relations and syllogisms, descriptions and explanations, causes and reasons, universal and particular statements ("All birds are blue" versus "This bird is blue"), the nature of hypotheses, and rules governing sentence reversal (for example, "All oaks are trees," but the reverse is never true). The five general program goals are improving (1) reasoning, (2) creativity, (3) personal and interpersonal growth, (4) ethical understanding, and (5) such philosophic thinking objectives as understanding alternatives, impartiality, consistency, giving reasons for beliefs, decision-making situations, and part-whole relationships. For further information, see Lipman, Sharp, and Oscanyan (1980).

Critical Thinking as Problem Solving

Budmen (1967) considered critical thinking to be virtually identical to problem solving or an act of inquiry. He emphasized, however, that critical thinking differs from more objective scientific problem solving in that critical thinking involves values, emotions, and matters of judgment. From this perspective, Budmen's message to teachers was that students should be taught that there are problems for which there is no single solution—only judgments and alternatives. Said Budmen, "What to consider in arriving at these judgments, how to identify the alternatives and make the choices, is what the process of critical thinking is all about." He outlined four steps which could be taught.

Budmen's first step is to identify one's basic assumptions, feelings, beliefs, and values relating to an issue. This was considered " . . . the heart of the process." The second step involves an examination of all sides of an issue. As a third step one examines all possible actions and their probable results. "More than anything else, students must understand that all behavior has consequences . . . " Finally, the process requires a choice among alternatives: a decision.

For teaching purposes, Budmen stresses that a solution resulting from these steps should be the best one for the particular student. Therefore, problems best suited for the development of critical thinking would be problems without a single right answer.

Also taking a problem-solving approach to critical thinking, Dressel and Mayhew (1954) reduced a long list of critical-thinking abilities to five central ones. The abilities follow a problem-solving format, but with considerable evaluation built into each step:

1. The ability to *define a problem,* which includes the abilities to define abstract elements in simple, concrete, and familiar terms; break complex elements into workable parts; identify the central elements of the problem; and eliminate extraneous elements from the problem.

2. The ability to *select pertinent information* for the solution of a problem, including the ability to distinguish reliable and unreliable sources of information; recognize bias in the selection and rejection of information; recognize information relevant to the solution of the problem; and select information from personal experience relevant to the problem.

3. The ability to *recognize stated and unstated assumptions,* including the ability to recognize unsupported and irrelevant assumptions.

4. The ability to *formulate and select relevant and promising hypotheses,* including the abilities to discover clues to the solution of the problem, select promising hypotheses for first consideration, and check hypotheses against the information and assumptions.

5. The ability to *draw valid conclusions* and to judge the validity of inferences, including the abilities to detect logical inconsistencies, recognize conditions necessary to verify a conclusion, and judge the adequacy of a conclusion as a solution to the problem.

By way of comment, if critical thinking reduces to good problem solving, as Budmen (1967) and Dressel and Mayhew (1954) argue, the teaching implication is obvious: teach problem solving. Now critically consider this possibility: As we will see in the next chapter, the process of creative thinking requires those same abilities we just listed for problem solving (see items 1, 4, and 5, especially). Logically then, critical thinking and creative thinking would be the same (if A is C and B is C, then A is B). Would the reader agree that critical thinking and creative problem solving are identical?

LEADERSHIP

Leadership and critical thinking have much in common: They are difficult to define, they can take innumerable forms, and virtually all educators agree they are important objectives for gifted and talented students—"tomorrow's leaders" (Lamb and Busse, 1983; Parker, 1983). As Passow and Schiff (Johnson, 1977) observed, our gifted leaders of tomorrow " . . . are intelligent, educated, and motivated to provide leadership through planning, creating, inventing, teaching, and building [and] exercise leadership by virtue of their superior achievement and performance in socially valuable areas." Given this core assumption of future leadership, it seems logical that leadership training should supplement the development of other cognitive and affective skills and gifts.

The following two subsections review definitions of *leadership* and then turn to specifics of what is taught when you "teach leadership."

As an overview, first, definitions of leadership typically amount to lists of characteristics of leaders. Second, leadership training in the schools, when it is attempted at all, typically takes one of two main approaches. (1) Students are put into leadership situations with the hope that leadership characteristics somehow will be strengthened. Discussions of leadership dynamics and leadership traits sometimes accompany this "on-the-job" leadership experience. (2) Alternatively, students receive training in component leadership skills, such as communication (public speaking, discussing), creative problem solving, critical thinking, decision making, persuasion, group dynamics, and even understanding others' needs.

Definitions and Characteristics of Leadership

One definition of leadership is found in the Renzulli and Hartman (1971; Renzulli, 1983) *Leadership Rating Scale,* reproduced in Appendix 4.5, on which teachers evaluate potential G/T program candidates according to the following criteria. A student high in leadership:

1. Carries responsibility well and can be counted on to do what has been promised.
2. Is self-confident with both age-mates and adults; seems comfortable when showing personal work to the class.
3. Is well liked.
4. Is cooperative, avoids bickering, and is generally easy to get along with.
5. Can express him- or herself clearly.
6. Adapts to new situations; is flexible in thought and action and is not disturbed when the normal routine is changed.
7. Enjoys being around other people.
8. Tends to dominate; usually directs activities.
9. Participates in most school social activities; can be counted on to be there.

A rigorous definition of "extraordinary leaders" comes from Plowman (1981), who describes such people as:

> . . . persons who get other persons to act—often to accomplish specific short-term objectives. Extraordinary leaders are [able to] get other persons to resolve complex situations and problems and to attain long-range goals. They generate brilliant ideas and plans. The extraordinary leader uses expertise from a number of sources, discovers and develops latent capabilities of followers, ferrets out the real problem from a host of apparent problems, and is quick to communicate solutions. . . . this type of leader organizes work and solves problems in ways which seem bizarre, but which actually result in greater achievement than with traditional methods.

While this description would seem to make tough demands on the average mortal, Plowman notes that highly gifted/talented children tend to have the right traits. Specifically, they are able to:

1. Change their interpretation of the meaning and use of objects, processes, and systems.
2. Use facts and systems of facts in new ways.
3. Relate the apparently unrelatable.
4. Produce creative and valid solutions and products.
5. Move individuals and organizations toward agreed-upon goals.
6. Overcome apparently insurmountable obstacles.
7. Achieve needed change.

To further clarify the nature of leaders and leadership, Plowman (1981) itemized six aspects of leadership in the form of adjectives: *charismatic, intuitive, generative, analytical, evaluative,* and *synergistic.* All of these could be considered competencies upon which a leadership curriculum could be based.

Charismatic traits include an almost mystical ability to instill others (partly by example) with a sense of mission, and to energize them to think and act to achieve objectives. *Intuitive* characteristics include the ability to sense what is about to happen via an extrapolation of current events or a keen sensitivity to subtle cues. It includes the ability to sense the needs of individuals and groups and to respond to those needs even before they are expressed. The leader's intuition and forecasting ability helps others to see the rationality and validity of individual and group action. *Generative* refers to creativeness: defining problems in new ways and creating unusual ideas, processes, and courses of action. *Analytic* leadership includes seeing component parts of systems and analyzing their individual contributions. The *evaluative* involves judging the effectiveness or efficiency of activities or programs. The *synergistic* aspects " . . . are those which make the unbelievable happen"—goals are reached in half the expected time, or production is five or ten times what was expected.

Plowman (1981) also reported the results of a 1980 leadership session at the California Association for the Gifted Annual Conference in Los Angeles in which 16 traits of leadership were identified. Each trait was categorized as *cognitive* (C), *affective* (A), or *both* (B):

1. Assertive decision making (B)
2. Altruistic (B)
3. Persuasive/innovator (A)
4. Sensitivity to the needs of others (A)
5. Ability to be a facilitator (B)
6. Goal oriented (C)
7. Strong communication skills (B)
8. Integrity (A)
9. Organization ability (C)
10. Resourceful (B)
11. Risk-taker (B)
12. Charisma (A)
13. Competence (knowledge) (B)
14. Persistence ("hangs in there") (A)
15. Accepts responsibility (B)
16. Creative (B)

Only two traits were rated as *cognitive*, indicating both the importance of affective characteristics in leadership and the complexity of the traits.

Importantly, each of these traits, as with the traits and "aspects" in the previous lists, could be seen as objectives or competencies of leadership curricula, competencies to be strengthened by leadership experiences.

Leadership Training

We noted previously that one popular leadership-training strategy is simply putting students into leadership situations. This can include giving them responsibility for a variety of small-group projects, for example, panel discussions or the preparation of a joint report, a joint science or other research project, and so on. Following this general strategy, Magoon (1980) recommended:

1. *Classroom monitorships,* in which students assume responsibility for regulating the behavior of peers (for example, in lineups), record keeping (roll taking), or other jobs (blackboard or A-V duties). Such activities teach leadership and followership, including the notion that there are menial tasks which must be carried out for the system to function.
2. *Mentorships,* in which gifted and talented students tutor peers or younger students. The mentors learn to communicate in an acceptable and challenging manner.
3. *In-school leadership projects,* identified via brainstorming, such as improving student behavior (for example, in the halls or cafeteria), improving the physical plant (classrooms, bathrooms, or temperature or noise levels), or solving problems related to curriculum, instruction, or administration (rules, management practices).
4. *Community projects,* in which students take on neighborhood problems or undesirable conditions. This activity requires the development of communication skills, tact, diplomacy, and patience.
5. *Simulations,* which can involve, for example, establishing "banks" and "stores," making rules, and establishing a legal system for maintaining the rules.

Said Magoon, these five strategies are " . . . based, in part, on a leadership program that has been classroom tested with talented and gifted students for over three years with exciting results."

Plowman (1981) recommended strengthening leadership with exercises aimed at developing the component skills of critical thinking, decision making, persuading, planning, and evaluating. More complex objectives included helping students understand others' needs, exploring patterns of individual and group behavior, and showing students ways that changes are made in political, social, economic, and other spheres.

Parker (1983) suggested that leadership could be trained by strengthening the four component skills of *cognition* (especially, research, exploration, and investigative skills), *problem solving* (including creative thinking), *interpersonal communication* (including self-awareness, concern for others, cooperation, and conflict resolution), and *decision making.*

Generally following the Plowman and Parker component-strengthening strategy, Magoon (1981) proposed that students be exposed to the "topic and content" of leadership itself. For example, training can include teaching students about leadership and followership, principles of participatory democracy, group processes, and characteristics of leaders, along with developing communication skills.

Maker's (1982) suggestions for leadership training include both practice in leading and the deliberate teaching of component skills. First, she notes that as the school year progresses, the teacher should gradually become a sideline facilitator, and the gifted and talented students should learn to become leaders. Students can be asked to teach small groups of students, a task which intrinsically requires leadership, and to take responsibility for various projects. Also, deliberate, awareness-raising discussions of leadership can include listing qualities of leaders, followed by discussions of which qualities help to make leaders successful. The teacher also can foster discussion skills, public speaking, and group control and group dynamics skills.

Role playing may be used to shed light on some facets of group dynamics. For example, each student in a small discussion group can be privately instructed to play a particular role, positive or negative: One person tries to get the job done by initiating, encouraging, and giving and asking for information; one person disagrees with everything, seeks attention, and tries to block progress; one person keeps looking at his or her watch and wants to quit; one person agrees with conflicting views; and so on (Bushman and Jones, 1977; Maker, 1982). Post-hoc analysis of roles and dynamics are naturally part of the educational process.

Gonsalves, Grimm, and Welsh (1981) described an Oakland, California, program for developing social leadership skills in seventh- and eighth-grade students, their parents and their teachers. It was a learning-by-doing approach, with the learners divided into *political, media, social welfare, environment,* and *education* groups. Each group had an adult leader and an elected student leader. Each group was charged with completing a special project for the group or for the school community; that is, they were given responsibilities requiring problem solving, decision making, and leadership.

As an indication of the types of leadership projects, consider the model phone call planned by one 12-year-old member: "About 10 of us will be there tomorrow at noon, and we want to discuss community problems with the Mayor (or the Superintendent of Schools, or the Members of the Central Labor Council)." The media group visited major newspapers and radio and TV stations; the art group painted a mural, and volunteered to paint scenery for a school play. At general meetings all students listened to and questioned local political leaders. Fund raisers faced a real problem—raising $4,000 to pay for a week-long camp for the participants.

Before the camping trip students and adults discussed camp rules, organized equipment, and made general plans for the trip. At camp, various courses focused upon academic topics not necessarily related directly to leadership, for example, art, language, geography and map reading, photography darkroom techniques, watercolor painting, and fly tying (which was tested in local streams.)

By way of evaluation, the authors concluded that, despite problems of defining and evaluating social leadership, "for everyone involved—it worked." More specifically, students in the leadership program began running for student body officer positions; they entered academic and nonacademic contests; many who previously saw school as dull now saw its possibilities and opportunities; many tried out for school productions; they registered for a normally avoided journalism class; and importantly, many became more likely to speak out about their concerns and to organize plans of action. See Gonsalves, Grimm, and Welsh (1981) for further details.

SUMMARY

Affective learning, critical thinking, and leadership all are goals of programs for gifted and talented students.

Affective learning includes the topics of self-concepts, moral thinking, social adjustment, motivation, self-actualization, concern for others, and more. It is a crucial program goal.

High-achieving gifted students usually have good self-concepts, and gifted students usually attain higher levels of moral thinking. The self-concept is closely tied to success experiences, which makes feedback from schoolwork and the teacher extremely important for children. Academic failure implies low self-worth.

Developing good self-concepts is a goal in itself. We have many "selves" (academic, social, emotional, physical). The self-concept is organized, stable, and evaluative. Underachieving G/T students have poor self-concepts. The self-concept may be formed according to "mirrored" reflections from others. Achieving students are confident and use failures constructively.

Because self-esteem is highly valued, failure-oriented students will use defense mechanisms, such as deliberate underachieving, setting goals impossibly high or too low, setting a wide "confirming interval," and attributing failures to external causes.

Individualized learning, with realistic goal-setting, is one solution to self-defeating defensive behaviors.

Kohlberg's six stages of moral development are considered "true," invariant stages. In the Preconventional level, right action avoids punishment and satisfies one's own or the needs of others (who will reciprocate). In the Conventional level, correct behavior is defined by strict social conventions.

In the Postconventional level, right action is defined by universal and self-determined principles. Children understand all previous stages and one more, and prefer this next one. Research is mixed regarding sex differences in moral development, and whether or not gifted adolescents truly do think at the Postconventional level.

Children should be exposed to moral thinking at the next higher level. They should have opportunities to think about moral problems, for example, using moral dilemmas. Kohlberg's stages themselves can be taught.

Fantini emphasized teaching "caring" values; exposing students to problems of the elderly and handicapped, to examples of humanistic thinking, and to social issues; and involving students in community service programs, which G/T students can design and carry out. Values clarification strategies and the Magic Circle technique help students understand and accept values.

Davis suggested using creativity strategies for teaching affective and humanistic values, for example, brainstorming, empathy, metaphorical thinking, mental visualization, "What would happen if . . . ?," questioning, and role playing.

The humanistic teacher has a good self-concept, likes others, initiates change, and is honest and genuine, forward-growing, sensitive, creative and adventurous, confident, and open to other viewpoints.

To increase achievement motivation, McClelland recommended teaching students to think like achievement-oriented people, for example, by teaching them that achievement is important and possible.

Among many other definitions, critical thinking may be defined as evaluative thinking or problem solving.

Allen recommended teaching students to evaluate such matters as a speaker's biases and qualifications; the adequacy of information, unstated assumptions, the validity of reasoning, and others. Ennis's similar principles emphasized teaching students to look for ambiguities, contradictions, reliability of statements, unwarranted conclusions, adequacy of definitions, and others.

Philosophy courses for children may teach ethical principles, logical reasoning, and critical thinking.

Critical thinking defined as problem solving suggests, according to Budmen, that students should be taught to identify assumptions, examine all sides of an issue, and examine the likely results of various actions.

Dressel and Mayhew itemized five main critical thinking abilities: the ability to define a problem, select pertinent information, recognize stated and unstated assumptions, select relevant hypotheses, and draw conclusions.

Leadership is important in G/T education, but difficult to define. Definitions of leadership usually amount to characteristics of leaders, for example, high responsibility and confidence, being well-liked, good verbal ability, adaptability, sociability, and tendencies to dominate and direct.

Plowman's definition of extraordinary leaders included the abilities to identify the "real" problem, generate brilliant ideas, get other persons to accept goals and to act, and to solve problems in "bizarre" ways. Plowman states that G/T children often have these traits.

Six "aspects" of leadership (Plowman) included being charismatic, intuitive, generative (creative), analytical, evaluative, and synergistic. These and other cognitive and affective traits could be used as objectives and competencies for creating a leadership curriculum.

Leadership training typically involves putting students into leadership situations, or else teaching such component knowledge and skills as communicating, creative thinking, problem solving, critical thinking, decision making, planning, evaluating, persuasion, group dynamics, principles of participatory democracy, interpersonal skills, understanding others' needs, understanding leadership itself, and others.

Magoon described five leadership training activities: classroom monitorships, mentorships, in-school leadership projects, community projects, and simulations.

An Oakland, California, leadership-training program required middle-school students and their parents to assume responsibility for projects. Students increased dramatically in their school participative and leadership activities.

10

CREATIVITY I:
The Creative Person,
The Creative Process,
and Creative Dramatics

There can be no more important topic in the education of gifted and talented children than *creativity*. Indeed, the two interrelated purposes of gifted education are (1) to help these children and adolescents develop their gifts and talents and realize their potential—that is, to help them become more self-actualized, creative individuals; and (2) to better enable them to make creative contributions to society.

Overview

This chapter and Chapter 11 are designed to help the reader better understand creativity and creative students, and to suggest ideas for stimulating creative growth. This chapter will review some basic features of creativity: (1) traits and characteristics of creative people, including the relationship of creativity to intelligence, and some important creative abilities; (2) the nature of the creative process; and (3) creative dramatics. The important topic of testing for creative potential was discussed earlier in conjunction with identification. Chapter 11 will focus more specifically on teaching for creative development.

CHARACTERISTICS OF CREATIVE STUDENTS

Chapter 2 summarized recurrent personality, motivational, and biographical characteristics of creative children and adults. To briefly review, creative people are frequently high in self-confidence, independence, risk-taking, energy, enthusiasm, adventurousness, curiosity, playfulness, humor, idealism, and reflectiveness. They tend to have artistic and aesthetic interests and be attracted to the complex and mysterious. Most of these traits were uncovered by Frank Barron (1969) and Donald MacKinnon (1978) in their classic Berkeley studies of creative architects, writers, and mathematicians.

Further, as we also noted earlier, some traits will be troublesome to teachers. Especially, the admirable characteristics of *independence* and *high energy*, combined with the nonconformity and unconventionality intrinsic to creativeness, may lead to stubbornness, resistance to teacher (or parent) domination, uncooperativeness, indifference to accepted conventions, cynicism, too much assertiveness, sloppiness, low interest in details, and a tendency to question rules and authority (Smith, 1966).

The biographical traits listed earlier included some unsurprising ones, namely, a background filled with creative activities and hobbies. Frequent performances in dramatic productions is a very strong indicator of creativeness, since such performances necessarily require important creative traits (humor, energy, aesthetic interests and risk taking, for example). More subtle biographical characteristics of creativity include a background of traveling, living in more than one state, preferring friends who are younger and older, having had an imaginary playmate as a child, and a tendency to believe in psychical phemonena (and a higher than average likelihood of having psychical experiences). Naturally, not all characteristics apply to all creative students.

Many of these traits can probably be enhanced in a more creative direction. Indeed, as we will see in the next chapter, there is every reason to believe that both attitudes and personality traits can be changed to produce a more flexible, creative, and self-actualized person. For example, where feedback and reinforcement help reduce anxiety and improve confidence, independence, and a better self-concept, an increase in creative productivity is likely. Participation in creativity courses often strengthens self-confidence and independence along with creative potential (Parnes, 1978); it is a chicken-egg problem as to which causes which. A teacher might also cultivate curiosity and an interest in art, and encourage and reinforce new activities, exploration, adventurousness, and even humor.

Other Indicators of Creativity: Torrance

Torrance (1981b) analyzed letters from 150 parents of creative children describing characteristics and behaviors of their offspring. Note that

© 1967 United Feature Syndicate, Inc.

some of these traits are certain to cause personal or social adjustment problems for the child:

Is overactive physically and/or mentally
Is annoyingly curious
Is forgetful and absentminded
Daydreams; gets lost in thought
Mind wanders too much
Has good sense of humor
Does not participate in class
Enjoys nature and the outdoors
Won't join Scouts
Friends think him/her slightly queer
Likes to work by him/herself
Imaginative; enjoys pretending
Is sensitive
Likes color
Is uncommunicative
Is a "What if?" person
Feels left out of things
Loves to read
Is good only in science (or art, music, etc.)

From teachers, counselors and school administrators participating in a creativity seminar, Torrance extracted another list of behaviors which also may be taken as "non-test indicators" of creativity. In edited form to reduce redundancy:

Sees relationships
Is full of ideas; high verbal or conversational fluency
Experiments, tries new ideas, new products, and so forth
Flexibility of ideas and thoughts
Persistent, persevering, unwilling to give up
Constructs, builds, or rebuilds
Prefers the complex, copes with several ideas at once, is irritated and bored by the routine and obvious
Can occupy time without being stimulated
Prefers to dress differently
Goes beyond assigned tasks
Is able to amuse himself or herself with simple things in imaginative ways
May appear to be loafing or daydreaming when actually thinking
Experiments with familiar objects to see if they will become something other than what they were intended to be
Is a window watcher during class, but keeps up with what's going on in class
Makes up games in the schoolyard
Enjoys telling about his/her discoveries and inventions
Comes up with ways of doing things that are different from standard directions
Is not afraid to try something new
Draws in his/her notebook while the teacher is giving a lecture or directions
Draws elaborate pictures
Goes further with games than specified in the accompanying directions
Uses all senses in observing
Does not mind the consequences of appearing different

Torrance (1979) itemized still other nontest indicators of creativeness and responsiveness in the kinesthetic and auditory areas:

Shows skillful, manipulative movement in crayon work, typing, piano playing, cooking, dressmaking, and so on.
Shows quick, precise movements in mime, creative dramatics, and role playing
Works at creative movement activities for extended periods of time
Displays total bodily involvement in interpreting a poem, story, or song
Becomes intensely absorbed in creative movement or dance
Interprets songs, poems, or stories through creative movement or dance

Writes, draws, walks, and moves with rhythm and is generally highly responsive to sound stimuli

Creates music, songs, etc.

Works perseveringly at music and rhythmic activities

The characteristics listed here are intended to help the reader recognize creative children and adolescents in the classroom. The lists also might increase one's patience with the obnoxious kid who shows a few too many of the negative traits. Perhaps the creative energy, unconventionality, stubbornness, inquisitiveness, and so forth, require rechanneling into constructive outlets.

Creativity and Intelligence

The relationship between creativity and intelligence is an old and continuing issue (see, for example, Getzels and Jackson, 1962; Keating, 1980; Wallach, 1970; Wallach and Kogan, 1965). On one hand, most of us would agree that creative talent and intelligence definitely are not one and the same—the highly creative person and the highly intelligent person are not necessarily the same person. At the same time, however, it is obvious that students or adults who produce excellent and innovative artistic, literary, scientific, or other creative products are usually fairly bright. Few major socially relevant creative contributions come from the ranks of mentally deficient citizens. There is a good argument supporting a *moderate* relationship between creativity and intelligence, even though they clearly are not the same animal.

Research generally bears out this relationship. Most comparisons of creativity scores with IQ scores show low positive correlations. For example, correlation coefficients between scores on the *Torrance Tests of Creative Thinking* and scores on a variety of group and individual intelligence tests typically fall between about .15 and .40 (Wallach, 1970; Yamamoto, 1966). Getzels and Jackson (1962) similarly found correlations from .12 to .39 between their divergent thinking tests and group and individual intelligence measures. A correlation between the elementary school *GIFT* creativity scores and *Slosson Individual Intelligence Test* scores was a statistically significant .33 (Rimm and Davis, 1980). Rimm also found a significant .39 correlation between *GIFT* scores and scores on the *Kranz Talent Identification Instrument.* These relationships support the idea that although creativity clearly is different from intelligence, the two constructs are correlated to a moderate degree.

One good resolution to the creativity-intelligence issue lies in the *threshold* concept (MacKinnon, 1978). The argument is that over the wide range of intelligence, from mental deficiency through the normal ranges to genius levels, there certainly is a moderately good relationship between creativity and IQ scores. However, at *high* levels of intelligence—namely, above a threshold IQ score of about 120—there is no relationship at all. That is, above this intelligence level, neither a person's IQ score nor school grades will predict his or her level of creativeness. One implication of the threshold concept is that if students selected for a gifted program are in the top 1 to 5 percent in intelligence, the large majority of creative students will be missed!

The threshold position has both high intuitive appeal and research backing. For example, Reis and Renzulli (1982) found no differences in the quality of creative products produced by students in the top 5 percent in intelligence or achievement compared with students in the top 25 percent, that is, the other students in the talent pool.

The difference between the bright students who are creatively productive versus those who are just bright lies in the very important personality, motivational, and dispositional characteristics discussed above. As an intimately related consideration, many bright students are *capable* of creative productivity—they simply are not *predisposed* to think creatively or to engage in creative activities. A central goal of all gifted education programs, of course, is to correct this deficiency—to stimulate intelligent students to attain higher levels of "creativity consciousness" and creative productivity.

Another well-known position regarding creativity and intelligence seems inconsistent with the threshold notion. Wallach and Kogan (1965) argued strongly that when creativity tests are (1) untimed and (2) administered in a relaxed, gamelike atmosphere, the usual correlation between intelligence test scores and creativity test scores disappears. That is, when pressured, testlike conditions are removed, the influence of intelligence upon divergent-thinking scores also is removed. If scores on their divergent-thinking tests (for example, listing unusual uses for a tire) translate accurately as *creative ability,* then their argument directly implies that creative ability and intelligence are, in fact, independent in children in regular classrooms.

However, the present authors are reasonably convinced that, if real creative products are the measure of creativeness, brighter students also will produce more original and better products in art, writing, composing, designing, acting, science, and so on. While intelligence and creativeness definitely are different, they nonetheless seem to be moderately related over the wide range of intellectual ability. In accord with the threshold notion, they likely are independent at high levels of intellectual ability.

As a final note, we also should emphasize that many academically "below average" students will demonstrate marvelous creative talent, for example, in art, dance, or any other area in which the student possesses special knowledge and skills.

Creative Abilities

There are a great many intellectual abilities that contribute in one way or another to creative potential. Indeed, it would be difficult to isolate mental abilities having absolutely nothing to do with creativeness. The list below includes the most seemingly important creative abilities. Most have appeared elsewhere in the creativity literature, usually in Torrance's work (for example, Torrance, 1962, 1979, 1980, 1984). The first four are the classic Guilford/Torrance *fluency, flexibility, originality,* and *elaboration* abilities which are measured by the Guilford (1967) tests and the *Torrance Tests of Creative Thinking* (Torrance, 1966). Some people have mistakenly assumed that these four are a definitive and exhaustive list of creative abilities, which is not true at all.

Fluency. The ability to produce many ideas in response to an open-ended problem or question. The ideas may be verbal or nonverbal (for example, mathematical, musical, and so forth). Pseudonyms include "associational fluency" or "ideational fluency."

Flexibility. The ability to take different approaches to a problem, think of ideas in different categories, or view a situation from several perspectives.

Originality. Uniqueness, nonconformity in thought and action.

Elaboration. The important ability to add details to a given idea, which includes developing, embellishing, and implementing the idea.

Sensitivity to problems. The ability to find problems, detect difficulties, detect missing information, and ask good questions (Dillon, 1982).

Problem defining. An important capability that includes the abilities to: (1) identify the "real" problem, (2) isolate the important aspects of a problem, (3) clarify and simplify a problem, (4) identify subproblems, (5) propose alternative problem definitions, and (6) define a problem broadly. Abilities 5 and 6 both open the door to a wider variety of problem solutions.

Visualization. The ability to fantasize and imagine, "see" things in the "mind's eye," and mentally manipulate images and ideas. According to some, this may be the single most important creative ability.

Ability to regress. The ability to think like a child, whose mind is less cluttered by habits, traditions, rules, regulations, and the firm knowledge of "how it ought to be done" and "how we've always done it"—strong barriers to creative thinking.

Metaphorical thinking. The ability to borrow ideas from one context and use them in another context; or the ability to borrow a solution to one problem and transfer it to another problem.

Evaluation. The very important ability to separate relevant from irrelevant considerations; to think critically; to evaluate the "goodness" or appropriateness of an idea, product, or problem solution.

Analysis. The ability to analyze details, analyze a whole into its parts.

Synthesis. The ability to see relationships, to combine parts into a workable, perhaps creative whole.

Transformation. This includes the ability to adopt something to a new use, to "see" new meanings, implications, and applications, or to creatively change one object or idea into another. Guilford (1983) considers transformation ability to be extremely important for creativity.

Extend boundaries. The ability to go beyond what is "usual," to use objects in new ways.

Intuition. The ability to make "intuitive leaps" or see relationships based upon little, perhaps insufficient information; the ability to "read between the lines."

Predict outcomes. The ability to foresee the results of different solution alternatives and actions.

Resist premature closure. This is another important ability, and one in which many students are deficient. It translates simply as "not jumping on the first idea that comes along."

Concentration ability. The ability to focus on a problem, free from distraction.

Logical thinking ability. The ability to separate the relevant from the irrelevant, to deduce reasonable conclusions.

Some personality traits could also be viewed as "creative abilities," for example, sense of humor, curiosity, artistic interests or talent, tolerance for ambiguity, spontaneity, and perhaps others. In addition, the 24 divergent-thinking abilities in Guilford's (1967, 1979b) *Structure of Intellect* (SOI) model, reviewed in Chapter 7, include abilities that overlap with the above list. As you may recall, Guilford's 24 abilities are combinations of four contents (figural, symbolic, semantic, and behavioral) and six products (units, classes, relations, systems, transformations, and implications). *Humor,* for example, is an SOI ability involving the "divergent production of semantic transformations" (DST). Further, there are innumerable learned skills and abilities in every social, scientific, business, or artistic field that are essential for creative thinking within that particular knowledge area (Keating, 1980).

THE CREATIVE PROCESS

There are several ways to view the creative process. First, the traditional approach is to describe a sequence of *stages* through which one might proceed in solving a problem creatively. Second, the creative process can be viewed as a *change in perception*—literally "seeing" new idea combinations, new relationships, new meanings, new implications, or new applications that simply were not perceived a moment before. These approaches to the creative process will be briefly summarized subsequently.

A third approach to understanding the creative process is to examine creative thinking *techniques*—strategies used by creative individuals to produce the new idea combinations and relationships that comprise creative ideas and products. This topic is postponed until Chapter 11.

Steps and Stages in the Creative Process

The Wallas model.   The best-known set of stages in the creative process is the *preparation, incubation, illumination,* and *verification* stages suggested in 1926 by Graham Wallas. The *preparation* stage includes clarifying and defining the problem, gathering relevant information, reviewing available materials, examining solution requirements, and becoming acquainted with any other relevant innuendos or implications, including previous unsuccessful solutions. This stage basically involves clarifying "the mess."

The *incubation* stage may best be viewed as a period of "preconscious," "fringe conscious," "off-conscious," or even "unconscious" activity which takes place while the thinker, perhaps deliberately, is jogging, watching TV, playing golf, eating pizza, walking along a river bank, or even napping. Guilford (1979a) suggested that incubation takes place during reflection, a pause in action, and that some people are simply more reflective than others.

The third, *illumination* stage is the sudden "Eureka, I found it!" or "Aha!" experience. A solution appears, usually suddenly (although it may follow weeks of work), that seems to match the requirements of the problem.

The final *verification* stage, as the name suggests, involves checking the workability, feasibility, and/or acceptability of the illumination.

The reader may note that these stages resemble steps in the classic scientific method: state the problem, propose hypotheses, plan and conduct the research, then evaluate the results. Note also that the stages are not an invariant sequence. Some stages may be skipped or the thinker may backtrack to an earlier stage. For example, the process of defining and clarifying the problem (preparation) often leads directly to a good, illuminating idea. Or if the verification confirms that an idea will not work or will not be acceptable, the thinker may move back to either the preparation or the incubation stage.

Actually, one of the most important steps in creative thinking was ignored in the Wallas model: implementation. The idea must be developed and elaborated upon, and the solution carried out. Perhaps this step was assumed.

The Fabun model.   Fabun (1968) added three enlightening stages to the Wallas model. His first stage was labeled *desire*. A problem, by virtue of being a problem, disturbs the equilibrium of the thinker, who becomes motivated to find a solution and restore the equilibrium (Davis, 1973). Fabun's second stage is *preparation,* paralleling Wallas's. In the third stage, *manipula-*

tion, the thinker often actively manipulates ideas or materials. For example, an artist, photographer, or interior designer will experiment with colors, subjects, and arrangements; a writer or poet will toy with different words, phrases, characters, plots, or topic arrangements; a composer, scientist, or engineer will try many idea combinations and arrangements to find one that is interesting, effective, or aesthetically pleasing.

Fabun's fourth stage, *incubation,* is followed by his interesting *intimation* stage—the nice warm feeling that you are getting somewhere; you are not there yet, but it looks like something good will happen soon. Gordon (1961) labeled this good feeling a "hedonic tone," noting that it occurs frequently when closing in on a creative problem solution. The sixth and seventh stages in Fabun's revision are *illumination* and *verification,* as in Wallas's original model.

A two-stage model.   Often, the creative process seems to involve two fairly clear steps: The *big idea* stage and an *elaboration* stage (Davis, 1983a). The big idea stage is a period of fantasy in which the creative person is looking for a new, exciting idea or problem solution. After the idea is found, perhaps using a personal creative thinking technique, the elaboration stage requires idea development, elaboration, and implementation. The artist must assemble his or her materials, do preliminary sketches, and create the final work; the novelist must create characters and plot; and the research scientist or business entrepreneur must organize the details and carry out the work necessary to implement the big idea.

The Creative Education Foundation stages: Parnes.   An extremely useful set of stages are the five outlined by Parnes (1981; Parnes, Noller and Biondi, 1977; see also Treffinger, Isakson, and Firestien, 1982): *fact finding, problem finding, idea finding, solution finding,* and *acceptance finding.* These five steps are useful because they guide the creative process; that is, they tell you what to do at each immediate step to eventually produce one or more creative, workable solutions. Another unique feature is that each step first involves a divergent-thinking phase, in which lots of ideas (facts, problem definitions, potential solutions) are generated, and then a second convergent phase in which only the most promising ideas are selected for further exploration.

The first stage, *fact finding,* involves "listing all you know about the problem or challenge" (Parnes, 1981). For example, let's say the problem is thinking of ways to stimulate creativity in an elementary school resource room G/T program. An individual or group first would list all of the facts they could think of relating to training creative thinking and perhaps to the nature of creativity and creative abilities. The list of ideas is then convergently narrowed to a smaller number of facts that might be especially productive.

The second stage, *problem finding,* involves listing alternative problem definitions. One principle of creative problem solving is that the definition of a problem will determine the nature of the solutions. It helps to begin each statement with, "In what ways might I (we) . . . " (for example, find lists of strategies, locate someone who knows about training creativity, locate books on the topic, have someone else do it, have the kids themselves solve the problem, and so on).

One or more of the most fruitful definitions is selected for the third stage, *idea finding.* This is the divergent-thinking, brainstorming stage; ideas are freely listed for each of the problem definitions accepted in the second stage.

In the fourth stage of *solution finding,* criteria for idea evaluation are listed; for example: Will the strategy strengthen important creative abilities? Will it strengthen good creative attitudes? Will it teach usable creative thinking techniques? Will it cost too much? Will it take too much time? Are the materials available? Will the principal, other teachers accept it? Will the children cooperate? And so on. The list may be reduced to the most relevant criteria.

Sometimes, an *evaluation matrix* is prepared, with possible solutions listed on the vertical axis and the criteria across the top (see Figure 10.1).

FIGURE 10.1 Example of an Evaluation Matrix. Each idea is rated on a 1 (low) to 5 (high) scale according to each criterion. Total scores are then tallied.

	Strengthen Abilities?	Strengthen Attitudes?	Teach Techniques?	Cost Too Much?	Use Too Much Time?	Materials Available?	Principal, Teachers Accept It?	Children Cooperate?	Total Score
Use Brainstorming									
Teach Techniques									
Use Synectics									
Find Exercises									
Creative Drama									
Art, Handicrafts									
Creative Writing									
Research Projects									

Each idea is rated according to each criteria (perhaps on a 1 to 5 scale), the rating scores are entered in the cells, and then the scores are totaled to find the "best" idea(s).

Finally, *acceptance finding* (or implementation) amounts to thinking of " . . . ways to get the best ideas into action" (Parnes, 1981).

In his inspiring book *The Magic of Your Mind,* Parnes leads the reader through problem after problem with the goal of making the five steps habitual and automatic. That is, when encountering a problem, challenge, or opportunity, one quickly would review relevant facts, identify various interpretations of the problem, generate solutions, evaluate the ideas, and speculate on how the solution(s) might be implemented and accepted. After 25 years as president of the Creative Education Foundation, and much experience teaching creative problem solving, learning these steps is Parnes's best recommendation for becoming a more creative problem solver and a more effective, self-actualized human being.

In the classroom, Parnes's stages would be used to guide a creative-thinking session that (1) improves students' understanding of the creative process, (2) exposes them to a rousing creative-thinking experience, and (3) solves a problem. With much practice with the steps, students might become habitual creative thinkers, as Parnes intended.

Parnes (1981) noted that "the five steps are a guide rather than a strict formula. Frequently, a change of sequence may be introduced into the process; and it is always advisable to provide plenty of opportunity for incubation." In conversation, Parnes told the authors that people tend to use the five stages too rigidly. He suggested a star-shaped model enclosed in a circle (Figure 10.2), emphasizing that—if it helps the creative process—one may flexibly move directly from any one step to any other.

Keating's four stages in socially relevant creativity.   Keating (1980) proposed that the act of producing socially relevant creative innovations involves more than just divergent thinking. His four components take " . . . a vaguely temporal sequence. . . . " Component 1, *content knowledge,* is based on the assumption that it is virtually impossible to advance beyond the status quo in a field unless one has a thorough working knowledge of the particular discipline or art form. A deep familiarity with the work of one's predecessors in any field is " . . . if not an absolute prerequisite, at least a virtually universal concomitant of creative breakthroughs." Said Keating, whether learning is an exciting activity or mundane drudgery, it is a prerequisite for socially relevant creativity.

Component 2 is *divergent thinking,* which Keating identified mainly with ideational fluency and flexibility. He considered divergent thinking to be about equal in importance to content knowledge. In one debatable statement Keating claimed, "The promotion of ideational fluency in the absence of solid content acquisition is of unknown worth, and may be more

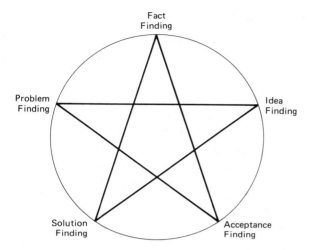

Fact
Finding

Problem
Finding

Idea
Finding

Solution
Finding

Acceptance
Finding

FIGURE 10.2 An alternative conception of the Creative Education Foundation Stages emphasizing that one may flexibly move from any stage to any other.

harmful than helpful." His position on this point is too extreme. The authors and others (for example, Feldhusen and Kolloff, 1978; Torrance, 1984) would argue that "content-free" classroom creativity exercises teach important creative attitudes, such as valuing creativity, having confidence in one's ideas, and a general creativity consciousness and predisposition to think creatively. Exercises also can teach creative-thinking techniques and strengthen any or all of the creative abilities listed earlier in this chapter.

Component 3 is *critical analysis*. Noted Keating, it is inaccurate to assume that critical thinking is the antithesis of creative thinking. As colorfully stated by Keating, "Critical analysis has an undeserved reputation as the tough heel on the fragile throat of creativity." Rather, " . . . some judgments must be made so that highly promising ideas may be separated from unpromising ones." Critical analysis thus involves avoiding wasting intellectual effort on dead-end ideas, yet avoiding the danger of prematurely discarding preposterous ideas that may lead to a major advance. According to Keating, consumer gullibility to advertising claims and the equally frequent belief in parapsychological phenomena are evidence that solid critical skills are not a product of the existing educational system.

Finally, component 4, *communication skills*, assumes that an idea or artistic conception that exists only in the head of the potential creator is not "creative" in the strict sense. "Something must be made, produced, concretized in some fashion before it has a chance to succeed in contributing to the collective human experience." Communication skill was interestingly seen as the mirror image of critical analysis; that is, one should be a "competent sender" as well as a "thoughtful receiver."

An important message in Keating's "vaguely sequential components" is simply that programs for teaching creative thinking should not focus totally on his component 2, divergent thinking. For "real," socially relevant creative contributions, the components of background knowledge, critical thinking, and communication skills also are essential.

The Creative Process as a Change in Perception

Many creative ideas are the result of a change in perception—the usually abrupt "seeing" of new idea combinations, new relationships, new meanings, new applications, or new implications. This phenomenon occurs whether the "illumination" is a simple modification of a cookie recipe (perhaps substituting mint candies for chocolate chips), or an unfathomably complex discovery in mathematics, physics, medicine, or astronomy.

One simple way to illustrate the sudden perceptual change is with visual puzzles. For example, look at Figure 10.3. There is one main, meaningful figure, created in fact from a photograph. After you find this figure, try to locate: (1) a flying pig, (2) an Al Capp *Li'l Abner* character with a snaggle lower tooth, (3) a woman with her hair in a bun reclining on a sofa (she is in white). If you can find these easy (?) ones, you may proceed to (4) the Road Runner, (5) Harry Belafonte, (6) Popeye, (7) Blackbeard the Pirate, (8) a side profile of Jesus, (9) right next to Jesus a lady in a bouffant hairdo, and (10) E.T. You will find yourself exclaiming, "Oh! There it is!" or "Now I see it!" The solutions are outlined at the end of this chapter.

We do not understand this sudden perceptual change very well. In some cases it may be due simply to viewing (or thinking of) one or two

FIGURE 10.3 Visual Puzzle.

stimuli and then mentally modifying them, combining them, or otherwise detecting a new meaning or relationship. For example, a candy bar mogul, always alert for new products, may receive a sample package of macadamia nuts on an airline flight and instantly "see" a chocolate/macadamia treat. A Silicon Valley computer chip expert, upon checking his wristwatch, may suddenly visualize a baseball game or some other video game incorporated into the wristwatch. A novelist may "see" an intriguing story take shape as the result of a visit to Cuba or Grenada, or from reading about a Middle East battle.

The creative change in perception is indeed a complex, mysterious, and elusive process. Krippner (1972), for example, has described the possible roles of extrasensory perception (ESP), precognition (seeing into the future), the unconscious mind, and even mind-altering psychedelic drugs in achieving creative insights. He cited physicist Max Planck and mathematicians Evarist Galois and Bernhard Reimann as three highly creative persons whose early intuitive visions led to marvelous creative breakthroughs. In all three cases, principles said to be necessary for their respective discoveries were not yet known. Citing Hadamard (1945), Krippner proposed that these " . . . discoveries were made intuitively and imaginatively with the aid of deep unconscious processes."

Torrance (1980) similarly described the "supra-rational" nature of "insight, intuition, and revelation" that happens in an instant. Said Torrance, these phenomena do not fit into the rational model of science and therefore have not been scientifically studied.

The discussion of creative thinking techniques in the next chapter will outline some unconscious creative processes that have been made conscious, knowable, and teachable. As we will see, most creative thinking techniques are based on forcing the thinker to consider (or "see") new relationships among ideas.

CREATIVE DRAMATICS

Creative dramatics most definitely is a unique classroom activity. According to Way (1967), it is "the education of the whole person by experience." As with other creativity exercises, creative dramatics stimulates divergent thinking, imagination, and problem solving. It also may strengthen sensory awareness, concentration, control of the physical self, discovery and control of emotions, humor, self-confidence in speaking and performing, empathic and humanistic understanding of others (Davis, Helfert, and Shapiro, 1973; Way, 1967), and even critical thinking (Carelli, 1982). The reader also will discover that creative dramatics is as fun as it is beneficial. Furthermore, sessions are not difficult to lead; the two main requirements are a good sense of humor and enough energy to crank up a people machine or wade through a peanut butter swamp.

Although creative dramatics may lead to a stage performance, a production in front of an audience is unusual. Typically, an audience is not needed or desired, since it would interfere with the imaginative, concentrated and sensitive involvement necessary for successful creative drama. Creative dramatics thus may be distinguished from children's theatre. With the latter, a published play is obtained, or written by a teacher, the very best actors are selected and trained (to impress the principal and parents), and everyone else finds props, paints scenery, sells tickets, does makeup, and at show time hands out programs or operates the lights and tape player. Creative dramatics is for all students, not just for a handful of talented actors and actresses.

Beyond warmups (next section), there are three main categories of creative drama activities: movement exercises, sensory and body awareness exercises, and pantomime and playmaking.

Warmup Exercises

Any creative dramatics session must begin with some simple loosening up exercises, movements that stretch a few muscles but require little or no thinking. Some suggestions are:

Holding up the ceiling.   As the leader narrates, the students strain to hold up the ceiling, slowly letting it down (to one knee), then pushing it back up into place.

Biggest thing, smallest thing.   Another easy one is to have everyone stretch his or her body into the "biggest thing" he/she possibly can. No one has any trouble guessing what the second part of the exercise is.

Stretching.   There are many ways to stretch. One strategy is to have students begin with their heads and work down, stretching then relaxing every part of the body. Vice versa, begin with the toes. Either may be done lying down.

Warmup at different speeds.   Children run in place in slow motion, then speed up until they are moving very fast. Variations include jumping, skipping, or hopping.

Movement Exercises

Circles.   The group stands in a large circle. Each participant, in turn, thinks of a way to make a circle by using his or her body. It may be a fixed or moving circle, using part or all of the body. All others must make the same circle. Names add to the fun—for example, "This is a halo circle,"

"This is a shoulder circle," "This is a chicken circle," "This is a Steve Martin circle." Circles will be more original if originality is clearly encouraged.

Mirrors. Everyone needs a partner. One person becomes a mirror who mimics the movements of the partner. Roles are reversed in about three minutes.

Circus. Each child becomes a different circus performer or animal. Variations include the leader directing what every one should be, for example, tightrope walkers, trained elephants, lion tamers, jugglers, and so forth.

People machines. This is everyone's favorite. There are two main strategies. Students can form *groups* of six to twelve students and take 10 or 15 minutes to design and practice their machine. They are performed one at a time for the others, who try to guess what the machine is. Alternatively, with the *add-on* method an idea for a machine is agreed upon and then one person starts the action. Others add themselves. Sounds—beeps, dings, buzzes, pops, and so on—are recommended. One of the best is an old-fashioned pinball game, which can absorb fifty volunteers.

Obstacles. With chalk, the leader draws a "start" and "finish" line on the floor, about eight feet apart. One at a time, each student makes up an imaginary obstacle that he or she must climb over (past, through, under, around) to get from start to finish. Since only one person participates at a time, it works best with small groups.

Gym workout. Participants pantomime activities as if they were in an imaginary gym. They run in place, lift weights, roll a medicine ball, climb a rope—all at once or one at a time.

Robot walk. Each person is a robot with a unique sound and walk. Whenever one robot touches another robot, both stop, sit down, and begin again to rise with a new sound and a new walk.

Balloon burst. There are two main versions. First, each person is a balloon who is blown up, and up, and up. The balloon can be released and zip around the room, or else blown up until it pops. In the second version the entire group is one balloon that is blown up to the limit, then bursts.

Creative locomotion. Have children walk like a Crooked Man, the Jolly Green Giant, Raggedy Ann, a robot, and so forth; run like a squirrel, mouse, Miss Muffett frightened by a spider, or the fattest person in the world running for a bus; jump like a kangaroo, popcorn, a jack-in-the-box; or walk through a peanut butter swamp, flypaper, a jungle, tacks, deep sand, or deep Jell-O. The leader and students call out new characters, animals, substances, surfaces, and so on.

Making letters.   Have individuals or two people shape their bodies to become alphabet letters. Others guess the letter. A small group can spell a word.

Imaginary tug-of-war.   Ask for ten volunteers (or pick them, if reluctance prevails). They are divided into two five-person teams. The leader narrates: "This side is struggling hard and seems to be winning. Now the other side is recovering. Look out! The rope broke!" Warn them to listen to the narrator, and be sure they hear the last instruction.

Sensory and Body Awareness

Trust walk (or blind walk).   This is an absolute must. Each person has a partner. The member with eyes shut, or blindfolded, is led around the room, under tables and chairs, and allowed to identify objects by touch, smell, or sound. Students walk down the hall, get a drink of water, try to read names or numbers on doors (such as "Boys"), go outside and explore trees, the sun, shade, a flower, and so on. Ask about experiences and discoveries in a follow-up discussion.

Body movement.   Children discover their moving parts when the teacher asks them to move their fingers, then hands, wrists, elbows, shoulders, neck, head, face (chew, makes faces, bat eyelashes), back, hips, legs, ankles, feet and toes. Variations: Ask students for more ideas; ask students to keep all parts moving as more are added.

Exploring an orange.   Give everyone an orange to examine closely. How does it look, feel, smell, taste? What is unique about "your" orange? Take the orange apart and examine and discuss the colors, patterns, and textures. Eat the orange.

Empathic vision.   Ask students to inspect the room through the eyes of an artist, a fire inspector, lighting engineer, some ants. Look at today's weather from the point of view of a bicyclist, a pilot, a duck, a field mouse, a skier. Who else?

Listening.   Have students sit (or lie) silently, listening first for sounds that are close, then for sounds that are far. Encourage concentration, letting sounds evoke associated images and memories. With all eyes shut, students can describe the sounds with their hands, communicating nonverbally.

Smelling. Small bottles are prepared in advance, with such familiar scents as vanilla extract, Vicks Vaporub, peanut butter, used coffee grounds, cinnamon, cloves, rubbing alcohol, lipstick, and so on. In small groups the scents are passed around and students discuss the memories that are stimulated by each smell.

Touching. Have students touch many surfaces, concentrating fully on the feel. Use strange objects (for example, a piece of coral) and familiar ones (for example, a piece of paper). A paper sack or box may be used to hide the objects from sight.

Pantomime and Playmaking

Many of the movement and sensory exercises cited thus far also include an element of pantomime (for example, the tug-of-war, robot walk). With more "serious" pantomime, students create appropriate positions, physical movements, and even eye movements as they perform in an imaginary environment. With encouragement, students can use their faces, hands, and bodies to express sadness, glee, love, fear, and so on. Pantomime can include relatively simple, short-term involvement, or else lengthier mini-plays without lines.

Some pantomime activities include:

Invisible box. Six to ten students form a circle. In turn, each person lifts the lid on an invisible box (or trunk), removes something, does something with it, then puts it back in the box and closes the lid. The action may go around the circle two or three times.

Invisible balls. An invisible ball is passed from person to person several times around a small circle (or up and down each row in a class). As each person receives the ball, it changes size, shape, weight, smell, and so forth.

Inside-out. Children become fish in a tank or zoo animals in cages. Others look in.

Animal pantomimes. Each child moves to the center of the circle to pantomime his or her animal. Others guess the animal. For variety, two or three animals can act out a simple plot, for example, a cat sneaking up on a mouse; a bear looking for honey but finding bees; a bull spotting some picnickers; a squirrel and a bluejay both trying to get the same piece of bread; a rabbit and a turtle preparing for a short race. Students can think of more.

Creating an environment.   This exercise is much like an add-on people machine. Students think of and create an environment, such as a bowling alley, fishermen in a boat, a playground, ballet class, sea fish and animals, gym class, football team warming up, farm animals, an assembly line processing freshly caught salmon, and so on. The class will think of more possibilities.

Miscellaneous pantomime.   Many brief sketches may teach characterization. With no lines allowed, students pay high attention to movements and expressions. As some examples: a jolly MacDonalds counterperson waiting on two or three impatient customers, a fussy person trying on hats or shoes, scared mountain climbers unable to go up or down, three stooges hanging wallpaper or performing heart surgery, a grouchy cab driver in 5 o'clock traffic getting a worried person to the airport, the President of the United States being locked out of the official airplane, and others.

Playmaking involves acting out stories and scenes without a script. To improve the expressiveness of movements and gestures, a sketch may be practiced without lines, that is, in pantomime. With one straightforward strategy, students are given a simple scene (plot), characters are explained, and then students improvise the action.

Way (1967) suggested that mini-plays need not be silly. They can involve, for example, miners working against time to reinforce a mine about to cave in; slow-moving astronauts assembling something on the moon; toyshop toys or museum displays coming alive at the stroke of midnight; Californians experiencing an earthquake; or witches and goblins cooking up a magic brew with improvised important ingredients. Historical episodes, folklore, mythology, fairy tales, nursery rhymes, and animal stories also present possibilities: for example, the Boston Tea Party, Columbus discovering America, Goldilocks and the Three Bears, Cinderella, and others.

A more structured playmaking strategy might run as follows. After a few warmup exercises, the leader tells a story. Then leader and students review the sequence of events—what happened first? Second? The group then discusses characterization, considering physical, emotional, and intellectual qualities (limping, slow, quick-stepping, nervous, angry, happy, excited, calm, conceited, dull-witted, scientific-minded). The play typically is broken down and worked out scene by scene. The group may first act out a scene without dialogue, to explore the movements, expressions and general believability of the characters. After improvements, it is replayed with improvised dialogue. A given scene may be replayed many times, with different students trying different roles. As noted above, ideas may be found in historical or mythological material, or in children's books, nursery rhymes, or other stories. Also, brainstorming may be used to generate plots and ideas.

For playmaking with gifted students, Carelli (1981) mentioned that the students may select the theme, assign responsibilities, plan and implement the activities, including researching the particular historical or mythological event, and evaluate both the process and the final product.

To conclude, creative dramatics is a worthwhile activity which may be used at any age level, from the elementary school pullout program to the high school drama class. By giving students a perfectly logical reason to be silly, feelings of self-consciousness and fear of failure are reduced, and confidence is built. Humor, as we noted earlier in this chapter, is a common component of creativeness, and certainly one encouraged in creative dramatics sessions.

SUMMARY

Creative students tend to be independent, risk-taking, energetic, curious, witty, idealistic, artistic, and attracted to aesthetic interests and to the complex and mysterious. However, they also may be stubborn, resistant to domination, and indifferent to conventions. They usually have a background of creative activities.

Torrance concluded that creative children may be annoyingly curious and forgetful, not participative in class, imaginative, flexible, sensitive, avid readers, uncommunicative, and "What if" persons. They also may be perceptive, full of ideas, persistent, and tend to daydream, go beyond assigned tasks, and make up games.

Creativity and intelligence are different, yet related. The threshold notion suggests that over the wide range of intelligence, creativity and intelligence are moderately related; above a threshold IQ of about 120, they are independent. Personality and motivational traits influence which bright students will be creatively productive.

Wallach and Kogan argued that if creativity tests are untimed and administered in a friendly, gamelike atmosphere, the correlation between creativity scores and IQ scores will disappear.

Creative abilities include more than fluency, flexibility, originality, and elaboration. Some examples: sensitivity to problems, the ability to define a problem well, the ability to resist premature closure, and visualization, regression, metaphorical thinking, evaluation, analysis, synthesis, transformation, concentration, and logical-thinking abilities. Some personality traits may be considered abilities (humor, curiosity, artistic interest, etc.).

The creative process may be viewed, first, as stages in creative problem solving. Wallas's four stages included preparation, incubation, illumi-

Solutions to Visual Puzzle.

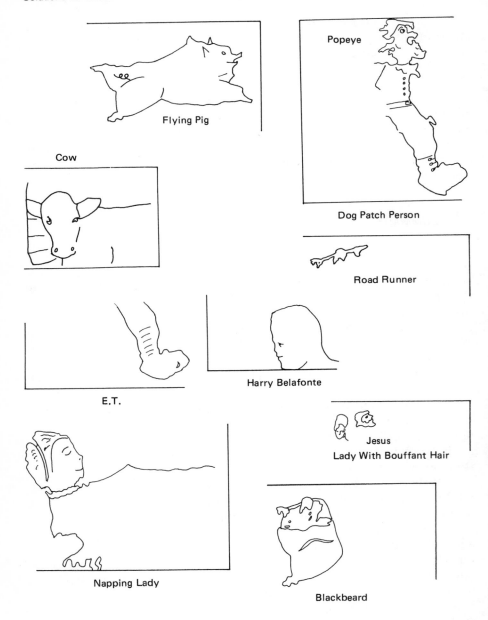

Flying Pig

Popeye

Dog Patch Person

Cow

Road Runner

E.T.

Harry Belafonte

Jesus
Lady With Bouffant Hair

Napping Lady

Blackbeard

nation, and verification. Fabun inserted desire, manipulation, and intimation. A two-stage model included a big-idea stage followed by an
elaboration and development stage.

Parnes's Creative Education Foundation stages included fact finding,
problem finding, idea finding, solution finding, and acceptance finding.
With practice, these can become habitual, creative responses to problems
and opportunities.

Keating's four components of socially relevant creativity included
content knowledge, divergent thinking, critical analysis, and communication skill.

The creative process also may be viewed as a change in perception,
seeing new idea combinations, new relationships, new meanings, new implications, and new applications. This sudden change in perception is not
well understood, leading to speculations of possible roles of ESP or supra-
rational thinking.

Creative dramatics seeks to strengthen divergent thinking, imagination, problem solving, and sensory awareness, as well as discovery and control of emotions and the physical self, humor, self-confidence, and
empathic understanding. There are three main categories of activities,
including movement exercises, sensory and body awareness exercises, and
pantomime and playmaking.

11

CREATIVITY II:
Training Creative Thinking and Creative Teaching

CAN CREATIVITY BE TAUGHT?

Attitudes, Abilities, Techniques

The authors frequently are asked a key question: Can creativity be taught or are you born with it? The answer is an unequivocal yes and yes. Some people, of course, are born with creative genius, along with other necessary talents and drives we do not thoroughly understand. The names of DaVinci, Picasso, Curie, Edison, and Einstein come to mind. No amount of creativity training can elevate the average person to such lofty creativeness.

However, it is also absolutely true that everyone's personal creativity can be improved. In the case of gifted and talented children, efforts to strengthen their creative abilities—and get them to use the abilities they were born with—sometimes have dramatic effects.

If we pause for a moment and reflect on what actually is taught in creativity courses—elementary, secondary, college, and professional—the answer is not too mysterious. All the suggestions in this chapter for stimulating creative thinking will be aimed at strengthening *attitudes* conducive to creativity, *abilities* that seem to underlie creative potential, and *techniques* for producing new idea combinations.

First, creative *attitudes* are taught in every program, and for good reason. To think creatively a person must be consciously aware of creativity. He or she must value creative thinking, appreciate novel and far-fetched ideas, be open-minded and receptive to the zany ideas of others, and be mentally set to produce creative ideas; in short, the person must be *creativity conscious*. Improving creative attitudes and awarenesses probably is 90 percent of the problem of stimulating people of any age to think more creatively. Sometimes, the attitude changes resulting from creativity training produce significant changes in personality traits and dispositions related to creativity (Davis and Bull, 1978; Parnes, 1978).

Second, creative *abilities* and skills can be strengthened via practice in much the same way that practice and repetition will improve violin playing and arithmetic ability. The practice may include mind-stretching divergent-thinking exercises, some of which are similar to items from divergent-thinking tests (for example, thinking of unusual uses, improvements for products, and outcomes of "What would happen if . . . ?" events). Guilford (1962), in fact, recommended that creativity might be strengthened by giving exercises similar to the tests that measure those abilities. The Guilford/Meeker *Structure of Intellect* approach includes creativity exercises designed to remediate specific creative abilities shown by the *SOI-Learning Abilities* tests to be weak. Samples of the many types of classroom creativity exercises will be itemized later.

Perhaps best of all, involvement in activities requiring creative thinking—art, design, writing, filmmaking, science, theatre—are intuitively sound ways to build fluency, flexibility, elaboration, visualization, metaphorical thinking, problem definition, evaluation, and other creative problem-solving abilities and skills.

Third, creative thinking *techniques* for producing novel idea combinations may be developed. Davis (1981a, 1983a, 1984) divided these into (1) *personal* creative-thinking techniques—unique, individual strategies that are developed and used by every creatively productive person; and (2) *standard* creative thinking techniques, taught in every creativity course and most books on the topic (for example, Davis, 1983a; Feldhusen and Treffinger, 1980; Shallcross, 1981), including at least one children's workbook (Davis and DiPego, 1973). For example, brainstorming, the grandfather standard creative-thinking technique, not only helps thinkers to produce new ideas and idea combinations, but fosters creative attitudes and strengthens divergent-thinking abilities and skills as well. Both personal and standard creative-thinking techniques will be described shortly.

THE MODEL AUTA

Davis's model *AUTA* (Awareness, Understanding, Techniques, and self-Actualization; Davis, 1982, 1983a; Davis and O'Sullivan, 1980) is a four-step taxonomy of creative development that describes (1) steps in becoming a more creative person, and therefore (2) an instructional sequence for teaching for creative development. It also (3) imposes some structure on the amorphous topic of "creativity." The model thus outlines a reasonable sequence of content and activities aimed at strengthening creative attitudes and awarenesses, abilities and skills of creative thinking, and creative-thinking techniques.

Awareness.   The first step in becoming a more creative person involves increasing one's creativity consciousness. Most students simply do not think about creativity or becoming more creative. The learner must come to appreciate the importance of creativity to one's personal growth—for developing one's talents, for self-actualization, for mental health, and for simply getting more out of life. The learner also should grasp the role of creative innovation in the history of civilization and in solving society's present and future problems. Indeed, without creative innovation people still would be living in caves during their short, sick lives, scrounging for roots and berries and clubbing slow rodents for breakfast.

Understanding.   Any creativity training will have more impact and make a more lasting impression if students are helped to understand the topic of creativity. There is a large body of information that contributes to this understanding. Despite its importance, the limited space and scope of Chapters 10 and 11 have permitted us only to scratch the proverbial surface. Some main topics are:

> Characteristics of creative people
> The nature of creative ideas as modifications and combinations of other ideas
> The nature of the creative process
> Creative abilities
> Theories of creativity
> Tests of creativity
> Creative thinking techniques
> Creativity exercises, methods, and materials

The lives of well-known creative people provide one useful way to teach about desirable creative attitudes, habits, and lifestyles. And the *Torrance Tests of Creative Thinking* may be used as the basis for a lesson in the meaning of *fluency, flexibility, originality,* and *elaboration* and their importance in creative thinking. Further information regarding the above topics may be found in Davis (1983a), Feldhusen and Treffinger (1980), Parnes (1981), Shallcross (1981), Torrance (1962, 1979), Treffinger (1980), and Treffinger, Isakson, and Firestien (1982).

Techniques.   There are personal creative thinking techniques, developed and used by every creatively productive person, and there are well-known standard techniques, both of which will be elaborated in the next section of this chapter.

Actualization.   This final step in the model AUTA is the desired outcome of the entire sequence. A more creative student is more self-actualized—a more capable, confident, productive, well-adjusted, empathic, democratic, and forward-growing person who is using his or her capabilities to become what he or she is capable of becoming. In the words of Carl Rogers (1962), "The mainspring of creativity appears to be the same tendency which we discover so deeply as the curative force in psychotherapy—man's tendency to actualize himself, to become his potentialities." Maslow (1971) defined self-actualized creativity as the mentally healthy tendency to live all aspect of one's life in a flexible, open, and creative fashion.

In one study of college students (Buckmaster and Davis, in press), scores on the *How Do You Think?* inventory (Davis, 1975), which measures creative personality and biographical characteristics, were compared with scores on Buckmaster's *Reflections On Self and Environment* (ROSE), which was designed to assess Maslow's (1954, 1968) fifteen characteristics of the self-actualized person. The correlation was a solid .73—the two tests were identifying the same people. Moreover, scores on both tests were statistically correlated with creativity ratings of students' creativity projects.

PERSONAL CREATIVE THINKING TECHNIQUES

This and the following section will elaborate on the third step of the model AUTA: personal and standard techniques of creative thinking. *Personal* techniques are methods that are developed and used, consciously and unconsciously, by every creative person regardless of the subject or content of his or her creations. This topic lies at the core of central questions such as "Where do ideas come from?" and "What is the nature of the internal creative process?"

When readers become sensitive to the notion of personal creative thinking techniques, they will see them continually. Seeing a movie, a paperback book, or a new consumer product, or hearing a new hit tune, the reader will sometimes understand where the author, inventor, or composer found the idea. The particular innovation may be a recognizable spin-off, a modification, or a combination, or the innovator may have extracted the idea from a news event, an historical event, an earlier book or movie, and so on.

An important point is that every one of the *standard* techniques described in the next section originated as a personal creative-thinking technique—a method that some creative person used in his or her day-to-day high-level creative thinking. The standard techniques are unconscious methods made conscious, knowable, and teachable.

To present the flavor of personal creative-thinking techniques, let's look at a few familiar examples. In science, Einstein used what he called "mental experiments." For instance, he would fantasize a trip through space in an elevator at the speed of light in order to produce new perceptions, new relationships, and new ideas.

In art we find recurrent subjects and styles with every famous painter, reflecting their personal creative thinking techniques. Picasso, for example, is known for his African, harlequin, blue, and pink (rose) periods, during which his paintings were inspired by particular themes. He also deliberately disassembled faces and other pictorial elements and put them back together in more original arrangements. Paul Gauguin painted South Pacific natives in his unique style, time and again. Edgar Degas is noted for his graceful ballerinas. Renoir's trademark is his soft pastel, female subjects and still lifes. Georges Seurat used a "dot" painting style (pointillism), often with water and sailboats as subjects. The unique style of Toulouse-Lautrec's heavily outlined, tall and cartoonlike subjects in evening dress is also familiar. Maurice Utrillo used simple street scenes. Even the great Leonardo da Vinci reportedly wandered Italian streets, sketchbook in hand, to locate interesting faces for his painting *The Last Supper.* Throughout art history, ideas for paintings have been taken from mythology, the Bible, or historical events.

In music, all of Franz Liszt's *Hungarian Rhapsodies* were drawn from the folk tunes of Hungarian gypsies. The waltzes of Brahms and Beethoven were also built on folk melodies, and Tchaikovsky, too, developed folk tunes into symphonies. Each small section of Moussorgsky's symphony *Pictures at an Exhibition* was inspired by a painting by his friend Victor Hartmann. The most famous theme from Ferde Grofé's marvelous *Grand Canyon Suite* came from clopping mule hooves.

Political cartoonists continually use a deliberate metaphorical thinking strategy for finding ideas. They take ideas from one situation and transfer them to a new situation, namely, whatever political topic they wish to comment on. For example, when the movie *Shogun* was first televised, one cartoonist used a "Shonuff" theme to criticize Jimmy Carter; in rerun two years later, *Shogun* was used to comment on "Reagun's" MX missile ideas. A picture of Leonid Brezhnev as Darth Vader, with the caption "The

Empire Strikes Back," was used to comment on the Russian clamp down on strikes and demonstrations in Poland.

The same deliberate metaphorical technique is used in the daily cartoon section of the newspaper. *Alley Oop,* for example, in recent years built stories around *Alice in Wonderland,* Count Dracula, escalation in the arms race, football, American politics, and the Olympics.

Columnist-humorist Art Buchwald also uses deliberate metaphorical thinking—borrowing ideas and concepts from one area and using them to make a humorous political comment in another. In one column he borrowed ideas from TV soap operas and used them to discuss a new "Seamy, Steamy Tale of Power and Greed—The Budget of the United States Government Fiscal Year 1984":

> I couldn't put it down. I kept turning the pages to see what government programs would be cut next. It's more frightening than *Rosemary's Baby.*
> You mean it's a thriller?
> It's more of a whodunit. Or, specifically, who's doing it to whom. It's about money and power, the struggle for survival, death and taxes and man's fate in a world he never made.
> Any sex?
> The military chapters are very sexy, particularly the love scenes between the President of the United States and the new weapons that the Pentagon has seduced him into buying.
> You mean the President is in bed with the military-industrial complex?
> All through the book! Some of the scenes are so hot that Tip O'Neill has threatened to ban the book in Boston . . . *

Toward the end of the sixteenth century, Holinshed's *Chronicles,* a history book, was published. William Shakespeare used it extensively as a source of ideas for *Macbeth, Henry IV, Henry V, Henry VI, Richard II,* and others. He drew from Plutarch's *Lives* to write *Antony and Cleopatra* and *Coriolanus. Troilus and Cressida* came from various accounts of the story of Troy. Astronomer and science fiction writer Isaac Asimov (1978) details other of Shakespeare's sources in *Asimov's Guide to Shakespeare.* Scholars in literature do studies to trace the sources of Shakespeare's ideas and the ideas of other classic writers.

Contemporary writers continue to use identifiable procedures to inspire novels and movies. For example, Truman Capote used a Midwest murder as the inspiration for *In Cold Blood.* The Normandy invasion was the basis of the novel and movie *The Longest Day;* Pearl Harbor was the source of ideas for *Tora, Tora, Tora!* and *From Here to Eternity.* Another movie, *All the President's Men,* was based on Watergate. In a recent interview the screenwriter of *High Noon* confessed that the inspiration for his award-

---

*Reprinted by permission of Art Buchwald.

winning suspense western came from the intimidation of writers and actors in Hollywood by organized crime in the 1950s. Countless other ideas for movies and novels have been found by looking at Greek and Roman history (*I, Claudius,* for example), Biblical history (*Moses*), American history (*Gone with the Wind*), Egyptian history (*Cleopatra*), and so on. In fact, it would be rare to find a major novel or Hollywood movie that did *not* have a clear metaphorically related source, if the author were asked.

The most successful Hollywood motion pictures to date comprise the *Star Wars* series—based partly on an effective personal creative thinking technique used by the creator George Lucas. While writing the script for *Star Wars* Lucas read books on mythology. Said Lucas in a *Time* magazine interview, "I wanted *Star Wars* to have an epic quality, and so I went back to the epics." Thus we find a young man who must prove his manhood to himself and to his father; who rescues a princess in distress; who has an older and wiser mentor (actually two, Ben Kenobi and Yoda); and who battles with a villain, Darth Vader. Some western movies have been built deliberately around the same principles.

Professional comedians also use personal creative-thinking techniques, both for their unique type of humor and for their original delivery. Norm Crosby uses malapropisms: In one commercial he is "very enameled" of his Light Beer; he also has a "great affliction" for Johnny Carson. The comedian Don Rickles insults people, using the same insults again and again ("Shut up dummy, you're makin' a fool of yourself!").

Rodney Dangerfield's "I don't get no respect" theme makes him one of the most successful American comedians. He continually puts himself down: "When I was born the doctor told my mother, 'I did everything I could, but he's gonna' be okay.' " "Dad took me to the zoo. They said, 'Thanks for bringing him back.' " "I couldn't play hide-and-seek 'cause nobody wanted to find me!" "Once I swallowed a can opener. Mom said, 'Don't worry, we got another one.' "

The list of personal creative-thinking techniques could be endless. The main point is that *ideas come from somewhere.* Photographers develop pet techniques and subjects; clothes designers and architects extract ideas from museums and history books; rock musicians have borrowed from classic standard tunes; and so on.

Developing Personal Creative Thinking Techniques

There are several ways students may be encouraged to develop personal creative thinking techniques. First, students should understand how even extraordinarily creative people have "found" ideas. This demystifies creativity and helps convince students that they also can legitimately build upon existing ideas without feeling "uncreative." After all, if William

Shakespeare, Franz Liszt, George Lucas, and Art Buchwald can borrow plots, tunes, and ideas, so can they. Many young writers, artists, and composers are erroneously convinced that their ideas must be 100-percent original and never inspired by a recognizable source.

Second, some recurrent personal creative thinking techniques may be teachable. For example, some techniques that have been in the literature include:

1. Deliberately looking for metaphors
2. Adapting solutions from similar types of problems
3. Modifying, combining, and improving present ideas
4. Starting with the goal and working backward to deduce what is required to reach that goal
5. Beginning with an "ideal" or "perfect" solution—such as having the problem solve itself—and again working backwards to design a creative solution
6. Asking yourself how the problem will be solved 25, 100, or 200 years from now

Third, since personal creative thinking techniques develop (1) in the course of doing creative things or (2) from instruction by people who use and understand such techniques, G/T students should become actively involved in such inherently creative activities as art, photography, creative writing, acting, journalism, independent science, or other activities requiring creative thinking and problem solving.

The necessary creative involvement certainly would come from self-directed projects of the Renzulli Type III variety. Many enrichment plans do this. Pullout and mainstreaming strategies frequently include independent, creative projects. Special classes, special schools, and Saturday and summer programs also foster the development of personal creative thinking techniques if they permit independent creative work, preferably guided by an expert. Mentorships may be the best approach, since they involve many hours of direct, personal work with a creative professional. Field trips lead to exposure to experts, to creative ideas, and to sophisticated elaborations and embellishments of ideas.

Visitors can also teach personal creative thinking techniques. For example, a visiting artist program can help children understand the creative processes of a professional artist or writer. School districts in some states contract with a different visiting artist or writer each school year. In this way children have a close view of, and learning experience with, a variety of artists during their school years. University and industry researchers and other creative professionals may also be invited to share their experiences related to creative discoveries and creative thinking. Creative artists and scientists serve as real-life models of creativity to whom gifted children are rarely exposed.

STANDARD CREATIVE THINKING TECHNIQUES

There are several well-known methods for producing new ideas and new idea combinations which, as we mentioned, are taught in most university and professional creativity training courses. The strategies also may be taught to middle and high school students, and to gifted and talented elementary students. One lively workbook, *Imagination Express* (Davis and DiPego, 1973), incorporates standard creative thinking techniques into a fantasy story about a Saturday subway ride from Kansas City to Pittsburgh to Dublin to Tokyo to Santa Monica and back. It also teaches good creative attitudes and awarenesses. The workbook was written for approximately the seventh-grade level, but older students (including teachers) and younger students seem to benefit as well.

It is worth repeating that every "standard" creative thinking technique began as a personal technique which some perceptive person identified, explained, and thus made conscious and teachable.

Brainstorming

In the case of brainstorming, it was Alex Osborn, cofounder of the New York advertising agency Batten, Barton, Dursten and Osborn and founder in 1954 of the Creative Education Foundation, who identified the conditions and listed the rules for brainstorming. The main principle is *deferred judgment*: Idea evaluation is postponed until later. Note that this principle implicitly creates a receptive, *creative atmosphere* and teaches good creative attitudes: receptiveness to and appreciation for novel, perhaps far-fetched ideas. Carl Rogers (1962) referred to this essential creativity ingredient as *psychological safety*. Osborn (1963) observed that any type of criticism or evaluation interferes with the generation of imaginative ideas, simply because you cannot do both at once. The purpose of any brainstorming session is to generate a long list of possible problem solutions.

Brainstorming is an effective procedure that may be used in the classroom for (1) teaching a creative thinking technique, (2) practicing creative thinking (thus strengthening attitudes and abilities), and/or (3) solving some pressing school problem, such as high absenteeism, messy school grounds, drug problems, traffic problems, bicycle thefts, raising money, selling play tickets, and so on. The four ground rules are quite simple:

1. ***Criticism is ruled out.*** This is deferred judgment, which contributes to the creative atmosphere so essential for uninhibited imaginations.
2. ***Freewheeling is welcomed.*** The wilder the idea the better. Seemingly preposterous ideas sometimes lead to imaginative yet workable solutions.

3. ***Quantity is wanted.*** This principle reflects the purpose of the session: to produce a long list of ideas, thus increasing the likelihood of finding good problem solutions.

4. ***Combination and improvement are sought.*** This lengthens the idea list. Actually, during the session students will spontaneously "hitch-hike" on each other's ideas, with one idea inspiring the next.

Variations on brainstorming include *reverse brainstorming,* in which new viewpoints are found by turning the problem around. For example: How can we *increase* vandalism? How can we *increase* the electric bill? How can we *stifle* creativity? How can we *decrease* morale? Reverse brainstorming quickly points out what currently is being done incorrectly, and implicitly suggests specific solutions. With *Stop-and-Go* brainstorming, short (about 10-minute) periods of brainstorming are interspersed with short periods of evaluation. This helps to keep the group on target by selecting the apparently most profitable directions. In the *Phillips 66* technique small groups of six brainstorm for six minutes, after which a member of each group reports either the best ideas or all ideas to the larger group.

It is easy to run a classroom brainstorming session. The teacher begins by discussing creativity and creative ideas, which leads to brainstorming as one method that stimulates creative thinking. Rules are discussed, a problem selected—such as "How can we turn the classroom into a foreign planet?" or "How can we raise money?"—and a volunteer scribe lists ideas on the blackboard. The teacher-leader's role is to frequently ask, "Anyone else have an idea?" Or the leader might specifically ask the quieter students if they have ideas they wish to contribute. If a serious problem (for example, messy hallways) is the focus, the leader can give the group 48 hours advance notice of the nature of the problem. Gifted and talented students can learn to organize and lead brainstorming sessions.

Critical to the brainstorming atmosphere is the monitoring of criticism. Children often forget themselves and begin criticizing each other's ideas, which has an immediate stifling effect on those who were just beginning to contribute. The teacher occasionally may need to inject something like, "Remember, during brainstorming we don't criticize any ideas," "The best ideas come when we welcome all ideas," or "Sometimes ideas that seem wild or silly will lead to good ideas that work."

Idea evaluation. Merely listing wild ideas does not represent the complete problem-solving process. Therefore, a brainstorming session sometimes is profitably followed by an idea evaluation session. Idea evaluation would be most important if the class intended to present the school principal (or the mayor) with some blue-ribbon solutions to a real current problem. If a teacher wishes to be systematic then, and increase students' knowl-

TABLE 11.1   Example of Evaluation Matrix

IDEAS	CRITERIA						
	Cost	Effect on Teachers	Educa- tional Effects	School Spirit Effect	Effect on Students	Effect on Community	Totals
Buy class sweatshirts	+3	+2	+1	+3	+3	+3	15
Establish school baseball team	−2	+2	0	+2	+2	+2	6
Start interclass competition	0	0	+1	+3	+2	0	6
Get new school building	−3	+3	+2	+3	+3	−2	6
Get rid of "hoods"	−3	0	−3	+1	−3	−3	−11

POSITIVE EFFECTS

+3 = Excellent
+2 = Good
+1 = Fair
 0 = Not Applicable

NEGATIVE EFFECTS

−1 = Slightly Negative
−2 = Somewhat Negative
−3 = Very Negative

edge of an organized evaluation process, the group can brainstorm evaluation criteria, such as: Will it work? Can the school afford it? Will the community (parents, principal, mayor) go for it? Is adequate time available? Are materials available? And others.

As we saw in the previous chapter, the most relevant criteria would be listed across the top of an *evaluation matrix,* the specific ideas in rows down the left side. Table 11.1 shows one evaluation matrix that was constructed to evaluate ideas brainstormed for the problem "How can we build school spirit?" The numerical row totals provide a guide to the ideas that students may wish to realistically pursue.

The use of objective criteria for the evaluation process serves many purposes. (1) It helps the class objectively evaluate ideas, of course. (2) It helps students learn to evaluate as part of the overall creative problem-solving process. (3) Evaluation requires students to consider many components of the problem. (4) The use of criteria helps prevent the evaluation from becoming a personal attack on specific children. (5) In some cases an objective evaluation can help the group explore its value system relative to the problem at hand. Finally, (6) idea evaluation can help children understand that thinking of "silly" and "far-fetched" ideas truly can result in good and practical solutions to problems.

Evaluation sessions may follow the use of any of the creative thinking techniques described in the following section.

<hr>

INSET 11.1 DEMONSTRATING EVALUATION AND DEFERRED JUDGMENT

One interesting classroom exercise demonstrates both the creative and the practical value of deferred judgment in creative problem solving. It also demonstrates an objective idea evaluation procedure.

Students are asked to list ways to improve their present classroom according to these instructions. Step 1: they must list each idea, evaluate it immediately, and cross it off if it does not seem practical. Step 2: they are to forget about the first activity and as a class make a list of all the ways they can think of to improve the classroom with no consideration given to practical evaluation. Step 3: subgroups of five or six students work together in a brainstorming session listing whatever ideas occur to them and building upon each other's ideas, again with no evaluation. Step 4 requires the use of an evaluation matrix to determine which ideas have practical value (see Table 11.1).

The class probably will find that Step 2 produced more creative and practical ideas than Step 1, and that Step 3 produced the best ideas of all.

<hr>

Attribute Listing

Robert Crawford (1978), designer of *attribute listing,* argued that, "Each time we take a step we do it by changing an attribute or a quality of something, or else by applying that same quality or attribute to some other thing." Attribute listing thus is both a *theory* of the creative process and a practical creative thinking *technique.* Following Crawford's definition, there are two forms of attribute listing: (1) attribute modifying and (2) attribute transferring. Either strategy may be used individually or with a group.

Attribute modifying. The problem solver lists main attributes (characteristics, dimensions, parts) of a problem object, then thinks of ways to improve each attribute. For example, a group of students might invent new types of candy bars or breakfast cereals by first writing important attributes (size, shape, flavor, ingredients, color, texture, packaging, nutritional value, name, and so on) on the blackboard, and then listing specific ideas under each main attribute. Particularly good combinations may be picked out of the lists of ideas. In university design engineering courses, this strategy is called the *substitution method* of design.

Attribute transferring. Here we have a pure case of metaphorical thinking—transferring ideas from one context to another. We noted above how deliberate metaphorical thinking is used by artists, cartoonists, composers, writers, and others. As one classroom application, ideas for a truly memorable parents' night or open house might be found by borrowing ideas from a carnival or circus, Disneyland, E.T., the Wild West, a funeral parlor, MacDonald's, or a *Star Wars* or *Frankenstein* movie.

Morphological Synthesis

The *morphological synthesis* technique is a simple extension of the attribute listing procedure (Allen, 1962; Davis, 1973, 1983a). Specific ideas for one attribute or dimension of a problem are listed along one axis of a matrix, ideas for a second attribute are listed along the other axis. Plenty of idea combinations are found in the cells of the matrix. One sixth-grade class invented new sandwich ideas with the morphological synthesis technique (see Figure 11.1). With a third dimension (for example, type of bread) you would have a cube with three-way combinations in each cell.

In fact, the method may be used with a half-dozen or so dimensions by listing ideas in columns. Shallcross (1981), for example, described how Fran Stryker, creator of the *Lone Ranger* radio and TV series, quickly generated ideas for 30-minute daily episodes by listing ideas for *characters, goals, obstacles,* and *outcomes* in four columns, then with eyes shut picking one idea from each column. If the idea combination seemed uninteresting, another could be found in seconds. Inspirations for short stories in a creative-writing class could be found in the same way, while simultaneously teaching students a creative thinking technique.

Idea Checklists

Sometimes, one can find a *checklist* which suggests solutions for your problem. For example, the *Yellow Pages* are often used as a checklist for problems like "Who can fix my TV?" or "Where can I get a haircut?" High school counselors have used the *Yellow Pages* for career counseling ideas. A Sears or gift store catalogue may be used to solve a gift-giving problem.

Some idea checklists have been designed especially for creative problem solving (see Davis, 1973). The most popular of these is Alex Osborn's (1963) *73-idea-spurring questions* (see Table 11.2). Take a few extra seconds as you read through this list and think of how a mouse trap, a back pack, a can of soda pop, or a poster advertising a school play might be improved by the suggestions on the list. Ideas will be elicited virtually involuntarily.

Synectics Methods

Synectics, taken from the Greek word *synecticos,* means the joining together of apparently unrelated elements. It was his work with creative-thinking groups that led William J. J. Gordon, originator of the synectics methods, to identify strategies that creative people use unconsciously. He

FIGURE 11.1 A Morphological Sandwich.

A sixth grade Milwaukee class used the morphological synthesis method to generate 121 zany ideas for creative sandwiches. Can you find a tasty combination? A revolting one? If you add a third dimension, with five types of bread, how many total ideas would you have?

New Companions to Add Zest

	Celery	Applesauce	Cucumbers	Peppers	Tomatoes	Raisins	Nuts	Dates	Bananas	Cottage Cheese	Cranberry Sauce
Liversausage											
Egg Salad											
Chicken											
Tuna Fish											
Peanut Butter											
Jelly											
Sardines											
Deviled Ham											
Corned Beef											
Salmon											
Cheese											

Standard Sandwich Favorites

Ratings of Various Spreads

Flavor	1st	2nd	3rd	4th	5th
Super Goober (Peanut Butter/Cranberry)	17	2	1	0	4
Charlies Aunt (Tuna and Applesauce)	3	16	2	2	1
Irish Eyes are Smiling (Corn Beef and Cottage Cheese)	0	0	16	2	6
Cackleberry Whiz (Hard Boiled Eggs/Cheese Whiz)	1	3	2	14	4
Hawaiian Eye (Cream Cheese and Pineapple)	3	3	3	6	9

(Header: Choices)

From G. Davis, *Creativity is Forever* (Dubuque, Iowa: Kendall/Hunt, 1983). Used with permission.

TABLE 11.2   Osborn's "73 Idea-Spurring Questions"

Put to other uses? New ways to use as is? Other uses if modified?

Adopt? What else is like this? What other idea does this suggest? Does the past offer a parallel? What could I copy? Whom could I emulate?

Modify? New twist? Change meaning, color, motion, sound, odor, form, shape? Other changes?

Magnify? What to add? More time? Greater frequency? Stronger? Higher? Longer? Thicker? Extra value? Plus ingredient? Duplicate? Multiply? Exaggerate?

Minify? What to subtract? Smaller? Condensed? Miniature? Lower? Shorter? Lighter? Omit? Streamline? Split up? Understate?

Substitute? Who else instead? What else instead? Other ingredient? Other material? Other process? Other power? Other place? Other Approach? Other tone of voice?

Rearrange? Interchange components? Other pattern? Other layout? Other sequence? Transpose cause and effect? Change pace? Change schedule?

Reverse? Transpose positive and negative? How about opposites? Turn it backward? Turn it upside down? Reverse roles? Change shoes? Turn tables? Turn other cheek?

Combine? How about a blend, an alloy, an assortment, an ensemble? Combine units? Combine purposes? Combine appeals? Combine ideas?

made these strategies conscious and teachable in a form for adults (Gordon, 1961) and for children (Gordon and Poze, 1980). His workbooks, *Making It Strange, Books 1–4* (Gordon, 1974), give children first-hand experience with the fascinating synectics problem-solving methods of direct analogy, personal analogy, and fantasy analogy.

Direct analogy.   With this method the thinker is asked to think of ways that similar problems are solved in nature by animals, birds, flowers, weeds, bugs, worms, lizards, and so on. For example, ideas for conserving energy could be found by asking how animals keep warm in winter.

In a creativity workshop for the elderly, many expressed concern for their personal safety. With a synectics approach the problem became, "How do animals, plants, birds, etc., protect themselves, and how can these ideas help the elderly?" The list included spray cans of skunk scent, slip-on fangs and claws (mildly poisonous), a compressed air can that screams, an electronic transmitter that secretly "yells" for police assistance, traveling only in groups, camouflage or disguises (for example, wearing a police uniform), and others.

Personal analogy.   Imagine you are a piece of candy sitting quietly with your candy friends on the shelf of the local drugstore. A little boy walks in, places two cents on the counter and points at you. How do you feel? What are your thoughts? Describe your experiences for the next fifteen minutes. The purpose of such exercises, similar to the "be the thing" exercises in Gordon's *Making It Strange* workbooks, is to give elementary students practice with the *personal analogy* creative thinking technique. With this strategy, new perspectives are found by becoming part of the problem, usually a problem object. What would you be like if you were a highly efficient can opener? A captivating short story? A truly exciting and valuable educational learning experience for children?

Fantasy analogy.   Problem solvers think of fantastic, far-fetched, perhaps ideal solutions which can lead to creative yet practical ideas. Gordon sees fantasy analogy as a type of Freudian wish fulfillment. For example, one can ask how to make the problem solve itself: How can we make the hallways keep themselves clean? How can we get parents to want to attend open house? How can we get the School Board to want to give us a new instructional materials center? Some years ago, design engineers probably asked: How can we get refrigerators to defrost themselves, make their own ice cubes? How can we get ovens to clean themselves? Automobile brakes to adjust themselves? This was employing fantasy analogy.

The synectics methods have given professional problem solvers many good ideas. Synectics, Inc., for example, helped invent NASA space suits and a space feeding system, disposable diapers, the trash masher, *Pringles Potato Chips,* an ice maker, an electric knife, an accelerated wound-healing system, and a constant speed device. The strategies can be used in the classroom either as (1) creativity exercises or (2) material for lessons in techniques of creative thinking.

CREATIVITY-STIMULATING ACTIVITIES AND EXERCISES

Involvement in Creative Activities

The G/T teacher-coordinator should be continually alert for opportunities to exercise creative thinking and problem solving in content areas. Available opportunities might also be expanded. Are music, science, and art programs adequate? Are materials and instruction available? Are creativity-stimulating learning centers available? Are students encouraged to become involved in scientific and aesthetic activities? Are community resources and mentors being used to good advantage?

Creative Thinking Exercises

There are a variety of classroom exercises that (1) acquaint students with creative thinking, thus increasing creativity consciousness and bending attitudes in a creative direction; (2) strengthen creative abilities and skills; and (3) teach creative thinking strategies. For example, any of the creative thinking techniques just discussed, particularly brainstorming, may be used in classroom creativity exercises.

There are also many types of questions and problems that implicitly require creative ideas and creative attitudes. Students can work on these as a class, perhaps following brainstorming rules, or else individually. One of the best and most involving methods is to divide students into problem-solving teams. All teams work on the same problem and then report all or the best ideas to the entire class. Students often are surprised at the different problem interpretations, approaches, and ideas from the other groups.

Some useful types of creativity exercises are:

1. The *"What would happen if . . . ?"* future projection in which students list consequences for unlikely events. The events may be imaginary or potentially real. What would happen if each person had an eye in the back of his or her head? If dinosaurs roamed America? If elves stole everyone's buttons? What would America be like if the British had won the Revolutionary War? If Lincoln had remained a log splitter? If the earth shifted and Brooklyn became the North Pole? What would we do without numbers? Automobiles? Music? TV? Peanut butter? MacDonald's? Football?

2. Thinking of *product improvements* is another type of open-ended question. Students may be asked to think of improvements for any product or process—pencils, desks, jogging shoes, classrooms, bicycles, pianos, school lunches, soda pop, ice cream treats, computers, a bathtub, and so on.

3. Thinking of *unusual uses* for common objects is probably the single oldest creativity test item; it also makes a good exercise. How might we use discarded rubber tires? A coat hanger? Empty plastic gallon milk containers? A wooden stick? A sheet of paper? Leftover and wasted cafeteria food?

4. Posing *problems and paradoxes* is intrinsically interesting and challenging. A problem may require a solution, or a puzzling situation may require a logical explanation. The problem may be realistic or fanciful. For example: How can bicycle thefts be eliminated? How can the lunch menu be improved? What can we buy for parents for Christmas/Hanukah for five dollars? How can the school (family) light bill be reduced. How can our health be improved? What can be done for Mr. Smith, a former night watchman who is 50 years old, out of work, and has no special skills? How could we remove a stubborn elephant from the living room? How can we keep gremlins from stealing the melons from the melon patch? How can the three bears prevent burglaries?

Here are some examples of problems requiring explanations: The principal suddenly cancels recess. Why? The grass behind billboards in pastures is often lush. Why? Ten paintings were discovered missing from the art gallery, but there was no sign of a break-in. How could they have disappeared?

5. *Design problems* are a category by themselves. Students can be asked to design an ideal school, an airplane for hauling nervous kangaroos, a better lawn mower, more functional clothes, safer ways to travel, a more efficient way to serve lunch in the cafeteria, new sandwiches or other treats for MacDonald's, a better mouse trap, and so on.

A workbook by Helman and Larson (1979) lists hundreds of creativity-stimulating problems, exercises, and projects. One of the authors' favorite creative writing exercises involves giving students an unusual newspaper headline and then asking them to write the story. The tabloids found in grocery stores are full of ideas. For example, the front page of the January 4, 1983, issue of *Weekly World News* included these winners:

Magic Bracelet Turns Skinny Kid Into a Battling Superman

Hungry Man Jailed—For Eating His Neighbor's Dog

Soviets Plan Beast Army—By Mating Men to Animals (The permutations here are endless!)

Heartbroken Woman Sobs: "I Was Fired for Being Too Ugly"

Bride Runs Off With Best Man: "We Planned Our Getaway at the Reception," Says Happy Couple.

Shallcross (1981) itemized a variety of exercises that could be integrated into specific subject matters. For example:

1. Sculpt something using leaves, rocks, paste, and a paper bag (art).
2. List ways to get children to enjoy brushing their teeth (health).
3. Invent a one-step "meal-in-one" (home arts).
4. Plan a mystery or soap opera series using the morphological synthesis approach (language arts).
5. Think of new ways to measure time, water, air, or height (math).
6. Have someone strike three notes on a piano. Use them as the basis for a melody (music).
7. Invent stretching exercises for joggers (physical education).
8. Brainstorm ways endangered species might be preserved (science).
9. Brainstorm ways different cultures could learn to understand each other better (social studies).

Treffinger, Isakson, and Firestien (1982) described creative-thinking exercises at three levels resembling the Renzulli (1977) Enrichment Triad Model and the Feldhusen and Kolloff (1981) three-stage enrichment model. At Level I, *Divergent Functions,* some comparatively simple exercises Treffinger et al. recommended were:

Brainwriting, which is like brainstorming except that participants write down their ideas.

Slip writing, another written brainstorming procedure in which students think of ideas for a problem, write one idea on each card, and then share the cards with other participants who look for promising combinations or applications.

Five senses, in which nonverbal ideation is stimulated, for example, by music, photos, slides, films, or odors.

Opportunity search, in which (1) new opportunities and ideas are sought, followed by (2) an evaluation of the need for each opportunity or idea, and then (3) the production of more ideas for how specifically to respond to the needs (DeBono, 1980).

Webbing (idea networks), used to identify topics and subtopics for reading or research. Beginning with a general category word (for example, space), students associate progressively more specific topics and subtopics (for example, rockets, other planets, UFOs, conditions for life).

Level II, *Complex Thinking and Feeling Processes,* included, for example:

Confronting the unexpected, which involves working on puzzles, paradoxes, apparent contradictions, or issues that involve tension, stress, or conflict.

Itemized responses, an evaluation procedure in which thinkers first list useful aspects of an idea and then their concerns or problems with the idea.

Problem redefinition, aimed at having students produce and consider alternative problem definitions, involves asking "Why?" after each problem statement is given. Each successive statement usually is a broader definition than the preceeding one (Dillon, 1982).

Excursion, based on synectics methods (Gordon, 1961; Prince, 1970), involves selecting a setting entirely unrelated to the problem at hand, free associating ideas related to that setting, then relating or "force fitting" the ideas to the original problem.

Because the Treffinger et al. Level III activities, *Involvement in Real Problems and Challenges,* is very similar to the Renzulli Type III enrichment and stage three of Feldhusen's enrichment model, the strategy need not be duplicated here (see Chapter 8). The teacher's role in Level III activities is, for example, to expose students to many possibilities for projects, help them find material and human resources, provide constructive criticism, and help find outlets and audiences for projects.

The possibilities for mind-stretching exercises truly are endless—with a little brainstorming by the G/T teacher.

Implementation Charting

Thus far, this chapter mainly has emphasized the earliest steps of the complete creative problem-solving process—the production of new and different ideas—with the goal of strengthening appropriate creative attitudes and abilities and perhaps teaching creative thinking techniques. However, when students work on "real-life" problems and projects, the ideas also must be evaluated and implemented. Gifted children need to be encouraged to develop the skills and confidence to carry through their creative ideas.

Implementation charting will help gifted children see implementation as the realistic next step in creative thinking, following the generation of ideas and the evaluative selection of one or more workable solutions. With implementation charting students are taught to prepare a chart specifying both (1) the persons responsible for implementing components of the idea(s), and (2) a completion deadline. For example, if the best idea for increasing school spirit was to sell school sweatshirts, then an implementation chart such as the one in Table 11.3 might be suitable.

Note also, there is more than one role of *evaluation* in creative problem solving. In the present example, the initial ideas were evaluated in an evaluation matrix (Table 11.1). However, after the idea(s) are selected and the project implemented, another evaluation must determine if the project was effective and successful and if it should be continued. Perhaps the group will be ready to implement a second idea, for example, for encouraging school spirit.

TABLE 11.3   Implementation Chart for Selling School Sweatshirts

ACTIVITY	PERSON RESPONSIBLE	TIME FOR IMPLEMEN-TATION
1. Ask permission for project	Ron	March 10
2. Design sweatshirt	Mary, Ruth	March 15–20
3. Approve design	Student Council	March 22
4. Review possible sweatshirt sellers	Barb, John	March 15–20
5. Make recommendation to Student Council	Student Council	March 22
6. Order sweatshirts	Barb, John	March 24
7. Organize student sales campaign	Tom, Mary & Allan	March 22–31
a. Posters	Bob, Andy	March 25
b. Article in school newspaper	Alice	March 25–31
c. Article in community newspaper	Allan	March 28
8. Actual beginning of sales	Tom, Mary & Allan	April 10
9. Student Sweatshirt Day	Ron, Mary & Ruth	April 12
10. Evaluation of success of project	Original Brainstorming Group	April 20

CREATIVE TEACHING AND LEARNING

Torrance (1977b) stated that " . . . people fundamentally prefer to learn in creative ways." These ways include exploring, manipulating, questioning, experimenting, risking, testing, and modifying ideas. Said Torrance, learning creatively takes place during the processes of sensing problems, deficiencies, or gaps in information; formulating hypotheses or guesses about a problem; testing the hypotheses, revising and retesting the hypotheses; and then communicating the results. He explained that problems arouse tension, thus motivating the learner to ask questions, make guesses, and test the adequacy of the guesses, correcting errors and modifying conclusions if necessary. Further, when something is discovered we are inspired to " . . . want to tell someone about it." Creative learning, observed Torrrance, is superior to "learning by authority." While creative learning strengthens such abilities as problem sensitivity, fluency, flexibility, originality, elaboration, and redefinition, learning by authority seems to strengthen primarily memory and logical reasoning (Torrance, 1977b).

Torrance (1981a; 1981c; Torrance and Myers, 1970) takes a marvelous humanistic approach to creative development with his descriptions of creative teaching. It goes beyond merely stimulating imagination and problem solving. Indeed, the core purpose of creative teaching is to create a "responsive environment," and one of his principles is "Love children and let them know it."

Some recommendations for creative teaching included the following:

Maintain high teacher enthusiasm.
Accept individual differences, for example, in preferred ways of learning, learning rates, faults, and so forth.
Permit the curriculum to be different for different pupils.
Communicate that the teacher is "for" rather than "against" the child.
Encourage and permit self-initiated projects.
Support students against peer conformity pressures.
Allow or encourage a child to achieve success in an area and in a way possible for him or her.
Respect the potential of low achievers.
Do not be blinded by intelligence test scores; they do not tell the whole story.
Do not let pressure for "evaluation" get the upper hand.
Encourage divergent ideas; too many "right" ideas are stifling.
Do not be afraid to wander off the teaching schedule and try something different.

Torrance (1981a, 1981c) summarized some signs that creative learning is taking place, which partly represent benefits of creative teaching and learning. These include improved motivation, alertness, curiosity, concentration, and achievement; a charged atmosphere "tingling with excitement"; the combining of activities that cut across curriculum areas, and a continuity of activities, one leading to another; improved communication of ideas and feelings; a "boldness" in ideas, drawings, stories, and so on; improved self-confidence; improved creative growth and creative expression; and importantly, a reduction of unproductive behavior, behavior problems, hostility, vandalism, and apathy, and an increase in enthusiasm about school and learning and improved career aspirations.

Creativity training and creative teaching can indeed make a difference, for gifted, normal, and even troubled students.

SUMMARY

Teaching creativity includes teaching creative attitudes, strengthening creative abilities, and helping students develop creative thinking techniques.

The model AUTA, which outlines steps in becoming more creative, emphasizes the development of an *Awareness* of the importance of creative development, an *Understanding* of the topic of creativity, developing *Techniques* for finding ideas and, the goal of it all, becoming more *self-Actualized*.

Personal creative thinking techniques are methods developed and used by creative people in every arena of creative endeavor. Students may be helped to develop personal creative thinking techniques by teaching them to look for metaphors, work backwards from the goal, look for ideal solutions, ask how the problem will be solved in the future, and others. Involvement in creative activities, preferably directed by creative mentors, is a highly desirable way to teach personal creative thinking techniques.

Standard creative thinking techniques are taught in virtually every creativity course and training program. Brainstorming is based on deferred judgment, which contributes to a creative atmosphere. Osborn's brainstorming rules include: (1) no criticism or evaluation is allowed, (2) wild ideas are encouraged, (3) many ideas are wanted, and (4) participants should look for idea combinations and improvements. Variations include reverse brainstorming, stop-and-go brainstorming, and the Phillips 66 procedure.

When leading a brainstorming session, discuss the rules, present the problem, encourage quieter participants, and monitor criticism. Give advance notice when the topic is a serious one. The creative thinking session may be followed by idea evaluation, perhaps using a systematic evaluation matrix.

Attribute listing includes (1) modifying important problem attributes and (2) transferring attributes from one situation to another (metaphorical thinking). Morphological synthesis is a matrix approach to generating ideas. Idea checklists may be used to find ideas. One idea checklist designed expressly for creative problem solving is Osborn's "73 idea-spurring questions."

Three synectics methods included direct analogy, looking for ways that similar problems are solved in nature, for example, by animals, birds, worms, flowers, lizards, and so forth; personal analogy, in which new viewpoints are found by becoming a problem object or process; and fantasy analogy, in which the thinker looks for far-fetched, perhaps ideal problem solutions.

Involvement in creative activities in content areas is perhaps the best way to stimulate creative thinking, strengthen creative abilities, skills, and attitudes, and nurture creative thinking techniques.

Classroom creativity-stimulating exercises include using standard creative thinking techniques (particularly brainstorming), the "What would happen if . . . ?" approach, thinking of improvements for products, thinking of unusual uses for common objects, posing problems and paradoxes, solving design problems, writing stories to fit newspaper headlines, and many others.

Shallcross suggested specific types of exercises for various subject matters.

Treffinger and his colleagues itemized creativity exercises at three levels: divergent functions, which included comparatively simple divergent-thinking exercises; complex thinking and feeling processes, in which students deal with more complex problems, paradoxes, idea evaluations, problem restatements, and others; and involvement in real problems and challenges.

Implementation charting teaches students to plan the timing and responsibility for implementing the best idea(s) generated for a real problem.

According to Torrance, creative teaching and learning includes exploring, questioning, experimenting, testing ideas, and other activities. Creative learning includes sensing a problem, formulating hypotheses or guesses, testing, revising and retesting the hypotheses, and communicating the results.

Recommendations for creative teaching included high teacher enthusiasm, the acceptance of individual differences, encouraging self-initiated projects, looking beyond IQ scores, encouraging divergent thinking, and others.

Creative learning can result in improved motivation, achievement, creativity, self-confidence, school attitudes, and others.

12

CULTURALLY DIFFERENT AND ECONOMICALLY DISADVANTAGED CHILDREN: The Invisible Gifted

The scene is the principal's office in an inner-city elementary school. The principal, a black woman, is bright, determined, dedicated, and very professional; she has been carefully selected from among many competitors to lead a daring new approach to educating inner-city youngsters. Many of these children, with learning and social problems, had been written off as "nonlearners" by teachers in other schools. Today, several members of the school board who are interested in the goals and methods of this innovative "fundamental" school program interview the principal. Their questions begin with the who's, why's, and how's of this unique school. She answers that the school is based on certain fundamentals: carefully selected staff, parent involvement, basic skills, mastery learning, firm discipline, and homework.

Then a significant question:

"Ms. Jones, how will you teach your gifted students?" And the response:

"In this school we have no gifted children."

Culturally different and economically disadvantaged black, Hispanic, Native American, and white children living in large urban centers, in poor rural areas, and on Indian reservations rarely are identified or described as "gifted" or "talented." Their formal educational needs are assumed to be only in basic skills areas; and their adjustment to school and learning almost always involves strict discipline. Their cultural or language differences plus their lack of exposure to mainstream American culture usually combine to obscure from society the gifted children among them. These gifted minority and disadvantaged children typically proceed invisibly through school until they drop out or, with luck, graduate.

Overview

Because culturally diverse and economically disadvantaged children and adolescents rarely are identified for their giftedness, they seldom are included in G/T programs. Furthermore, because their families and peers typically do not reinforce the development of their intellectual or creative talents, they are especially in need of strong school support. This chapter will discuss (1) the special needs of these children, (2) methods for identifying them, and (3) relevant programming strategies.

SPECIAL NEEDS

In 1977 Congresswoman Shirley Chisholm introduced legislation to include funding for gifted and talented minority and culturally different children within the Elementary and Secondary Education Act. She immediately was confronted with the reality of widespread misunderstanding of these students (Chisholm, 1978). She pointed out that her white colleagues did not seem to recognize the existence of *gifted* minority children, and that they assumed that all minority children were in need of academic remediation. Her black colleagues, with little apparent support, questioned her sponsorship of programs which " . . . did nothing but promote (discriminatory) IQ testing and money for affluent white children." In her keynote address before the National Forum on Minority and Disadvantaged Gifted and Talented, Chisholm (1978) lamented the failure of our educational institutions to nurture the talents of gifted disadvantaged students. She faulted American education for (1) inadequate methods for recognizing talent among culturally different children and (2) insufficient funding to provide special programs for these children.

The late 1960s and the 1970s saw the introduction of major educational and social programs to improve opportunities for minority, culturally different, and economically disadvantaged children. The Elementary and Secondary Education Act, Head Start programs, educational TV programs for children ("Sesame Street," "Electric Company"), bilingual educational funding, and court-ordered desegregation all contributed to enhancing educational preparation and opportunities. The actual educational and social impact of these investments has been both controversial and difficult to evaluate. However, some statistics are very encouraging;

for example, the percentage of minority students who graduate from high school has increased dramatically. According to a 1977 U.S. Department of Commerce report, in the mid-1950s only 50 percent of black youth and less than 40 percent of Hispanic youth graduated from high school. By 1977, however, 76 percent of black and 58 percent of Hispanic students were graduating. For white students in a similar time period, graduation rates increased from just under 80 percent to 87 percent.

Another indication of a closing gap comes from an analysis of black-white achievement test scores from the National Assessment of Educational Progress. Burton and Jones (1982) found that during the 1970s, for youth tested at ages 9 and 13, the discrepancy between black and white achievement scores had become smaller in five major subjects: writing, science, mathematics, social studies, and reading. In areas where achievement had declined, it declined less for blacks than for whites. Burton and Jones concluded that efforts to provide equal educational opportunity may indeed have reduced black-white achievement differences. These important findings, demonstrating improvement in basic skills, may affect opportunities for the culturally different gifted learner in a very important way, to which we now turn.

Maslow's Hierarchy of Motivation and Rimm's Hierarchy of Cognitive Needs

In the context of teaching a badly underachieving but gifted eight-year-old Pima Indian boy, Scruggs and Cohn (1983) stated as a major implication of their work, "Ability training in skill deficit areas should be among the very highest of priorities. If the child is to function at top efficiency, that child must have the tools with which to work." To illustrate how the improvement of basic skills will aid the culturally different gifted child, it may be helpful to compare the gifted child's cognitive and creative growth with Maslow's (1954, 1968) hierarchical theory of human motivation (Figure 12.1).

In describing his hierarchy of human needs, Maslow explained that persons cannot grow toward self-actualization—the full development of one's capabilities and talents—unless lower-level needs are met first: those related to physiological needs, safety, belongingness and love, and esteem. The motivation to provide for these needs was entitled *deficiency* motivation mainly because the needs require frequent attention and, furthermore, if deficiencies in these needs are not removed, human behavior will come to resemble low-level, survival-based animal behavior. However, when the basic deficiency needs are met, *growth* motivation will direct behavior toward fulfilling higher-level needs, needs to know and understand, needs for order and beauty, and, at the pinnacle, needs for self-actualization.

In the same way, the "three R's"—basic reading, writing, and

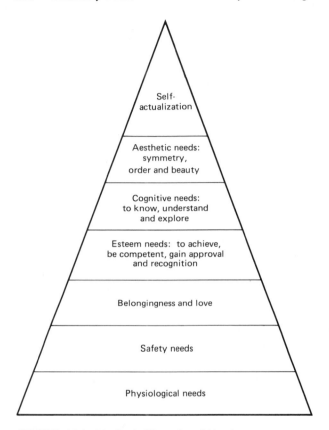

FIGURE 12.1 Maslow's Hierarchy of Needs.
A. H. Maslow, *Motivation and Personality* (New York: Harper & Row, 1954). Used with permission.

arithmetic—sit at the base of a hierarchy of intellectual needs (Figure 12.2). These *basic skills* are prerequisite to the middle levels of the hierarchy, *knowledge and its application,* and the *analysis, synthesis, and evaluation of ideas,* which in turn are required for the top level of the hierarchy, *creative production.* All gifted and talented children should be encouraged to move toward higher levels of the hierarchy. However, they cannot achieve the higher growth levels if they have not mastered the deficiency level of basic skills. If the deficiency needs are not met, the gifted child is likely to perform as a child with average or below-average abilities and therefore will not be identified as gifted.

Three real-life examples will illustrate the dramatic effects of removing educational deficiencies on cognitive and creative growth—and the "discovery" of giftedness. The first example comes from the school described at the outset of this chapter. The reader will recall that the principal

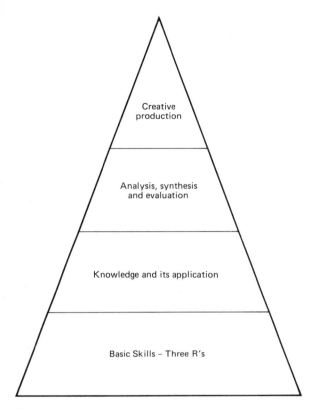

FIGURE 12.2 Rimm's Hierarchy of Cognitive Needs

had indicated in her interview that "no gifted children" were in her school. Three years later, this same principal described with pride the artwork and creative writing of students who had won city-wide contests, as well as the drama talent and the high basic-skills achievements of her "gifted" students. These talented children were there all along; they could grow toward creativity only when deficits had been removed.

A second example comes from a fifth-grade teacher in an urban parochial school that also considered itself a "fundamental" school. The student population of this school was composed almost entirely of minority children who were relatively poor. During its initial years, this school also was assumed to have no gifted children; teaching the Three R's—and doing it well—was seen as its only mission. Within two years the faculty became aware that among these children, who had been assumed to be average or below in ability, there again were intellectually and creatively gifted children. As this teacher added creative-thinking activities to her daily lesson plans, she discovered even more gifted children.

A demonstration exercise with a group of her students made this new-found creativeness clearly visible. The students, using a technique called *random juxtaposition,* were demonstrating one type of unrehearsed creative thinking. They were to select one article from a grab bag and "tell how this article was like themselves." A black child who had been a serious behavior and learning problem before he had come to the school selected an orange from the bag. On the spot, he created this humorous comparison: "This orange is like me because its skin is tough on the outside and I am tough on the outside. When you get inside the orange, it's good and sweet and I'm good and sweet on the inside too."

Yet another example, the Native American boy evaluated and taught by Scruggs and Cohn (1983), although only a single case, nicely illustrates the importance of strong training in the basics for gifted culturally different children. Eight-year-old Vernon was reading at a grade equivalent of 1.6, showed minimal single-digit addition and subtraction ability, was classified as "learning disabled," and had been required to repeat second grade. But a *WISC-R* test showed a verbal IQ of 102 and a performance IQ of 130, the latter being two standard deviations above the national mean (top 2 percent) and two and one-half standard deviations above the mean for Native Americans. A ten-week program at Arizona State University focused on remediating reading and math deficiencies, applying reading, writing, and language skills to a favorite topic (animals, particularly dinosaurs), along with activities designed to develop Vernon's general knowledge and increase his enjoyment of the university environment. In brief, his math and, especially, his reading ability improved substantially and his "prognosis for further achievement was judged to be very favorable."

These examples illustrate how reducing basic skills deficits of gifted disadvantaged youngsters is indeed an important step, but one which is preliminary to identifying these children and providing programs for them. While Vernon is a rare exception, schools often default in providing the next logical step—the G/T services themselves. After deficient learning needs are remedied, gifted disadvantaged children become more easily identifiable and could be directed toward a challenging and intellectually stimulating program. Instead, however, they typically are promoted out of the specially funded program which has served them so well and placed in a mainstream program that provides no special opportunities for developing their newly discovered abilities.

An example of one such situation comes from five years of evaluation reports of an Hispanic bilingual program in a major midwestern city. Each year the evaluator (Rimm) commended the program staff for the large gains in basic skills shown by a small proportion of the children. Each year the evaluator recommended that these fast learners be channeled into a bilingual program for gifted children. However, despite the recommendations and despite the continued needs of these youngsters, they were dropped from the program because, according to government definitions and regulations, they no longer showed basic skill deficiencies and therefore could no longer be served. Since there was little or no government money for special services for these gifted minority children, they would no longer be aided in any special way and they would be less likely to develop their higher-level cognitive abilities and move up the hierarchy of cognitive needs (Figure 12.2).

As a final comment on the needs of disadvantaged gifted students, it has been established (to no one's surprise) that early childhood experiences are critical to cognitive development and to success in school. Bronfenbrenner (1974, p. 181), for example, indicated that "while excellent early development does not guarantee lifelong excellent development, poor progress during the early years seems to be remarkably difficult to overcome." However, while a culturally impoverished childhood is hardly an asset, it does not totally prevent the later development of skills and abilities. Ogby (1981), in his cross-cultural research into the origins of human competence, concluded that early cultural deprivation does not necessarily limit the later development of skills and competencies. Said Ogby, "Given the opportunity, one does not have to be born and raised in a white middle-class home or receive 'supplementary childhood care' to become a doctor, lawyer, or professor in the Western social and economic system" (p. 416). Connolly and Bruner (1974) also argued that formal school learning is both reasonable and effective for children of widely varying backgrounds.

Surely the upward mobility and career success of thousands of disadvantaged and minority persons is strong evidence for the feasibility of overcoming unfavorable early environments. Gifted programs for disadvantaged, minority, and culturally different children can provide an important, sometimes pivotal boost to the development of undiscovered potential and can help these invisible gifted children become part of tomorrow's promise.

IDENTIFICATION

As noted earlier, minority and culturally different gifted children are not easily identified. Indeed, because of cultural bias in test instruments and other identification methods, many typical procedures actually obscure students' giftedness—by "proving" these children are *not* gifted. Because actual achievement often is not outstanding, identification must be based upon superior *potential* instead of superior performance (Scruggs and Cohn, 1983). This section will review typical identification methods and evaluate their usefulness for culturally different and economically disadvantaged populations. It also will recommend other identification procedures that in some cases may be more effective.

Intelligence Tests

High intelligence test scores on either group or individual tests are one valid way to identify intellectually gifted minority youngsters. However, an average or even low IQ score may be a poor or misleading indicator of student ability if the child comes from a culturally deprived or culturally different environment.

This issue is exceedingly complex. There are frequent and continuing debates regarding *cultural bias* in mental testing and the dust is far from settled. For example, some argue that the lower average scores of minority groups are simply evidence of discriminatory test bias. From this perspective, intelligence tests " . . . have devastating labeling—and pigeon-holing—effects . . . and they are nothing more than an Anglo yardstick designed to make whites look ingenious and blacks and other minorities stupid" (Clifford, 1981; Hoffman, 1964; Zacharias, 1977). For another view, Arthur Jensen (1976), known for his "racial differences" hypothesis, argues that intelligence tests " . . . show practically no evidence of differential culture bias . . . ," by which he means that the tests do in fact predict school success for both minority and majority cultures.

In an article entitled "The Trouble With IQ Tests," physics professor Zacharias (1977) made a number of specific complaints about intelligence tests: (1) They demand an understanding of the tester's jargon, proper guessing of what the tester wants, and tolerance for boredom; (2) test items often are ambiguous, illogical, meaningless, irrelevant to what the student knows or cares about, time wasting, overprecise or not sufficiently precise, and tricky in appearance even when they contain no tricks; and (3) the tests tend to be frightening, penalizing, damaging to a student's self-image, and misleading for tracking or assigning students to grade levels. Zacharias's opinion is clear enough.

More optimistically, Thorndike and Hagen (1977) argue for the usefulness (prediction ability) of intelligence tests, but further note that (1) the tests do not determine a person's ability, they simply suggest strengths and weaknesses; (2) they describe how a person is doing at the present time; and (3) we should consider the cultural, personal, and family background in interpreting test scores. Thus controversy around this subject continues.

Educators and psychologists—whether liberal or conservative, black or white—will agree that culturally different students are more likely than the average student to have a difficult time when taking tests of *verbal ability* (vocabulary, comprehension). These tests, of course, are based upon middle-class English. The problem is that subcultural languages such as black English (Baratz, 1974; Labov, 1974), Hawaiian pidgin, Navajo or other Native American languages are different, and so the person's linguistic structures, categories, and associations are also different. Group intelligence tests depend heavily on language ability and therefore are more likely to be biased than individually administered tests. The *WISC-R* separates subtests and IQ scores into *verbal* and *performance* (nonverbal) components, thereby allowing a bright child with deficient English to score high. Scruggs and Cohn (1983), Kryaniuk and Das (1976), and Schubert and Cropley (1972) have commented upon the large verbal/performance discrepancies of Native American children, due at least in part to language and cultural differences.

Witty (1978) noted that bias comes from other testing subtleties in addition to the language problem. For example, minority children may have lower expectations of success, lower test-taking motivation, and higher test-taking anxiety, particularly when the administrator is middle-class white. High anxiety is known to lower any type of human performance or test score (Weiner, 1980; Cronbach and Snow, 1977).

In sum, a high IQ score is convincing evidence of high intellectual ability among culturally different and poor children, just as with majority children. However, many gifted minority and economically disadvantaged children will be overlooked if intelligence tests are used as the only or the most important identification instrument. Their use is recommended, but average or low scores should be interpreted with caution, and in consideration of the language, cultural, and family background and the circumstances of testing.

Achievement Tests

Achievement tests typically are administered at regular intervals in virtually every school system, and so achievement information usually is readily available. However, while standardized achievement tests are highly recommended as an identification tool for most populations, with culturally different students they are plagued by exactly the same problems as intelligence tests. Therefore, while it is critical that achievement scores not be misused because of cultural bias, it certainly is reasonable to use them as one index of gifts and talents for minority children. As with IQ scores, children who produce high scores on achievement tests are showing good evidence of special kinds of giftedness. However, in culturally different populations, there are likely to be gifted children who may not score high on these tests despite their giftedness. Many teachers, for example, have observed children who randomly complete answers on achievement tests because of low interest and low motivation. Achievement tests alone, then, are not a sufficient measure for the identification of gifted minority and poor children.

Teacher Nominations

In many instances, teacher nominations of giftedness are a highly suspect and invalid identification strategy (Gallagher, 1966; Martinson, 1974; Rimm, 1977). Nonetheless, it continues to be the most popular identification method used. For minority and poor children, the teacher nomination method creates special hazards. "Teacher pleasers," who are neat and clean, nicely dressed, have nice manners, who speak middle-class English, and who turn in their work neatly done and on time, are likely to be named as "gifted." Other students—poor, black, Hispanic, or Native American—are automatically "disadvantaged" by many teachers in the nomination process.

On the other hand, a sensitive and caring teacher who is knowledgeable about characteristics of gifted children may, in fact, be the very best identifier of the culturally different gifted child. Furthermore, such a teacher may be able to guide and inspire a talented child who does not score high on any ability or achievement test. In the hands of a sensitive and aware teacher, then, the teacher nomination procedure can be a potentially important way to locate economically disadvantaged and culturally different gifted children.

The nomination procedure will be greatly improved by educating teachers regarding characteristics of gifted and talented minority children, some of which are different than usual characteristics of giftedness. For example, Gay (1978) researched common characteristics of gifted children and compared them to parallel characteristics of gifted black children. Her list of 11 characteristics stems from twenty years of teaching experience with black children and three years of teaching in a program for the gifted and talented (see Table 12.1).

The present authors might repeat an earlier warning in relation to Gay's item 11 in Table 12.1. Gifted black children may perform only at an average level in school because of socioeconomic, language, motivational, personal, or cultural handicaps. Therefore, students should be considered potentially gifted if they earn high ratings on many of the first ten characteristics, with or without actual "good" school achievement.

Swenson (1978) constructed a helpful list of characteristics of creativeness in a culturally different and socioeconomically deprived urban school area. Her list came from information generated by 36 teachers and was based on observed original behavior related to classwork, art, and antisocial—yes, *antisocial*—behavior (see Table 12.2). Note that because teachers are accustomed to disciplining children for antisocial behavior they may overlook the creativity exhibited in such behavior (see especially items 2, 9, 18, 23, and 24 in Table 12.2).

TABLE 12.1   Comparative Characteristics of Giftedness

CONCEPTS FROM THE LITERATURE	MANIFESTATIONS OF GIFTED CHARACTERISTICS IN GIFTED BLACK CHILDREN
1. Keen observation	Picks up more quickly on racist attitudes and practices; may feel alienated by school at an early age.
2. Interest and ability in perceiving relationships	Seeks structure and organization in required tasks; may be slow to motivate in some abstract activities.
3. Verbal proficiency, large vocabulary, facility of expression	Many black children have large vocabularies inappropriate for the school setting; thinking in black English may hinder the facility of expression in standard English.
4. Breadth of information	Difficult to determine many areas of experimental knowledge for black children.
5. Questioning, curious, skeptical	Though some ask too many "wrong" questions, some may have been conditioned to suppress questioning behavior.
6. Critical, evaluative, possessing good judgment	Explores (in perception of relationships) better or wiser choices; reads behavioral implications.
7. Creative, inventive, original	Makes up games and activities; expresses original ideas in other ways.
8. Power of concentration, long attention span	May find some have extremely strong concentration due to persistent noise in environment; may also express displeasure at having to stop an activity.
9. Independence	Need for less supervision is especially pronounced in black gifted.
10. Diversity of interests and abilities	Frequently has artistic, musical, creative writing, psychomotor, or leadership talent in addition to global intellectual ability; may neglect school work due to other interests.
11. Academic facility and strength	Good at basic school tasks; may not have expected achievement due to inferior schooling.

From J. E. Gay, "A Proposed Plan for Identifying Black Gifted Children," *Gifted Child Quarterly, 22* (1978), 353-59. Reprinted by permission.

As a final note on the teacher nomination procedure, Kranz (1981) has argued that teachers can be trained to identify and accurately rate gifted and talented students. Her *Kranz Talent Identification Instrument* was designed to assist teachers in identifying culturally diverse, minority, immigrant, and poor gifted children, as well as middle-class gifted children.

TABLE 12.2   Characteristics of Creativity in Culturally Different Students

1. Repeats activities so that he/she can do them differently.
2. Invents imaginative lies.
3. Shows that he/she sees hidden meanings, cause and effect relationships that are not obvious.
4. Writes and illustrates stories without being asked to do so as an assignment.
5. Utilizes free time by making up games or making something from paper and material scraps as opposed to more structured activities.
6. Finds many answers to a situational question.
7. Lets his/her imagination "run" when writing a story; sees more possibilities.
8. Finds activities for spare-time work with little or no additional help.
9. Decorates the border of his/her paper when doing an assignment.
10. Doesn't copy other children's ideas in art.
11. Builds and constructs things using unusual materials; uses ordinary materials in different ways.
12. Interrelates his/her experiences and draws on them with ease in discussions.
13. Doesn't let classroom events go unnoticed; questions them.
14. Accomplishes things on his/her own without help.
15. Writes poems and stories in his/her spare time.
16. Asks unusual questions during class discussions.
17 Makes up his/her own ideas when the class does a project together.
18. Suggests to the teacher alternate ways of doing an activity.
19. Is willing to risk friendship to express his/her feelings or thoughts.
20. Enthusiastic about new activities in music and art.
21. Goes beyond what is required in class assignments; makes his/her work "fancier."
22. Comes up with fresh, original comments or an unusual correct answer when there is more than one correct answer.
23. Finds new ways to get attention.
24. Tries original ways to get out of work he/she doesn't want to do.
25. Takes the initiative when he/she wants to know something; reads or asks questions without prompting.

From J. E. Swenson, "Teacher-assessment of Creative Behavior in Disadvantaged Children, *Gifted Child Quarterly,* 22 (1978), 338-43. Reprinted by permission.

Creativity Tests

Creativity tests, both divergent thinking tests and self-descriptive inventories (see Chapter 4), can be very helpful in selecting minority and culturally different children for participation in G/T programs. Specifically, they are useful in identifying highly creative children who are not motivated to achieve and who may not score high on ability or achievement tests. For both kinds of tests, there has been research with minority children that supports their use.

The *Torrance Tests of Creative Thinking* (Figural Form, particularly) have been used in several research projects with minority children. For example, Solomon (1974), in an analysis of 722 test scores, found that minority children scored higher than other children in some areas of creative thinking in grades 1 and 3. At the fifth-grade level there were no significant differences between scores of minority and other children. Torrance (1971; see also Torrance, 1977b) summarized the results of 16 different studies designed to evaluate racial or socioeconomic differences in Torrance Test scores. The results varied, with some favoring the minority children and others favoring majority children, but overall his conclusions supported the notion that there is no racial or socioeconomic bias in open-ended tests of creative thinking. Both Verbal and Figural (nonverbal) test forms apparently are good instruments for screening for creative talent regardless of racial or socioeconomic backgrounds.

As mentioned earlier, the *Group Inventory for Finding (Creative) Talent* (GIFT) and the *Group Inventory For Finding Interests* (GIFFI; Rimm, Davis, and Bien, 1982) are self-report inventories that evaluate personality characteristics, attitudes, interests, and biographical information known to be associated with creativeness. Studies by Rimm and Davis (1976, 1980) indicated that GIFT and GIFFI are valid for identifying creative potential in both rural and urban socioeconomically disadvantaged populations, as well as among specific ethnic groups, including black, Hispanic, and Native American minority students.

Chambers, Barron, and Sprecher (1980) confirmed that considerable information has been collected to show that some motivational and personality characteristics are indeed related to creativeness. They used this information to help identify gifted Mexican-American elementary students, and concluded that " . . . the abilities and traits necessary for future high-level intellectual/creative contributions appear to be similar for both culturally similar and culturally different persons."

Central to the appropriate use of divergent thinking tests such as the Torrance Tests or personality/biographical inventories is the recognition that (1) scores from a single creativity test should be combined with other information, such as teacher ratings of creativity or scores on a second creativity test, in order to reach a valid decision, and (2) low creativity test scores absolutely must never be used to eliminate children from G/T programs. Creativity tests are not perfect; there simply are too many types of creativity and creative people. However, creativity tests can identify creatively gifted children, majority and minority, who may not be identified in other ways.

Parent Nominations

As indicated earlier in this text, parents typically know a lot about their children's gifts and talents. For years they may have watched their energetic children create games and stories, invent things, build things, solve problems, create humor, and produce original artwork, writing, musical compositions, mechnical gadgets, and/or scientific products. Parents also

will be able to identify specific culturally valued giftedness—for example, caring for siblings and fixing dinner while waiting for Mom to come home from work—better than a person outside of the cultural system. Parents should indeed be given an opportunity to nominate their children for par-
/ ticipation in a G/T program.

Peer Nominations

Peers of the economically deprived or culturally different gifted child usually do not place a high value on school achievement. However, they are as aware of gifts and talents among their friends and classmates as are other young people. Bernal (1978; see also Bernal, 1979), for example, noted that members of a particular ethnic group almost always can identify the "smartest" among their peers.

In order to identify unusual intellectual, creative, or leadership ability, it may be necessary to look beyond the classroom to the out-of-school cliques and crowds. One interesting approach is to meet with students named by peers as out-of-school "leaders." These leaders can explain characteristics of culturally valued giftedness within their own peer culture (Bernal, 1979; Bruch & Curry, 1978), gifts which might qualify the person for the special opportunities of a G/T program. In inner-city areas, for example, creative approaches to self-maintenance or even survival may be reasonable arenas in which to discover giftedness. Culturally valued art and music talent, which is known to peers but not expressed in the classroom, also would be important information for the identification of giftedness. Finally, the "different" or lonely child in a minority culture, even though he or she does not value intellectual pursuit, may be considered suspect for unusual talent. The child may well have special interests and talents, suppressed due to peer pressures, that should be cultivated in a G/T program.

A Quota System

One reasonable solution to minority representation in a G/T program is the quota system. A fixed percentage of culturally different children are included in a program, based upon the percentage of those students in the school or district. The quota system assumes that the *same percentage* of minority students are gifted and talented as majority students, and should therefore be included in the program regardless of comparative test scores or grades. As one might guess, this is a much debated assumption. A central issue is the fairness to majority students who are excluded and who, according to objective criteria, appear more qualified. Although there remain problems of finding effective instruments and procedures (Hersberger and Asher, 1980), using a quota system has proven to be a successful and educationally beneficial strategy for the minority and poor children so identified (Berliner and Rosenshine, 1977; LeRose, 1978). It is a useful approach to identifying the "invisible" gifted minority children and including them in G/T programs.

PROGRAMMING FOR CULTURALLY DIFFERENT GIFTED STUDENTS

Programming for culturally diverse and socioeconomically disadvantaged gifted and talented children can include any of the curriculum options for acceleration, enrichment, and grouping described in earlier chapters. However, there are important additional components of such programs that should be given special consideration: (1) maintaining ethnic identity, (2) extracurricular cultural enrichment, (3) counseling, (4) the use of parent support groups, and (5) career education. While it may not be possible to include all of these components at the outset, it is highly desirable to eventually include *all* of them if minority gifted children are to have an optimal opportunity to develop and use their abilities.

Maintaining Ethnic Identity

The *assimilationist* position holds that upward mobility in the United States requires conformity to the language, culture, and rules of the majority Anglo population. Assimilationists further point out that minority subcultural values prevent or at least discourage integration into the majority community, and thus limit the minority person's educational and socioeconomic opportunities (Banks, 1979). Exum (1983) noted that assimilationist attitudes of black families, who wish to succeed and be accepted in the white world, not only may be pro-white, but even anti-black.

On the other hand, the *cultural pluralist* emphasizes the importance of pride in one's ethnic identity as an important part of educational and career achievement. Cultural pluralists note the close relationship of ethnic pride to the development of healthy self-concepts, and therefore consider heterogeneity and diversity to be beneficial to both individual and cultural growth. There has been no particular resolution to the basic argument between the assimilationist and cultural pluralist positions, and the debate continues to affect the education of persons in minority communities.

One main arena of controversy, for example, is found in questions related to bilingual-bicultural education programs for Hispanics, Asians, and Native Americans. Assimilationists oppose such programs, indicating that they slow the process by which the culturally different child is integrated into the mainstream culture. They claim that precious time is wasted in teaching children about their heritage and in their own language. Instead, they maintain that this time should be more profitably used for teaching basic skills—in English. However, cultural pluralists argue that the positive self-concepts derived from ethnic pride are extremely important to the minority children's educational and life achievements.

The results of research studies evaluating the effects of bilingual programs on achievement in basic skills have been mixed. The Department of Educational Research and Program Development (1974) in Milwaukee and Rimm (1977) found that children in Hispanic bilingual programs showed better achievement test gains, in both Milwaukee, Wisconsin, and St. Paul, Minnesota, than Hispanic children not in the programs. However, many other school districts have found no significant measurable advantage for students involved in bilingual programs. It already has been pointed out that the mastery of basic skills is a minimal prerequisite for the identification of giftedness. Therefore, gains in basic skills are extremely important for culturally different gifted students who may have basic-skills deficiencies. However, evaluations of bilingual education programs have not indicated a clear, unambiguous avenue for strengthening basic skills, nor a clear resolution to the assimilationist/pluralist debate.

Nonetheless, the cultural pluralist position seems innately more reasonable. People cannot totally separate themselves from their cultural backgrounds, and if they view that heritage as somehow negative or derogatory they will see themselves as second-class persons who are restricted in ability, opportunity, or both. In contrast, if a person values his or her ethnic identity, then the pride, confidence, and feelings of acceptance—all of which are basic to constructive mental health—should help motivate the person toward personal growth and achievement.

As a general principle, educators committed to providing programs for the gifted and talented necessarily support the development of diversity. That is, they intrinsically agree that each gifted child is different and therefore requires educational opportunities that fit his or her special strengths and talents. By the same reasoning, it would seem that G/T educators also should value the differences inherent in ethnic cultures, and should recognize the personal growth, mental health, and educational advantages that accompany pride in one's culture.

Banks (1979) developed an enlightening five-stage framework for understanding ethnicity and the development of ethnic identity and pride.

Stage 1, ethnic psychological captivity.   This is a stage of negative self-concepts. Individuals in this stage have internalized the negative stereotypes about their own ethnic group. They show strong out-group identification and strive vigorously to become assimilated.

Stage 2, ethnic encapsulation.   Interestingly, this stage most often characterizes members of the majority Anglo-American group. In this stage individuals interact only with members of their own ethnic group. Further, they believe their group is superior to other groups. Asian Americans, blacks, Hispanics, and Native Americans manage to exhibit ethnic pride without attacking Anglo-Americans; unfortunately, the reverse has not been true.

Stage 3, ethnic identity clarification.

Individuals in this stage have clarified intrapsychic conflicts about who and what they are and have developed positive attitudes toward themselves and their own ethnic group. This self-acceptance is a prerequisite to accepting and responding positively to others.

Stage 4, biethnicity.

Individuals in the biethnic stage possess a positive sense of ethnic identity and pride, but also have the skills needed to participate in another ethnic culture as well. While there is double membership in this stage, reference-group orientation—one's primary identity—is with one's own ethnic group. Importantly, there is no reference-group conflict in deciding where one's primary membership and allegiance should be—it is with one's own ethnic group.

Stage 5, multiethnicity.

Banks describes this stage as the idealized goal for all persons in a pluralistic society. Individuals at this stage are able to function within several ethnic sociocultural environments, and they understand and appreciate the variations and differences among the several cultures.

Banks's typology would appear to have direct application to the development of ethnic identity programs, with his Stage 5 as the goal of such programs. Gifted and talented children should not only acquire constructive and unprejudiced attitudes (as all children should), but should learn to function effectively within multiple sociocultural environments.

One might operationalize the Banks model, for example, by identifying the ethnic development stage in which most students in a classroom or G/T program are functioning, and then create an ethnic component designed to help those students move toward higher stages. For secondary and perhaps younger students, the Banks model itself could comprise an eye-opening part of the curriculum, one in which the "highest level of thinking" is in the multiethnic Stage 5.

If a G/T program serves students in a multicultural area, explicit objectives of the program should include the provision of multiethnic experiences and, for minority persons especially, the development of positive ethnic identity.

Extracurricular Cultural Enrichment

The cultural enrichment that comes from attending concerts, theatre, and ballet and visiting exhibitions, art galleries, and museums usually is provided by the families of middle-class gifted children. For the socioeconomically deprived child, these experiences typically are nonexistent or else limited to occasional school excursions. Exposure to the arts can be a valuable experience for economically deprived gifted children, as well as a good reinforcement for their participation in the gifted program. Importantly, such exposure would strongly reinforce students' own artistic or scientific efforts and talents. The individualized program for the gifted Native American boy described earlier (Scruggs and Cohn, 1983) included visits to a gallery exhibit of children's art, the Arizona State University Art Museum, the Life Sciences Zoological Exhibits, the ASU Anthropology Museum, remote sites of University Computer Services, a microcomputer laboratory, a studio of the local PBS TV station, and the ASU Instructional Resources Library.

For maximum benefit, art or science experiences should be tied to other knowledge, skill, or creative components of the G/T program. For example, historical backgrounds of particular artists, composers, or scientists would add knowledge and depth to the experiences. Also, discussions of the antecedents and idea sources of particular products or performances, or comparative evaluations of various works, would further embellish the event. "What would happen if . . . ?" or "In what other ways might we . . . ?" questions add creative and futuristic thinking to the experiences. Students also can do further research, prepare written or oral reports to the class, or write stories, newspaper columns with photos, or news reports about a person or event, and so on. Finally, as we noted earlier, field trips are the most beneficial when students are armed with specific objectives to be met and questions to be answered before they climb onto the bus.

School funding for many enrichment experiences is certain to be limited or even absent. Ideally, travel and admissions monies would be built into the original program budget. If not, local industries, businesses, or civic groups may be encouraged to fund specific trips. For the business owner, such sponsorship has the attraction of combining a small tax-deductible investment (bus costs plus admission fees) with a superb public relations opportunity (news coverage). Parents too, with advance notice, usually can put together the few dollars necessary for a good enrichment experience. Note also that, at least in medium to large cities, many museums, galleries, and university facilities are free, reducing expenses to bus fares and the required candy and soda pop.

Counseling

The support that comes from an intact and secure family structure may be less available to many economically disadvantaged or culturally different students. While family problems are not unique to students in these groups, it is true that complicated and temporary marital relationships, alcohol abuse, mobility, and other forms of stress and instability are common. According to a 1981 U.S. Census, for example, 36 percent of black families are single-parent, female-headed. Health, hygiene, and nutritional values may be minimal. Peer pressure not to achieve is strong. In some difficult circumstances, and in accord with Maslow's hierarchy (Figure 12.1), survival itself takes strong precedence over educational achievement and developing gifts and talents.

Such children need "shelters," persons to whom they can go when intellectual, social, developmental, and even safety and survival needs are threatened. This shelter should include an adult—an empathetic and professional counselor—who understands the local economic and ethnic realities and who cares about the welfare of all children. Exum (1983) recommended that counselors in minority areas should, first, increase their knowledge about the school community, for example, by becoming acquainted with population characteristics, availability of resources, availability of public transportation, community leadership styles, and the particular types of problems that frequently come to the counselor's attention. Second, Exum noted that the counselor's credibility and trustworthiness will be enhanced if he or she becomes more visible in the community, perhaps by serving on multicultural committes and by patronizing minority businesses. A third recommendation was for counselors to be flexible in scheduling appointments—using evenings and weekends—because so many parents of minority children cannot attend counseling sessions during the regular work day. Generally, said Exum, counselors should seek to build personal relationships with minority families, because "parents are much more responsive to counselors whom they believe have a genuine personal interest in their children."

The counseling shelter also should provide a peer support group comprised of other gifted children, many of whom will share similar problems. Generally, individual and group counseling and organized peer support groups are very important for the culturally different gifted child, and should be a high priority of any G/T program in a culturally diverse area.

Parent Support Groups

Although every gifted program should encourage parent education and involvement, parents of socioeconomically deprived and culturally different children have a special and greater need. These parents will become supportive and involved only if (1) they understand their child's gifts and talents and (2) they understand the opportunities available to the gifted in our society. Further, they are more likely to assist their children and contribute to the G/T program if they do not see the program as elitist (for example, for WASPs only) or as threatening. For example, parents may resist a G/T program if they believe the program will psychologically separate them from their children or cause their children to respect them less. It may be frightening to parents with little education to learn that their child is very bright and on a track toward a middle-class education that, they believe, could alienate the child from them.

On the other hand, if the program emphasizes *positive cultural identity,* fears of alienation should be reduced. Parents also will have an avenue for relating to and making contributions to the program. Parent meetings, in which the G/T program and activities are explained and the above problems addressed, and in which parents share problems and optimism, will benefit the program and the gifted children involved.

Career Education

Career education is an important priority in all education. One problem for disadvantaged gifted students, however, is that "career education" traditionally focuses on occupations and careers which seem suitable or available to the majority of children in a particular school. Thus a curriculum program in a middle-class high school will feature college preparatory coursework and a professional career orientation. A high school in a minority or economically depressed area will focus on blue-collar occupations, with strong offerings in welding, machine shop, auto mechanics, and typing. There is a noticeably reduced awareness and valuing of college training and professional careers, and thus a reduced opportunity for the necessary preparation.

Career education for the gifted child in a lower-SES environment, of course, should stress the *professional opportunities available* and the necessary *educational preparation.* However, a realistic career education program also must emphasize the life-styles, values, ethics, and goals that accompany particular professional careers (Moore, 1979). To compete successfully, the disadvantaged gifted child must acquire the many subtle attitudes and skills that accompany a given profession—attitudes and skills learned at home by children of educated professional parents.

An important—indeed, crucial—component of career education is the involvement of suitable *models.* These are professional persons of similar ethnic backgrounds who have, in fact, emerged from difficult socioeconomic circumstances. They need to share their experiences, their problems, and their strategies for success with gifted young disadvantaged people. One cannot expect these children and adolescents to be career oriented and motivated unless they know that success is possible and that higher education is both reachable and worth the effort. Presentations, mentorships, and on-the-job visits are good ways to provide gifted youth with a taste of career and life goals worth working for. The models also can help students understand that within the professional areas there *will* be support; and further, that once high-level positions are attained, both intrinsic and extrinsic rewards will make the educational and economic struggle worthwhile. Professional persons from disadvantaged backgrounds typically are very sensitive to the problems of culturally different and poor gifted youth and are motivated to help.

As we have seen, career education for gifted minority, economically deprived, and culturally different students usually must be *broader* than typical career education programs. While college-educated parents automatically provide good models and informal information and values to their middle-class children, it is rare for culturally different students to have such models in their immediate families or even neighborhoods. Their parents usually are not aware of the opportunities and obstacles related to a high-level professional education. Therefore, a good career education program for these students will need to provide considerable and detailed direction. For example, these young people must learn about colleges and universities that will support both their professional and their ethnic needs. They will require direction in finding scholarships or other funding assistance. They will need to learn how to prepare for entrance examinations and personal interviews. They also must be reassured about the social environment they may encounter.

The extraordinary value of a well-designed career education program for gifted disadvantaged youth is that it may guide very talented persons to become fulfilled and productive individuals, individuals who will make those "valuable contributions to self and society." However, if these gifted youth meet only dead ends and frustration and have no outlet for the development and expression of their talents, society will not only lose their positive professional contributions, but will likely be taxed (literally) by their negative contributions. Farley (1981) argued that high energy levels can be channeled either into creative and productive outlets or, in the case of many low-SES adolescents, into delinquency and self-destructiveness. Their energy, talents, and frustrations may combine into antisocial behavior—perhaps in a leadership capacity—which constitutes an obviously serious and unnecessary waste of human potential.

SUMMARY

Due to cultural and language differences, culturally and economically disadvantaged students rarely are identified as "gifted."

Some statistics indicate that educational and social programs for disadvantaged and minority students have led to reduced dropout rates and have reduced achievement differences between black and white students.

Modeled after Maslow's theory, Rimm's hierarchy of intellectual needs emphasizes that good preparation in basic skills is prerequisite to the application of knowledge, the analysis, synthesis, and evaluation of ideas, and creative production. Further, the lack of such skills obscures the giftedness of culturally different youth. Examples demonstrated how intellectual and creative giftedness was revealed when deficiencies were removed, thus allowing the identification of culturally different gifted students. One danger is that when deficiencies are remedied, gifted students are no longer eligible to receive special services.

While early childhood experiences strongly influence later academic and career success, deprived environments do not totally prevent the development of talent.

Low IQ and achievement test scores may be misinterpreted to "prove" the absence of giftedness. Since such average or below-average achievement can be common among the gifted disadvantaged, identification must be based upon potential rather than actual academic performance. A high IQ score remains a valid indicator of giftedness, but an average or low score may be misleading. Cultural and family background, including language differences, and testing circumstances, such as motivation and test anxiety, must be considered.

While high achievement is good evidence of talent in particular areas, achievment test scores suffer from the same problems as intelligence test scores.

Teacher nominations may favor members of the majority culture; however, a sensitive teacher who understands characteristics of gifted students may be an excellent identifier of gifts and talents of minority students. Gay compiled a list of characteristics of gifted black children and Swenson itemized characteristics of creativity in culturally different students. The Kranz Talent Identification Instrument includes training teachers to validly rate all students, including minority and poor ones.

Research indicates that creativity tests, such as the Torrance Tests of Creative Thinking and the Rimm and Davis GIFT and GIFFI inventories, are good instruments for identifying creative disadvantaged and minority students. Parent and peer nominations also are good identification strategies. One may need to look outside the school to identify artistic and creative talent in culturally different and disadvantaged students.

A quota system assumes that gifts and talents exist in equal proportions in all cultural groups and assures their representation in G/T programs. Programming options described in earlier chapters also may be used with disadvantaged and minority students.

In order to support personal mental health via ethnic pride, the maintenance of ethnic identity was recommended, which is consistent with the cultural pluralist position. *Assimilationists* argue that bilingual programs interfere with the integration of culturally different children into the mainstream. *Cultural pluralists* feel that ethnic pride is central to self-esteem and educational and career success. Research on the benefits of bilingual programs is mixed.

Banks's five stages of ethnic identity included (1) ethnic psychological captivity, characterized by negative self-concepts; (2) ethnic encapsulation, basically the majority tendency to assume superiority over minority groups; (3) ethnic identity clarification, the development of positive attitudes toward oneself and one's ethnic group; (4) biethnicity, which includes ethnic pride and the ability to participate in another culture; and (5) multiethnicity, the ability to function in several ethnic environments. In teaching an ethnic component, a teacher might identify students' ethnic stages and attempt to move them toward higher stages.

Extracurricular cultural enrichment is important for socioeconomically deprived and minority gifted students. Such experiences can include other knowledge, skill, and creative objectives.

Troubled students need understanding, including help from a trained and empathetic counselor. Exum recommended that a counselor learn about the local community, become more visible, and be flexible in scheduling appointments. A support group of gifted peers also is beneficial.

Parents will support G/T programs if they understand the importance of the program for their child's future, and if they are not threatened by the program or its possible effects on their child. Parent meetings will aid in educating parents regarded G/T programs and will allow parents to share problems and optimism.

Career education must include not only career options and the preparation needed to attain them, but the life-styles, ethics, and goals that accompany various professions. Models—professional persons from similar disadvantaged backgrounds—are a vital component of a successful career education program.

If gifted disadvantaged and minority students are not helped to develop their skills and receive professional training, they may channel their talents into antisocial and self-destructive behaviors.

13

UNDERACHIEVEMENT:
Diagnosis and Treatment

The underachieving gifted child represents both society's greatest loss and its greatest potential resource. The child has the potential for high achievement and significant contributions, but is not using that talent in productive ways. Since the child's special abilities are recognized, the nonproductiveness often leads to frustration by parents, teachers, and even the child him or herself. However, if the underachieving pattern can be reversed, the child frequently makes unusual progress in skill acquisition and in positive, productive work. In view of the child's history of underachievement, the extent of positive change after appropriate intervention usually is quite surprising.

Overview

This chapter will review characteristics, causes, and dynamics of underachievement, along with a strategy for reversing this costly syndrome.

DEFINITION AND IDENTIFICATION OF UNDERACHIEVEMENT

Underachievement is defined as a discrepancy between the child's school performance and some index of his or her actual ability, such as intelligence, achievement, or creativity scores, or observational data.

Test Scores

The chief index of actual ability is test scores. Despite all the faults and problems related to testing, despite test unreliability and measurement error, and despite all the biases which need to be considered related to low test scores, it seems apparent that children cannot score extraordinarily high on tests purely by accident. Test-taking skill is certainly one factor to consider, but it alone cannot account for test scores that consistently fall two or more standard deviations above the mean, that is, above the ninety-seventh percentile. Unusually high scores then, whether on intelligence achievement, or creativity tests, indicate special abilities or skills not apparent in the underachieving child's usual schoolwork.

Intelligence Test Scores

If a child is identified as gifted, even based on intelligence test scores alone, it is important to compare the child's *actual* school performance to the performance that would be *expected* based on those IQ scores. There are several statistical concepts that may be used in this kind of comparison, especially *grade equivalent scores, mental age* (MA) *equivalents, stanines,* and *percentiles.* For example, a third-grade child of 8 years 6 months may produce intelligence test scores in the ninth stanine (top 4 percent) or a mental age equivalent score of 10 years 2 months, but his or her usual classroom performance might range between the fourth, fifth, and sixth stanines— strictly at grade level. Any of these statistical yardsticks are satisfactory for helping to operationally define underachievement in order to identify children who need help.

A frequent error in the identification of underachievers is to use a *fixed* number or months of years below grade level as a criterion of underachievement. For example, first-grade children who are six months below their expected achievement level will have far more serious underachievement problems than eighth graders performing one full year below the expected level. For the younger children six months may represent being 50 percent behind where they should be; for the eighth-grade children one year represents only 12.5 percent behind where they would be expected to be performing. The main problem related to using a constant number of months is that younger children with underachievement problems are likely to be overlooked because the discrepancy between actual and expected achievement does not appear to be large enough in terms of actual months, even though the problem is quite serious. Since underachievement can be treated more easily when diagnosed early, it is critical to recognize this common identification error.

Achievement Test Scores

Many schools do not routinely administer group intelligence tests, but virtually all schools regularly use published (standardized) and/or teacher-made achievement tests. These provide an objective basis for determining the levels of information and skills that a child has mastered. The teacher is in the uniquely best position to compare actual school performance (for example, the quality of reports, projects, homework, math or reading proficiency, or class participation) with the achievement test scores.

The clear determination of underachievement by comparing achievement test scores with usual classroom performance is problematic and at least partly subjective. For example, if grade equivalent scores are used and a child scores three grades above average in reading achievement, this should not be interpreted to mean that the child should be reading at exactly three grade levels above the rest of the class. However, it does indicate that he or she should be reading above grade-level material comfortably. If the child seems able to read only grade-level material in class, he or she is underachieving.

Creativity Test Scores

High scores on divergent-thinking tests such as the *Torrance Tests of Creative Thinking* (Torrance, 1966) or on creative personality inventories such as *GIFT* and *GIFFI* (Davis and Rimm, 1979; Rimm, 1976; Rimm and Davis, 1980) strongly suggest that the child has talent in the area of creative and productive thinking. However, high creativity scores do not assure high achievement. On the contrary, some fairly common characteristics of creative students—such as nonconformity, resistance to teacher domination, impulsiveness, and indifference to rules—may cause the creative child serious difficulties in achieving within the classroom structure. Some highly creative students are dramatic underachievers, since their personalities and thinking styles may be quite at odds with that required for classroom success. Other creative students, however, apply their unique talents to classroom assignments and requirements and achieve at the level of students with much higher tested intelligence (Getzels and Jackson, 1962).

Children with high creativity scores but only somewhat above average IQ scores (110–130) have very high potential for making creative contributions (Reis and Renzulli, 1982; Renzulli, Reis and Smith, 1981; Torrance, 1971). If students in this category are not achieving at least at grade level in school, they should be identified as gifted underachievers, even though their intelligence and achievement test scores may not be in the "gifted" range. Chances are excellent that such students will flourish in the less restrictive, more self-directed environment of the gifted education program.

Observation

Some underachieving gifted childen do not perform well on any test due to poor test-taking habits. For example, they may not be motivated to do well. On a group test some students may answer questions randomly; on an individually administered test they may "play dumb." Teacher and parent observations provide the only basis for identifying these gifted children; there will be little or no objective criteria.

Teachers may note class behaviors, comments, or vocabulary which suggest that the child has much more intellectual, creative, or artistic potential than he or she is exhibiting in school-related work. Teachers, however, can recognize these behaviors only if they are aware of characteristics of gifted children. Teachers must remain open to the possibility of discovering giftedness in children already labeled as "average" or "below average." Many such gifted underachievers are never discovered.

Parents are in a unique position to observe the talents and capabilities of their own gifted children, even if the children are not high achievers. Note that teachers and principals often feel threatened by parents who insist their child is "gifted." Such parents are often inappropriately described as "pushy." Educators should assure these parents that their perceptions will be given full consideration if they can provide specific examples of behaviors that would be evidence of their child's giftedness. If the anecdotal material appears reasonably convincing, further testing may indeed furnish supportive data for the parents' observations. If the anecdotal material does not suggest giftedness, the teacher or principal can explain why such behavior does not represent special talent by comparing it to anecdotal material about typical children and highly talented children.

CHARACTERISTICS OF UNDERACHIEVING GIFTED CHILDREN

Studies of gifted underachievers have identified characteristics that are typical of these children. Joanne Whitmore (1980) has summarized some of the most important traits in an identification checklist (Table 13.1). If ten or more of these characteristics are checked, she suggests this would indicate that the child should be further evaluated to determine if he or she is indeed a gifted underachiever.

TABLE 13.1   A Checklist to Identify Gifted Underachievers

Observe and interact with the child over a period of at least two weeks to determine if he or she possesses the following characteristics. If the student exhibits ten or more of the listed traits, including all that are asterisked, individual intelligence testing (Stanford-Binet or WISC-R) is recommended to establish whether he or she is a gifted underachiever.

_____   *poor test performance
_____   *achieving at or below grade-level expectations in one or all of the basic skill areas: reading, language arts, mathematics
_____   *daily work frequently incomplete or poorly done
_____   *superior comprehension and retention of concepts when interested
_____   *vast gap between qualitative level of oral and written work
_____   exceptionally large repertoire of factual knowledge
_____   vitality of imagination, creative
_____   persistent dissatisfaction with work accomplished, even in art
_____   seems to avoid trying new activities to prevent imperfect performance; evidences perfectionism, self-criticism
_____   shows initiative in pursuing self-selected projects at home
_____   *has a wide range of interests and possibly special "expertise" in an area of investigation and research
_____   *evidences low self-esteem in tendencies to withdraw or be aggressive in the classroom
_____   does not function comfortably or constructively in a group of any size
_____   shows acute sensitivity and perceptions related to self, others, and life in general
_____   tends to set unrealistic self-expectations; goals too high or too low
_____   dislikes practice work or drill for memorization and mastery
_____   easily distracted, unable to focus attention and concentrate efforts on tasks
_____   has an indifferent or negative attitude toward school
_____   resists teacher efforts to motivate or discipline behavior in class
_____   has difficulty in peer relationships; maintains few friendships

From Joanne Whitmore, *Giftedness, Conflict, and Underachievement* (Rockleigh, N.J.: Allyn & Bacon, 1980). Copyright © 1980 by Allyn & Bacon, Inc. Reprinted by permission.

Characteristics of underachievers can be categorized in three different levels in terms of their causes and visible symptoms. The primary characteristic is *low self-esteem,* which appears to be at the root of most underachievement problems. The low self-esteem seems to lead to the secondary characteristics of *academic avoidance* behaviors, which in turn produce the visible tertiary traits of poor study habits, unmastered skills, and social and discipline problems. However, these causes and effects are at least partly bidirectional. That is, like the chicken-egg problem, each set of characteristics tends to determine the others.

Primary Characteristic of Underachievers: Low Self-Esteem

The characteristic found most frequently and consistently among underachieving children is low self-esteem (Fine and Pitts, 1980; Rimm, 1983; Whitmore, 1980). Not believing themselves actually capable of accomplishing what their family or teachers expect of them, they may mask their low self-esteem with displays of bravado, rebellion, or with highly protective defense mechanisms (Covington and Beery, 1976; Fine and Pitts, 1980; Rimm, 1983). For example, they may openly criticize the quality of the school or the talents of individual teachers, or else claim that they "don't care" or "didn't really try" in regard to a mediocre test score or class grade.

Related to their low self-esteem is their sense of low personal control over their own lives. If they fail at a task, they blame their lack of ability; if they succeed, they may attribute their success to luck. Thus they may accept responsibility for failure, but not for success (Felton and Biggs, 1977). As we saw in Chapter 2, strong feelings of *internal control* are characteristic of gifted achievers, but not underachievers.

This attribution process in educational achievement has been related to the original theory of *learned helplessness* earlier advanced by Seligman (1975). If a child does not see a relationship between his efforts and the outcome, he is likely to exhibit characteristics of learned helplessness and will no longer make an effort to achieve. This pattern is characteristic of many gifted underachievers. Weiner (1974, 1980) also noted that a child's subsequent performance will be strongly influenced by whether he or she attributes successes and failures to ability, effort, task difficulty, or luck. Especially, attributing success to *effort* leads to further effort, while attributing success to *task ease* or *luck* does not.

Secondary Characteristics of Underachievers: Avoidance Behavior

Low self-esteem leads the underachiever to nonproductive avoidance behaviors both at school and at home, secondary characteristics of underachievement (Whitmore, 1980). For example, underachievers may avoid making a productive effort by asserting that school is irrelevant and that they see no reason to study material for which there is no use. Students may further assert that when they are really interested in learning, they can do very well. These kinds of avoidance behaviors protect underachievers from admitting the lack of self-confidence, or worse, the feared lack of ability. If they studied, they would risk *confirming* the possible shortcomings to themselves and to important others. If they do not study, they can use the nonstudying as a rationale for the failure, thus protecting their valuable feelings of self-worth (Covington and Beery, 1976).

Additional defensive avoidance behaviors that operate in a similar fashion to protect underachievers include intense interest or even leadership in out-of-school activities which are less threatening. These successes essentially compensate for academic failures.

Extreme rebellion against authority, particularly school authority, provides another route to protect the underachiever. The student seems eager to tell teachers, the principal, the superintendent, even the Board of Education, exactly how they ought to run the school. Faulting the school helps the underachiever avoid the responsibility of achieving by blaming the system.

Expectations of low grades and perfectionism—though apparent opposites—also serve as defense mechanisms for the underachieving child with low self-esteem. If the underachiever expects low grades, he or she lowers the risk of failure. Note that low goals are consistent with a poor self-image and low self-confidence.

On the other hand, perfectionism provides a different protection. Since perfection is unachievable, it provides the child with a ready excuse for poor performance. For example, students can assert with bravado that they set their goals higher than most people, so of course they cannot be expected to always succeed. The students thus provide a rationale for failure and do not need to label themselves as incompetent (although they may indeed feel incompetent).

By contrast, achieving children set realistic goals which are reachable, and failures are constructively used to indicate weaknesses needing attention.

Tertiary Characteristics of Underachievers

Because underachieving children avoid effort and achievement to protect their precarious self-esteem, tertiary characteristics arise which support the pattern of underachievement. These include deficient school-related skills (Fine and Pitts, 1980), poor study habits, peer acceptance problems, poor school concentration, and home and school discipline problems. It is critical to recognize that these tertiary indicators of underachievement are the visible "tip of the iceberg," characteristics that mainly result from the secondary avoidance behaviors which protect underachievers from the primary problem, low self-esteem.

To reverse the pattern of underachievement, the educator will need to address the problem at all three levels. The visible tertiary characteristics will need correction, as well as the secondary avoidance behaviors. The most important goal, however, is to help the underachieving child deal with the core problem, low self-esteem (Rimm, 1983).

ETIOLOGIES OF UNDERACHIEVEMENT

Children are not born underachievers; there is no nature/nurture debate relative to underachievement. It is *learned* behavior, and therefore it can be unlearned. Underachievement can be taught by families, by schools, or by cultures. The last, cultural underachievement, its etiology and treatment, is discussed in Chapters 12 and 14 focusing on culturally different students and females. The following sections will describe rituals and reinforcements that maintain patterns of underachieving in the home and school. Recognizing factors that cause, support, and reward underachievers should help the reader understand the dynamics of underachievement and therefore should assist in reversing the problem. A better understanding of the supporting rituals and reinforcements also should make it possible to help prevent potential underachievement.

FAMILY ETIOLOGY

When families of underachieving children are compared to families of achievers (Frazier, Passow, and Goldberg, 1958; Zilli, 1971), certain characteristics become apparent. Some of these characteristics are difficult to alter, but some can be easily changed by concerned parents once they are aware of the dynamics. Among the characteristics resistant to change are general poor family morale and family disruption (French, 1959) caused by death or divorce. Among those that can be changed relatively easily are parent overprotection, authoritarianism, excessive permissiveness, and inconsistencies between parents. These frequently result in manipulative rituals and parent identification problems that almost always can be recognized.

It is helpful for teachers to be familiar with "problem family" patterns, because an understanding of these patterns will help the teacher communicate with parents more effectively. Also, many family patterns which include manipulations by a child are extended by the child into the classroom. Thus a sensitivity to underachieving patterns can help the teacher avoid being manipulated by the student.

Identification and Modeling

The Terman and Oden (1957) study of underachieving gifted showed that most underachievers were boys and that the most significant characteristic of these boys was *non*identification with their father. Rimm (1984), a private practice psychologist specializing in underachieving gifted children, similarly found that underachievers frequently did not identify with the same-sexed parent. Interestingly, however, some identified very strongly with a same-sexed parent—if that parent appeared from the child's perspective to also be an underachiever or to be giving the child messages that schoolwork avoidance is acceptable.

Freud (1949) explained identification with the same-sexed parent as a product of the resolution of the *Oedipal* or *Electra* complexes. During the phallic stage of development (ages 3 to 5), said Freud, the child finds him-

or herself romantically attached to the opposite-sexed parent. Recognizing that the parent already has a partner, the child sees the impossibility of the affair and resolves the issue by unconsciously identifying with the same-sexed parent. This identification purportedly causes the child to adopt the behaviors, conscience, and appropriate sex role of that parent. The three-year-old boy walking in Daddy's shoes or the girl imitating Mommy's telephone conversation is said to be evidence of the early identification process.

While conceding that it is nice for children to love their parents, contemporary social learning theorists question whether identification truly stems from the unconscious resolution of a sexual conflict. Rather, they describe identification and imitative behavior in terms of *modeling* (Meichenbaum, 1977). Research by Mussen and Rutherford (1963) and Hetherington and Frankie (1967) indicate that the parent model chosen for identification and imitation depends largely on a combination of three variables, *as perceived by the child*: (1) nurturance, (2) power, and (3) similarities between the parent and child.

The *nurturance* variable is very straightforward. The child tends to identify with, and model the behavior of, the parent who is highly nurturant. The parent may not be warm and loving in general, but there may be an especially warm, loving relationship between the parent and a particular child or children in the family. If that parent is an underachiever, or does not stress achievement, the child may adopt similar attitudes.

The way that *power* influences identification, imitation, and underachievement is sometimes direct and at other times more complicated. In the most direct way, if one parent is definitely more powerful from the child's perspective, but does not value education or school achievement, the identifying child is not likely to perform well in school. Teachers need to be aware of this pattern because they may see only the concerned mother of an underachieving boy at parent conferences. However, it may be the *father* with whom the conference should be taking place. It is difficult to motivate a boy who identifies with his father, if the father and the boy view education as "women's work."

Some typical, more complicated power patterns that foster underachievement in children are described by Rimm (1984) as "Father is an Ogre," "Daddy is a Dummy," and "Mother is an Ogre." In the first pattern, "Father is an Ogre," the father is viewed as successful and powerful, the mother as kind and caring. Often, a closer view of the home life shows a father who wears a big "No!" on his forehead. That is, he firmly prohibits many of the activities the children wish to pursue. However, the children learn to bypass his authority by appealing to their kind, sweet mother. Mother either manages to convince Dad to change his initial decision, or surreptitiously permits the children to carry out their desired activities anyway. Children quickly learn the necessary manipulative maneuvers.

The ritual worsens because as the children grow older the father begins to recognize his lack of power over his family, and he becomes more and more authoritarian as he tries to cope with his powerlessness. In response to his increasing authoritarianism, mother feels an increasing need to protect and defend her children. In desperation she invents new approaches to sabotaging her husband's power in the belief that she is doing the best thing for her children. Although girls in this family are likely to be achievement-oriented because they see their mother as powerful and positive, boys will tend to underachieve. They see no effective model in their father, who appears both hostile and powerless. They may fear and resent him, but are not likely to want to emulate him.

"Daddy is a Dummy" is a slightly different but equally disruptive ritual. This syndrome is often discovered in homes where Mother has a college education which includes courses in education and psychology. Dad has no college education or one that did not include psychology. Mother is certain that she knows the "correct" way to bring up the children which, according to her training, should include an important father role. However, whenever Dad attempts to play his parent role, Mother corrects him and explains a better way in which he can play his part. Dad feels uncomfortable and powerless in handling the children and makes every effort to withdraw, sometimes to 70 hours at the office. If Mother insists that he come home, the television screen becomes his escape. Sons again tend to be the underachievers in this family since they see their father as either powerless, absent, or as expressing passive-aggressive behavior. These underachieving boys often assume the same passive-aggressive posture in front of the television screen.

In the third parenting pattern, "Mommy is an Ogre," we find a disciplinarian mother and a kind, sweet, but undisciplined father. This results in at least two more poor patterns for identification. (1) If the disciplinarian mother is viewed by the children as fair and strong and supported by "kind father," this provides a weak male image for the sons, but a strong mother figure for female identification. (2) However, if the mother's discipline is overruled by the father, we have potential models for underachievement for both male and female children. The boys may identify with Father because he is viewed as powerful, but he models some characteristics and habits which make for underachievement—ignoring or violating (Mom's) rules, procrastination, and lack of discipline and perseverance. To the girls, Mother may be viewed as insignificant sound and fury, and therefore cannot become the model for an achieving daughter because of the children's perceptions of both her powerlessness and her continuous anger.

In addition to nurturance and power, the third variable that affects identification is the *similarities* the child sees between him or herself and a parent. This similarity provides a strong basis for sex-role identification. High similarity between mother and daughter or between father and son strongly support same-sex identification when nurturance and power of the parents are equal. However, unusual similarities in appearance, abilities, interests, or personality between boys and mothers or between girls and fathers frequently leads to cross-sex identification. Cross-sex parent identification can contribute strongly to either achievement or underachievement. Achievement motivation may be strengthened by female identification with a powerful and effective father if he is intellectually oriented, but weakened if he is not intellectually oriented. However, underachievement appears to be fostered by the cross-sex identification of sons with their mothers.

Other research has produced several findings that relate child-parent identification to achievement and underachievement. For example, Lamb (1976) and Zilli (1971) found that if Father is absent from the home boys are more likely to be underachievers. Parish and Nunn (1983) discovered that males and females whose fathers left home (or died) before the age of 13 tended to be low in internal locus of control, a trait strongly related to achievement. In relation specifically to quantitative abilities, if Father is absent boys' and girls' math aptitudes and achievement are more likely to be weak (Carlsmith, 1964). However, girls and boys who identify strongly with father are more likely to have good problem solving, math, and science skills (Helson, 1971; Milton, 1957).

As we will see in Chapter 14, Rodenstein and Glickauf-Hughes (1979) found that a girl's attitude toward a career will be strongly and positively influenced by a successful working mother. However, this holds true only if there is a good family attitude toward Mother's employment and Mother's role conflict is minimal. Almquist and Angrist (1971) similarly emphasized that in order to aspire to a career, young women need good role models who can demonstrate that marriage and a career can be successfully combined.

In summary, the identification literature clearly supports the significance of identification with good parent models as an important family factor in high achievement. The lack of that identification, or the identification with a poor parent model, seems to be clearly related to underachievement. Parents who view their own lives as interesting and successful and who model an equitable and respectful husband-wife relationship provide ideal role models for both male and female children.

Manipulative Rituals and Counteridentification

The situation in which a parent identifies with his or her child is known as *counteridentification*. The parent who counteridentifies with the child invests him or herself in the child's activities and empathically shares efforts, successes, and failures. A familiar example of counteridentification is the vociferous father who argues desperately with the referee at the Little League baseball game, as if it were he who had been unfairly called "out." Counteridentification is not always bad. Many parents vicariously enjoy seeing their children excel in sports or other talent areas, attend prestigious colleges, or travel, activities which the parents missed in their own youth.

Counteridentification has not been thoroughly explored in research, but it appears to have the potential to influence either high achievement or underachievement. The potential for positive contributions to achievement comes mainly from the parents' sharing of skills and their investment of time and resources. As mentioned earlier in this book, Bloom (1981; Bloom and Sosniak, 1981) found that the early training of talented mathematicians, pianists, and swimmers included coaching by one or both parents who had a strong personal interest in the particular talent field. Bloom emphasized that the parent provided an early and influential model for the child. Based on Bloom's descriptions, it also is likely that most of the parents counteridentified with their talented child.

On the negative side, several forms of counteridentification can lead to manipulative rituals by children, supporting underachievement. Two such rituals begin with kind, empathic parents who try to be helpful to their children and try to understand their point of view. In one negative ritual rooted in counteridentification the child manipulates parents into completing his or her homework. This extremely common problem begins innocently enough. The child does not understand an assignment and goes to the parent for an explanation. The counteridentifying parent not only explains the assignment, but in order to prevent the child's "suffering" continues to work with the child. The parent explains the assignment step by step, over and over. The child soon learns that he or she needs only to briefly express confusion and the parent is brought quickly to his or her side for the evening. Together they complete the daily assignments. When father or mother does not cooperate, the child may punish the parent by failing the assignment, thus encouraging the parent to be more helpful with the next homework.

It is not surprising that as time progresses the child finds the assignments more difficult and takes longer and longer to complete the work. Not only has the child found comfortable reinforcement in the form of attention from mother or father, the child loses confidence in his or her ability to achieve independently. Since mother or father is now carrying the responsibility for much of the work, the child may no longer believe it is possible to learn the required skills.

An early manifestation of this dependent pattern in the classroom is a child seeking continuous aid from unsuspecting teachers. For example, this is the child who typically waits until instructions have been given twice and then raises his hand and innocently announces, "Ms. Jones, I just don't understand what I'm to do."

This dependent pattern sometimes has its origins in an early teacher recommendation to a parent. For example, in a primary grade a teacher may have suggested that a parent regularly help the child with homework. Teachers should be cautious in making such recommendations, and should be explicit in the kinds of help that they suggest so that this help does not lead to overdependence.

This dependent ritual is relatively easy to change if identified early, but very resistant to change in the high school years. By then, there is a sizeable gap between the student's developed skills and those necessary to succeed in high school. Furthermore, by this time the youth has little remaining confidence in his or her school-related competence.

The second maladaptive ritual that stems from counteridentification is one in which parents convey *too much power* to their gifted children and the children become aggressively manipulative. Because the children appear so bright, and because they use adult vocabulary and adult reasoning, parents find themselves interacting with them almost as adult peers long before the children have attained the wisdom to match their verbalizations (Fine and Pitts, 1980). Parents and sometimes teachers may be awed by the child's "adultized" rationalizations for why they need not perform routine school tasks. To their own detriment, these children thus learn to manipulate their parents and teachers, frequently bypassing skill development because the work is "boring" or "irrelevant." Further, they may claim there is "no reason" to write material that they can answer orally, and they may depend on their verbal precociousness until written skills actually become deficient. The following is a favorite story of such a child:

> David, an only child, had been surrounded by an adult world since infancy. As a fourth grader with an IQ of 138, he was determined not to memorize arithmetic facts. He explained to the psychologist that there was absolutely no reason for him to learn math since he had already finalized his career choice: "I expect to become a fireman and therefore, it will only be necessary to learn the chemistry of extinguishing fires." After further discussion, David did acknowledge laughingly that at an earlier age he had preferred owning a candy store because he believed as an owner he would have a continuous candy supply. The psychologist pointed out his first career change and David hesitantly acknowledged he might make some future changes and might even need to learn basic mathematics, a skill which he had largely managed to avoid.

The teacher who works with students such as David must recognize that the verbally powerful child needs to be carefully led to the conclusion that he must learn and study. Opposing this child will only lead to a no-win battle, and antagonism is the likely result. Recognizing the power pattern that exists at home can help the teacher guide this child in the classroom and help avoid an adversary relationship. This adversary interaction, which occurs frequently between gifted children and their teachers, is one main cause of some teachers saying they don't like gifted students. These gifted students will also say that particular teachers "don't like" them.

SCHOOL ETIOLOGY

The gifted child is exposed to what is frequently known as the "good year, bad year" syndrome. It has been estimated that at least 80 percent of the teachers in this country have had absolutely *no* exposure to teaching methods for the gifted child. Some of these teachers supply most of the "bad years." However, other teachers, even without G/T training, do detect and provide for the special needs of the gifted child, creating the "good years" in school. Fortunately, not all "bad years" are devastating. Most gifted children are resilient enough to function well even in a less than responsive environment. However, certain personal and classroom conditions seem to create problems for the gifted child and seem to initiate or accelerate underachieving behavior patterns.

School Climate

Whitmore (1980) described classroom environments that appear to cause and support underachievement. The main characteristics she discovered were a lack of respect for the individual child, a strongly competitive climate, emphasis on outside evaluation, inflexibility and rigidity, exaggerated attention to errors and failures, an "all controlling teacher," and an unrewarding curriculum. One needs to view the school environment in relationship to the dynamics of underachievement to understand how it provides behavioral patterns and rituals that reinforce underachievement. We will look more closely at the effects of inflexible and competitive classrooms.

Inflexible classrooms. The inflexibility and rigidity which demonstrate lack of respect for the individual child provides a strong reinforcement for underachievement by the gifted child. The intellectually gifted child learns faster and integrates information more easily. The creatively gifted child thinks differently and asks frequent questions. The rigid teacher, however, adheres to an organized schedule that allows little flexibility for those who differ in speed or learning style. The gifted child quickly discovers that rapid completion of assignments usually leads to more assignments. These tyically are not more challenging or more exciting, but represent "busy work" to keep the active gifted child occupied.

Initially, the gifted child may be pleased and motivated by the special treatment by the teacher. Eventually, as the child finds the busy work unchallenging and boring, he or she determines that these additional assignments are punishment for rapid work. To avoid the punishment, the child slows his or her pace and no longer completes assignments before the rest of the class. However, since the student's mind remains active and alert, he or she usually must find other diversions such as daydreaming, troublemaking, or surreptitiously reading an exciting book. In some cases the diversions become powerful reinforcers that distract the child from completing even the regular assignments, which appear dull by comparison. Consider this actual case:

> Robbie, 8 years old, was a highly verbal child with an IQ in the very superior range. However, he was two years behind in mathematics and never completed his math assignments. His problem became clear after he was observed in class by the psychologist. On his lap, hidden from the teacher's view, was a book he was reading while the teacher explained the math assignment. The book was shifted to underneath the math book while students were to be doing math written work. Robbie moved further and further behind in mathematics, which was taught too slowly for his quick mind, but he read many exciting books. He was referred to the psychologist as having a "learning problem."

In addition to busy work, other ritual punishments tend to discourage the gifted child from achieving in the rigid, inflexible classroom. For example, if the gifted child responds too frequently in class or asks too many questions, he or she is not called on to speak. However, if the ignored child waves his or her hand too enthusiastically, calls out answers, or talks excitedly to a neighbor, he or she is rewarded with a scolding. The scoldings may serve either to reinforce or punish the child. If the child views them as punishment, he or she stops responding, deciding that such enthusiasm is somehow inappropriate to the school setting. If the child views the scoldings as reinforcing, he or she increases the talking out of turn and the hand waving, which become nuisances to both teachers and peers. Either way, enthusiasm for learning and thinking is diminished.

Gifted children in inflexible classrooms may adopt a variety of maladaptive behaviors that get attention (reinforcement), but contribute to underachievement. Poor handwriting, sloppy or incomplete work, not following teacher directions, noncompletion of homework, or aggressive behavior and fighting in the classroom or on the playground sometimes produce more attention and rewards in an inflexible classroom than independent thinking, questioning, enthusiasm, or the speedy completion of tasks.

Competitive classrooms.   The classroom where comparative evaluation is heavily stressed and where there is extraordinary emphasis on competition is exemplified in the not-too-fictitious story, "Congratulations Miss Smithersteen" (Rimm, 1980; see Appendix 13.1). The announcement to the class of grades, the comparison of students' test scores, the announced surprise expressed by a teacher when a student scores higher or lower than expected, and the continuous ranking of students all foster extreme competition within the classroom. That competition is attached to extrinsic evaluations of performance based on objective criteria that, from the perspective of the child, are viewed as the "true" measure of his or her competence and worth. Children who are already strong achievers and continue to find themselves at the top of the class may become even more motivated to achieve in this very competitive environment. However, even for highly motivated children too much emphasis on extrinsic rewards may detract from the intrinsic rewards of learning and creativity.

It is underachievers, of course, who are most dramatically affected by the severe competition (Covington and Beery, 1976). Underachievers, who do not have a clear sense of their own competence, are informed on a daily basis that they are not measuring up to the standards of excellence of the classroom. These children are given objective evidence of average or below-average abilities. Since competitive achievement is the only source of teacher recognition and rewards in the classroom, and since these children do not believe they are capable of attaining that recognition, they search for other classroom rewards or other evidence of personal worth, or adopt the defensive measures noted earlier in this chapter and in Chapter 8.

A highly competitive environment may be a "good year" or a "bad year" for the achieving gifted child. For the underachieving gifted child it is always a "bad year," since it provides convincing evidence of his or her own incompetence. An actual case:

> Despite her IQ in the very superior range, five-year-old Bonnie's underachievement was encouraged very early by her competitive kindergarten classroom environment. Bonnie had been a spontaneous and enthusiastic child in her nursery school class, where her teacher had described her as very bright and happily adjusted. In kindergarten she was referred to the psychologist because her mother reported that "she did not like to go to school." Her kindergarten teacher described her school performance as poor. She rarely completed her work, did not seem happy, and tended not to participate in class activities. Classroom observation revealed the competitive environment that gave Bonnie her sense of failure and motivation to slow her pace.
>
> The children sat on the floor around the chalkboard for their letter-printing lesson. The teacher announced the letter to be printed and some children enthusiastically raised their hands. After the selected child printed the letter on the chalkboard, the children were asked if it were printed well. In chorus, they exclaimed an enthusiastic "yes" if it were and a punishing "no" if it was poorly executed. The teacher would agree or disagree with the children, pointing out the good qualities or the problems related to the printing of the letter. When Bonnie, with her hand barely raised, was selected to perform, the inadequate execution of her letter brought the "no's" that she had come to expect. Further, the "in seat" handwriting exercise that followed was carefully monitored by open teacher evaluation of each child's performance. It was not surprising to observe Bonnie's very slow performance and her nonsuccessful efforts at the perfection which she could not achieve.

In this highly competitive kindergarten class, Bonnie already was being taught that she could not succeed in a classroom environment. Fortunately, in first grade Bonnie was placed with a supportive teacher who fostered a noncompetitive environment and Bonnie developed confidence and enthusiasm again. The underachievement syndrome was reversed by a "good year."

Negative Expectations

Rosenthal and Jacobson's (1968) book *Pygmalion in the Classroom* inspired a landslide of research, much of which strongly supports the notion that a teacher's expectations can have a dramatic impact on children's self-concepts and school achievements (see Cooper, 1979, or Davis, 1983b, for reviews). The problem is that for children, teachers and school success are the major—if not the only—source of feedback concerning one's ability, competence, and worth (Covington and Beery, 1976). The teacher who sends messages of negative expectations will frequently find exactly what he or she expects: Both regular and gifted students will underachieve. As a perhaps surprising source of negative expectations, Felton and Biggs (1977; p. 7) concluded that, "remediation, as it is sometimes practiced, may help the student to label herself as *stupid,* and this, in turn, may affect the teacher's attitudinal responses to that individual. This means that underachievement may be caused directly in the classroom and in the 'helping' provided there."

Not all gifted children will respond to the negative attitudes and expectations of a teacher by poor achievement. Some few may see this attitude as a special challenge and make additional efforts to meet that challenge. However, the underachieving gifted child, whose self-concept already is poor, normally will perceive the teacher's expectations of failure as a confirmation of his or her own poor self-evaluation. Another true story:

Carla, a minority student, entered college with reasonable expectations of success. Although she had been a poor student in elementary school, hard work in senior high school showed her that she could do well. Her high school grades were very good and she felt excited about the challenge of college. Based on an English entrance examination, she was placed in a small remedial English class. Most students in the class were on probation and the English teacher made a similar assumption about Carla. When Carla came for help, it was because she worried that perhaps she did not have the ability she had only recently come to believe she had. It was the expectations communicated to her in the English class that threatened her precariously held positive assumptions about her own abilities. Fortunately, another teacher had confidence in Carla's ability and convinced her that she was indeed a very capable student, and that it would only take a small compensatory effort to learn some skills she had missed earlier in her education.

It was her minority status together with some very real educational gaps that set the stereotype for negative expectations of Carla. After her confidence was restored, Carla easily learned the necessary English skills and continued college as a very successful student.

An Unrewarding Curriculum

Although the complaint from the underachieving gifted child that the school curriculum is irrelevant, dull, or unchallenging may only be a defensive avoidance ritual, it is often a real difficulty. Gifted children are particularly vulnerable to the "unrewarding curriculum" problem because of their intellectual and creative needs. Gifted children are often anxious to question, criticize, discuss, and learn beyond the levels that are appropriate for most students in the class. If the students are not challenged by the curriculum, they will find stimulation outside of the curriculum, and school will indeed be viewed as dull and boring. It is not uncommon for gifted underachievers who perform poorly in school to achieve excellence in non-school-related activities where they create their own rewarding curriculum. Consider the case of Ron:

> Ron was described as a poor reader and disinterested in school. In fourth grade he completed assignments rarely, daydreamed, performed his class work sloppily, and in general was considered a below-average student. At home he was immersed in comic books or baseball. He literally read and enjoyed thousands of comic books. As for baseball, he had easily committed to memory baseball statistics of the previous 20 years and talked knowledgeably about batting averages and pitching records that involved mathematics well beyond what he had learned in school. The same skills he seemed unable to apply in the classroom setting were readily exhibited in his areas of true interest—comic books and baseball. A more rewarding curriculum could have brought together Ron's interests and abilities and expanded both.

THE TREATMENT OF UNDERACHIEVEMENT

As we have seen, the underachieving gifted child continues to underachieve because the home, school, and/or peer group support that underachievement. The student is not motivated to achieve, and there probably are deficiencies in skills necessary for achievement. Working below one's ability affects both immediate educational success and eventual career achievement; it is an important problem requiring attention.

While it may seem like a tall order to reverse a long-standing pattern of underachieving, Rimm's strategies have proven successful in case after case (Rimm, in preparation). She has found that the treatment of underachievement involves the collaboration of school and family in the implementation of five important steps:

1. The assessment of skills, abilities, and home and school reinforcement contingencies.
2. The modification of reinforcements at home and school.
3. Changing the expectations of important others.
4. Improved model identification.
5. Correcting skill deficiencies.

Most of these concepts have been described in this chapter. It is important to note that, to reverse underachieving patterns, all five steps must be implemented approximately simultaneously.

Biographical studies of achievers who indicate they previously had been underachievers show that all five steps usually are included in the change process. These "spontaneous changers" typically initiated their turnabout with Steps 3 or 4, the discovery of a positive model for identification or a change in expectations of important others, for example, a teacher, boyfriend, girlfriend, or spouse. These relationships, which are common in spontaneous underachievement conversion, need to be recognized as important elements in the deliberate treatment of underachievers. Parents and teachers must remain very aware of the critical role they play in the implementation of the critical five steps, particularly in the areas of setting expectations and finding or becoming a good model.

Step 1: Assessment of Skills, Abilities, and Reinforcement Contingencies

The first step in the underachievement reversal process is an assessment that involves the cooperation of the school psychologist, teachers, and parents. The school psychologist should have primary involvement in this process. However, since few school districts allocate time for gifted children within the psychologist's role, it may be necessary for the guidance counselor, G/T coordinator, or classroom teacher to assume some of the responsibility. Ideally, the person should (1) have some background in measurement, (2) be sensitive to varying learning and motivational styles and problems, (3) be knowledgeable in behavioral learning theory, and (4) be aware of the special characteristics of gifted and creative children. *Objectivity* also is an important qualification. These characteristics make it difficult for the regular classroom teacher to be effective in this role. However, a teacher who has made a special effort to educate him- or herself in the area of gifted education, together with a psychologist or qualified counselor, may be able to conduct such an assessment.

The *individual* intelligence test is a highly recommended first assessment instrument. That venerable IQ number has the potential to communicate important expectations related to the child's true abilities. Since the child has not been motivated, it is likely that *group* intelligence test scores have underestimated his or her intellectual potential. Also, it is characteristically difficult to score above 125 on some group intelligence tests, a serious problem for intellectually gifted students. Therefore, the *WISC-R* or the *Stanford-Binet* must be individually administered by the psychologist. The *Slosson Individual Intelligence Test* could be administered by a teacher or counselor with practice. There also are other individual intelligence tests that can be administered by a psychologist to evaluate learning potential for culturally deprived, nonverbal, non-English-speaking, blind, or deaf gifted children who also may need to be individually assessed. Some of these instruments are questionable in terms of their equivalence to the most conventionally accepted tests, namely, the Wechsler and Binet scales, but all provide a reasonably acceptable estimate of the child's school-related capability.

During testing the examiner must be especially aware of particular task-relevant characteristics of the child: symptoms of tension, attention to the task, perseverance at the task, responses to frustration, problem-solving approaches, and responses to personal encouragement by the examiner. These reflect, in miniature, approaches to educational tasks that the child very likely uses in the classroom and home environments.

Intelligence testing should be followed by individual achievement tests to clearly assess strengths and deficits in basic skills, particularly reading and math.

A creativity test or inventory, which can be administered by the teacher or a psychologist, also should be part of the assessment. These produce not only a norm-referenced creativity score, but also descriptions of abilities, characteristics, and interests that are relevant to understanding the child's personality, creative potential, and learning style. The *GIFT* and *GIFFI* tests include dimension scores such as *Independence, Self-confidence,* and *Risk-taking* that provide important insights to understanding underachievement.

A *learning contingency recording form* provides critical guidance for the discovery of ritualized reinforcement contingencies that may be motivating and supporting the child's underachievement (see Inset 13.1). Such a form can be completed by the classroom teacher to map school contingencies and by a parent to map home contingencies. A school psychologist or G/T coordinator who is sensitive to reinforcement contingencies would be the ideal person to complete such a form, based upon his or her objective classroom observations. These professionals would also be able to analyze the forms completed by classroom teachers or parents.

Finally, a parent interview also can be very helpful in identifying underachieving patterns unintentionally maintained at home and school. Ideally both parents should be at the interview. If only one appears, it would be important to ask about the other parent's relationship to the child. Overall, the analysis of student abilities and home and school rein-

---

INSET 13.1   *EXAMPLE OF A HOME CONTINGENCY RECORDING FORM*

A home contingency recording form permits a parent to record the day's activities for a child. By noting the order, time, and place of activities, it is possible to analyze the reinforcements which may be maintaining underachieving behaviors. What kinds of changes might you recommend to this parent?

	ACTIVITY	APPROXIMATE TIME	PLACE
1.	Arrives home from school	3:30–3:45	
2.	Snack	3:45–4:00	Kitchen
3.	Watches TV with brother	4:00–6:00	Living Room
	Has argument with brother about show they wish to watch. Argument gets louder and I ask them 3 times nicely to quiet down. Finally, I lose my temper and yell at Bobby who is punching Johnny while Johnny is screaming for help. I command Bobby to let Johnny watch his TV program this time and recommend that Bobby have a turn later tonight.		
4.	Dinner—whole family eats	6:00–6:30	Kitchen
	Bobby brings up earlier fight. Argument begins again and spouse sides with Bobby on his position, but ends by leaving table distressed and angry at me for not being able to control the boys.		
5.	Boys return to TV. I do dishes	6:30–7:00	Living Room
6.	Bobby does homework	7:00–8:00	Kitchen Table
	I supervise Bobby's homework. He works slowly, asks for help often and seems to be daydreaming. He doesn't understand the math assignment and isn't concentrating.		

---

forcement contingencies is critical to the second step of the underachievement modification program.

Step 2: Modification of Reinforcements at Home and School

The behavioral analysis in Step 1 will certainly identify some of the manipulative rituals discussed above in the home and school etiology sections. These behaviors need to be modified by setting important long-term goals and some short-term objectives that can ensure immediate small successes for the child both at home and at school. These successful experiences should be reinforced by rewards, anything from gold stars or extra art time to special outings with parents or money.

There are several considerations in determining the rewards to be used. First, they must be meaningful to the child. Money may seem unimportant to a six-year-old, while stars are not particularly motivating to the adolescent. They must also be within the value system and range of possibility for the givers of the rewards. Schools do not usually use money as a reward, and parents may not want to pay (bribe) their children to learn. There are, however, effective rewards within the value system of parents and within the capabilities of teachers to administer—for example, free time. The rewards should not be too large. In fact, they should be as small as possible yet effective enough to motivate behavior. They can be increased in value as necessary; but if one has already used large rewards, small rewards will no longer be effective. It is important always to supply the rewards agreed upon, and to pay them on a regular basis immediately after the activity is successfully completed. Rewards may be based on activities completed, or based on the quality of the activity. Rewards should never be paid for incomplete work or when the work is not attempted. A sample *activity chart* appears in Inset 13.2, along with a guide for using the activity chart. Such a chart may be used to coordinate rewards with academic and nonacademic accomplishments.

INSET 13.2 ACTIVITY CHART

ACTIVITY	MON	TUES	WED	THUR	FRI	WEEKEND
Homework						
Reading	5	X	6	4		5
Math	5	5	5	10		5
Spelling	2	X	2	X		2
Social Studies	X	2	2	X		X
Science	X	X	X	2		X
Language	2	2	X	2		X
Extra Work						
Reading	15	10	8	5		15
Writing	X	3	5	X		5
Math	X	5	X	X		X
Home Responsibilities						
Wash dishes	5	5	X	5		
Pick up bedroom	5	5	5	5		
Total	39	37	33	33		32

Instructions to Parents for Charting Activities

1. You and your child need to determine a specific minimum daily study time. Twenty minutes for first and second graders, one-half hour for third to fifth graders, one hour for sixth and seventh graders, and one and a half hours for grades 8–12 can be used as a guideline. This amount of time may vary with the child and the school. Five days a week for study are recommended.

2. The place of study should be a desk or table in the child's own room or in a quiet area away from the television and family activities.

3. Children may not watch television until study time is complete and work is reviewed.

4. Review the child's study accomplishments and points earned daily. If possible the same-sexed parent should monitor the work and review the study chart with the child.

5. A guideline for giving points is one point for each page read, two points for each page written (for example, workbook or copying material), five points for each page of math work or creative writing. The parent may add bonus points for unusual improvement in work or for especially good quality work. Points will be exchanged for tangible rewards.

6. Daily rewards should be used for very young children (stars, stickers, baseball cards). Weekly rewards are preferred by older children (trips, special privileges, money).

7. Rewards should always be paid if earned and not withdrawn based on some other inadequate behaviors.

8. Rewards should never be paid if they are not earned.

9. Clear, brief messages of praise for work well done or disappointment at work inadequately completed should be given daily by the parent.

10. Consistent and orderly monitoring of work will need to continue until the child's performance has shown consistent improvement. Eventually children will not need the external monitoring and reward system since intrinsic rewards such as satisfaction with work well done, interest in content, and positive expectations will suffice. Time needed will vary with the child's age and type of problem.

Step 3: Changing the Expectations of Important Others

Parent, teacher, and peer expectations are difficult to change. As noted above, IQ scores, if higher than anticipated, are very effective in modifying expectations. Anecdotal information also can provide convincing evidence of the child's abilities. For example, a teacher convincing an adolescent or his or her parents of the child's mathematical talent can explain that the child solves problems in an unusually clever way or seems to learn math concepts more quickly than anyone else in the class. A psychologist trying to convince a teacher that a child has unusual talent can describe the unusual vocabulary or problem-solving skills that the child revealed during testing. *Specific* descriptions of unusual strengths are good evidence of giftedness.

It is very important to underachieving children that parents and teachers be able to honestly say to them that they believe in their ability to achieve (Perkins and Wicas, 1971). The expectations of these important others are basic to the personal change in self-expectations that is necessary to reverse from underachievement to high achievement. Jackson, Cleveland, and Mirenda (1975) showed in their longitudinal research with bright fourth-, fifth-, and sixth-grade underachievers that positive expectations by parents and teachers had a significant long-range effect on achievement in high school.

Because it is difficult to change the expectations of persons who know the child, changing the child's school environment sometimes is an effective measure. Changing schools is a drastic step to take, unless one is reasonably certain that the change will make a worthwhile difference. If extraordinarily gifted children are stifled by school environments that set only average goals and expectations, the children sometimes will change their entire achievement pattern when put in an environment that expects and values high achievement. However, for most children it is more realistic to try to change relevant expectations within the school.

Step 4: Model Identification

A critical turning point for the underachieving child is the discovery of a *model* for identification. All other treatments for underachievement dim in importance compared with strong identification with an achieving model. As noted above, Bloom's (1981; Bloom and Sosniak, 1981) biographical research with highly talented students showed that parents modeled the values and the life-styles of successful achievers in the talent area. Radin (1976) argues that the best family environment for a gifted boy is provided " . . . when a father is perceived as competent and strong, is pleased with his job, and permits his son to master tasks independently." Since this ideal situation is rarely provided for the gifted underachiever, parents and teachers need to manipulate the environment, using information that we know encourages identification, to help the student find a good model for identification.

Research on parent identification (for example, Mussen and Rutherford, 1963) indicates that the selected parent identification figure is nurturant, powerful, and shares common characteristics with the child. These same characteristics can be used to locate an appropriate, achieving model for the underachieving gifted child. As a warning, however, an underachieving adolescent sometimes selects a powerful, nurturant model who shares the *underachieving* characteristics of the adolescent. This person then becomes a strong model for underachievement.

Underachieving children should be matched with an achieving person to serve as a model for them. The person selected can serve in a model capacity for more than one child. His or her actual role may be tutor, mentor, companion, teacher, parent, sibling, counselor, psychologist, minister, scout leader, doctor, and so on. However, the model should have as many of the following characteristics as possible:

1. *Nurturance.* The model must care about the child assigned. Many adults are pleased to encourage youth with whom they can counteridentify.
2. *Same sex.* Although identification with an opposite-sexed model is possible, the similarity in sex facilitates identification.
3. *Similarities to child.* These may include religion, race, interests, talents, physical disabilities, physical characteristics, socioeconomic backgrounds, specific problem experiences, or any other characteristics that will create the necessary easy rapport. When the child realizes that the model can be truly understanding, empathic, and sympathetic—because the model has experienced similar problems—rapport is more easily established and the process of identification is facilitated.
4. *Openness.* A model's willingness to share his or her own real problems in establishing him or herself as an achiever is important for encouraging communication and identification, and for motivating the underachieving child.
5. *Willingness to give time.* Achieving adults frequently have shortages of this most precious commodity. However, it is not possible to be an effective, positive model without providing time. It can be work time, play time, or talk time. Models who work on tasks with their child or play with their child can be most effective. It becomes possible for the child to see first hand such important achievement characteristics as responding to challenge, winning and losing in competition, reasoning styles, leading, communicating and relating to others, and experiencing successes and failures. The child is helped to learn the skills necessary for achievement without necessarily viewing this as a conscious learning experience.
6. *Sense of positive accomplishment.* Although the model's life need not be perfect, the model must exhibit to the child the sense that his or her achievements have been personally fulfilling. Achievement involves sacrifice and postponed gratifications. The underachiever must recognize that these costs and postponements are worthwhile.

Step 5: Correcting Skill Deficiencies

The underachieving gifted child almost always has skill deficiencies as a result of inattention in class and poor work and study habits. However, because he or she is gifted, the skill deficiencies can be overcome reasonably rapidly. This is less of a problem for a very young child because the deficiencies are less likely to be extensive. An outside tutor, either peer or adult, can help to bridge the skills gap. The tutoring need only be on a weekly basis, and the tutor should not be a parent. The correction of skill deficiencies must be conducted carefully so that (1) the independent work of the underachieving child is reinforced by the tutor, (2) manipulation of the tutor by the child is avoided, and (3) the child senses the relationship between effort and the achievement outcomes. Charting progress during tutoring helps visually confirm the rapid progress to both child and tutor.

Treatment Beyond Home and School

The preceding recommendations for the treatment of underachievement at home and school are effective with many children and adolescents if the underachievement is not complicated by heavy involvement in drugs, alcohol, crime, or serious depression. However, even the adolescent who shows a long history of "complicated" underachievement may also be able to reverse the underachieving pattern, as well as the drug, crime, or other problem. In addition to the parent and educator working together, this youth is likely to need attention by a psychotherapist specializing in adolescent problems. One excellent alternative for such an adolescent is a residential school which combines individual and group therapy, including behavior modification techniques, and provides a controlled environment with educational opportunities aimed at overcoming underachievement (Peterson, 1978). Residential schools combining education with psychological treatment are listed in a book entitled *Handbook of Private Schools,* available in most public libraries.

SUMMARY

Underachievement by gifted students is a great potential loss that can be reversed. It is defined as a discrepancy between students' high ability and mediocre or poor school performance.

Intelligence, achievement, and creativity scores can be used to help diagnose underachievement. If the gifted student is a poor test-taker, observation by teachers or parents is necessary for determining giftedness.

Whitmore prepared a checklist of characteristics of gifted underachievers. The authors describe three levels of characteristics: (1) low self-esteem, which is the most basic; (2) defensive avoidance of threatening academic tasks; and (3) poor study habits, peer acceptance, school concentration, and discipline.

Underachievement is learned.

Gifted underachievers are less likely to identify with their same-sexed parents, unless the parents also are underachievers or do not value achievement. Freud explained identification as an unconscious product of resolving Oedipal or Electra complexes. Social learning theorists emphasize the importance of a nurturing relationship, perceived power in the parent, and similarities in child-parent characteristics.

Several parent-power patterns foster inappropriate identification and underachievement. Research shows worse male achievement for males in father-absent homes, and worse math and problem-solving skills for both sexes in such homes. Successful career mothers serve as effective models for achieving girls.

Counteridentification can lead parents to spend time with their children and reinforce the development of academic, artistic, or athletic skills. It can also lead to manipulation by children and to underachievement. If parents complete the child's homework it will encourage excessive dependence. If parents give their highly verbal children too much power, the children may manipulate their environments to avoid effort.

Teachers who recognize and provide for gifted students create their "good years"; other teachers who cannot, their "bad years." Inflexible teachers, who may pile on extra busywork, encourage underachievement. Attractive diversions also may reward underachieving.

Teachers may ignore or scold the hand-waving, question-asking gifted student, who then stops responding in class. Counterproductive behaviors, such as sloppy or incomplete work or aggressive behavior, may be rewarded by valuable teacher attention.

Heavy emphasis on competition tends to minimize intrinsic rewards of learning and creating. Competition is devastating to underachievers, whose self-concept is damaged by repeated evidence of incompetence.

Negative expectations by teachers become self-fulfilling prophecies. Remedial work also may label a student as inept.

An unrewarding curriculum prevents the gifted child from fulfilling needs to question, discuss, criticize, and so forth. Challenges may be found outside of school, for example, in hobbies or athletics.

The treatment of underachievement requires five steps: (1) evaluating the students' abilities with intelligence and creativity tests, and determining school and home reinforcements that support underachievement; (2) changing the school and home reinforcers to support academic achievement; (3) changing the expectations of significant others; (4) locating a good model for identification; one who is the same sex, powerful, similar, open, and nurturant—and an achiever; and (5) correcting the skill deficiencies.

APPENDIX 13.1 CONGRATULATIONS, MISS SMITHERSTEEN, YOU HAVE PROVED THAT AMY ISN'T GIFTED

"What makes you think Amy's gifted anyway?" Miss Smithersteen's words echoed through the stillness of the empty classroom. It was parent conference day and two adults sat at the front of the large recently vacated classroom. Mrs. Robertson, Amy's mother, was there to talk to Miss Smithersteen, Amy's teacher.

A pregnant silence followed while "Amy" images flashed through Mrs. Robertson's head. Comical baby Amy, balancing a book with her bottle. Two-year-old, wise Amy, unsolicited, carrying a towel to Grandma to dry her hands since Grandma had to run to the telephone with wet hands. Four-year-old, independent Amy telling her playmates, "Yes, I can be a doctor even if I am a girl." And ten-year-old, absorbed Amy, immersed in hours of reading each night before bedtime.

Mrs. Robertson didn't really know how she could answer Miss Smithersteen's question. She really wasn't sure that Amy was gifted. She knew Amy wasn't the highest achiever in her class, but she was also the youngest child in the class. Amy had always been a really good reader and oh yes, now she remembered, it was that I.Q. test a few years ago. . . . And then Mrs. Robertson added hesitantly, "Well, Miss Smithersteen, I know there are children in Amy's class who may be more gifted than Amy, but I do think that an I.Q. around 140 means that she's fairly bright."

Miss Smithersteen responded defensively and continuously. "I.Q.'s really don't mean much, you know. She doesn't seem gifted to me. She has trouble sequencing; you see I looked through her reading workbook and she has all the sequencing mixed up and she only scored ninth on her quarter textbook test and she never even speaks up in class and she is a *B* student."

The stress of Miss Smithersteen's last statement presented an image of a *B* indelibly written on Amy's forehead and Mrs. Robertson really felt that there was nothing more constructive she could say. But she did need to explain one thing about Amy, so she began again.

"Miss Smithersteen, Amy may not be quite herself for a few days since, as you know, she's in the high school play and is staying up late for rehearsals during this last week before the play."

"Oh yes, that's another thing, Mrs. Robertson." Miss Smithersteen's booming voice continued, "She should be working on basic skills and not wasting time on school plays. I'm giving the gifted children plenty to do. They're working on mythology now and Amy is only a *B* student."

Mrs. Robertson, thinking about the positive experience the play was for Amy, sensed an urgent need to leave the classroom. She also knew that it was equally critical to say something positive to Amy's teacher.

"Miss Smithersteen, I do want you to know that Amy really likes school and enjoys your teaching and thank you very much for your time." Mrs. Robertson was being truthful. Amy did enjoy school. And she even had said that Miss Smithersteen was interesting and that she was enjoying the special extra assignment in mythology where she could read all the mythology she wanted and just tell the teacher the pages to get extra credit.

As Mrs. Robertson walked the block to her car, she wondered about why that conference had gone so wrong. Every other "Amy" conference in Amy's school life had gone beautifully. It had started when she had asked about Amy's *B* grade in reading. She really wasn't worried about Amy getting a *B* but she wanted to tell Miss Smithersteen that it didn't seem quite fair. The fifteen best readers of the ninety children in the fourth grade were identified for special accelerated reading group. All had been *A* reading students in their regular reading groups and now only six had received *A*s. It seemed to her that the children were being punished for being bright and she had dared to express that opinion to Miss Smithersteen. Mrs. Robertson realized that the conference had deteriorated rapidly from that moment. During the drive home, Mrs. Robertson vowed quietly that she would, in the future, keep her opinions to herself. She really did want to keep a positive relationship with Amy's teacher.

Three days later the typically enthusiastic Amy leaped off the school bus with the news of her school day. "Mom," she exclaimed, "you'll never guess what happened today in school. Miss Smithersteen announced the grades of our reading unit test and she said to the whole class, 'You'll never guess who had the second highest score,' and it was me, Mom. I guess I really surprised her."

Mrs. Robertson was delighted at the news. It seemed like a quiet victory after her conference just a few days earlier. She knew Amy was a good reader and since all the students in the special class were, it seemed logical that the order of their scores would vary from time to time. Anyway, it was good for Amy's confidence, even though Miss Smithersteen had made the announcement as if Amy's skill was unexpected.

The next school quarter went well for Amy. She was as enthusiastic as ever about school projects and was also pleased about her good grades, especially in reading. At the end of the quarter when Miss Smithersteen calculated the total reading scores, she announced the grading cutoff points to her class. Amy came home a little despondent that day without her typical joyful leap off the bus.

"Mom," she said, "it doesn't really seem fair. I missed an *A* by just one point. Only three kids got *A*s this time and what I don't understand is that last quarter, when Debbie missed an *A* by one point, Miss Smithersteen gave her an *A* anyway."

Mrs. Robertson reassuringly said to Amy. "I'm really pleased with your work. It's really important that you're trying your best and that you're really learning."

"But Mom," Amy resignedly added, "I just hate all the workbook work. It's so boring."

Amy walked quietly out of the kitchen and Mrs. Robertson sighed. She knew that there was nothing that she could do about an indelible *B* and felt almost sure that Amy was resilient enought to successfully negotiate the routine reading workbook page days ahead. And to be fair to Miss Smithersteen, Mrs. Robertson acknowledged to herself, Amy had come home on many days with much enthusiasm, so there was certainly more to her school days than reading workbooks.

Third-quarter teacher conference time arrived and Mrs. Robertson resolved to make this a positive parent conference. She promised herself she would only *listen* to Miss Smithersteen's description of Amy's work and then only ask about how Amy was getting along with her peers. She would make absolutely no comments about grades.

Miss Smithersteen's welcoming smile announced to Mrs. Robertson that she too was determined to make this a positive conference. Together they reviewed Amy's papers and Mrs. Robertson felt assured that Amy was continuing to do fine school work until Miss Smithersteen announced that, of course, Amy hardly ever spoke up in class. Mrs. Robertson reflected for a few seconds and then responded a little tensely, "That isn't like Amy. I have never heard that from any of Amy's other teachers. It means that Amy doesn't feel very confident. Miss Smithersteen, I would really appreciate it if you could help Amy build her confidence. She really has much that she could contribute and perhaps I should talk to Amy and ask her why she doesn't speak up in class. Oh yes, Miss Smithersteen, I wanted to tell you that I noticed that Amy is speaking with excellent vocabulary since she's been in your class and I wanted to thank you."

Miss Smithersteen enthusiastically agreed to try to help Amy speak up in class, but she did want to show Mrs. Robertson one more of Amy's papers. She selected a reading test from the back of a pile of papers and showing it to Mrs. Robertson, she announced confidently, "You see, Mrs. Robertson, this is an important reading test and as you can see, Amy earned a *B* on this test. I want you to understand that Amy is really a *B* student in reading."

"Oh, yes, I see," Mrs. Robertson responded forcing a cheerfulness into her voice. Thanking Miss Smithersteen for the conference, she moved toward the door. She imagined Amy again with an indelible *B* placed neatly on her forehead.

Despite the indelible *B* reading test, Mrs. Robertson felt some triumph. She had succeeded in keeping the conference mainly positive and had even communicated with the teacher about both of them making efforts to build confidence in Amy relative to speaking up in class. It had not been a bad conference and at least teacher and parent would be working together *for* Amy.

Mrs. Robertson postponed talking to Amy about class participation for a few days mainly because the days were full of other activities and also because she wanted to think more about what she wanted to say. It was a not-so-bouncy day when Amy came in from the bus and Mrs. Robertson asked the usual questions about Amy's day at school that provided a natural introduction to the subject.

"Things went okay, I guess," Amy said. "But today in reading group, Miss Smithersteen gave us a grade for class participation. I answered a really lot of questions, but Mom, she only gave me a *B*. I thought I deserved an *A*."

"Oh well, Amy, don't worry about the grade. I'm really happy to hear you're answering questions in class," Mrs. Robertson responded making an effort to sound enthusiastic.

"Amy," she continued, "Miss Smithersteen did tell me at our conference that you don't speak up in class very much any more. Is there any special reason why you don't?"

Amy looked puzzled and hesitated before she answered. "You know, Mom," she said, "I always raise my hand when I know the answer, but Miss Smithersteen hardly ever calls on me. Then sometimes I'm not sure of the answer and so I don't raise my hand. It's funny—that's when she calls on me. I wish she wouldn't do that. And Mom, did you ever ask Miss Smithersteen why I didn't get an *A* in reading?"

Mrs. Robertson, taken somewhat by surprise by the last question, responded honestly. "Yes, I did," she said, "but that was way last fall."

"Well," continued Amy seriously, "I wish you wouldn't ever do that again because today Miss Smithersteen said to our reading group that there were some mothers who wanted to know why their little babies weren't getting *A*s in reading and, Mom, she looked right at me."

Amy's last sentenced trailed off as she quietly left the room to busy herself with her afterschool activities. She seemed to have already forgotten the incident, but Mrs. Robertson, frustrated at her own communication failure, whispered to herself, "I'm sorry Amy." Then she wrote the following never-to-be-sent imaginary letter.

Congratulations, Miss Smithersteen, you've proved Amy isn't gifted. Each year Amy's confidence and competence have grown. She came into your class a confident and eager little student. She loved learning and school and reading and felt really bright and capable. She still loves learning and school and reading, but has lost the sense of classroom competence. You engraved an indelible *B* on my child's forehead and have pushed her down all year and refused to let her grow. Yes, Miss Smithersteen, you are right—you have proved yourself right, but that is not a fine teacher's mission. With only the same effort you could have continued to elevate Amy, to facilitate her eagerness, to enjoy her enthusiasm and to delight in her giftedness. Together we could have enjoyed the results of your successful performance and your contribution to Amy would have been immeasurable.

Congratulations, Miss Smithersteen, you are right. For this year Amy is a *B* student. The indelible letter is engraved on her forehead. She is not gifted. But Amy is resilient and Amy is bright and Amy is excited about learning and in future years, Miss Smithersteen, Amy will have different teachers and then Miss Smithersteen, Amy *will* be gifted again.

From Sylvia Rimm, "Congratulations, Miss Smithersteen, You Have Proved Amy Isn't Gifted," *G/C/T Magazine,* Sept.-Oct. 1980, 22–24. Reprinted by permission.

14

THE CULTURAL UNDERACHIEVEMENT OF FEMALES

The expectation that gifted females will utilize their talents should be set into motion as early as possible in the young gifted child's experience. (Wolleat, 1979)

The education of gifted women has been a low priority throughout history, a matter that has led to wholesale female underachievement. Many gifted girls have been, and continue to be, systematically discouraged by peers, family, and sometimes teachers and counselors from using their talent in productive ways. Schwartz (1980) noted that even though more doors are open today to gifted women than ever before, they still find themselves in a no-win conflict between professional interests and education, on one hand, and pressure to fill the traditionally appropriate sex role, on the other. Observed G/T educator Lynn Fox (1977a), "I [have] wondered how many written articles or presented papers on the topic 'The Gifted Child' would have been more realistically entitled 'The Gifted Male.' "

It used to be much worse. History shows that leading educators and psychologists have played a deliberate role in limiting educational opportunities for females. While many early educators simply ignored the education of females, some were explicit in designing education to maintain women's subservience to men. Smith (1981) quoted one of the most influential educators of the eighteenth century, Jean Jacques Rousseau, regarding his theory for the education of "Sophie," the ideal girl.

> Women's entire education should be planned in relation to men. To please men, to be useful to them, to win their love and respect, to raise them as children, care for them as adults, counsel and console them, make their lives sweet and pleasant. These are women's duties in all ages and these are what they should be taught from childhood on.

Smith also reminds us that Sigmund Freud and Carl Gustav Jung, leading psychoanalytic psychologists of the late nineteenth century, described what they perceived as inferior female characteristics. Freud noted the main traits of femininity as narcissism, masochism, and passivity. Jung described the mentally healthy female as being more emotional and less rational and logical than an equally mentally healthy male.

G. Stanley Hall (1844–1924), another leading psychologist and educator, reflected Freud's views in recommending that education for women " . . . should aim at nothing but motherhood." Edward L. Thorndike, early in this century, progressed only slightly beyond Hall, suggesting that education is not likely to "harm women's health" and that some women could even be educated toward careers, provided those careers involved nurturing roles (Smith, 1981). All these quaint views both reflected and reinforced prevailing social attitudes.

Stereotyping, Bias, and Discrimination

Carrelli (1982) noted that the correction of sex inequities requires attention to three interrelated types of limitations: sex role *stereotyping*, sex *bias,* and sex *discrimination.* Sex role *stereotyping* takes place whenever specific behaviors, abilities, interests, or values are attributed to one sex. For example, boys are stereotyped as strong, independent, unemotional, and achievement oriented; girls as weak, dependent, nonaggressive, nurturant, and emotionally expressive. We might add that "women are terrible at math" and "women are indecisive, ineffective leaders" are two more stereotypes. The stereotypes are culturally defined and reinforced by parents, teachers, counselors, and even students themselves.

Sex *bias* refers to treating the sexes differently, usually based upon the above sorts of stereotypes. For example, based only on a gifted girl's sex—and with no knowledge of her specific talents—a teacher or counselor might advise a young woman to avoid math, physics, and chemistry courses and the scientific careers that require them. Carelli noted that if female students ignore stereotyping and bias, and engage in masculine activities, the result can be criticism, labeling, and social ostracism. Because bias is rooted in stereotypes, when stereotypes are gone bias will also disappear.

Sex *discrimination* is the denial of opportunities, privileges, or rewards to a person or a group because of their sex. Of course, it is a violation of federal law. Carelli described the case of an artistic male with talents in drama and costume design. Although he convinced his friends they were stereotyping costume design as "women's work," he could not convince the school guidance counselor, who denied him admission to a sewing class that he needed.

Sex role stereotyping, sex bias, and at least subtle forms of sex discrimination continue to the present. However, the changing role of women, which began in the late 1960s and early 1970s, provides us with unmistakable evidence that women have the potential to achieve and to contribute much more to society than they have in the past. More than ever, women are entering and succeeding in "men's" professions—law, medicine, business, engineering, and others. Furthermore, in making career-related contributions to society, they also are enhancing their own lives and achieving greater personal fulfillment.

Overview

This chapter will review some statistics and opinions regarding the present status of sex inequities in the work world and life satisfactions of working versus nonworking women. It also will review arguments and data regarding biological sex differences, along with information regarding the other viewpoint—that observed differences are sociocultural in origin and are maintained by mechanisms that support female underachievement. Suggestions for teaching and counseling gifted females and for reducing sex role sterotyping, bias, and discrimination also will be itemized. Finally, we will extend the school-home model for modifying general underachievement, described in Chapter 13, to reversing underachievement patterns in gifted girls.

PRESENT STATUS OF WOMEN: WOMEN IN THE WORK FORCE

An analysis of the present status of women in the work force provides the best documentation for the argument that many gifted women are indeed functioning as underachieving adults. They often occupy sex-role sterotyped careers and occupations and receive inequitable salaries and responsibilities. Noted Jones (1978; Schwartz, 1980), only " . . . nine percent of the nation's labor force of doctoral scientists and engineers are women." Rudd and McKenry (1980) noted that 80 percent of the women in their study were involved in just 20 of 500 possible job categories. The sex-role sterotyped careers—for example, teaching, nursing, clerical work, factory work, bookkeeping, and secretarial work—were mainly low-salaried jobs and, with the exception of teaching and nursing, not considered a "profession." Armstrong (1979) found that one-tenth of 1 percent of America's engineers and 2 percent of the physicists were women. Allain (1981) similarly pointed out that female college graduates earn approximately $7,000 less per year than male college graduates. In 1977 the U.S. Department of Labor reported that female college graduates earned an average of just $300 more per year than male high school dropouts.

These figures suggest that education is less important for upward mobility and high career achievement than *sex*, and that many talented females are indeed underachieving. Said Wolleat (1979), ". . . despite twenty or more years of formalized guidance services in most high schools, sex remains the best single predictor of who will enter many occupations . . . "

The status of women in education further documents female underachievement. Elementary and, to a lesser degree, secondary teaching have long been known as female sterotyped professions. In 1980, approximately two-thirds of all K–12 educators were female (Smith, 1981). However, the upper echelon of power in elementary and secondary education is predominantly male and again reflects dramatic achievement inequities for females: Only 15 percent of school principals are women, and just a handful of women serve as school superintendents. Leadership in teachers' organizations shows similar inequities, with most local, state, and national positions held by men.

Higher education is dominated by men in numbers, rank, and salary. Most professors are men. According to some 1977 U.S. Department of Health, Education and Welfare statistics, only at the lower faculty levels, such as instructor or lecturer, do the numbers of female faculty approach equality with males. The disproportionate number of male college professors is even more alarming in light of Tidball's (1973) conclusion that the number of women faculty at a given college is an excellent predictor of how many career women the college will produce.

Women also tend to be found in lower ranks and in less prestigious institutions, compared with men of similar educational preparation (Giele, 1978). Vetter and Babco (1975) reported that at four-year universities, 60 percent of the male faculty were professors and associate professors compared with only 30 percent of the female faculty. Salary inequities show a similar pattern, with women's salaries at 78 percent of men's salaries (Kilson, 1976).

Of course, part of the sex differences in numbers, rank, and salary could be due to the more recent influx of women into college teaching, leading logically to lower average ranks and lower average salaries. Affirmative action committees, particularly at major universities, try to prevent blatant sex discrimination. However, a University of Minnesota study (reported in a 1972 *Time* magazine article) indicated that even at equal ranks, female faculty salaries were 32 percent lower than those of males.

College administration has been a virtual *no-woman's land*. The same

TABLE 14.1 Males and Females Receiving Degrees in Traditionally Male Fields in 1970–71 and 1979–80 (From the National Center for Educational Statistics)

		1970–71				1979–80	
	N	MALE	FEMALE	N		MALE	FEMALE
Bachelor's Degrees		%	%			%	%
Agriculture	12,672	96	4	22,802		70	30
Business Management	115,527	91	9	186,683		66	34
Engineering	50,046	99	1	68,893		91	9
Physical Sciences	21,502	86	14	23,410		76	24
Health Professions	25,226	23	77	63,920		18	82
Professional Degrees							
Dentistry	3,745	99	1	5,258		87	13
Medicine	8,919	91	9	14,902		77	23
Veterinary Medicine	1,252	92	8	1,835		67	33
Law	17,421	93	7	35,667		70	30

1972 *Time* magazine article recommended, "If a woman wishes to become a college president, she is advised to become a nun." At the time, just 1 percent of college presidents were women, and virtually all of these were nuns. Frazier and Sadker (1973) reported that 100 percent of the presidents of coed universities were male, and so were 97 percent of the graduate deans, 91 percent of the deans of students, 95 percent of the admissions directors, and 96 percent of the registrars. On the positive side, as in other traditionally male professions, the number of women entering college administration appears to be increasing.

Some 1982 figures from the National Center for Educational Statistics, U.S. Department of Education, document dramatic changes in the numbers of women receiving bachelor's or professional degrees in traditionally male-dominated fields (see Table 14.1). However, except for *health professions*, the percentage of females continues to remain much lower than that of males. While these trends are in a positive direction, the figures still clearly document the underachievement of gifted and talented women.

LIFE SATISFACTIONS OF WOMEN

In the postwar years, even a woman who attended college was expected to achieve life satisfaction vicariously through her husband's career. Her success was tied to his success, along with success in the wife, mother, and home manager role she would play. Qualities of being "good-looking" and "sexy" were part of her definition as a woman (Graham, 1978; Schwartz,

1980). Her primary allegiance was toward her family, while the primary allegiance of her husband was toward his career (Coser and Rokoff, 1971).

Eminent developmental psychologist Erik Erikson (1959) described the *identity crisis*—deciding who and what you are—as being resolved later for a woman than for a man, and as tied directly to marriage, her husband's career, and the birth of the first child. Identity was wrapped in the nurturing role. Adams (1971) suggested that women were caught in a "compassion trap," based on the belief that their most important function was to provide tenderness and compassion.

Note, too, that sociocultural sterotypes allowed a man to receive encouragement and support for his demanding career and professional accomplishments. However, a talented woman did not have a nurturing and supporting "wife" available, nor was anyone particularly anxious to take over home and child-rearing responsibilities for her.

This dramatic waste of the talents and contributions of women might be justified if women perceived themselves as fulfilled and happy in their housewife role. Surely, the nurturing of future generations is a critically important contribution to society, as is the support of men who make professional contributions. Research indicates that while some women do find high life satisfaction as homemakers, on the average life satisfaction—including self-esteem and feelings of competence—is greater for working and career women (Birnbaum, 1975). Bernard (1972), for example, found that housewives who derived their identify solely from their role as wife and mother were most likely to suffer the effects of *housewife syndrome*. This syndrome includes a sense of helplessness and hopelessness, depression, and a loss of self-esteem. The years devoted to caring for one's family seem to deprive many women of their sense of autonomy, leaving them with feelings of complete dependence. On the other hand, career women usually derive much satisfaction from their work and the recognition they receive (Rodenstein and Glickauff-Hughes, 1979). Nadelson and Eisenberg (1977) reported that husbands of professional women found them to be "more stimulating" people.

With working-class women, Feree (1976) found that, on the average, wives who held even low-prestige jobs were happier and more satisfied with their lives than women who were full-time housewives. She made the interesting proposal that the low satisfaction reported by housewives was due to performing a job that has no clear criteria of "success," resulting in feelings of low recognition and a poor sense of accomplishment. Three out of four housewives and two out of three employed wives reported that they felt incompetent relative to their homemaker role. In contrast, none of the employed wives reported feeling incompetent relative to their jobs, and more than half believed they were "extremely good" in their work.

Shaver and Freedman (1976) also documented the sense of competence stemming from outside employment. Housewives reported feeling lonelier than employed wives (44 percent versus 26 percent), more anxious and worried (46 percent versus 28 percent), and more "worthless" (41 percent versus 24 percent). These figures suggest that not working outside the home almost doubles the likelihood of unhappy feelings about oneself.

Women returning to college and the work world after five to ten years of full-time devotion to wife and child-rearing roles provide rich anecdotal material regarding the dramatic changes in their lives. The following story, shared by a young woman married to a successful physician, reveals the frustration some of these women feel.

> I had worked previous to having had my family and had received recognition and promotions for my accomplishments. When my husband completed medical school and we had our family, I reluctantly gave up my job. There were three children in rapid succession, and although I enjoyed mothering, I became more and more frustrated with my own sense of personal accomplishment. I kept telling my husband that I was anxious to return to college. One day while bathing the baby, I made the decision. I packed my suitcases and set them in the hall. When my husband came home, I simply said, "Either I return to school or I'm leaving." My husband looked strangely at me and said he hadn't realized that I wanted to go back to school, but that I certainly could. I couldn't believe his response, because I had been telling him this all year. I guess he didn't really believe me, and I had to do something really dramatic for him to hear what I was saying.

The Home-Career Conflict

Although working outside the home usually provides more self-satisfaction and life satisfaction, gifted women are caught in a very common conflict. The alternative to the *housewife syndrome* is the *working wife* or "Queen Bee" (Staines, Tavris, and Jayaratne, 1974) syndrome, a demanding superwoman role that requires women to meet the obligations of a challenging and worrisome job plus fulfill the traditional responsibilities of cleaning, shopping, cooking, laundry, and child care—and be a loving and supportive wife as well. Great mental stability is required.

Poloma (1972) interviewed 53 couples in which the wives were involved in the male-dominated professions of law, medicine, and college teaching. These women used one or more of the following four techniques for managing the home-career conflict.

1. *They looked at the **benefits** of combining a career and a family, rather than the costs.* As one woman explained, "I am a better mother because I work and can expend my energies on something other than over-mothering my children."
2. *They decided in advance which role came **first** in the event of conflicting demands.* In virtually every case, family crises took precedence over career crises. If the baby sitter did not show up or a child got sick, the wife, not the husband, missed work that day.

3. *They* **compartmentalized** *the two roles as much as possible, keeping work and family distinct.* Few of the women brought work home with them, for example, although their husbands often did.

4. *They* **compromised.** The wives controlled the extent of their career commitment to fit the circumstances of their family lives—how the husband's work was going, his income, the ages and number of children, the husband's support (or lack of it), and so on. "When one or more of these factors is out of kilter, the wife makes the necessary adjustment to manage role strain," Poloma found.

Some women felt compelled to make unreasonable concessions. For example, a lawyer would not talk about her practice at home, so that " . . . the children would not think that her work was more important than their father's." Others expected little and asked virtually nothing of the family to help them adjust to the double demands of family and career.

For the professional woman with a family, there is no easy solution to the continous conflict of her roles. If she is committed to her career, she feels guilty for not fulfilling her nurturing commitment to her family. If she considers family first, she is criticized and feels guilty for not being sufficiently dedicated to her career. One apparently successful solution, used by one married pair of professors known to the authors, is to split the household and child-care duties down the middle. The father not only does his share of the cooking and housework, but is equally likely to take a day off to tend to a sick child. However, university people may be more accepting of such role division than people in a nonuniversity community. There may be very few working couples who divide home responsibilities equally.

Despite the difficulties of the double-role commitment, Birnbaum's (1975) study provides encouraging statistics for gifted young women who choose to combine *marriage and a career* or choose *careers only*, compared with becoming *housewives only*. Of the three groups, the housewives showed the lowest average self-esteem. Only 14 percent of the housewives, compared to 54 percent of the married professionals and 54 percent of the single professionals, reported "good" to "very good" self-esteem. Seventy-two percent of the housewives, compared with 36 percent of the married professionals and 73 percent of the single professionals, reported "feeling lonely" fairly often. Forty-two percent of the housewives indicated that they missed challenge and creativity, compared to just 4 percent of the married professionals and none of the single professionals. Sixty-one percent of the housewives, 12 percent of the married professionals, and 58 percent of the single professionals viewed themselves as "not very attractive" to men. Interestingly, while 52 percent of the housewives considered themselves happily married, 68 percent of the married professionals rated themselves as happily married. Although the "working wife" syndrome will pose problems for gifted women, these figures again indicate that it beats out other alternatives in terms of personal life satisfaction.

Rodenstein and Glickauf-Hughes (1979) reported similar statistics with 201 women graduates of the University of Wisconsin, ages 24 to 35. The *single* and the *married* career women rated themselves higher in "work satisfaction" and "recognition for accomplishments" than the *homemaker* group. Perhaps not suprisingly, while 96 percent of the homemaker and married career women indicated that children were a satisfying aspect of their lives, only 1 percent of the single career women indicated satisfaction in this area. It is noteworthy that 38 percent of the single career women planned to have children at some point in their lives; they were not rigidly locked in to a single, childless career-only life-style. They retained their flexibility and kept their options open; they could change their minds and their life-style if they wished.

As a final note, the present authors agree that society is the loser when any gifted and talented person, male or female, elects not to become a contributing professional. At the same time, it is true and acceptable that some women, gifted and "normal," do find a wife-mother-homemaker role satisfying, and free from the pressures and anxieties of job responsibilities and the career-homemaker conflict. None of the research in this section claimed that 100 percent of all housewives were unhappy and unfulfilled. Aesthetic and creative needs may be met in developing high-level home-making and child-care skills, in artistic and creative hobbies, and in clubs and community work. It is important, however, that all young women, and especially high-potential ones, have both the encouragement and the opportunity to receive training, develop their talents, and become professionals if that is their choice. The research reviewed in this section suggests it is the best choice. The doors must remain open, and gifted females must have the support of parents, teachers, school counselors, future partners, and society (for example, business, industry, and government).

DIFFERENCES BETWEEN THE SEXES

Comparisons of biological versus sociocultural differences between the sexes should provide a good basis for determining the extent to which the underachievement of women can be modified. The proportion of sex differences that are biologically determined could be viewed as limiting the potential achievements of gifted women. However, sex differences related to sociocultural norms—stereotypes, bias, and discrimination—can be changed, and the correction of these problems may be seen as freeing women to achieve equally with men.

Biological Differences

Velle (1982) recently reviewed research on biologically-based behavioral differences between the sexes, differences that conceivably could limit achievements of women. Although some of the research was based on animal behavior, some also involved human subjects.

Levels of physical activity.   Velle attributes high levels of male physical activity to hormonal influences in the brain during fetal development. He cited research with horses (Schafer, 1974) and monkeys (Goy and Resko, 1972) that supported greater hormone-related physical activity in males. He also reminds us that castration of male domestic animals invariably produces quieter animals. His only example of actual human sex differences in activity came from research reported by Restak (1979), which showed that hyperkinesis (abnormally high levels of physical activity) is found in boys much more frequently than in girls. Of course, the hyperactivity that accompanies about 50 percent of common learning disabilities in school children is known to be largely a boys' problem (Davis, 1983b).

Aggression.   Velle cited various animal studies linking the male hormone testosterone with aggression (for example, Bronson and Desjardins, 1968, 1971; Edwards, 1969; Goldberg, 1973). He also documented human studies (Freedman, 1974; Conner, Levine, and Wertheim, 1969; Goldberg, 1973; Moyer, 1974) which indicated that boys display more aggressive behavior than girls, and suggested that this is related to adolescent competitive behavior. One interesting study (Yalom, Green, and Fisk, 1973) reported the results of giving synthetic estrogen (a female hormone) to pregnant diabetic women. Their sons showed significantly less aggressive behavior at age 16, compared with same-aged boys of normal mothers and of untreated diabetic mothers.

Tomboyism.   *Adrenogenital syndrome* is an abnormal condition in girls characterized by masculinization of external genital organs. It apparently is caused by excessive androgen hormones during fetal development (Liddle, 1974). Girls with this syndrome always have corrective surgery and are raised as girls. However, despite their female socialization, most of them show characteristics usually considered masculine, such as preference for boy playmates, interest in sports and athletics, preference for boys' clothes and toys, preference for a professional career to marriage, higher physical activity levels, and a lack of interest in caring for small children, hence the nickname *tomboyism* (Money, Hampson, and Hampson, 1973; Money and Schwartz, 1978). These findings support the reality of biologically determined sex differences which, in these tomboyism cases, can override environmental and sociocultural influences.

Cerebral dominance differences. In the past three decades, specialization of the left brain hemisphere for speech and verbal abilities and logical and sequential thinking, and the right hemisphere for spatial and other nonverbal abilities, has been continuously researched and written about. Assumptions about abilities related to sex differences based on the more specialized use of one side of the brain or the other are highly controversial and not well supported by any documented research. However, Levy-Agresti and Sperry (1968; see also Benbow and Stanley, 1980, 1981; Kolata, 1983) reported finding stronger right-hemisphere dominance for males, resulting in higher spatial abilities. Buffery and Gray (1972), in clear contradiction, argued that the better male bilateral development—equal development of both sides of the brain—is responsible for the apparently superior spatial skills of males.

If there are hemispheric differences between the sexes, no research makes it clear whether the hemisphere differences cause the differential spatial ability, or whether cultural conditions cause the differential hemispheric development. Camille Benbow (Benbow and Stanley, 1981), however, even though she would *like* to find an environment difference that has been overlooked, concluded that the superior verbal skills of girls and the superior math and spatial skills of boys are tied to differential hemispheric functions, and the difference is genetic. She reported one study in which a group of girls were specially taught spatial skills, but even that made little difference in their measured spatial ability.

Durden-Smith and DeSimone (1982) recently itemized some apparently biological differences between the sexes that, on balance, make females look noticeably superior—physically, psychologically, and socially. Consider these differences:

Men are more likely to be sexual deviates or psychopaths.

Women are stronger in verbal and communication abilities, but suffer more from phobias and depression.

There are more males at both ends of the intellectual spectrum—retardates and geniuses.

More males have heart attacks, since testosterone apparently increases cholesterol and hardening of the arteries.

Girls develop faster.

More males are spontaneously aborted during pregnancy, are born dead, or die in the first month of life.

More males have major birth defects.

Males are born less sturdy.

Boys are four or five times more likely to be *autistic* (being mute or having bizarre speech) or *aphasic* (unable to produce or comprehend speech; aphasia also includes emotional and thinking disorders).

Boys are much more likely to be unable to read (*dyslexia*), unable to do arithmetic (*dyscalculia*), or to have other learning disabilities.

Boys are five times more likely to stutter.

Males commit almost all violent crimes.

Males are more prone to alcoholism.

Males are more prone to schizophrenia.

We also might mention some traditional observations: Boys are more likely to be hyperactive, disruptive, and aggressive in class. Girls have better handwriting and better teeth and, when they get older, they have more hair and they live longer.

Sociocultural Differences

The investigation of sociocultural differences in the treatment of the sexes—and all of the resulting differences in behaviors, attitudes, and abilities—clearly has been spurred by the feminist movement. Although these differences can be described and to some extent even quantified, research cannot delineate the exact extent to which specific differences are cultural versus biological in origin. However, studies of the changing role of women in society provide good documentation that many differences are indeed *not* biologically based.

The pink or blue blanket that identifies sex differences almost at birth is the first step in giving differential direction to the sexes. Next comes the infant's nursery, with pastel colors, lace, frills, and dolls for girls and bright colors, football heroes, space ships, and dump trucks for boys. The expectations of *docility* and *conformity* for girls throughout early childhood initiate the gifted girl to her eventual underachieving role in society.

In the process of developing her *Bem Sex-Role Inventory*, Bem (1974) itemized stereotyped characteristics associated with men and women. Interestingly, characteristics considered "masculine" also are typical of successful people, for example: *aggressiveness, ambitiousness, analytical ability, assertiveness, competitiveness, leadership ability, independence,* and *self-reliance.* Characteristics in the "feminine" column included those which might be associated with mothering or, at best, a narrow range of nurturant, female-dominated occupations, for example: *affection, cheerfulness, compassion, gentleness, love of children, shyness, understanding,* and *warmth.* Parents who teach *only* these characteristics to females by their expectations, by parent sanctions of appropriate behavior, and by modeling also are systematically teaching their daughters to underachieve.

Bem's sex-role stereotyped traits are further reinforced by textbooks, literature, and the media. In an analysis of one third-grade reader, Allain (1979) found that men were described as involved in 33 occupations compared with only 6 for women. Further, these occupations were clearly sex-role stereotyped, for example: doctor, minister, cowboy, inventor, and mayor for men; and teacher, princess, seamstress, and secretary for women. Weitzman and Rizzo (1974) claimed that science texts " . . . give children the impression that no woman has—or can—play a role in building our scientific knowledge." Children also are guided toward sex-role stereotyped books. There are "girls' books," such as *Little Women* and *Little House in the Big Woods,* and "boys' books," which include tales of mystery, adventure, risk-taking, and accomplishment (Sadker, Sadker, and Hicks, 1980).

Television, so pervasive in the lives of children, further reinforces sex-role stereotypes. Sternglanz and Serbin (1974) analyzed sex-role stereotypes of ten of the then most popular children's shows. They found half to have no female characters at all, while the others had twice as many males as females. Furthermore, females were portrayed as not making or carrying out plans; they were punished if they were too active or aggressive; and they continuously deferred to males. Male characters were highly active, aggressive, and socially dominant, and they made plans and carried them out.

The influence of movies and television on the aggressiveness and morals of children is an important and continuing issue. On the side of strong effects, Bandura and Walter's (1963) classic research on the effects of modeling showed that filmed models were as effective as live models in influencing physical aggressiveness in children. Even closer to the present problem, Pingree (1978) found that five-minute commercials were effective in influencing children to accept either traditional or nontraditional roles of women.

Can gifted girls overcome the impact of families, schools, and sex-role stereotyped literature and media on their own self-perceptions? Only with high levels of awareness and some deliberate "counterconditioning."

Differences in Abilities

Jensen (1980) presented a comprehensive review of studies of sex differences in tested abilities. Table 14.2, adapted from Jensen, reflects the percentages of studies indicating superior performance by either sex and the percentages showing no significant sex differences. Based on these studies, there is no overwhelming support that any ability is totally and exclusively sex related. However, there is evidence that females may outperform males on tests of *verbal ability, verbal divergent thinking,* and *general intelligence,* while males may outperform females on tests of *quantitative*

TABLE 14.2   Numbers of Studies of Sex Differences and Their Outcomes on Various Types of Tests Published Since 1966

TYPE OF TEST	N	Significant Difference in Favor of		
		NEITHER	MALE	FEMALE
		%	%	%
General Intelligence	58	69	5	26
Verbal Ability	131	62	10	28
Quantitative Ability	35	43	46	11
Visual-Spatial (nonanalytic)	35	68	26	6
Visual-Spatial (analytic)	63	55	40	5
Reasoning (nonverbal, nonspatial)	38	69	18	13
Piagetian Tests of Conceptual Level	51	80	12	8
Divergent Thinking (verbal)	32	50	16	34
Divergent Thinking (nonverbal)	23	30	35	35

Adapted with permission of The Free Press, A division of Macmillan, Inc., from *Bias in Mental Testing* by A. R. Jensen. Copyright © by A. R. Jensen.

and *visual-spatial* abilities (Bee, 1974; Benbow and Stanley, 1980, 1981, 1983b; Block, 1976; Callahan, 1979; Maccoby and Jacklin, 1974). In addition, girls generally score higher on achievement tests, get higher grades, and as mentioned above, have fewer learning disabilities, repeat fewer grades, and cause less trouble in class (Brophy and Good, 1970; Lips and Colwill, 1978; Maccoby and Jacklin, 1974). The higher grades may be due to their acquired attitudes of dependence, conformity, and desire to please (L. W. Hoffman, 1972).

Incidentally, in reviewing sex differences in scores on standardized tests, keep in mind that some sex differences actually could be artificially reduced during the test construction process itself. Test items that appear to yield sex-biased scores often are eliminated during the construction of a test, selectively leaving items which do not discriminate by sex.

Mathematics Ability

The most prominent and heated argument related to differential abilities regards whether males have superior mathematical abilities (Armstrong, 1979; Benbow and Stanley, 1980, 1981, 1982, 1983b; National Assessment of Educational Progress, 1975; Pallas and Alexander, 1983; see also Stanley and Benbow, 1983).[1] The math difference seems to widen over the years, becoming quite prominent by junior high school

[1]Interestingly, no one seems to dispute the possibility that girls have superior verbal abilities, higher IQ scores, better overall academic records, plus other superior features noted above.

(Hilton and Berglund, 1974; Leinhardt, Seewald, and Engel, 1979; Maccoby and Jacklin, 1974). Giele (1978) and Fennema (1980), in fact, concluded that male and female math abilities are about equal in childhood, but at about age 12 or 13 boys begin to show superiority.

Camille Benbow and Julian Stanley (1980, 1981, 1982, 1983b)—basing their work on years of Scholastic Aptitude Test-Mathematics (SAT-M) scores collected for thousands of students in Stanley's *Study of Mathematically Precocious Youth* (SMPY)—concluded that their data support a biological superiority of male math ability, which could be related to male superiority in spatial tasks. They indicated that environmental influences are not likely to so dramatically affect the "extreme absence of extraordinary female talent" among students involved in the SMPY talent search. A November 1983 Associated Press news release, based upon a recently published article in *Science* magazine (Benbow and Stanley, 1983b), noted that in the years 1980, 1981, and 1982 Benbow and Stanley found that the average SAT-Mathematics score for 19,883 gifted seventh-grade boys was 416. For 19,937 gifted girls the average score was a noticeably lower 386. Average SAT-Verbal scores were almost identical, 367 for boys and 365 for girls. Further, boys outnumbered girls by better than 2 to 1 among those scoring above 500; by better than 4 to 1 among those who scored over 600; and by almost 13 to 1 in the group scoring 700 or higher (113 boys, 9 girls). Benbow and Stanley " . . . could not find substantial differences in attitude, background, or previous mathematical training between boys and girls." See Inset 14.1 for one possible physiological explanation of sex differences in mathematical talent.

Jensen's (1980) data in Table 14.2 shows that visual-spatial (analytic) skills favored males in 40 percent of the studies reviewed, while just 5 percent favored females. We noted before that the superior male visual-spatial ability has been used to explain their apparently superior mathematics ability. Based on his inbreeding study in Japan involving marriages between cousins, Jensen (1982) proposed that visual-spatial ability is a sex-linked recessive trait. He explained that inbreeding has the effect of improving a skill that is recessive, but decreasing a skill that is dominant. Since visual-spatial abilities seemed to increase with inbreeding, he concluded that the trait must be a biologically determined, sex-linked recessive characteristic carried through females to males. It is a creative argument, one difficult to grapple with.

The counterarguments to a biological explanation of male math superiority, which mainly assert that mathematics ability is cultural in origin, also are creative and impressive.

Cultural stereotypes. Usiskin (1982) found that in the area of geometry proofs there were no ability differences between males and females. Usiskin argued that no sex differences were found in this area because it is

---

INSET 14.1 DOES MATH GENIUS HAVE A HORMONAL BASIS?

In recent years, Harvard Medical School neurologist Norman Geshwind has proposed that excess testosterone or unusual sensitivity to testosterone during fetal life can alter brain development (Kolata, 1983). Specifically, the right hemisphere of the brain (instead of the usual left) becomes dominant for language abilities, and the person is likely to be left-handed. Further, such individuals—mainly boys, of course—are predisposed to (1) such speech abnormalities as autism, dyslexia, or stuttering, (2) certain kinds of giftedness, particularly artistic, musical, or mathematical, and (3) disorders in the body's immune system. Said Geshwind, "If you get the mechanism adjusted just right you get superior right hemisphere talents, such as artistic, musical, or mathematical talent. But the mechanism is a bit treacherous. If you overdo it, you're going to get into trouble. It's a funny mechanism. At first, it looks like you have to deliberately produce damage to produce giftedness."

According to *Science* magazine writer Gina Kolata, Benbow and Stanley were intrigued by this possible explanation of male superiority in math talent, and promptly contacted their very best students (those who scored above 700 on the SAT-M) to see if they were left-handed or had immune system disorders. "To their surprise and delight, they find that Geshwind's predictions hold up beautifully in their group" (Kolata, 1983). Twenty percent of the mathematically talented students are left-handed, which is more than double the proportion of left-handedness in the general population. A full 60 percent have immune system disorders (allergies, asthma)—which is five times the expected rate.

When Benbow and Stanley contacted students in their list who were less mathematically talented, the students also were less likely to be left-handed or to have immune disorders.

While Geshwind agrees that the data for the precocious students "fit in perfectly, to put it bluntly," he also concedes, "There's been—understandably—an enormous degree of skepticism."

---

a kind of mathematical reasoning that is "environmentally pure." That is, it is not taught at any earlier time in school nor is it used in the child's home environment, and therefore it is not subject to environmental sex-role stereotyping.

During adolescence, when sex differences in math skills begin to become especially prominent, males and females also begin their heterosexual interests. Society encourages boys more often than girls to show superior intellectual ability to attract members of the opposite sex. However, girls, in accord with cultural stereotypes, may believe that boys do not like girls who excel in math, and therefore do not seek to develop mathematical abilities (Fox, 1977a, 1977b).

Unequal math training. Based upon her review of research on mathematics learning, Fennema (1980) argued that conclusions about male superiority often have been based on studies in which the number of previous math courses has not been controlled; that is, males with more math background have been compared to females with less background. However, Fox (1980, 1981a; see also Benbow and Stanley, 1980, 1981, 1983b) emphasized that the mathematics talent searches conducted at Johns Hopkins University for the SMPY program were at grades 7 and 8, when males and females had equal math training.

Jacquelynne Parsons (1982) has argued that the spatial skills leading to strong math problem solving can be trained, and that sex differences would be removed if the training were at least equal.

Father identification. As we saw in Chapter 13, several studies (for example, Sutton-Smith, Rosenberg, and Landy, 1968) reported that early father absence, before age 8 or 9, has a depressing effect on later math scores of both males and females. They hypothesized that children learn a mathematical problem-solving thinking style from their fathers. Helson (1971) similarly reported that creative women mathematicians and scientists tended to identify with their fathers. It is possible then that learning mathematical thinking and problem solving may take place informally in the family through the process of identification with the father. Since boys are more likely to identify with their fathers than girls (Hetherington, 1972), boys logically would acquire superior mathematics abilities.

Different toys. Still another hypothesis is that sex-role stereotyped toys improve visual-spatial abilities for boys more than for girls. Trains, model airplanes, race cars, trucks, electrical sets, Legos, Tinker Toys, and other construction toys all are more likely to be played with by boys. These toys may enhance spatial skills more than the typical dolls, tea sets, coloring books, jump ropes, and needlecraft supplied to girls.

Teacher expectations. Mathematics has been considered a male domain by both students and teachers. Ernest (1976) found in interviewing teachers that 41 percent thought boys were better at math than girls, while none thought girls were better. Since teacher expectations may affect achievement by as much as 20 percent (Brophy, 1982), the *self-fulfilling prophecy* might easily help perpetuate mathematics as a male domain.

Also rooted in cultural stereotypes and expectations, Brody and Fox (1980) found that parents of gifted boys were more likely to see a career in mathematics for their son than were parents of gifted girls.

School support.   In an analysis of schools that successfully teach math and science to girls, Casserly (1979) found that teachers in those schools were not threatened by mathematically gifted girls, that they used older females to tutor younger girls, and that they began good programs before the sixth grade—before girls come to view math as a male subject. Fox (1974) similarly found that girls were successful in a math program for the gifted when school personnel were enthusiastic and supportive of the girls.

The mathematical sex differences issue obviously is involved and confusing, in view of conflicting research data, different interpretations of the same data, and of no small importance, different philosophical commitments—which frequently are quite fixed before the scholars even look at the data.

Importance of the Math Differences Hypothesis

Differential skill in mathematics is a critical issue in relation to the professional development of gifted females. Male-dominated fields that convey high status and good financial rewards (for example, medicine, engineering, architecture, pharmacy, computer sciences, and all physical sciences) *require skill in mathematics.* Sells (1976) found that male and female applicants for admission to the University of California–Berkeley differed significantly in their math preparation. Sixty-eight percent of the females, compared with 35 percent of the males, did not qualify for college calculus. At the University of Maryland, Sells (1976) found that only 15 percent of the white females and 10 percent of the black females had the math prerequisites necessary for a mathematics or science-related major. This lack of preparation clearly prevents most females from *ever* entering many challenging and rewarding professions. Said President Reagan in his 1983 State of the Union address to Congress, "If a child has not acquired a good mathematical training by age 16, he or she will never be able to enter the fields of engineering or science."

Differences in Leadership Ability

Apart from mathematical abilities, and without getting into the nature-nurture debate, Linda Addison (1979) proposed that females are weak in characteristics contributing to good leadership; namely, females:

1. Are weak in the ability to project themselves into the future, to see the unforseeable, and to anticipate problems and predict consequences and trends.
2. Are weak in the ability to use many cues in decision making.
3. Have a tendency to fear and avoid risk situations, rather than to weigh dangers against opportunities.

Good leaders, said Addison, are " . . . able to set goals, plan, establish priorities, and set a course of action. Further, women do not see themselves as leaders and are unable to project themselves into these positions." One solution she described was a simulation game that rewards females for participating in leadership experiences; more specifically, for predicting and evaluating the consequences of changes and decisions, and for thinking analytically and critically.

DIFFERENCES IN EXPECTATIONS, ACHIEVEMENT ORIENTATION, AND ASPIRATIONS

Differences in mathematical preparation and perhaps leadership propensities provide real barriers to the entrance of females into many male-dominated professions. In addition, there are also culturally imposed sex differences that discourage females from seeking high career achievement. Family, school, and peer expectations discourage a strong achievement orientation, risk-taking, independence, and self-confidence in girls. These pressures can lead to low aspirations which, in turn, result in underachievement.

Family Expectations and Identification

High educational achievement and high career aspirations begin at home. Both mother role-modeling and father expectations have a compelling and documented influence on the achievement orientation of gifted girls. For example, in regard to identification with mother, Shaw and White (1965) found that high school girls with high grades viewed themselves as more like their mothers than their fathers, compared with lesser-achieving females. A study of college freshmen by Teahan (1963) also showed that high-achieving females saw themselves as being much like their mothers, while low-achieving females did not.

In regard to career aspirations, many researchers (for example, Almquist and Angrist, 1971; Altman and Grossman, 1977; Frieze, Parsons, and Ruble, 1972; Marini, 1978; Radin, 1974; Sutherland, 1978; Tangri, 1972) concluded that career modeling by mothers motivates females to have higher educational and career aspirations. As for the specific nature of their career choices, however, Rodenstein and Glickhauf-Hughes (1979) found no effect at all of mother's or father's career on the career choices of gifted women at the University of Wisconsin.

Fathers' direct expectations of their daughters also may influence female achievement. Radin and Epstein (1975) found that fathers' short- and long-term academic expectations of their daughters were positively correlated with measures of the girls' intellectual functioning. There may be a chicken-egg problem, however; that is, do higher expectations produce the higher intellectual functioning, or is it vice versa?

Sex-stereotyped expectations of girls—and all women—by their fathers (Lynn, 1974) and dominating fathers (Teahan, 1963; Heilbrun, 1973; Heilbrun, Harrell, and Gillard, 1967) appear to have a negative effect on girls' achievement.

Research on the comparative importance of the mother versus the father role-model for female achievement is not always consistent, nor are the dynamics uncomplicated. We noted earlier that Helson (1971) found that creative women mathematicians tended to be oldest daughters who identified with their fathers. Bardwick (1971) also emphasized the importance of girls' identification with their fathers in order to learn important achievement traits such as independence and self-esteem. Drews and Teahan (1957) and Pierce and Bowman (1960), however, concluded that mother dominance was critical in encouraging girls to become career-oriented achievers. On the other hand, some women have sought careers in a direct response to what they perceived as their mothers' "empty lives"— their mothers served as models of what *not* to do.

In conclusion, despite some special circumstances and exceptions, career-oriented mothers do indeed provide strong role models that, along with positive and supportive father expectations, influence educational and career achievement of gifted girls.

Peer Expectations

From early adolescence, and sometimes before, peer expectations play a very strong part in directing achievement. Because high intelligence and an achievement orientation sometimes are considered masculine characteristics, girls risk being considered "unfeminine" if they become too involved in school achievement. The following retrospective statement by a female college student in a class given by one of the authors (Rimm) exemplifies the pressure on female students not to achieve:

> In junior high I was still interested in sports, as an active participant and a spectator. I also did very well in school, with my favorite subjects being math and science. By eighth grade, however, I realized that "dumb blonds" were the most popular with boys. Therefore, without lessening my achievement, I became very modest, trying to downplay my intelligence.
>
> In high school, the outlet for my interest in sports changed from being a basketball player to being a cheerleader, the more feminine role. I left it to the boys to do the aggressive work while I looked "pretty" jumping and cheering. While I still remained in the top portion of my class, always trying to do my best in school, I continued to be modest, acting dumber than I was.

Ruth Duskin Feldman, former Quiz Kid and author of the book *Whatever Happened to the Quiz Kids* (1982), shared an anecdote with the author (Rimm) that shows only a small change in peer expectations of gifted females. As a college student, she was asked by a male friend if she would rather be told she was smart or beautiful. Her response at that time was, "Beautiful—I know I'm smart!" A recent sequel to this conversation occurred in her daughter's gifted class. The teacher asked the females in the class if they would rather be beautiful or valedictorian. They all indicated they would prefer the latter. She then asked the males how they would feel about dating the class valedictorian. The boys concluded that dating the valedictorian would be fine, provided she was pretty. If peer pressure to achieve has changed for gifted girls, it has changed mainly from the female perspective. Even bright males continue to rank attractiveness ahead of intelligence.

By college age, parent attitudes toward gifted women's career choices appear less important than peer attitudes (Parsons, Frieze, and Ruble, 1978), especially those of male peers. In a clever study by Farmer and Bohn (1970), female college students were administered the *Strong Vocational Interest Blank,* an assessment of career interests, at two different times and with two different sets of instructions. The first administration included regular instructions. The second administration used role-playing instructions: The women were to imagine that men liked intelligent women, and that women could successfully manage both careers and families. Career interest scores rose in six occupations, including artist, psychologist, lawyer, physician, and life insurance salesperson. Trigg and Perlman (1976) similarly found that females were more likely to apply to graduate school in less traditional areas if their male friends encouraged them to do so. Horner's (1969, 1972a, 1972b) classic "fear of success" syndrome, in which girls suppress high achievement and success because of their fear of "failing as a female," will be discussed later. As one immediately pertinent finding, Horner found that females who received career encouragement from their male friends were less likely to experience fear of success.

School Expectations

From nursery school onward we find continuous documentation of school biases that deter an achievement orientation for females. Serbin and O'Leary (1975) compared differential treatment of boys and girls in 15 nursery school classes and recorded the following behaviors that they felt would reinforce aggressiveness, confidence, and independence in boys, but not girls.

1. Boys were encouraged to work on their own much more often than girls.
2. Teachers rewarded girls for being dependent by responding more when they were near, but gave similar attention to boys regardless of physical distance.

3.   All 15 teachers gave more attention to boys than girls, including more individualized instruction and more tangible and verbal rewards.
4.   Girls were rebuked quietly; boys were scolded publicly.

When teacher feedback is given to children, Dweck and Bush (1976; Nichols, 1979) found that poor performance often is described as "lack of ability" in girls, while similar poor performance is noted as "not working hard enough" with boys. This difference is important. If poor performance is seen by students (girls) as lack of *ability,* then increased effort will not solve the problem. However, if poor performance is interpreted as lack of *effort,* then the students (boys) will be motivated to work harder to achieve (Weiner, 1980).

Fox (1981b) interestingly noted that the "critical thought and questioning mind" of the young boy is likely to be described as "insolence" or an "argumentative nature" in a girl.

Casserly (1979) reported sex differences in willingness to take Advanced Placement courses. Although girls outnumber boys in traditionally "female" Advanced Placement courses (for example, English, Spanish, and French), girls usually take fewer Advanced Placement courses than boys in math, history, classics, German, and all sciences. In analyzing differences between schools that produce high-achieving girls and those that do not, Casserly identified two disarmingly simple factors: (1) The schools producing high-achieving girls used a tracking program that made Advanced Placement classes a natural sequence, and (2) teachers both actively recruited girls for the Advanced Placement classes and expected them to be high achievers.

School counselors have been found to possess sex stereotypes that work against female achievement. In one survey, Petro and Putman (1979) found that both male and female school counselors agreed that girls are more " . . . easily excitable in a minor crisis, easily influenced, home-oriented, passive, noncompetitive, indecisive, and easily hurt." Other evidence shows that female counselors often project their own fears of science and math into girls, cautioning them that they may not get good grades if they take difficult math and science courses (Casserly, 1979).

Counselors also suggest to girls, more often than to boys, that they need time for their social lives and/or that they should avoid courses in math and science. Quoting one counselor, " . . . there are so many fun things going on. I think they'll be busy enough and they [girls] can get into the serious work in college" (Casserly, 1979). The following quote was considered by Casserly to be representative of male counselors: "There are men with Ph.Ds in physics all over the place who can't get jobs. Why should we encourage girls?"

From preschool to college, then, and despite improvements in recent years, many teachers and counselors by implication and by action discourage females from developing their talents equally with males (Casserly, 1979; Donahue and Costar, 1977; Fitzgerald and Crites, 1980; Fox, 1977a; Schwartz, 1975; Wolleat, 1979).

Self-Expectations

Female aspirations and achievement orientations surely are changing. This change must include altered self-perceptions and self-expectations. If gifted females are to develop their talents and make their contributions to society they must acquire confidence and strong achievement needs, and they must make plans for a sound education.

Research suggests four important factors that seem to be linked to the lower self-expectations and aspirations of females: (1) a lower sense of competence, (2) the tendency to attribute failures to oneself and successes to external factors, (3) lower achievement motivation, and (4) the "fear of success" syndrome mentioned above. These undoubtedly are interrelated, and together decrease the likelihood of gifted women aspiring to challenging professions. We will examine each of the four.

Low sense of competence. First, studies of the sense of competence among women repeatedly show that, on the average, women exhibit lower feelings of competence than do men. For example, Stake (1981) found that females tended to score lower than males in predicting their future ability to perform well in high-level careers. Crandall (1969) discovered that when college students were asked to predict future test grades, women usually expected to do worse than in the past while men expected to improve (despite the fact that the women actually did as well as the men or better). Addison (1981) similarly found that in evaluating their own performance females tended to underestimate their degree of success while males tended to overestimate it.

In a program in which gifted seventh- and eighth-grade students were given an opportunity for grade acceleration, only 54 percent of the girls chose acceleration, compared with 73 percent of the boys (Fox, 1977b). Said Fox, girls were less confident in trying something new and were more fearful of failure. They also experienced more problems of self-esteem—which were unrelated to actual ability—and were more fearful of peer rejection. Hall (1982) similarly reported that girls were less likely than boys to enter college early.

A classic study by Goldberg (1968) indicated that women also seem to lack confidence in other women. College students were asked to rate a written work as to its value and its author's competence. Some were told that the author was a female, others that the author was a male. College women rated the work more highly when the author was identified as male.

Maccoby and Jacklin's (1974) conclusion that boys are more intensely socialized toward competition and success provides a reasonable explanation for their developing a stronger sense of personal competence.

Attributional differences.   The lower confidence that females exhibit is also reflected in studies of the causal attributions they make. Studies of both children and adults report a similar sex-related tendency (Deaux, 1976; Frieze, 1975; Post, 1981). Females tend to attribute their successes to hard work or to luck, but their failures to lack of ability. Males tend to follow the reverse attribution process, blaming others, bad luck, or their lack of effort for failures, but crediting their own high abilities for successes.

An extreme form of this attribution difference is found in the *imposter* phenomenon, in which women who have achieved success indicate that they do not believe they are capable of being in their position, and that their inability will somehow be discovered. It is surely an example of extremely low confidence when women who receive recognition for their achievements still are unable to attribute this success to their own ability.

Low achievement motivation.   Our third factor in female underachievement is low achievement motivation. A basic premise of achievement motivation theory (Atkinson, 1974; McClelland, 1976; McClelland, Atkinson, Clark, and Lowell, 1953) is that persons with strong needs to achieve will strive to succeed in situations requiring intelligence and leadership. The need to achieve is a highly consistent personality trait that, according to Veroff (1969; Feld, Ruhland, and Gold, 1979; Ruhland, Gold, and Feld, 1978), begins developing as early as the second grade.

Efforts to teach achievement motivation basically encourage the learner to think as achievement-oriented individuals do; that is, to (1) value success and achievement, (2) accept moderate risks, (3) set realistic and achievable goals, and (4) feel confident that he or she can achieve these goals.

We have seen throughout this chapter that cultural stereotypes, biases, and home and school expectations have worked to reduce female independence and aggressiveness, and, consequently, their needs for high-level academic and career achievement. Achievement motivation leaders McClelland (1976) and Atkinson (1974) also attribute needs for achievement to learning, rather than heredity, and point to parental influence in childhood as the crucial factor.

As an interesting historical fact, in an 873-page compilation of research into achievement motivation, a single footnote commented on achievement motivation research with women (Atkinson, 1958).

Fear of success.   As early as 1935 Margaret Mead observed that " . . . the achieving girl [is threatened that she] will never be chosen by a member of the opposite sex." More recent research on women's fear of success (Horner, 1969, 1972a, 1972b; Zinberg, 1974) suggests that in mixed sex competition, women are motivated to *avoid* success. Horner hypothesized that aggressiveness traditionally is considered a masculine characteristic. Since competitiveness or being too intellectual is not ladylike, women fear that success in the achievement domain may mean failure as a female.

In Horner's research, 90 female college students were asked to respond to the statement below with "Anne" as the character, while 88 males responded to the same statement with "John" in it:

> After first term finals Anne (John) finds herself (himself) at the top of her (his) medical school class.

The scoring of the stories showed that 90 percent of the males described rosy futures for John—but a full 65 percent of the females predicted an unhappy outcome for Anne. Anne's academic success was described as bringing her social rejection in the form of unpopularity, loneliness, lack of femininity, and low marriageability. Success in competition with males thus was seen as leading to feelings of anxiety, guilt, despair, and doubt about femininity and normalcy. Based on these sad predictions for bright women, Horner coined the phase *fear of success* and explained that this paradox in women's achievement motivation would cause many women to feel defensive about their achievements if they are successful, and sometimes will prevent them from achieving in the first place.

Lavach and Lanier (1975) discovered that Horner's fear of success was particularly prevalent among high-achieving white adolescent girls. The anxiety was aroused especially when in direct competition with males, and it increased from grades 7–9.

To be fair, we must note that in the dozens of follow-up studies of women's fear of success, the results have been inconsistent or else have demonstrated qualifying circumstances. For example, both Alper (1974) and Katz (1973) found that fear of success scores are considerably lower when the situation is less threatening. For example, when reference to "medical school" was omitted (Alper) or when it was noted that half of "Anne's" medical school classmates were women (Katz), fear of success scores dropped considerably. A replication of the Horner study by Hoffman (1974) showed that more males (77 percent) than females (65 percent) showed fear of success, although the men's reasons were different than for women. While women feared that success would mean social rejection, men tended to question whether the success was worth the tremendous effort.

EDUCATING GIFTED FEMALES

Society no doubt will continue to improve in providing a support system in which gifted women may develop their potential equally with men. Schools, however, must take a leadership role in fostering this equal development.

In this section the model explored in Chapter 13, dealing with underachievement, will be used to provide some realistic guidelines that can help teachers, counselors, and parents reverse underachievement in females. That model includes the following five steps:

1. Assessing skills, abilities, and home and school reinforcement contingencies
2. Modifying reinforcements at home and school
3. Changing the expectations of important others
4. Improving model identification
5. Correcting skill deficiencies

Since cultural underachievement is a more extensive problem than individual underachievement, there will be some additional special problems that educators must consider in programming for underachieving girls.

Assessing Skills, Abilities, and Reinforcement Contingencies

School district administrators, principals, teachers, counselors, and others need, at the minimum, to ask the following questions:

1. Are sex-role stereotyped books, films, and other media avoided in the classroom and library?
2. Are spatially oriented activities, such as mathematics and computer work, introduced early so that both girls and boys can begin learning these skills before peer pressures intervene?
3. Are females equally encouraged to participate in competitive activities?
4. Are counselors and teachers being educated in the opportunities for and abilities of females?
5. Are students and their parents being educated regarding the broad range of opportunities for females?
6. Are girls encouraged to take leadership roles in the school?
7. Are gifted girls encouraged to take advanced courses in all curricular areas?
8. Are students exposed to a variety of successful, professional female models?
9. Are opportunities available for assertiveness training for females?
10. Are some all-female group guidance experiences being provided, so that girls may deal with problems related to femininty, self-confidence, and an achievement orientation?
11. Are efforts being made to erase the stigma of a high achievement orientation for females?
12. Are the rewards for career achievements for females being stressed equally with those for males?

To the extent that answers to these questions reflect nonencouragement of high-level educational and career aspirations for gifted girls, suitable changes should be initiated.

Modifying Reinforcements at Home and School

While it is difficult enough to modify reinforcements for females at school, it is even more difficult for a teacher to encourage such reinforcement among parents and peers. A series of short letters to the parents of gifted students, including some specific suggestions of ways in which parents can help encourage sex equity and female talent development, may help. One example of such a letter appears in Inset 14.2. Notice that only one topic is addressed in this letter, encouraging girls to take higher-level mathematics and science courses. Other topics for brief letters could include strengthening the girl's career orientation, building confidence, the value of higher education, the role of some risk-taking in success, and perhaps even the eventual division of household chores. In each case, it is important to emphasize the rewards available to females who develop their abilities, and to encourage parents to reward girls for accepting special challenges. This is a difficult message to give parents; they have been socialized in a culture that has fostered underachievement in women, and therefore they themselves usually are guilty of reinforcing sex-role stereotypes.

Peer reinforcements are perhaps the most difficult to manipulate. One effective way to encourage peer reinforcement is to provide coeducational group meetings for gifted students, both educational and semisocial. The kind of rapport and mutual support that usually develops in such meetings encourages all gifted students to challenge themselves. Discussions in which students air their concerns (for example, regarding risk-taking or the career-homemaker conflict) may help give females the support they will need. Discussions of careers that are appropriate for all gifted students will emphasize the acceptability and desirability of female talent development. The rapport established among gifted peers can also create a more supportive and rewarding social life for gifted girls, which is an important variety of peer reinforcement.

Changing the Expectations of Important Others

Teachers, parents, and girls themselves must acquire the expectation that females can achieve. Providing teachers, parents and gifted students with evidence of female achievement in traditionally male-dominated fields is a most effective method of changing expectations. Internship programs (in which girls work with women executives and other women professionals), career women guest speakers, and field trips to see the accomplishments of talented women all provide living evidence of female accomplishment. Local professional women's organizations, such as American Association of University Women or the local chapter of the National Organization for Women, may be pleased to cooperate with such projects.

INSET 14.2 CHALLENGE SENIOR HIGH SCHOOL, EVERYTOWN, WISCONSIN

Dear Mr. & Mrs. Kirpatrick:

We would like to recommend that your daughter Sara select Calculus, Advanced Biology, and Advanced Chemistry among her courses in grade 12. Her past performances in mathematics and science suggest that she would benefit from these challenging courses. These courses are complex and do involve more homework than some other selections that she might make. As a result, some high school students, particularly females, are hesitant in selecting them for fear that they may not perform as well as they typically have performed. Mainly these students worry about a negative effect on their grade-point average or about peer pressure which may make high-level science or math courses appear to be more male related.

We hope that Sara will be encouraged to select these courses because advanced courses in science and math can provide many more career options for her. Challenge Senior High School has taken the following steps to encourage capable girls to select these difficult courses:

1. Course grades are weighted so that a "B" grade in these courses is the equivalent of 4 points or an "A" in easier courses.
2. Courses are taught by both male and female teachers who were selected based on their willingness to provide extra support and help for these challenging courses.
3. Guest lecturers from professional science and mathematics areas will provide information to students on career areas in science and mathematics.
4. Women guest lecturers will share with girls their experiences on how to combine careers and homemaking roles.
5. Students who select these courses will be eligible for Advanced Placement Testing and may therefore be able to earn college credits during their senior year in high school.

You or Sara may want to chat with me further about our special program to encourage bright female students to fulfill their intellectual potential. Please don't hesitate to call me to discuss Sara's special concerns. We will also be holding a special meeting for gifted girls and their parents in early March and I hope to meet you at that time.

Sincerely yours,

Margaret Nellon

Margaret Nellon
Guidance Counselor

Opportunities to hear, see and work with high-achieving women can be supplemented by reading and research projects that provide students with the opportunity to learn about achieving women and to understand the training and personality characteristics needed for high career achievement. The actual study of women's achievements in the arts, sciences, and in literature will help gifted girls, their teachers, and their families to recognize the reality of female talent and accomplishment.

Model Identification

Although there are fewer female models with whom gifted girls may identify—for example, women doctors, lawyers, researchers, or executives—they nonetheless can be located, even in small communities. Such persons provide the aspiring gifted girl with the assurance that it is possible for a woman to achieve a career goal and at the same time enjoy a satisfying marriage if she so chooses.

At extremely high achievement levels, however, the scarcity of female models can lead to doubly strong anxieties related to the conflict of successfully coordinating a marriage with a career requiring long, arduous preparation. The extent of this problem was recently shared by a woman M.D./Ph.D student at Harvard Medical School. She had failed to find even one woman, either at Harvard or in her research field, who had successfully combined marriage with a career in medical research. The recognition that she was investing so much time and energy to prepare for a career-marriage role, when virtually no evidence that success was possible existed, left her extremely frustrated. She wanted desperately to find a model who could provide encouragement.

Educators do need to help girls locate such models. The models can share with gifted girls the experiences, rewards, frustrations, and decision-making processes that accompanied their accomplishments. In view of their own difficult experiences, they often are eager to share insights with gifted young women.

Correcting Skill Deficiencies

The skill deficiencies of gifted girls usually are found in math and science. Such deficiencies can be prevented by encouraging high school girls to take the necessary advanced courses, which will permit their eventual entry into desirable college majors and prestigious careers.

One good approach to attracting girls to advanced math classes is to encourage women teachers to teach them. Also, reasonable grading criteria, good teaching, and smaller classes that allow individual attention can make these classes more attractive to all students, and less threatening to gifted girls. Many students, male and female, avoid math classes in fear of lowering their grade-point averages, which reduces their chances for high school awards and college admission and scholarships. If advanced math course grades could be weighted such that a *B* earns 4 points instead of the usual 3, gifted males and females both would be less intimidated by such courses. The greater complexity and competitiveness of these courses should justify a more lenient grading policy.

We should note that not all areas in which females are deficient are academic. In addition to providing experiences that will help academic and creative development, teachers and counselors must ensure that gifted girls are helped in developing *autonomy, self-esteem, self-confidence,* a *willingness to compete, leadership* and *assertiveness* (Addison, 1979; Fox, 1981b; Navarre, 1980; Wolleat, 1979).

Finally, the special problems that characterize the wide-reaching cultural underachievement of women require that all persons be enlisted in the task of changing the culture in order to support the development of women beyond their stereotyped nurturing roles. The rewards to individual women and to society will make the effort easily worthwhile.

SUMMARY

The education of gifted women historically has been largely ignored. Some early influential educators publicly specified a nurturing domestic role for women.

Carelli defined three interrelated problems as (1) stereotyping, the attributing of behaviors, abilities, or interests to one sex; (2) bias, differential treatment according to sex; and (3) discrimination, the denial of opportunity based on sex.

In the work force, women are dramatically underrepresented in traditionally male professions. Salaries also are comparatively poor.

Women are underrepresented in educational administration in elementary and secondary schools, in college teaching, and in college administration. While women's entry into "male careers" is improving, the percentage of women in these fields still is low.

Women's life satisfactions stereotypically have been tied to their husbands' career success plus success as a wife and mother. On the average, working and professional women show higher life satisfaction—greater self-esteem and greater feelings of competence—than full-time housewives.

The main problem is the home-career conflict. While there is no easy solution, some women decide in advance which role comes first (the family), compartmentalize the two roles, and often compromise to fit husband and family needs.

All gifted women should have the opportunity and encouragement to develop their talents and become professionals, if that is their choice.

Research suggests biological sex differences in levels of physical activity and aggression. Some scholars claim stronger right-hemisphere spatial abilities for males. Tomboyism, due to biological masculinization of sex organs, produces girls with many masculine interests and traits.

A list of sex differences in abilities and traits shows that, on the average, females tend to be physically, psychologically, and socially healthier. Sociocultural differences in the treatment of the sexes begin almost at birth. Differences exist in room decorations and toys and stereotyped characteristics, for example, as reflected in Bem's Sex-Role Inventory. Textbooks, literature, and the media, especially television, reinforce sex-role stereotypes.

Jensen's list of tested abilities showed women to be superior in verbal ability, verbal divergent thinking, and general intelligence.

The most heated debate centers on whether males have superior math ability, stemming from allegedly superior spatial abilities. Prominent in the issue are the Benbow and Stanley SAT-M statistics. Jensen proposed that the superior spatial ability of males is a sex-linked recessive trait.

Counterarguments propose that the math differences may be due to (1) cultural stereotypes, (2) unequal math training, (3) boys' identification with father, (4) different types of toys, (5) teacher expectations, and (6) lack of school support. The issue is made complex by inconsistent findings, different interpretations, and predetermined philosophical commitments. The issue is highly important because a lack of mathematical training will close—and is closing—permanently the doors to many high-status and well-paying male-dominated careers.

According to Addison, females tend to be weak in some leadership traits, including the abilities to predict problems, consequences and trends, to use many cues in decision-making, and to take risks.

High educational and career achievements are related to family expectations. Identification with mother, especially a career mother, appears important. Fathers' expectations of their daughters also influence achievement. Sex-role stereotyped family expectations work against girls' achievement. Research shows that creative women mathematicians tend to identify with their fathers. Traits of independence and self-esteem also may be learned from fathers.

Peer attitudes and expectations often depress female achievement. School expectations reward male independence, confidence, and aggressiveness, but reward female conformity. Likewise, female poor performance sometimes is attributed to lack of ability; male poor performance to lack of effort, leading boys to work harder.

Schools that successfully produce high-achieving girls make Advanced Placement classes a natural part of the sequence, and actively recruit girls for the Advanced Placement classes. School counselors sometimes perpetuate cultural stereotypes of male versus female traits, and often counsel girls to avoid math and science. Regarding self-expectations, women tend to have a lower sense of competence and self-esteem, attribute failure to lack of ability, and have lower achievement motivation. Horner's "fear of success" syndrome leads girls to view high achievement as unfeminine, that is, they fear "failing as a female."

Rimm's five-part model was presented as a guide for dealing with female underachievement: Step 1 included evaluating the school environment for factors that suppress or reinforce female achievement. Step 2 involved modifying school, family, and peer reinforcements. Step 3 included changing the expectations of teachers, parents, and the girls themselves. Step 4 involved finding suitable career women models. Step 5 focused on correcting skill deficiencies, particularly in math and science.

15

THE HANDICAPPED GIFTED CHILD

Typically, gifted children who are handicapped are recognized for their handicap, not for their gifts and talents. Their special needs stemming from the handicaps are provided for by mandated programs in special classes and special schools funded by state and federal government. Since most handicapping conditions do not preclude or prevent giftedness, it is logical to expect that one should find among handicapped children the same percentage of gifted and talented students as in the general population. However, labeling the child as "handicapped" plus attending to the priority needs of the handicapping condition usually obscures the creative, artistic, intellectual, or scientific talents of the child. They are thus much less likely than the nonhandicapped gifted child to be identified as gifted and included in a school program that helps develop their special talents.

Overview

This chapter will explore the needs and problems of handicapped children, their identification, and some programming ideas directed toward accommodating those needs.

NEEDS OF THE HANDICAPPED GIFTED

In 1975 the U.S. Office of Education estimated that slightly more than 12 percent of all children between ages 6 and 19 were handicapped (Ysseldyke, Algozzine, and Richey, 1982). In a 1979 report it was estimated that, nationally, 7.5 percent of our children were being served by special educational programs for the handicapped. In real numbers, Gearhart and Weishahn (1976) estimated the prevalence of handicapped children between ages 5 and 18 at between six and nine million. As for *giftedness*, Schnur and Stefanich (1979), estimating a conservative 2 percent of children as gifted, calculated that 120,000 to 180,000 handicapped gifted students are in our schools. A 5 percent cutoff would raise those figures to a more realistic 300,000 to 450,000.

Public Law 94-142, the "mainstreaming law," defines *handicapped children* as

> ... mentally retarded, hard of hearing, deaf, speech impaired, visually handicapped, seriously emotionally disturbed, orthopedically impaired or other health impaired children, or children with specific learning disabilities who by reason thereof require special education and related services.

Of these categories, it would seem that only mental retardation would preclude most forms of giftedness. Nonetheless, programs for handicapped gifted students are rare, even though state and federal funding agencies typically specify that handicapped gifted students be included in any funded G/T program. At the time Eisenberg and Epstein (1981) initiated their program they discovered that there were *no* special programs designated for handicapped gifted students in all of New York City.

Legislation clearly states that handicapped children must be served. However, Schnur and Stefanich (1979) pointed out that the handicapped gifted child may be omitted from special services (the special education class, a special education teacher, a reading teacher, psychological services, Individualized Education Programs) if he or she is functioning reasonably well within the regular classroom. This means that, for example, an intellectually gifted child who performs at grade level, but whose achievement nonetheless is depressed by his or her handicap, would not necessarily be provided with any special services because his or her performance is equivalent to that of average classmates. To the extent that the special services would individualize evaluation and instruction, help the gifted child remediate academic weaknesses, help the child compensate for the handicapping condition, and/or develop individual talents, such special attention is lost.

It is almost common knowledge that handicapped students have poor self-concepts, due to some amount of rejection by other students. Ironically, the labeling that is necessary to obtain funds for special services and equipment contributes to the social rejection and the poor self-concept (Hobbs, 1975). Several studies have shown that mainstreamed handicapped and emotionally disturbed children frequently are rated as the "least liked" in the classroom (Bruininks, 1978; Lansdown and Polak, 1975; Novak, 1974; Richardson, 1962, 1971). Burton and Hirshoren (1979) further found that the greater the severity of the problem, the greater the degree of social rejection. Bryan (1978) and Hoffman (1976) explained that some handicapped children—for example, physically handicapped or emotionally disturbed students—may visibly differ from peer group norms. Apparently, a "normal" child tends to feel that association with an atypical peer threatens the normal child's social image within his or her norm group. Sometimes, mainstreamed handicapped students are brutalized by other students, for example, by name calling or other insults, along with the social exclusion (Iano, Ayers, Heller, McGettigan, and Walker, 1974; Zigler and Muenchow, 1979). Handicapped children are under considerable stress, and strongly positive feelings of self-confidence and self-worth would indeed be surprising.

Maker (1977) suggested that gifted handicapped children themselves often are willing to accept inferior status because of their handicap, and despite their superior abilities and talents. Eisenberg and Epstein (1981) noted that even though most handicapped students do indeed have a poor self-image, in the special education room a gifted handicapped student might in fact be a leader.

Clearly, we are dramatically underserving a segment of the population that has high potential for personal development and achievement and for making high-quality contributions to society. Among outstanding creative individuals who were handicapped, Karnes, Shwedel, and Lewis (1983) listed Ludwig van Beethoven, Thomas Edison, Helen Keller, Vincent van Gogh, and Franklin D. Roosevelt. We might add the names of contemporary musicians George Shearing, José Feliciano, Stevie Wonder, and Ray Charles, all of whom are blind; violinist Itzhak Perlman, crippled by polio; and Hollywood personality Jack Paar, former "Tonight Show" host, who stutters. Unlike most gifted handicapped persons, these people are noted for their gifts and talents, not for their disabilities.

In sum then, gifted handicapped children continue to be ignored, programs for them are lacking, and their problems are compounded by sometimes severe social problems and rock-bottom feelings of self-worth and personal integrity.

IDENTIFICATION

Identifying the gifted handicapped child usually is difficult. A major problem is that their gifts usually remain invisible to teachers and sometimes even parents. As Maker (1977) reported, a concern expressed by gifted handicapped persons themselves is that they typically are noticed for their weaknesses, not their strengths. Eisenberg and Epstein (1981) described their G/T program for the handicapped in which forms for nominating handicapped gifted and talented students were sent to designated New York City schools serving a full 60,000 handicapped students. *Not one student* was nominated.

Another problem is that the handicap itself may obscure the *expression* of the special gifts and talents. For example, blindness, deafness, and some learning disabilities have the effect of slowing development and thus may result in deceptively lower IQ scores. For example, blind and deaf children, because of their sensory deficits, tend to be more concrete in their thinking, which will hardly help the abstract reasoning necessary for a high IQ score. Dyslexic children will certainly suffer on verbal components of an intelligence test, although Marx (1982) suggested that dyslexic children may have much higher than normal spatial-oriented giftedness. Other handicaps (for example, emotional disturbance or social maladjustments, orthopedic or health impairments, speech or language impairments) also can interfere with obtaining an accurate high score on an intelligence test.

In some cases then, the intelligence test—the most commonly used instrument for identifying gifted children—may add a handicap to the discovery of giftedness among already handicapped children. In other cases, however, and as with culturally different and underachieving students, intelligence tests scores can provide eye-opening insights into the true intellectual potential of handicapped children.

Karnes (1979) reported that identifying handicapped gifted children through observation was more difficult than with "normal" children. She found that a prolonged observation was necessary for accurate identification. Providing in-service workshops for teachers of the handicapped, which focus on characteristics of giftedness and the identification of gifted and talented children, should help the teacher identification and nomination process. Teachers who are trained to work with handicapped children rarely have training in the specific area of giftedness. Eisenberg and Epstein (1981) noted that in their search for gifted handicapped children, teachers would select conforming students, not the highly active, energetic ones. Concluded Eisenberg and Epstein, teachers definitely needed direction.

In observing possibly gifted handicapped children, one would, of course, watch for the types of characteristics and behaviors described in Chapter 2, along with an additional interesting one. As Eisenberg and Epstein described their gifted handicapped children, they " . . . understand faster, ask questions, zip through math—and they are terribly disruptive." With "normal" gifted students, disruptiveness is a trait that sometimes appears because the child is bored or frustrated in school. Because frustration and stress can be everyday matters for many handicapped gifted students, it is not surprising that *disruptiveness* can be a good indicator of giftedness with these children.

The identification procedure successfully used by Eisenberg and Epstein (1981) included IQ and achievement scores, which conveniently were already on file. They also used the Renzulli-Hartman (Renzulli, 1983) *rating scales,* not only the frequently used Learning, Motivation, Creativity and Leadership scales, but the less well-known Art, Music, Drama, and Communications scales as well. As noted above, when first approached via a mailing of nomination forms, not one teacher of handicapped students spontaneously nominated a single child for participation in the Eisenberg and Epstein program. However, after looking over the Renzulli-Hartman rating scales, many began *calling* (not writing) the program coordinator with the same urgent message: "Hey, I think I've got a kid for you!" The rating scales themselves served as quick in-service training for identifying gifted handicapped children.

Especially good indicators of giftedness from the Renzulli-Hartman Learning scale were:

2. Possesses a large storehouse of information about a variety of topics (beyond the usual interests of youngsters his/her age).
4. Has rapid insight into cause-effect relationships; tries to discover the how and why of things; asks many provocative questions (as distinct from information or factual questions); wants to know what makes things (or people) "tick."
6. Is a keen and alert observer; usually "sees more" or "gets more" out of a story, film, etc., than others.

Especially good items from the Motivation scale were:

1. Becomes absorbed and truly involved in certain topics or problems; is persistent in seeking task completion. (It is sometimes difficult to get him/her to move on to another topic.)
5. Prefers to work independently; requires little direction from teachers.

Eisenberg and Epstein also found peer nominations and self-nominations to be valuable; more valuable, in fact, than teacher nominations. The peers knew who were bright, creative, and fast-learning. Many handicapped students *nominated themselves* as gifted or talented, and " . . . nine out of ten were right!" In one case, a student nominated himself for the program, and shortly after had himself *decertified*—examined and taken out of the special education class.

Karnes and Shwedel (1981) created a *Talent Screening Checklist* designed especially for identifying handicapped gifted preschool youngsters. Corresponding to the U.S.O.E. definition (Marland, 1972), the checklist included the six areas of intellectual ability, specific academic talent, creativity, leadership, visual or performing art talent, and psychomotor ability. The checklist was completed by both a teacher and a parent, and if either rated the child in the top 25 percent the child was moved to the second step of the identification process. This second step involved guided observation of the child in one or more semistructured *Activities for Talent Identification* (Karnes and Shwedel, 1981). One of the Activities for leadership is shown in Table 15.1. Performance in the top 10 percent of the class constituted elibility for the program. Case conferences or a diagnostic evaluation by a psychologist were used if questions about particular children remained. Karnes and Shwedel pointed out that their identification approach minimized the risks of overlooking any truly gifted handicapped child; further, it also did no harm to any participants.

To help in the identification of gifted handicapped children, Maker (1977) recommended that (1) handicapped students should be compared with others who have the same handicap, and (2) characteristics that enable the handicapped child to effectively compensate for his or her handicap should be weighted more heavily. For example, if an orthopedically impaired student cannot write, his compensating verbal and cognitive abilities

TABLE 15.1   Activities for Talent Identification: Leadership

LEADERSHIP STYLE

Task
Teach the child to make paint by mixing water and dry paint. Then ask the child to pick two other children, a girl and a boy, and have the child teach them to mix the paint.

Criteria

1. Was the child willing to choose partners?   Yes(1)___   No(0)___
   If not, why?

2. How did the child go about enlisting others?
   (a) Did he/she invite or ask others to participate in a positive manner (1) or order or command in a negative manner (0)?   (1)___   (0)___
   (b) Did the child make the task seem exciting to the others?   Yes(1)___   No(0)___

3. How did the child go about the teaching task?
   (a) Did he/she verbally describe the sequence of steps?   Yes(1)___   No(0)___
   (b) Did he/she demonstrate the sequence of steps?   Yes(1)___   No(0)___
   (c) Did he/she monitor the work of the others?   Yes(1)___   No(0)___
   (d) Did he/she offer praise and/or encouragement to the others?   Yes(1)___   No(0)___

4. Did at least one of the children succeed at the new task?   Yes(1)___   No(0)___

Minimum Passing Score = 4

From M. Karnes, "RAPYHT Activities for Talent Identification: Leadership." Reprinted by permission.

should receive more weight; if a student cannot speak, his written, artistic, and creative talents should be examined.

As for creativity, the Renzulli-Hartman Creativity Scale mentioned above apparently is useful. The *PRIDE* (Rimm, 1982), *GIFT* (Rimm, 1976) and *GIFFI* (Davis and Rimm, 1980, 1982; see Chapters 2 and 10) creativity inventories have been specifically validated for use with children with learning disabilities and also should be usable with students with other handicaps.

Finally, as with the similarly difficult challenge of identifying gifted disadvantaged and minority children, using a *quota system* will ensure that handicapped children are examined closely for gifts and talents, and that many will be placed in programs if they show these. The identification of gifted handicapped students will continue to be difficult. However, a sensitivity to characteristics of giftedness and a willingness to look beyond the too-visible handicap will aid in the discovery of talent.

CRITICAL INGREDIENTS OF PROGRAMS FOR THE GIFTED HANDICAPPED

Programming for the gifted handicapped child may vary in type and content to the same extent as for other gifted children. It can include the same acceleration, enrichment, grouping, and counseling tactics, and with the same view toward developing the child's strengths, promoting high achievement, and enhancing creative and other high-level thinking skills. However, the program also must include some special components based on additional needs related to the handicapping condition.

Instead of categorizing the student first as handicapped and second as gifted, the G/T program should view the child primarily as a gifted child, but one who may need some special assistance because of his or her handicap. The primary emphasis thus should be on the recognition and facilitation of the child's strengths. A secondary focus is to prevent the child's handicap from becoming a deterrent to the development and expression of his or her talent.

Although different handicaps create different obstacles, there are a core of obstacles that appear to be critical for almost all handicapped children. It is these that we address as priorities for gifted programs that include children with handicaps.

REDUCING COMMUNICATION LIMITATIONS

Countless high-achieving handicapped college students have learned effective and socially acceptable ways to compensate for their handicapping condition. Blind students use tape recorders, study with sighted friends, and make easy arrangements to take exams orally. Severely visually impaired students will obtain (usually at government expense) head-mounted devices or other machines that magnify the pages of standard college texts. Deaf students will bring an American Sign Language interpreter to class, parking the smiling interpreter squarely next to the on-stage lecturer. Orthopedically impaired students scoot from building to building in electric wheel chairs; if they cannot write they also will use tape recorders and take exams orally. Dyslexic students pay maximum attention to lectures and illustrations, with little time devoted to frustrating printed words. On one hand, these handicapped students are admired for their courage and ingenuity. On the other, as energetic and talented individuals they simply are doing what they must do.

All handicapped persons must compensate as best they can for their limitations. In school, they must be able to perceive, respond, and express themselves; in short, they must be able to *communicate*. The regular and special education teacher must help ensure that technological aids and special training are available that will permit the handicapped gifted child not only to function "normally" in the regular class, but to develop his or her superior abilities and gifts. A short list would include wheelchairs, hearing aids, lip reading, sign language, braille training, braille texts, magnifiers, tape recorders, typewriters, artificial limbs and hands, paintbrush and pencil attachments for the head or arm, and microcomputers.

Microcomputers are presenting growing possibilities for extending the communication potential of handicapped children. For example, the computerized *Versa Braille* permits a child to type English letters and have them translated to braille, or to type braille letters and have them translated to English.[1] Other aids and devices are continually being developed, and a teacher of the handicapped should try to stay abreast of new developments.

In many cases, gifted and talented handicapped students cannot be identified without aids that allow them to communicate. For example, in Wisconsin teachers in the Arts for the Handicapped Project (O'Connell, 1982) designed several devices that served to free physically handicapped children from some limitations of their disabilities, permitting them to express themselves through art. The strategies allowed talented artists to be identified and they were taught advanced techniques and skills.

Some communication aids, incidentally, may have the initial effect of slowing down responding, learning, and cognitive functioning. However, once the communication skill is mastered, the handicapped child will have a vastly improved potential for in-depth development, achievement, and creative expression.

---

[1]*Versa Braille* is available from Telesensory Systems, Inc., 3408 Hillview Ave., P.O. Box 10099, Palo Alto, CA 94304.

The gifted handicapped child clearly needs to be provided with all possible resources to become a skilled user of substitute means of communication. Without the use of these aids, the expression of talent is impeded and locked within. Leaders of gifted programs not only must help obtain these resources, but must interpret to the community the beneficial effects of the aids and the potential talent that can be uncovered and developed when communication barriers are lifted.

SELF-CONCEPT DEVELOPMENT

We noted earlier that rejection by others, labeling, lowered teacher expectations, and the sense of being different combine to make the handicapped gifted child feel less capable and of less worth than other children. Because a poor self-concept is a primary characteristic of underachievement, dealing with the extremely poor self-images of these children should be a primary underlying goal of a gifted program for handicapped students.

In addition to feedback from others, the self-concept also is based upon a realistic appraisal of one's own skills and achievements. Therefore, program activities should be directed not only toward helping handicapped gifted children to achieve, but toward helping them to appreciate the worth of their achievements. Further, other students should be helped to recognize the quality of the handicapped students' work.

These achievements can be evaluated according to two sets of standards. The first set of standards would be the same as applied to nonhandicapped persons, which should make it clear to all that these contributions are valuable and even superior to the average. A second set of standards acknowledges the special talent and effort needed to overcome the handicap. If handicapped gifted children have high expectations placed upon them, and if communication barriers are removed, their academic and creative achievements in the arts, literature, mathematics, science, or social service can be as excellent as those of anyone else. And it is through the challenge of true high-level achievement that these children can realistically attain the positive self-concept they desperately need for their own personal growth. Appendix 15.1 presents a story written by a blind fourth-grade girl. It is an example of special talent as evaluated by both sets of standards.

Social Skills

Nonhandicapped children use all of their senses and their mobility to spontaneously learn social skills that permit them to be accepted by their peers. Handicapped children need to learn more concretely and specifically about the social life to which they, too, want and need to belong. This goal is indeed a challenge.

ndicapped students require social activities with other bright
children who have similar handicaps and similar goals and in-
s, so that they will not feel alone. Peer support and peer-support
groups have been recommended throughout this text as an effective solution to many self-concept and social problems of gifted students. Also, due
to lack of experience, gifted handicapped children may require "social
coaching" so they do not *guarantee* themselves rejection by, for example,
trying to show off, force themselves on a group, or withdraw completely.
These are common, self-defeating coping strategies adopted
unsuccessfully by many handicapped children and adolescents who so
strongly wish to be "part of the group" (Halverson and Victor, 1976).

The other children in the class, too, probably will require "sensitivity
training" and "values clarification" to help them empathize with the
handicapped child; that is, to help them understand the problems and feelings of handicapped individuals so they will *think* before mistreating or
excluding handicapped peers. Encounter-type groups—carefully monitored—which encourage open and honest communication between
handicapped and nonhandicapped youth can provide an important avenue for developing social skills and social relationships of handicapped
children, while providing unique sensitivity insights for the nonhandicapped child.

Classroom Tactics

Several classroom strategies may increase contact and positive feelings
between different student groups. For example, mixed learning teams,
which require all members to work together, have been successful in improving between-group attitudes and friendships. In Aronson's (Aronson,
Blaney, Sikes, Stephan, and Snapp, 1975) *jigsaw* method mixed groups of
six upper-elementary students are told that in one hour they will have a test
to see how well they have learned, for example, about the life of newspaper
publisher Joseph Pulitzer. Each of the six is given one paragraph covering
a different aspect of Pulitzer's career. To do well, each student must read
his or her own paragraph and then explain its contents to the others.
Cooperation and interdependence are the only route to success. With
mixed-race groups, teachers reported that changes in attitudes and self-
concepts—and an improved classroom atmosphere—were very impressive.

Peer tutoring also has the effect of increasing "liking" between different students. Normal gifted students may tutor handicapped gifted students, or the handicapped students may tutor others. The handicapped
students also may tutor younger children. Gartner, Kohler, and Reissman
(1971) stressed that when anxious, low-esteem, low-achieving students are
placed in the important and prestigious role of *teacher*, they learn new skills,

feel much better about themselves, and their attitudes toward school also improve. In addition, the younger children reap educational benefits, and also learn that handicapped persons are people too.

Encouraging Independent Learning

One-to-one attention is characteristic and often necessary for educational programs for handicapped students. However, these children sometimes become too dependent upon the individual attention and the continuous positive feedback that supports their learning. Such dependence will limit the motivation and achievement of any child. Therefore, handicapped children must be encouraged to develop both intrinsic motivation, with learning and success as their own rewards, and the ability to learn independently. Further, they need both independent, self-initiated learning experiences and cooperative small-group activities in which they can serve as leaders and as equal participants. Independent, self-initiated learning and learning as part of a class group are important for *all* children, especially gifted ones who will be faced with challenging college work and complex professions. We must be innovative in providing these independent and small-group learning opportunities for handicapped gifted children, just as they are provided for nonhandicapped gifted children.

HIGH-LEVEL, ABSTRACT-THINKING SKILLS

We noted earlier that limited sensory input may have the effect of depressing the development of high-level, abstract-thinking skills. Compared to persons with unimpaired senses, experiences of sensory handicapped students tend to be interpreted in a more concrete vocabulary. For handicapped children, a weakness in abstract and high-level thinking skill should not be viewed as "lack of ability," but as a deficiency that may require even more attention than with nonhandicapped gifted children.

Even more than for other gifted students, then, the gifted handicapped child must be exposed to programming methods that foster the development of such skills as *creativity, problem solving, critical thinking, classifying, generalizing, analysis, synthesis,* and *evaluation.* Encouraging such skill development is common in most gifted programs, but is doubly important for the handicapped gifted child.

Daniels (1983) itemized the following as curriculum and remediation methods specifically for teaching learning disabled children who are gifted and talented. Note the emphasis on abstract and high-level learning objectives.

Classification	Generalizing
Levels of abstraction	Learning concepts (not "words")
Appreciating relevancy	Vocabulary, spelling
Labeling	Writing, composition
Abstracting	Punctuation, proofreading

Some relevant bibliographic resources focusing on curriculum and teaching methods for use with handicapped children are listed at the end of this chapter.

PARENTING

Parenting is a critical component of any gifted program. However, parents of handicapped gifted children must deal with their child's special needs related to the handicap, as well as attend to his or her giftedness. Parents of handicapped children often devote resources, time, energy, attention, and patience far beyond that which is given to a normal child, which can result in advantages or, sometimes, disadvantages for the child. Consider these situations identified by Rimm in her psychology practice:

1. Intensive parental teaching of the child provided on a continuous one-to-one basis increases sensory awareness, knowledge, vocabulary, and skill development. The child will learn a great deal about his or her environment from this abundance of early teaching in the home. This obviously is an advantage.

2. Counteridentification, the parent's deriving of personal feelings of success and failure through the child's accomplishments, may cause a parent to do too much for the child. A too-helpful parent actually may rob the child of opportunities to learn skills and to build independence and self-confidence. In some cases a parent may even deny the existence of their child's handicap (for example, dyslexia, partial hearing loss). In other cases parents may use the child's handicap as an excuse for allowing the child to avoid responsibilities. Of course, the child soon learns to use the same kind of excuse to avoid unpleasant chores, for example, learning math `acts. Thwarting independence and skill development is a disadvantage.

3. Manipulation by the child also can be an outcome of counteridentification. Because the parent is so anxious for their united success, the child, perhaps unconsciously, learns that he or she can easily control the parent (for example, "I can't do it! You've got to help me!"). The manipulation skill acquired in the counteridentification process may be extended to teachers and peers. Manipulative attention-getting behaviors may take the form of overly dependent behavior, or a stubborn refusal to put forth effort in anything but the child's most preferred activities. This child and his or her parent will blame the school, the teacher, other children, and the

remainder of the child's world for not helping the child to learn, instead of encouraging the child to take responsibility for his or her own learning. Manipulation, dependence, and refusal to work also are disadvantages.

4. Involvement by one parent may be so intense that it precludes the other parent from participating. For example, special skills such as using braille, American Sign Language, or special teaching procedures may need to be learned by a parent. If the second parent (usually father) has not also learned these techniques, he may be omitted from the special relationship and may finally decide that he is not a very good parent. This is particularly a problem if the child is a boy and the close parent is a mother. The alienation of the father may deprive the boy of an important male identification figure and impedes his independence and growth. The boy, as he matures, will feel both grateful to his mother for her commitment, but angry and impatient with her for his dependence on her. Neither mother nor son will understand the deterioration of what was in childhood such a strong positive relationship. Excluding one parent from close family relationships will always cause a serious problem.

A parent involvement group always should be part of a gifted program that serves handicapped students. Such a group can help parents avoid some common problems. Such a group also can help parents to focus on their children's strengths rather than dwell on their handicaps.

The *Retrieval and Acceleration of Promising Young Handicapped and Talented* (RAPYHT) project (Karnes, Shwedel, and Lewis, 1983) is a program devoted to early education of gifted handicapped children. It includes an active and effective parent component. Noted Karnes et al., parent involvement helps maintain a consistent philosophy between home and school. In RAPYHT, parents participate in both indentification and training. The latter involves parents in helping their children compensate for their handicapping condition and develop in their areas of giftedness. Parents are encouraged to help in the classroom and are given suggested activities to be caried out with their children at home. Large-group meetings, small-group discussion sessions, individual conferences, a newsletter, and a parent library all are part of the family involvement. Although parents should always be involved in the education of their children, the special stresses and demands of parenting gifted handicapped students requires an even closer partnership between their formal and informal educators—teachers and parents.

SUMMARY

Gifted handicapped children typically are recognized for their handicap, not their gifts. Of the estimated 6 to 9 million handicapped children (age 5 to 18), 300,000 to 450,000 could be classified as gifted. Nonetheless, there have been few G/T programs designed for the handicapped gifted. Of the many varieties of physically and psychologically handicapping conditions, perhaps only mental retardation precludes most forms of giftedness.

Too often schools fail to accommodate the handicapped gifted. If the gifted child can function reasonably well, special educational services may be withdrawn. And due largely to social rejection, handicapped students frequently have poor self-concepts.

Identification is difficult. Handicapped gifted students tend to be unseen by teachers and even parents. Also, the handicap may obscure the expression of gifts and talents. While IQ scores can be extremely useful, they may be depressed by the tendency of sensory-impaired students to think less abstractly. In-service training dealing with characteristics of giftedness and identification methods is important. Disruptiveness may be a good indicator of giftedness, due to the frustration and stress experienced by gifted handicapped children.

Eisenberg and Epstein successfully used IQ and achievement scores, all Renzulli-Hartman rating scales, peer nominations, and self-nominations for identification. Maker recommended comparing handicapped students with other similarly handicapped students, and to heavily weight skills used to compensate. The Renzulli-Hartman Creativity Scale and the PRIDE, GIFT, and GIFFI inventories might be used for identifying creative giftedness. A quota system will ensure that handicapped students are examined for gifts and are included in programs.

G/T programs for handicapped gifted children can include the same acceleration, enrichment, grouping, and counseling components as other programs. Communication weaknesses must be compensated for via the use of mechanical aids and/or special training. Microcomputers especially seem potentially valuable. Some communication aids may initially slow learning until the new skill is mastered.

Developing positive self-concepts should be a main program goal of teaching the handicapped gifted. Learning to value their own superior achievements and talents should help their self-concepts. Helping other students to appreciate the achievements of handicapped gifted students also may be valuable. Peer support groups may help gifted handicapped students develop good self-concepts and social skills. "Social coaching" also may be needed.

Other children probably will require sensitivity and values clarification training to help them empathize with the handicapped. Learning teams may help improve attitudes towards handicapped students. Peer tutoring may improve social relationships and self-concepts.

Despite the necessity of one-to-one instruction for the handicapped gifted, the teaching of independent learning and learning in small groups is also necessary. Even more than with other gifted students, high-level abstract-thinking skills must be taught.

The great attention parents must pay to their handicapped child may result in superior learning and cognitive development. However, it can also lead to the suppression of self-confidence and independence, learning to manipulate parents, teachers, and peers, and the elimination of one parent from the family relationship.

Parent involvement groups are a critical component of a program for handicapped gifted students.

SUGGESTED READING

Visually Impaired

FUKARI, S. *How can I make what I cannot see?* New York: Van Nostrand Reinhold, 1974.
LOWENFELD, V. *The nature of creative activity.* London: Routledge and Kegan Paul, 1952.

Hearing Impaired

BRAGG, B. The human potential of human potential: Art and the deaf. *American Annals of the Deaf*, 1972, *117*, 508–511.

Other Handicaps

DANIELS, P. R. *Teaching the gifted/learning disabled child.* Rockville, Md.: Aspen, 1983.
FEINBERG, S. Creative problem-solving and the music listening experience. *Music Educators Journal*, 1974, *61*, 53–60.
GALLAGHER, P. A. Procedures for developing creativity in emotionally disturbed children. *Focus on Exceptional Children*, 1972, *4*, 1–9.

APPENDIX 15.1 SCRATCH AND SNIFF BOOK OF WITCHES

This story was written by Jenny Lehman when she was in fourth grade (age nine). Jenny was born without sight. Her parents made extraordinary efforts to educate her early to use her other senses to know her world. Jenny wrote this story in braille. She currently is receiving her education in a public elementary school in Watertown, Wisconsin, and has participated in the gifted program in that school. Jenny is continuing to write, but now has the use of *Versa Braille,* a computerized apparatus that translates typewritten braille into English letters, and typewritten English letters into braille.

She is bright and energetic evidence that handicapped children also may be gifted.

SCRATCH AND SNIFF BOOK OF WITCHES

Once there were two little girls whose names were Sandy and Candy Parker. Candy was eight and had long brown hair. She was tall for her age and was not too fat or too thin.

Sandy was five and had short dark hair. She was just the right height and weight for her age. The sisters liked each other a lot. They were more like best friends than sisters.

One day their mother said to them, "Why don't you go out and play for a while. You've been in the house so long."

Candy and Sandy skipped outside to play. But they got very bored playing by themselves. And they couldn't find anybody else to play with. So they decided to take a walk in the woods.

In the woods there were many different kinds of trees. But mostly there were pine trees. The children liked to smell the pine trees.

As they walked through the woods Sandy's imagination ran away with her. She thought she saw a face peeking out from a crotch in a maple tree. She asked Candy "C-C-C-Candy! a-a-are there any such things as witches!" "Awe don't be silly!" said Candy. But when she looked she saw that Sandy was very scared.

"L-l-l-look over there," whimpered Sandy. "Wow a cave," cried Candy. As they got closer to it they smelled peppermint cooking. As the girls got closer they heard a voice chanting, "Bat's wings and toad's feet! Make this candy good to eat. Good to eat for little children to turn them into rats and bats, pigeons and gnats! Oh I'm Elma the Witch and I'm terrible, horrible, and wicked!"

As if in a trance Sandy and Candy walked right into the cave. They walked up to a fire and saw an old woman bending over a pot making peppermint.

Candy shyly asked, "Are you really Elma the Wicked Witch." "No my dear child, I am really a poor candy maker. Would you and your sweet sister like some cherry candy?" "Yes, thank you very much," said Candy very politely.

The truth is that Elma was a very very very wicked witch! The cherry candy was enchanted. It would turn anyone who ate it into a frog.

Being in a trance they forgot all their mothers warnings and ate the candy! Immediately they were turned into two frogs.

The witch cackled, "Ha! ha! ha! ha! Those foolish children believed my chant! Now the only thing that will cure them will be a piece of black licorice. But they will never find one until they die. Ha! ha! ha! ha!!!"

"I think I will go and tell Zelda about my latest witchcraft. Ha! ha! ha!!!!" Then she flew away on her broom!

Sandy said, "Candy are you all right?" Candy answered, "I think so but I feel very hoppy!" "Let's see if there is any black licorice," said Candy. They looked and looked.

"Sandy do you think that is licorice in that sack over on that shelf?" asked Candy. "I don't know but I think I'll go and take a look," said Sandy. "Wait for me," said Candy. Then she discovered that it was licorice.

As soon as the girls put licorice in their mouths they became girls again. Sandy said "I liked being a frog! Can we do it again? It will be all right to take some home and when we want to get rid of mom and dad give them some."

But before the girls could escape they heard Elma coming back. She was bringing her sister Zelda to see the frogs. Quick as a wink Sandy spied a side tunnel. Pulling her sister they ran through it.

They ran through just in time for just then the witches came into the cave. "Why the frogs are gone!" cried Elma. "Quick!" cried Zelda, "bring me your book of magic spells. Maybe there's a spell that will help us find out where they went." Elma brought the book. Zelda found this chant.

"Uga bug, Clug! Put this candy into a jug. Make it act just like a drug. So I'll know why the children have gone." While she chanted this she was stirring up cinnamon and coconut. When she was done she ate it all. And this is what she saw—the children.

The children had ended up in a room where a man was bending over a fire. Looking closer she saw that it was Wonka Wizzard. She quickly opened her eyes. "Quick! We must go after them. They are with Wonka! He might destroy us!" cried Zelda. Meanwhile the girls were telling Wonka all their adventures. Immediately he said, "Hocus Pocus! Jiminy tread! Turn those witches into gingerbread."

Instantly the witches were gingerbread. Sandy and Candy and Wonka walked into the cave. They threw away all the candy except the gingerbread. That they cut into pieces and divided.

Then Wonka wished the girls home and he turned the cave and the whole part of the forest into a restaurant. It had very good food because Wonka was the cook and he could have wished anything and it would come true.

From Jenny Lehman, "Scratch and Sniff Book of Witches." Reprinted by permission.

16

PARENTING THE GIFTED CHILD

The "good parenting" any child needs is the main requirement for parenting the gifted child. However, there are some special obstacles, risks, errors, challenges, and joys that accompany being the parent of a child with unusual talents. Teachers should be sensitive to these matters in order to help guide parents of gifted children. For example: Contrary to popular belief, all parents everywhere do not believe their children are gifted. Some parents of gifted children will deny their children's special abilities in an attempt to keep them "normal" and "well-adjusted." Other parents, with the opposite attitude, seem to magnify their children's abilities and put excessive pressure on them for high achievement in all areas. This latter problem may include the tacit assumptions that (1) other children necessarily are inferior; and (2) by association, the parents also are superior. Either of these extremes, denying or magnifying giftedness, can cause problems for gifted children.

Overview

This chapter will emphasize some practical approaches to dealing with these and other special problems of parenting gifted and talented children. Although some concepts found here may apply to parenting all children, they are of special concern to parents—and therefore teachers—of gifted children.

THE "WHO'S IN CHARGE?" PROBLEM

> If God had meant gifted children to run their homes, She would have created them bigger. (Rimm, 1984)

As noted briefly in Chapter 13, children who show unusual verbal and abstract-thinking ability appear to be wise and mature beyond their years, and to a degree they are. These deceptive characteristics may obscure the lack of experience and maturity that is typical of all children. It sometimes happens that devoted parents, intent on providing an ideal climate for their gifted children, fall into the trap of believing that these little beings, by virtue of their extensive vocabularies and impressive speech and logic, are capable very early of making complex decisions and setting their own goals and directions. Their interests and concerns, of course, should be considered, but parents and teachers must not abdicate responsibility for guidance.

Regarding educational guidance, successful gifted achievers will usually agree that throughout their schooling they felt confident that (1) their parents and teachers were concerned and knowledgeable about an appropriate direction for their education, and that (2) following their lead was

---

INSET 16.1 A BILL OF RIGHTS FOR PARENTS OF GIFTED CHILDREN

1. Parents have the right to a free public education for their gifted children
2. The right to an education that enables them to learn all they are able to learn
3. The right to educators' awareness that gifted children learn earlier, better, faster and often differently from most other children
4. The right to be accepted and respected as parents of children with legitimate and special learning needs
5. The right to be involved in the planning for the education of their gifted children
6. The right to information in the child's file, and the right to explanation if that information is in unfamiliar terms
7. The right to freedom of expression as they voice the joys and problems of raising gifted children
8. The right to become change agents in the legislature and schools when gifted children are not adequately served
9. The right to an environment of acceptance and pride in what gifted children can accomplish for themselves, first, but also for the quality of all our lives.

From Gina G. Riggs, "Parents of Gifted and Talented Children: Unite!," *G/C/T Magazine,* January-February 1982. Reprinted by permission.

virtually always a wise decision. Note the following comment by a gifted high school student:

> As I grew more restless in public school, I decided to get out. My mother did the field work in finding out about a very special art school in town. That school changed my whole outlook on education. I dearly loved my art, and for the first time became interested in learning in general. If it had not been for my parents giving me the support I needed, I would have continued to deteriorate in a mechanical classroom setting. (Krueger, 1978)

Empowering children with adult decision-making provides power without wisdom. This can lead to formidable and continuing conflicts between gifted children and their parents as they compete for the power that parents give too early and try to recover too late. The resulting adversary mode may force adolescents to rebel too stubbornly, parents to respond too negatively, and both to lose the positive home atmosphere that can be so valuable in educating a gifted child.

PARENTING BY POSITIVE EXPECTATIONS

Parenting by *positive expectations* can be extraordinarily successful in guiding gifted children both in school and out. If high achievement, positive attitudes, and constructive behavior are expected and reinforced by parents, they will become internalized by the child, and the need for punishment usually will be negligible. How do some parents guide their children so well without punishment while others seem to need and use it so frequently?

Clear and consistent *messages,* agreed upon by both parents and transmitted to the child, are basic. For example, parental agreement on such underlying values as (1) the importance of study, learning and school; (2) respect for individuality; and (3) recognition of the need for reasonable amounts of recreation and fun seem to underly a positive and achievement-oriented atmosphere. Excessive double messages and half-truths related to these matters can cause problems for children. A *double message* is two contradictory messages given by one parent, or else opposite messages sent by two parents. A *half-truth* is a message that is partly true and partly false and therefore is easily misinterpreted by the gifted child. We will look at some common and troublesome parent-to-child messages.

DOUBLE MESSAGES AND HALF-TRUTHS

The "Yes-No" Message

The parent who loses his or her temper with a young child one moment, then apologizes and begs forgiveness immediately after, is giving a confused "yes-no" message to the child. The child does not really understand if the parent approves or disapproves of the behavior. However, the child does learn that the behavior has brought an inordinate amount of valued warmth and attention. Reasonably enough, the child may increase the kind of (undesirable) behavior that produces the attention. Punishments are thus punctuated by hugs and affection, and the child, persuaded by a strong basic need for love, may *increase* the troublesome behavior in a self-perpetuating, self-accelerating negative ritual.

As a variation, confusing yes-no messages also apply to misbehavior for which the child learns to apologize—and for which he or she receives forgiveness and affection. These children learn that virtually any behavior (for example, ignoring chores, misbehavior, or poor schoolwork) is acceptable, as long as it is followed by an apology or an "I'll study and try my best next time." Gifted children who use this strategy can become facile manipulators both at home and at school. For example, after each test they fail to study for they will have an excuse and an apology that the teacher frequently believes. The same manipulation ritual learned at home is thus transferred to the classroom. The dynamics of the situation confuse parents, teachers, and the gifted children themselves.

The "That's Good, but Don't Think You're Gifted" Message

This particular message may be transmitted by parents whose primary goal is to raise children who are "well-adjusted." Their expectations include an image of their child becoming a school class officer, a team sports player (preferably a star), prom king or queen, and other forms of leadership and popularity. Their expectations specifically exclude the image of their child being seen as the "brain" or "egghead," having a too-big vocabulary, having too many intellectual interests, and being socially excluded. In an unreasonable fear that their bright child may become too involved in academics, they will prefer that the child *not* be part of a gifted program. When the child does excel in academic contests or grades, they may respond with, "That's very good, but don't think you're gifted," or "I'm glad you're interested in reading, but you need to be well-rounded. How about the soccer team?"

This child usually begins school as a successful student and quickly finds him or herself identified as *bright*. If there is a gifted program, the child will be recommended for it. Although the teacher and the school send the child positive messages for his or her accomplishments, the parents' messages are ambiguous. In response, the child may become careless about schoolwork, and friends and playground activities take precedence. Grades and test scores begin to decline, but social leadership improves. Parents may be satisfied for a while—until in a parent-teacher conference the teacher explains that the child is not doing his or her homework and has careless study habits. Worse, he or she seems uninterested in school.

It is now time for a new message, inconsistent with the previous one. Parents now are disappointed with the laziness and poor study habits, and they may begin a withdrawal of privileges based upon grades. Popularity and leadership is suddenly a non-issue. Meanwhile, the child has lost confidence in his or her ability to achieve at a superior level, and the current skills gap may indeed make it difficult to perform well. Sports and friendships have become the highest priority—and these friends do not value "brains" and achievement.

At this point there no longer is a danger that the child will be labeled *gifted,* which, of course, was the parents' initial preference. However, they are not particularly comfortable with the *underachiever* label either. The double messages of "Achievement is fine, but being well-rounded is better" and later "Popularity is fine, but you're not achieving up to your capability" can lead to both irreversible underachievement and a strained parent-child relationship.

Incidentally, the threat to withdraw privileges is hardly unique to underachieving gifted children. A typical message given to many adolescents, it leads them to seek peer support against "unfair parents." Both children and parents lose in this unfortunate adversary game.

The "Let Me Help You Make It Better" Syndrome: Counteridentification

This double message is given by a parent who places a high value on the child's giftedness and also counteridentifies with the child. As we know, in counteridentification the parent sees him- or herself in the child and, perhaps unconsciously, lives through the child's experiences as if they were the parent's own. The child's accomplishments become the parent's victories; the child's losses are the parent's defeats. Parent involvement in the child's projects goes beyond guidance and mutual interest to active participation and, all too often, taking charge of the projects.

Each accomplishment of the child typically is followed by "helpful" parent criticism. This criticism involves more than just a small suggestion; it usually changes the child's original idea and remakes it into the parent's project. The completed project may indeed be of adult quality, and in fact wins praise from teachers or wins prizes in contests. The child receives a reputation for excellence, originality, and brilliance. The parents are pleased with the child's performance and deny, even to themselves, their involvement.

Unfortunately, the child acquires feelings of doubt and ambiguity about his or her own abilities. Although delighted with the successful outcomes, the child has difficulty defining his or her own contributions. Moreover, because parental standards are so high, new projects become difficult to start. And once a project is begun, the insecure child's goal becomes perfection and the work is meticulously slow and executed too carefully. Finishing the work thus is difficult because the child feels it will never be good enough.

Goal setting may become "defensive," aimed at protecting against feelings of failure and low ability (Covington and Beery, 1976). The activities the child selects are so easy that he or she cannot fail, or else so difficult that perfectionism and high standards may be used as excuses for not completing them. The child may also manipulate parents into more and more involvement in projects and activities, and since the parents cannot bear to see their child (or themselves) fail, they are pleased with the continuous opportunity to help.

The child can become fearful of the world's discovering somehow that he or she is not truly as bright as schoolwork and IQ and achievement tests indicate. And the child might write off the purported high ability, too, viewing it as only the ability to get good grades, but not meaning much else in the world.

The double message that counteridentifying parents give their child is that he or she is (1) gifted, but (2) still needs much help in order to perform at an acceptable high level. Such well-meaning parents rob their child of self-confidence, spontaneity, creative thinking, and independent work. Children can only build confidence from competent personal achievement.

This theme has many variations in terms of kinds of achievement (or lack of achievement), type of parental assistance, and the type of defense mechanisms used to cope with the feelings of doubt and ambiguity. However, underlying the observed behavior is a serious *lack of self-confidence*, making the child less resilient during normal failure experiences that are part of competing and achieving. Importantly, observers of this gifted child usually cannot understand the reason for the low confidence, in view of his or her superior talents and abilities.

The "Grades Don't Count—Or Do They?" Double Message

Messages from parents about grades often are inconsistent and confusing. Calling them "double" messages is an understatement because, in any one family, the messages are likely to vary with each parent, for each child, for different subjects, and at different times. For example, Mom might strongly reinforce an *A* on a social studies test, but a week later tell the same child that his or her *C* on the next test is " . . . fine, since it's a hard subject." Furthermore, to add to the child's confusion, still other ambiguous grade messages come from teachers, peers, siblings, and even grandparents.

How can we resolve this dilemma? As parents, we know that grades are the main communicators of achievement from teachers to children and parents. Parents need to consider several important realities:

1. Grades will always be used to evaluate performance, and thus will open and close opportunity doors.
2. Children will always be able to control their own grades to some extent, but never completely. The vicissitudes of teachers and evaluators will always be part of the outcome.
3. Children should be expected to earn the best grades they are able to earn. However, if the outcome is not satisfactory after trying their best, children should look first at their own work habits to determine if they are indeed studying as efficiently as possible. At the same time, it also is fair for them to examine teacher grading styles and possible teacher biases.
4. Children should not be urged to close doors on some types of schoolwork (for example, math, science) because of less-than-outstanding grades. This point will be addressed further when we discuss the "Winning Is Everything" message.
5. If low or mediocre grades do close one door for children, they need to learn to be resilient enough to search out other opportunities and to recognize that they need not view themselves as "failures" in schoolwork. Other "open doors" can be other subjects, other years, other teachers, and other eventual careers.
6. For gifted and talented students, high grades in core academic areas are important, even if the course content is seen as "boring"; however, high grades in all courses are not equally important. Thus gifted children should be expected to get good grades in math and reading, even though they may dislike math facts or those "dreadful" reading- and language-arts workbooks.

It is certainly all right for children to receive *A*'s in physical education, but unless they plan to direct their careers toward the sports world, *B*'s and *C*'s are acceptable, and enjoyable physical activity should be a more important goal than the grade. Gifted and talented children also should be relieved of strong pressure to earn straight *A*'s in home economics, manual arts, and perhaps even art, drama, and orchestra, unless these represent a central college or career direction.

It seems important to give gifted children a message of what is *central* to their education versus what is *peripheral* (that is, primarily valuable for one's general education, cultural enrichment, or even enjoyment). This message must come from parents, since teachers of "peripheral" subjects will have different opinions.

The "Winning Is Everything" Message

Competition in school presents multiple messages that can confuse both adults and children. For gifted children, competition provides special difficulties. Gifted children usually enter school as "winners" and often continue as winners with little effort. Because of their effortless successes, there is little early challenge and they may not easily see the relationship between competitive effort and achievement. However, at some point in their school career—for some gifted children by the second grade, but for others not until college—they discover that they are effortless winners no longer.

If they do not also discover that, with effort, they can again become winners, they may adopt maladaptive coping strategies. For example, they may write themselves off as school "losers" and *mentally* drop out. That is, they may choose sports, the drama club, or mischief as their area of winning, thus competing in nonacademic, noncareer areas. They might also stop competing completely and view themselves as "average kids" who do not need to compete, who do not need to work very hard to "get by." None of these self-messages encourages the gifted child to use his or her superior abilities.

In many cases, students' self-messages are a reflection of their parent's misleading messages. One such message is to "be a winner—and if not at academics, then at sports or something else." This message encourages the gifted child to redirect the efforts from the academic classroom to the gymnasium or athletic field, where the delighted parents can cheer their child's victories. A related and equally misleading message sent by parents is, "If you can't win, you're a loser." This message causes the gifted child to accept his or her losing status as evidence of lack of ability.

Neither message helps children see that there are many levels of winning other than being "Number 1." Also, children and adolescents should learn that using their superior abilities to succeed in school will sooner or later extend their options for important lifetime winning.

Of course, achievement involves excellence, and excellence certainly can be translated by children as "winning." However, if excellence and winning are viewed by parents only as achieving "first place," their children obviously run a high risk of failure. As a consequence, they will come to view their performances that are actually successful as less than adequate, and will continue to search in frustration for areas where they may compete to win *first place*. Alternatively, they may give up the competition entirely. Gifted teenagers, we might note, are overrepresented in the ranks of high school dropouts.

The "Mom (or Dad) Is an Ogre" Message: Parent Rivalry

Although much has been written about sibling rivalry, few parenting manuals devote much space to the rivalry *parents* can undergo for their children's favor, except perhaps in cases of separation or divorce. Even in good marriage relationships, however, there is often subtle competition between parents for the favor and control of children. The result, frequently, is "ogre games" (described in detail in Chapter 13), in which one parent takes for him or herself the role of "good, kind parent," leaving the spouse the role of disciplinarian—the *ogre* ("It's fine with me if you stay over at Susan's—but your mother doesn't want you to"). Gifted kids easily learn to manipulate this relationship very effectively ("Dad says it's okay, but you won't let me do anything!"). Playing one parent against the other almost always causes problems of stress and confusion for the child.

Of course, parents cannot ignore each other's opinions related to child rearing. However, as in all other components of a marriage, parents must make compromises in what they believe is good parenting, and they must support each other in their decisions. There is no one correct way for bringing up gifted children. However, if there is just one message from educational and clinical research that seems critically important to effective parenting, it is that two parents who show overt mutual respect for each other's opinions and each other's accomplishments provide ideal models for gifted children of both sexes.

What Can Parents Do?

Perhaps we first should accept the inevitable. As parents, we will not do and say what is "right" all of the time, nor do we need such absolute consistency. However, we do need to avoid a pattern of double messages that obviously causes problems for our children.

If the gifted child (or children) in the family are performing well, enjoying the expression of their talents, and growing positively in other ways, it is reasonable to assume that parents are doing their parenting job very well. Again, there is no one right way, but many. However, if the children (1) appear to be under stress, (2) are not achieving well and responsibly, (3) have serious social problems, and/or (4) have unusually difficult family relationships, one should look for a possible family pattern causing the problem. Our list of double messages and half-truths includes some common sources of such problems. When parents can clarify these messages, the results may profoundly help gifted children both in their family relationships and in the classroom.

A published comment by one gifted person may be relevant:

> My family has valued education and has strong interests in art, literature, and music. Because we are close, I've tried to emulate my parents. It is by imitating them, rather than from their telling me what to do, that I've developed a passion for learning and a compulsion to work in an organized manner. But I strongly believe that because of their love and affection, my parents gave me the self-esteem which is an essential element in constructive thinking. (Krueger, 1978)

COMPETITION AND PRESSURE

Competition encourages and motivates gifted children to perform to the best of their high ability, and the recognition they receive for their successes provides the motivation for continued competition. However, there are some negative side effects of extreme competitiveness. Several of these will be discussed separately.

Stress

The very competitive child may feel under continuous *stress*. Such children may exhibit symptons of tension such as nail biting, enuresis (bed wetting), extreme sibling rivalry, loss of appetite, irritability, stomach pains, headaches, or nightmares. These problems can complicate children's lives; they also can be highly informative to parents who are aware of the potential meaning of such symptoms. Of course, every normal child exhibits these symptoms occasionally. However, continued or increased symptoms very often can be attributed to competitive stress; they are physical ways of dealing with frustrations and anxieties.

Parents and teachers should try to help the child identify specific stressors, and then restructure tasks and goals to diminish the stress. For example, the parents or teachers of a high school student can help the student decide upon a sensible and tolerable academic load that challenges his or her abilities but is not overwhelming. Extracurricular activities must be made manageable. Even a gifted student cannot handle too many French clubs, drama clubs, forensics teams, volleyball teams, cheerleading squads, piano and dancing lessons, part-time jobs, and full social lives—along with an academic overload. Younger children also can find themselves under too much pressure, with plenty of homework, music lessons, Little League soccer, and trying hard to excel in all subjects and interests while simultaneously burdened with too many friends who have plenty of ideas of their own.

In some cases children who appear to "not get anything done" also may be feeling stress. The tension may stem more from worries about inadequacy and from work undone than by the actual hard work. Here are two documented examples:

> Bobby, a gifted fourth-grader, complained of stomach aches which he related to worrying about the difficulty of his mathematics. He said that even while he watched TV and tried not to think about his math, he felt sick to his stomach. It was recommended that Bobby change his study habits and do his math right after school, before watching TV and worrying. The stomach aches "miraculously" disappeared and Bobby found math to be much simpler than he thought.

Ron, a fifth grader, was in the lowest reading group in the class and was often teased about his poor reading skill. The recommended regimen of hard work, accelerated tutoring, and reading in an upper reading group was expected by his teacher to cause him even more tension. To everyone's surprise, Ron did not complain about all of the new homework, and the enuresis which had plagued him for many years suddenly disappeared.

If parents or teachers cannot identify the source of the stress, professional help from a guidance counselor or a school or clinical psychologist may be required. It is much easier to identify and treat a stress problem early than after it leads to habitual maladaptive coping patterns for the child.

A helpful way to understand the relationship between stress and efficient performance can be demonstrated by the classic *Yerkes-Dodson law* (Hebb, 1972; Figure 16.1). This principle holds that under very low stress (or motivation, or "psychological arousal"), persons perform inefficiently. As the stress or arousal level increases, efficiency also increases. Performance and efficiency peak at an intermediate level, which will vary somewhat for different persons and for different tasks. As stress continues to increase after that, efficiency decreases until, at extreme tension levels, performance is completely disorganized.

Any reader can relate to this experience. At some time, probably, you have studied very hard for an important and difficult examination, one which caused a great deal of stress. On examination day, you anxiously entered the classroom, stared at the examination on your desk, and for at least the first few minutes felt as if you could not recall any but the most simple ideas. Your stomach may have felt tight, and you probably felt hot or cold all over and slightly nauseous. Sometimes, the inability to perform will increase the anxiety and stress still further. Other times, one is able to

FIGURE 16.1   The Yerkes-Dodson Law Relating Stress (or Arousal) to Level of Effectiveness.

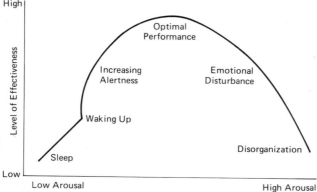

From *Textbook of Psychology,* 3rd ed. (1972), by D. O. Hebb. Copyright © by W. B. Saunders Co. Reprinted by permission of CBS College Publishing.

calm down to a more optimal level of arousal and then perform very well.

Competitive children—and most gifted children are competitive—are more vulnerable to stress. Parents and teachers cannot deliver them from stress, but they can model and teach stress reduction measures. Some simple approaches to dealing with stress include regular physical exercise, recreational and "fun" activities, and especially the availability of a safe and empathic environment where children can talk openly about their pressures and anxieties.

Webb, Meckerstroth, and Tolan (1982) recommend using humor to help reduce stress. For example, parents can be melodramatic about their own "intolerable" stresses and problems—making it clear that they are laughing at themselves. Parents can also encourage the child to "think out loud" about stress by gently raising questions such as, "What is the worst thing that could happen in that situation?" and "How big a catastrophe would that be?"

In sum, parents and teachers can best help children deal with stress from competition by (1) identifying the source of the stress and then helping the student redefine priorities to reduce the stress, (2) recognizing that a moderate and manageable amount of stress is necessary for peak performance, (3) helping provide outlets or "therapy" in the form of physical and other enjoyable activities, and (4) lending an understanding, empathic, and perhaps humorous ear. These techniques can be very useful in preventing deterioration of performance due to high stress.

Failure

Gail Sheehy (1982) in her book *Pathfinders* discussed differences among adults in handling their own development crises. In comparing adults who viewed themselves as successful and who led reasonably fulfilled lives versus those who saw their lives as filled with frustration and failure, she concluded that the main difference was the way in which they dealt with their *failures*. "Pathfinders," the term she used for the more satisfied persons, experienced just as many failure experiences as did the others; however, they were able to use those failures to grow and move forward. The less fulfilled persons, on the other hand, came to identify themselves as failures and remained in their less-than-satisfactory life positions.

It appears that gifted children, and perhaps all children, establish similar patterns. Children who are high achievers, creative, and success oriented, view their failures and losses as learning experiences (Covington and Beery, 1976). When failure occurs, they identify the problems, remedy the deficiencies, reset their goals, and then grow from the experiences. Failure is only a temporary setback, and they learn to attribute their failure to lack of effort, the unusual difficulty of a task, or perhaps the extraordinary skill of other competitors. As coping strategies, they may laugh at their errors, determine to work harder, and/or redesign their achievement goals. Importantly, they see themselves as falling short of a *goal,* not falling short as *persons.*

Other children, the nonpathfinders, usually take one of two main paths. Some children will persevere in the same direction, disappointed by their performance but determined to achieve that initial goal. If the goal is realistic, the renewed effort and determination may produce a satisfying success and they may feel like "winners" in the competitive game. If the goal is unrealistic, their continued efforts may fail and produce continued frustration and stress.

The other path is even more destructive. With failure, they become *failure oriented* (Covington and Beery, 1976). They come to view school as a competitive game they are incapable of winning, and so they logically decide that there is little purpose in playing. They learn to give up easily and they "get by" with a minimum of effort. The skill deficits increase, and these gifted children become underachievers who have little or no confidence in their ability to successfully compete in the school game.

To help their gifted child cope with failure, parents should first examine their own competitive style; the child may have learned maladaptive responses to failure from one or both parents. For example, parents may model an attitude of quitting too quickly if a problem gets difficult, of avoiding any type of competition, or of habitually blaming external sources for one's own shortcomings or lack of effort. A possible restructuring of parent attitudes and expectancies may, therefore, be the first item on the agenda for helping the gifted child who is not faring well in academic competition.

As another remedy, children may be taught to identify creative alternatives for their losses or failures. For example, they should recognize that normal people—even very talented ones—cannot be "Number 1" in absolutely everything, and that each has compensating areas in which they are quite outstanding. The child need not feel insecure or threatened by an occasional setback. Note, however, that a discussion of a child's failure may need to wait until after the emotional tension is reduced, to avoid defensive behaviors. Parents cannot expect rational perception or logical thinking during the immediate stress period following an upsetting defeat.

A questioning approach, rather than a lecture, may better help the child understand that (1) one cannot always win, (2) disappointment does not mean that he or she is a failure, (3) the particular experience simply was not as successful as he or she had hoped it would be, and especially (4) the central goal is to play the learning game at the student's best performance level, regardless of his or her competitive ranking.

Peripheral diversion.   It is important for parents to send a clear and direct message to their gifted child about the central role that school learning plays in their life. Indeed, if the child is to succeed academically in the way that both capitalizes on all of his or her abilities, and optimally prepares the child for higher education, then the "learning game" should be played above all others. As noted earlier, if parent messages stress that winning—regardless of the game—is all important, then winning at tennis, on the swim team, or in popularity contests may become too critical to the gifted child. A sad sight is unfulfilled adults in their twenties or thirties whose peak life achievement was election to junior class president or being star of the basketball team. Their competitive strivings helped them perform at their best, but in areas we might call peripheral. Of course, high school should not be all drudgery. However, with gifted and talented students who should be aiming at higher education and professional careers, academics should not play second fiddle to socializing or athletics.

Noncompetitive intellectual activities. Gifted high achievers and gifted underachievers both may be highly competitive and competition conscious. In the case of the high achievers, such competitiveness is functional. For underachievers it is dysfunctional, since they may perceive themselves as "losers" in the school game and therefore stop making an effort to compete.

For both groups, however, involvement in intellectual activities that are noncompetitive can be extremely valuable. Some examples of noncompetitive intellectual activities might include individualized self-paced instruction (for example, at learning centers or with language-learning cassettes), after-school clubs or interest groups, home hobbies or interests such as computers or reading, small-group field trips, independent research projects, or creative arts or writing. For the highly competitive achiever, such activities broaden knowledge and interests, encourage the "reflective pause" necessary for creativity, and provide a comfortable respite from the more highly competitive efforts. For underachievers, noncompetitive intellectual activities entice them into playing the learning/thinking game without fear of failure. To experience the joy of intellectual discovery is a critical goal for all gifted children, and noncompetitive intellectual activities is a good route to this goal.

Sibling Problems

Sibling rivalry seems inherent in Western civilization family structure. It can be minimized and adjusted for, but it will not disappear. The underlying cause of sibling rivalry is competition for parents' attention and, sometimes, resources. With gifted children, particular sibling combinations seem to cause special complications and therefore require special handling by parents and teachers. Several of these will be described shortly.

First, however, it is important to recognize a vital underlying principal for the care and handling of all children: Each and every child in a family should be provided the most ideal opportunity for intellectual and creative development for that particular child. Individual opportunities should not be eliminated because of a misguided democratic commitment to precisely equal treatment for every child. That is, opportunities for gifted children should not be avoided or ignored simply because less able and less interested siblings cannot participate in the same activity. Other children can be offered comparably attractive—but not necessarily identical—educational or recreational opportunities. For example, if one child strongly wishes to attend a Russian-language camp or a Saturday computer class, then an alternative in music, art, swimming, or tennis could be offered to a sibling who might feel cheated. Children have different abilities and different needs, and the most productive, and most fair, approach is to accommodate those differences.

Some typical sibling relationships that cause special problems for gifted children, and some suggestions for dealing with them, are outlined in the following.

The gifted child with less talented siblings. The gifted child with very high intelligence or an extraordinary special talent provides impossible competition in his or her area of giftedness for other children. The unique ability often requires an investment of an inordinate amount of time and resources to provide the special educational opportunities necessary to develop the talent and meet this child's unconventional needs. In the process, the gifted child naturally receives a large amount of attention and recognition. His or her brothers and sisters need to be able to admire the gifted sibling's success, but also recognize that a similar level of success probably is not attainable for them. They must use a different measuring stick to evaluate their own abilities, or they may fall into the trap of viewing their own real successes (and themselves) as failures. In the words of one successful and gifted "second sibling":

> Once I realized that there was nothing I could do to achieve as well as my sister, I decided to stop competing with her, to do the best I could, and to realize that what I was doing was really good too.

Although this youngster came to realize that he could be successful despite his being a "second place" student, that realization was not automatic. In addition to rewarding the victories of their most gifted child, parents also must recognize and reward the success of other siblings—basing those successes on each child's abilities and efforts.

The gifted child in a family of other achieving gifted children. It is not unusual to find that all of the children in a family are gifted; this could be due to genetics, a favorable environment, positive parent and teacher expectations, or, most likely, to all of the above. It is important to recognize that each child in the family will feel increased pressure to fulfill the expectations set by preceding siblings. The first day of school for "child two," "child three," or "child four" inevitably begins with, "Oh yes, I know your sister. She was such a good student!" If the child is gifted and confident, this identification may be pleasing because he or she recognizes that the teacher has expectations that can be fulfilled. Moreover, this early recognition may quickly produce privileges and trust that otherwise would take longer to earn.

On the other hand, a less confident child may see the early identification by the teacher as a threat, since the child may worry that his or her performance may be less adequate than that of the older sibling. A sensitive teacher will quickly learn to recognize the differences between siblings. Nonetheless, parents still may need to explain that "Mrs. Jones had Jimmy too, but she'll soon get to know that you're also a good worker, even though you're different than your brother."

Perhaps most important, parents of several gifted children may need to make a specific effort to ease the grade pressure for younger children. Parents should let them know that the parents understand the special pressures the children feel due to the inevitable comparisons with their siblings. The parent's "expectation message" should be that each child is expected to do the very best he or she can, and that the child's performance will be individually evaluated, not compared with the record of the older brother or sister.

The gifted child with a close-age older sibling of lesser ability.
Undoubtedly, one of the most difficult relationships exists when a younger gifted child has a brother or sister of average ability (or less) who is older by just one or two years. The most typical tendency is for parents to refrain from providing appropriate enriched opportunities for the gifted child in fear of embarrassing the inevitably insecure older child. For the gifted child, this strategy produces both frustration, from the reduced opportunities for skill development, plus pressure to underachieve and hide the high ability. The older child, of course, feels the sibling pressure anyway. In many cases, the older child also acquires lower achievement motivation due to the continual assurances that he or she is not really expected to achieve at a high level.

A better approach is to reinforce the gifted child's achievements, even if it means acceleration to the same grade as the older child. (Needless to say, it will be best if the siblings are *not* in the same classroom.) Also, parents absolutely must reinforce the older child's achievements according to that child's efforts and abilities. As the children become mature enough to discuss their differing abilities and the sense of competition they feel, open discussions of their feelings will help them deal with their sense of personal worth despite obvious differences in talent, school grades, and academic recognition.

Some parents will feel an altruistic commitment to "root for the underdog." While it's very American, this attitude can put unpleasant pressure on all children. Especially, the younger high achiever will not receive recognition at home for his or her superior achievements. In extreme cases, he or she may exhibit some of the symptoms of pressure described earlier (nail biting, nightmares, and so on), although he or she will continue to achieve. The less talented older child may become even less motivated to achieve, since he or she can earn more parent attention by not achieving. The child thus may learn to use the nonachieving behavior to manipulate and control the parents' attention.

Regardless of differences in sibling ability, it usually is better to acknowledge achievements and to reward them, relative, as we noted before, to each child's capabilities. Democratically pretending that differences do not exist, witholding important opportunities from the gifted child, or else accepting less than the best efforts from less capable children are common but unproductive responses of parents of gifted and talented children.

Generally, helping parents to deal with their children's competitive feelings—stress, failure, sibling rivalry—is a difficult problem. However, the patterns described in this section are common and recurrent ones, and the recommended solutions have proven effective again and again. The teacher should be aware of the patterns, set to recognize them, and prepared to make good recommendations to parents.

PEER PRESSURE

During early childhood, virtually all children are motivated by a desire to please parents and teachers and to be "good" children. Kohlberg (1974), in fact, titled this period the "good boy, good girl" stage in children's moral development. During these years, there is little peer pressure to distract the child from parental and school goals. Beginning usually in the preadolescent period, grades 4 or 5, however, the normal tendency to conform to peer norms and expectancies begins to exert its influence. The peer pressures become strongest and most influential in the adolescent years.

Adolescence marks the beginning of a crucial development phenomenon, the formation of a perhaps permanent *identity*—a personal knowledge of who and what one is and where one is going in life (Erikson, 1968). The youth who is changing rapidly, both physically and mentally, may have a difficult time during this "identity crisis" period. It is the structured standards of adolescent peers that often provide the needed direction, support, and strength. Close family relationships and good parent models will help to diffuse some of the ambiguity, but the necessary chore of establishing an identity separate from family ties will reduce parental influence during this period—and strengthen peer influence.

Every parent and teacher of adolescents is acutely aware of students' uniform dress standards and hair fashions, their shared tastes in popular music, and their overemphasis on athletic prowess. Unfortunately, a disdain for academics also is a common fashion in most junior and senior high schools. The unflattering labels for too-studious students may change from generation to generation—*egghead, bookworm, brain* or *nerd*—but the message is the same. The youth who is seen as too narrowly involved in studies and learning, and whose grades are consistently high, is likely to receive "corrective feedback" ranging from mild ribbing to complete social exclusion.

That pressures to be normal and to "fit" can be extreme is dramatically illustrated in the case of Dallas Egbert (Inset 16.2).

For the gifted child, who previously had taken pride in earning high grades, the victories in academic activities now present a difficult personal contradiction. For example, we earlier noted the "fear of success" syndrome among gifted females, the fear of seeming unfeminine and unattractive by being a competitive and successful high achiever (Horner, 1969, 1972a, 1972b). Other gifted students go through adolescence feeling very alone (see "It's Dumb to Be Smart," Appendix 16.1). However, the greatest tragedy occurs when the young person mentally drops out of school, literally accepting the peer mandate that "studying is not cool."

Uncomfortable peer pressures will be reduced if the scholarly adoles-

---

INSET 16.2 THE TRAGIC CASE OF DALLAS EGBERT

In Chapter 2, on characteristics of gifted and talented students, we emphasized how better adjusted than most they usually are, and how acceleration usually does them no psychological or social harm. The tragic case of Dallas Egbert, however, warns that such generalizations will not apply to every gifted child. Each is unique. While most are well adjusted, many are stress-ridden and highly susceptible to depression, drug abuse, and alienation (Webb, Meckerstroth, and Tolan, 1982).

Dallas Egbert was a young computer whiz with a tested IQ of 140. He entered the University of Michigan at age 16. When he disappeared six months later, friends initially assumed he had simply become carried away playing Dungeons and Dragons. A private detective found him in Texas two months later, and Dallas immediately began seeing a psychiatrist. The problem: He wanted to be normal. He felt despair and isolation because he was different, because he did not fit. Morose and disillusioned, he ended his problems with a bullet in the head on August 16, 1980.

---

cent can dissipate his or her brainy image with excellence in sports or drama, or has the good fortune to be physically attractive. Another important qualification for peer acceptance is skill in playing down one's academic ability and excellence, for example, by not using a sophisticated vocabulary, not showing high enthusiasm for high achievement, not carrying too many books at one time, and not mentioning one's large quantity of reading and studying or one's enjoyment of intellectual matters. A gifted student may continue to achieve, however.

As we have mentioned several times, probably the best way to stimulate gifted and talented students, particularly adolescents, is to help assemble a gifted cohort group. Such a group will encourage high achievement and reinforce the full use of one's talents. For example, youth symphony orchestras, high-level Saturday and summer programs in a variety of academic and art areas, special classes, and gifted-peer discussion groups help young people to value their talent and build constructive self-concepts and identities. It is also important for parents to value and support their children's talent during this precarious period in their development, and to not add to the pressures the child already is feeling, for example, by sending messages stressing high popularity and social success.

Finally, consider two tangentially related thoughts pertaining to peer pressures and the stresses of adolescence: First, if the gifted child has been accelerated, there is a tendency to blame difficulties of the adolescent period on the acceleration practice—"Well, skipping sixth grade just didn't work!" Maybe the acceleration was working, and the child might have been worse off without it. Second, if a gifted child is not achieving up to capacity—due entirely to an unchallenging curriculum—it is not unusual to blame anti-academic peer pressures rather than the educational deficiencies.

PARENT SUPPORT GROUPS

Since gifted children by definition are a minority, in most cases adequate educational opportunities will be provided for them only if there is a vocal and visible support group in the community. If adequate G/T programs are not available, joining or organizing a parent support group should be a top priority for concerned parents of gifted children and for teachers interested in gifted education. A fringe benefit of such visible membership is that parents make a clear statement to their children that education, cultural growth, and challenge are top priorities in family values. Names and addresses of three national organizations are listed at the end of this chapter. These organizations can direct parents and teachers to state and local groups. They are also a source of information and have publications on giftedness and gifted education.

As a teacher of gifted children, it is critical to recognize the important role of parent groups and parent support. Teachers must not view these parents as threatening, even though they are certain to make their desires known. Parent groups can help educate individual parents regarding the problems and needs of gifted children and the educational opportunities that are—or should be—provided to them. Parent groups can also help organize enrichment activities for gifted children, such as Saturday, summer, or mentor programs. Individual parents themselves may teach special art, music, math, or computer mini-courses. Parents also can serve as the important volunteer staff—tutoring, transporting, chaperoning—which will extend the opportunities that schools can provide to gifted and talented children.

Parenting gifted and talented children is an important job, and one that teachers can help make more effective.

SOME SPECIAL FAMILY CONCERNS: PREKINDERGARTEN EDUCATION

Apart from our discussion thus far, some other issues related to gifted children in the family must be addressed. Teachers can also be helpful in advising parents in these areas.

Preschool Learning

Parents of very young gifted children frequently ask teachers how they can best help their children before they enter school. It is an important matter, because research evidence clearly demonstrates the strong impact of early environment on language and cognitive development.

For example, White, Kaban, and Attanucci (1979) found in their Harvard Preschool Project that "live language" directed at the child during his or her first three years was the single most critical factor in the child's later competence in cognitive, linguistic, and social areas. Morrow (1983) compared the home environments of 58 kindergarten children showing high interest in reading with the homes of 58 children showing low interest. The high-interest children came from homes with supportive literary environments. That is, the family used the public library, parents did a great deal of reading, and parents read to children frequently; there were more books in the home and, specifically, in the children's bedroom. (As noted in an earlier chapter, Bloom and Sosniak [1981] stressed the pivotal significance of early parental influence—both encouragement and modeling—on the child's development of extraordinary talent in math, swimming, or music.)

The evidence provides a clear directive to parents regarding the need for early concentrated involvement with their child for the full development of both the child's language and nonlinguistic abilities.

Language experience is probably the most critical kind of involvement. Talking to the child, reading and telling stories, rhyming and imitation, word games, children's records, and even simply listening to children all increase the children's opportunities to learn communication and attention skills. Puzzles, blocks, and construction toys help them develop small-muscle coordination, spatial abilities, and concentration skill. Large toys (tricycles, wagons, riding horses) help the development of large-muscle coordination. Many games help children learn to follow directions and cooperate. Questioning, curiosity, and independence also should be encouraged.

Moss (1983) compared the maternal teaching strategies of 14 mothers with gifted preschoolers against those of 14 mothers with nongifted children of the same age. The first group of mothers tended to structure problems and then permit their children to derive their own solutions, learning to relate parts of the task to the goal. In the second group, mothers were more directive and actually tended to provide solutions to their children rather than permitting them to arrive at their own solutions. It seems important for gifted children to gain early experience in independent thinking and problem solving.

The following are a few more preschool precautions, some *do*'s and *don't*'s in helping gifted children. First, television watching, which is basically a passive-receptive activity, should be monitored and limited. In the Morrow (1983) study mentioned earlier, the high-interest kindergarten readers came from homes in which there were rules regarding television, and in which mothers watched less television than mothers in the homes of low-interest readers. However, educational programs would be an exception to this policy. Far too many children become TV junkies.

Second, overstimulation, for example, from too many peers or too much adult talk, can confuse children and detract from active involvement, concentration, and learning. While parent communication to the child is desirable, continuous talk and long abstract lectures to children are virtually meaningless, certainly boring, and exceed children's limited attention span. For some children, endless chatter will cause them to become restless and "hyperactive"; they know they should pay attention, but they cannot. For other children, overwhelming talking by a parent has the opposite effect, preventing the child's contributions and encouraging him or her to slow down and become very quiet. They give up trying to communicate with this parent.

Third, some daily "alone time" for a preschool child also is helpful. Interaction with peers and siblings is important to preschoolers, but some small amount of time each day for a child to play alone will encourage independent behavior and imagination. Creative persons of all ages seem to thrive on some amount of time alone.

All three of these precautions can help children very early to take initiative and to be active participants in their environments, rather than to receive stimulation only passively.

Day-Care and Nursery Schools

Day-care and nursery schools for preschool gifted children have become increasingly common as more women seek to combine careers with child rearing. The findings of previously discussed studies of the importance of language stimulation during early childhood seem to recommend a close parent-child relationship during this critical period. A day-care center on a full-time basis cannot substitute for that unique attentional experience, although part-time care may be satisfactory. A high-quality babysitter, who will talk to and interact with the child on a one-to-one basis, is a good alternative for a full-time working mother.

Attending nursery school for two or three half-days per week for a year or two before kindergarten can provide excellent language training and other forms of skill development and educational enrichment for any three- to five-year-old child. Note, however, that (1) the quality of the nursery school, (2) its sensitivity to the needs of very bright children, and (3) its encouragement of language and creative expression would be important considerations in making a selection.

In summary, the decision as to whether to place the gifted child in day-care or a nursery school is not an easy "yes" or "no" one. It must be a careful decision based on an examination of the particular needs of the child and the particular alternatives available for that child.

SUMMARY

Some parents will deny their child's giftedness; others may exaggerate it.

With the "Who's in Charge" problem, children are given too much adultlike decision-making power, leading to later conflicts.

Parenting by positive expectations includes expectations of high achievement, good attitudes and constructive behavior, and the minimizing of punishments, double messages, and half-truths.

The "yes-no" message includes punishing a child, then quickly apologizing. The child learns that misbehavior is rewarded with warmth and attention. The child also learns that any behavior is acceptable, if followed by an apology.

Parents who employ the "That's Good, but Don't Think You're Gifted" message overemphasize being well-adjusted and popular, and guide the child away from intellectual achievements. When underachievement results, parents may switch and begin punishing poor grades.

Counteridentification involves parents who vicariously experience their child's successes and failures. They may criticize, correct, and take over the child's homework and projects ("Let me help you make it better"), leading to feelings of doubt, ambiguity, and low confidence. Children may become perfectionistic and defensive.

There are also many double, inconsistent messages related to grades. Children should be expected to earn the best grades they can. Even with their best efforts, however, teacher biases and other circumstances put grades beyond children's complete control. When low grades occur, G/T children should learn (1) not to close doors entirely on the subject, and/or (2) to look for alternatives: new subjects, new school years that will be better, new teachers, or other career interests. While high grades in core areas are important, G/T children should be relieved of grade pressure in "peripheral" areas.

Gifted children usually have to learn that winning at academics sooner or later will require effort. Some parents send a "Winning Is Everything" message, which may redirect efforts from academics to athletics. Children need to learn that success need not include being "Number 1."

"Ogre games" occur when one parent competes for the child's favor by being the "kind and benevolent" parent and making the other parent the disciplinarian; children then learn to play one parent against the other. Parents should support each other's decisions.

If children show symptoms of stress, underachievement, and/or have social problems, a family pattern of double messages may be the problem. Clarifying the messages for parents will help.

Competitiveness motivates high achievement. However, feelings of competitiveness that are too strong cause stress, perhaps leading to loss of appetite, enuresis, nightmares, irritability, and so forth. Parents should help gifted children and adolescents to identify sources of stress and guide them in making the burdens more manageable.

As demonstrated in the Yerkes-Dodson law, an intermediate level of stress (arousal) produces optimal performances; stress beyond that level becomes counterproductive. Recreation, exercise, an empathic environment, and humor can help reduce stress.

Failure may be used as a learning and growing experience (by "pathfinders"), or it may lead to feelings of inadequacy (nonpathfinders). Failure will lead some children to persevere in the same direction, which may or may not produce success. Other children become "failure oriented"; they give up easily or get by with minimal effort. This attitude may be learned from parents.

Children should learn alternative coping strategies, such as: recognizing that they cannot be outstanding in everything; valuing their compensating outstanding achievements; and doing their best regardless of the competitive ranking. For gifted students especially, academics should be more important than, for example, social activities or even athletics.

Noncompetitive intellectual activities, such as individualized learning, clubs, hobbies, field trips, or independent research projects, lead to enjoyable experiences of intellectual discovery without fear of failure.

Sibling rivalry usually is due to competition for parents' attention or resources. One basic recommendation is that each child should receive individualized opportunities for creative and intellectual development; a democratic attitude of treating all children alike is counterproductive. Each child should be evaluated and reinforced for accomplishments relative to his or her own abilities and efforts.

With several gifted children in a family, the younger ones may feel strong pressure to meet the expectations of teachers familiar with their older siblings. An older, nongifted child learns that he or she is not expected to be a high achiever, and therefore may become an underachiever. The younger, gifted child may feel pressure to underachieve to hide the high ability, and may exhibit symptoms of stress.

Peer pressure, combined with adolescent identity formation, severely reduces parental influence. A disdain for academic accomplishment is a common form of peer influence that can lead to underachievement, that is, mentally dropping out.

The gifted student can learn to downplay his or her "brainy image" but still be a high achiever. The best solution is to help assemble interest groups of gifted peers who support the gifted student's achievement orientation.

Adolescent difficulties have been blamed on acceleration, often erroneously. Underachievement has been attributed to peer pressure, when an inadequate curriculum actually has been at fault.

Parent support groups can lead to the creation of G/T programs, teach children that parents value education, help educate individual parents, organize enrichment activities, teach mini-courses, and assist with the G/T program.

Preschool learning is critically important for language and cognitive development. Research indicates that habits of reading and skills of independent problem solving also are acquired in the early home environment.

Excessive TV watching and parent chattering should be moderated, and some daily time alone is recommended.

A babysitter who talks and interacts with a small child may be preferable to a day-care center. A good nursery school for two or three half-days per week can be immensely valuable.

NATIONAL GIFTED AND TALENTED
EDUCATIONAL ORGANIZATIONS

Council for Exceptional Children–Talented and Gifted (CEC-TAG), 1920 Association Drive, Reston, Va. 22091

Gifted Advocacy Information Network, Inc. (GAIN), 225 West Orchid Lane, Phoenix, Ariz. 85021

National Association for Gifted Children (NAGC), 5100 N. Edgewood Drive, St. Paul, Minn. 55112

APPENDIX 16.1 IT'S DUMB TO BE SMART (A NOT-SO-FICTITIOUS STORY)

"Jennie," Christi had blurted, "It's dumb to be smart! Why do you always have to use those big words? Nobody understands you anyway." Now the words resounded in Jennie's throbbing head.

"Dumb, dumb, dumb," Jennie whispered dully. Her tears soaked the pillow into which she had buried her head. Her bedroom door was closed and she hoped no one could hear her muffled sobs which escaped between whispered "dumbs." How could it be they felt that way? Jennie asked herself. She had tried so hard to be like the other kids. She had even made herself a long list of *don'ts* which she read to herself as a daily reminder.

Don't use your normal vocabulary.
Don't talk too much about your interests.
Don't talk about school work.
Don't talk about books.
Don't tell your grades.
Don't raise your hand more than twice in one class.
Don't talk to teachers when kids are around.
Don't show your excitement if you have a good idea.
Don't tell anyone how much you study or how you enjoy it.
Don't get into intellectual discussions with other kids.

"Dumb, dumb, dumb," Jennie repeated. Her *don't list* just didn't work. She knew that now. She couldn't fool anyone, least of all the other Junior High cheerleaders whom she wanted so much to have for friends. They had seemed so nice to her and she had thought that cheerleading was great because it had finally brought her real friends. Then last week it suddenly changed. Most of the girls had ignored her. They seemed to be having such fun, but they left her out. She knew they had gone for pizza with the team after the game, but they pretended they weren't going. This afternoon she had dared to ask Christi if she had done anything wrong and that was when Christi had told her it was dumb to be smart.

The sobs and tears had slowed now and Jennie lifted her head slowly from her damp pillow. Her printed bedspread blurred before her eyes but she knew she had to stop crying.

"There just isn't much sense in crying," she concluded. "I don't think Christi's right. It isn't dumb to be smart; there's so much that's exciting and interesting to learn. No, it isn't dumb, but it is lonely."

Jennie washed her face, combed her hair and carefully placed a determined smile on her reflection in the mirror. She didn't want her family to see the tears. They were understanding and felt badly for her, but they really couldn't help. She stared directly at her newly confident expression in the mirror and whispered, "Jennie, if no one likes you, that's your problem and you have to solve it." A solitary tear slid down the newly created expression betraying her precariously organized strength. The loneliness ached within her as she scrambled down the stairs, calling on her way, "Mom, need any help with dinner?"

Jennie always helped with the daily salad and she got busy scraping and cutting the carrot sticks while carefully averting her mother's eyes.

"Jennie," Mom asked, "How was school today—anything new?"

"No," Jennie responded staring at her carrots, "Nothing new—just a regular day." Then she added, thinking that she perhaps needed to sound more convincing, "Cheerleading was great; my new friends are so nice." "Nice" stuck in her throat a little and she could feel an *almost tear.*

"Dinnertime," mother called. Dad, Michael and Bruce emerged from the living room with a current of hungry comments related to the spaghetti to be served. Jennie set the salads on the table resolutely exhibiting her confident expression.

Michael, only slightly younger than Jennie, commented on the game.

"Hear the team won, Jennie. We have a great team."

"Must be the terrific cheerleaders," Dad added laughingly. Jennie and Bruce laughed, too.

"Did you go out for pizza with the team, Jennie?" Michael asked.

Jennie was startled by the question. "No, I didn't go," she hesitated. "I had too much homework," she lied and turned away as she spoke to surreptitiously hide a tear.

"Gee, Jennie, you're always studying. Why don't you have some fun? Study, study, study," Michael teased.

Mother added, "Jennie, it would be nice if you went out and had fun with your new friends. You do enough studying." Mother's voice trailed off as Jennie abruptly turned from the table. Her muffled sobs almost erupted as she dashed up the stairs to the protection of her room and the security of her still damp pillow.

"Dumb, dumb, dumb," she whispered to her pillow again. The door opened quietly and she knew her mom had come to listen again to her problems. The movement of the bed springs as Mom sat next to her seemed to initiate the explosion of tears and sobs that had been precariously submerged. She knew Mother would sit with her and wait patiently until the tears stopped and the words came. The tears and sobs continued until it felt to Jennie as if there were no more left inside her and then she lifted her head slightly to look at her now blurred mother.

Jennie managed the small smile that she knew her mother was hoping for and then repeated the story. "Mom," she said, "there's just no use trying—the kids don't like me. They think I'm a 'weirdo' just because I use three syllable words and I don't know how to fit in. I've tried and tried and they think 'it's dumb to be smart' and they don't want me to go for pizza with them or anywhere else, I guess. They even told me they weren't going. They just think I'm weird and I just don't know what to do anymore."

The tears were back but Jennie managed to stifle the sobs that wanted to come.

Mother looked directly into Jennie's tear-blurred eyes.

"Jennie," her voice was hushed but firm. "It's not dumb to be smart, not dumb at all, ever. But right now, at your age, it's hard. It's just hard for young people to be different. But you have such a good difference, such a lucky difference. It really is a gift—you have insights and thoughts and ideas and talents that hardly any 11 or even 13 and 14 year olds have and you must develop them. Your whole life will be fuller and richer and you can contribute so much more if you do. I know, Jennie, how lonely you feel and how hard it is, but hard things are worthwhile. Jennie, don't be afraid to be you. You are bright and unusual, and yes even different. But Jennie, it's a beautiful difference—be you."

Jennie thought to herself, "Not dumb, only lonely and Mom knows how I feel." Could she do it, could she be herself?

Aloud, Jennie only said, "Thanks, Mom. I guess I better do my homework now."

Jennie watched her mother as she left the room. She understood the frustration that her mother felt at being unable to help her. There didn't seem to be any way for anyone to really help her.

The sign on the door read, "Counselor Is In—Be Seated" and Jennie was seated in Mr. Jackson's outer office. Mr. Jackson was one of Jennie's favorite people and she stopped in frequently to talk to him about school. Yesterday she had stopped to tell him about her loneliness. Now he had called her down to his office.

The chair scraped the floor in the inner office. Footsteps approached the door and it was opened. Mr. Jackson walked out with Bob Johnson. Both looked serious, even sad. Jennie knew Bob Johnson. He was the school's worst trouble maker—always getting detentions, always starting fights. He teased Jennie, too. He was really mean and Jennie didn't even want to look at him. She was just thinking that the world would probably be a better place without people like Bob Johnson when Mr. Jackson smiled at her and signaled her into his office. To Bob, Mr. Jackson said, "Just sit out here for a few minutes and after that you and Jennie can use my office to talk."

"Talk?" Jennie thought to herself. "Why would I want to talk to Bob Johnson? I really hate him. He's mean, really cruel to me. Why would Mr. Jackson want me to talk to him?"

As soon as the door closed, Jennie's questions burst forth. "Mr. Jackson," she queried, "Why would you want me to talk to Bob Johnson? I don't like Bob Johnson and Mr. Jackson, I'm even afraid of him. He's big and mean and uses awful language and fights with everyone and I really don't see why you would want me to talk to him."

"Jennie," Mr. Jackson's voice was warm and friendly. "You and Bob both need help, more help than I can give either of you. And Jennie, I know you won't believe it, but you and Bob have a lot of the same problems. First of all, you're both very bright and thoughtful, truly gifted; second, you're both different from many students, and third, because you're different, you're both very lonely. And since I can't really help either of you, I thought maybe you could help each other. Jennie, will you give it a try?"

Jennie looked at Mr. Jackson in disbelief. "Could I really be like Bob Johnson? Bob Johnson, bright, thoughtful? Mr. Jackson, I don't mean to be disrespectful, but I believe you are mistaken. I mean I'll talk to him if you want me to, but I don't see how it can help either one of us."

"Good!" Mr. Jackson rose quickly, patted Jennie on the head, smiled and disappeared out the door leaving Jennie alone, startled and a little frightened.

Bob scuffed in and sat down across from her. Jennie didn't know what to say. She glanced at Bob quickly and then down at the floor. A childhood game silently flashed through her head. "Bob, begins with *B*—big, boisterous, bully, braggart, brutal, barbarious, bright and oh, yes, lonely. No, bright and lonely just don't fit with Bob," she thought.

"Jennie," Bob began gruffly, "Jackson says you're lonely. Can't be—you're smart and a cheerleader and on student council and teacher's pet and neat and clean and never in trouble. I think Jackson's just saying you're lonely cause I told him I was. Jackson's pretty decent to me but I think he doesn't understand kids. You're not lonely—you're lucky as hell!"

Jennie stopped looking at her shoes and now peered directly at Bob.

"Bob," she said, "I'm the loneliest person in this whole Junior High School. I try so hard to be like all the kids—not so smart so they'll like me, but it doesn't work. I don't have any friends—the kids think I'm weird because I use big words and because I like to read and if I couldn't talk to teachers—who could I talk to? But, Bob, you can't be lonely because I always see you smoking at the corner with a bunch of kids, and when you say something in class even if it's mean and hateful, all the kids laugh with you and everyone knows you're bigger and stronger than most anyone and besides, I never see you alone. How can you be lonely?"

A silence roared. Bob and Jennie seethed internally. Each struggled mentally trying to understand the other's position—to feel each other's loneliness. Bob put his face down into his open hands almost as if by obscuring his view he could see another picture. Jennie stared at the colorful bulletin board across the room as if the blended brightness might permit her to have an inner vision. The silence continued.

Bob exploded first, but Jennie vicariously experienced the insight.

"Jennie," he swallowed hard, and then confided, "Sometimes, I'm not lonely—when I tease you, when I hurt the kids, when I punch someone out, when I smoke with the gang, when I'm drunk as hell—when old man Jenks has me in his office, all those rotten things I do—they take away the loneliness. Then the loneliness is gone. Then people are with me—the guys and even the girls, they laugh with me and smoke with me and think I'm a super star and it feels good and the loneliness goes away. And when old Mr. Jenks has me in his office and my mom is there too, my mom is with me and we blame it all on Dad's drinking or on Mr. Jenks and then I'm not lonely and for a little while it feels good to not be alone."

By this time Bob's voice was loud and sounded victorious. It was Jennie's turn next and she was jubilant too.

"And Bob," she continued, "When my head is in a book or when I'm learning some new math or when I'm working on an experiment or when I'm excited about an idea or when I'm talking to a super teacher or when I play my flute with the orchestra, I'm not lonely and then it feels good not to be alone. It's like now—'cause we understand each other and it feels so exciting like your head is going to explode and it isn't lonely at all. . . . "

Jennie's voice trailed off and an embarrassed silence fell over the room once again. Jennie sensed she had said too much and turned away from Bob. Bob sensed his mask had been pierced and he ended the silence abruptly with his old bravado.

"This is all a lot of crap! I'm getting out of here. Why in hell would I want to talk to some brain, anyway?"

He stomped to the door, hesitated and turned toward Jennie. For an instant his mouth moved wordlessly as if he wanted to say one more thing—their eyes met in silence. It was a brief, almost imperceptible communication in the bluff of Bob's exit, but Jennie had received the message.

Mr. Jackson walked back into the office to find Jennie smiling to herself. "What happened to Bob?" he asked. "He stormed out of the office without a word."

"Mr. Jackson," Jennie said, "I think he was angry at me, at you, but mainly at himself. We had a really good talk and I understood his loneliness and he understood mine. I think, Mr. Jackson, that loneliness is really hard for both of us, but I can do better things because of it than Bob can. Mr. Jackson, I think that talk really helped me. Now I realize that there are other lonely kids who do different things to keep their loneliness away and just knowing that makes me feel not quite so lonely. And Mr. Jackson, I'm really happy that I have such good things to do to keep my loneliness away."

Jennie noted Mr. Jackson's pleased expression. She wondered if he knew this would happen. He really was a super guidance counselor. She wanted to lean over to kiss his smiling cheek to thank him but of course she wouldn't. Instead she rose to leave and on the way out said, "Thanks real much, Mr. Jackson, I really appreciate it."

From Sylvia Rimm, "It's Dumb to Be Smart," *G/C/T* (March/April 1981), 58–60. Reprinted by permission.

17

PROGRAM EVALUATION

WHY MUST PROGRAMS BE EVALUATED?

Traditionally, the systematic evaluation of gifted programs has been minimal. Developers of such programs typically feel that because they created a program in good faith, it necessarily is "successful"—besides, they prefer to spend their time planning and teaching. Another reason for the reluctance to evaluate is that "success" in teaching gifted and talented students is difficult to assess, compared with evaluating typical remedial or basic skills programs in which achievement test data provide straightforward and valid measure of the most important learning outcome. Generally, then, there has been a lack of program evaluation data, and a corresponding lack of accountability, pertaining to the effectiveness of G/T program components.

Overview

Although gifted programs are more difficult to evaluate than other programs, this evaluation is vital. Gifted programs come and go; the record of continuity is dismal. Therefore, if teachers and program directors hope to maintain or expand their programs, they must be able to demonstrate the success of the program to their administration, to school board members, to parents, and to state or federal funding sources. This is *accountability*. These publics will want to know who is being served by the program, how they are being served, and what beneficial effects the program is having. They also will want to know if the program is cost-effective—if the costs in time, personnel, and resources are producing optimal results. Equally important, teachers and program directors will need information allowing them to revise and improve the program. Beyond creating classroom quizzes or evaluating student papers and projects, teachers and coordinators usually have little training or experience in educational evaluation. This chapter is intended to simplify and clarify the evaluation of G/T programs and guide the teacher or coordinator in the evaluation process. Some additional books focusing on evaluation of gifted programs are listed at the end of the chapter.

EVALUATION DESIGN: BEGIN AT THE BEGINNING

Although evaluation is the topic of the last chapter in this book, evaluation of a gifted program belongs at the very *beginning* of program planning. At the outset, when setting goals and objectives for a G/T program, one should design a methodology for measuring whether or not those objectives are reached.

"Difficult" and "Easy" Evaluations

Some objectives may seem too subtle or nonobjective to be measured quantitatively. Some examples of *difficult* evaluations are improvements in leadership, self-awareness, self-concept, decision making, reasoning, analyzing, synthesizing, evaluating, social responsibility, intrinsic motivation, critical thinking, and creative thinking. Other objectives are comparatively *easy* to evaluate. Acceleration programs, for example, provide almost self-evident evaluation data. Did students succeed in the advanced classes, the college courses, or the correspondence courses? Did the grade-skipping or the early admission to kindergarten work well for the students involved? Enrichment plans that result in a bona fide product—a school newspaper, a report of a research project, a poetry book, a dramatic production, artwork, a movie—also provide relatively easy evaluation data. Such products reflect a clear change in student skills and performances that, most likely, would not have occurred without the G/T program (Renzulli and Smith, 1979). Whether objectives are difficult or easy to measure, we nonetheless must try to evaluate every planned objective.

EVALUATION MODELS

There are many models for structuring the evaluation of education programs. Several will be summarized here, in an admittedly oversimplified fashion. In all cases, the intrigued reader will need to explore the more complete, original statements.

Stufflebeam et al. (1971) described three seemingly sensible steps in evaluation, all of which aim at aiding program decision makers: (1) delineating the information to be collected, (2) obtaining that information, and then (3) providing it to the decision makers. The information supplied to decision makers must be *valid, reliable, timely,* and *credible.* Further, the information would bear on four types of program decisions: (1) *planning decisions,* which relate to the program objectives; (2) *structuring decisions,* which pertain to the program procedures; (3) *implementing decisions,* which relate to carrying out and refining the procedures; and (4) *recycling decisions,* which focus on evaluating and reacting to program achievements.

Provus's (1972) *discrepancy* model assumes five stages in the creation of a program. At each stage the reality of the program is compared with a standard, and any discrepancy is fed back in order to improve the program by, naturally, correcting the discrepancy. In Stage 1, *Design,* the initial program plan is compared with a set of theory-based design criteria, perhaps as defined by an outside consultant. If there is a discrepancy, the program plan is modified accordingly. In Stage 2, *Installation,* the actual reality of the program as it is implemented is compared with the design adopted in Stage 1. Again, any discrepancies between program design and installation would be used to guide changes. These could be in the actual installation or in the Stage 1 design criteria. In Stage 3, *Process,* the actual program activities are compared with the proposed program activities, and any discrepancies will result in corrective alternatives. Stage 3 is especially important for creating an effective, successful program. In Stage 4, *Product,* actual student products are compared with the planned ones. This is the main evaluation of program objectives. Stage 5, *Product Comparison,* involves a comparison of students' products and learning outcomes with those of other programs to determine program efficiency in the cost-benefit sense.

Part of Eash's (1972; see also Renzulli, 1975) *differential evaluation* model involves three considerations in the evaluation process: (1) *Effort*—how time is spent (that is, the program activities); (2) *Effect*—products and outcomes; and (3) *Efficiency*—the relationship of effort and resources to the quality of effects realized. As the program evolves from a newly planned, innovative program (initiatory stage), through the implementation and field testing of the program (developmental stage), to the established and stable level (integrated stage), more emphasis is placed on evaluating effects and efficiency (2 and 3).

Finally, and again oversimplified, the Renzulli and Ward (1969) DESDEG (*Diagnostic and Evaluative Scales for Differential Education for the Gifted*) model was designed specifically for evaluating programs for gifted and talented students. It also may be used for program planning and development (Renzulli, 1975). DESDEG includes a set of five published documents corresponding to the five parts of the model. Part I is the Manual, which explains everything you ever wanted to know about DESDEG. Part II, Evaluative Scales, includes scales for evaluating each of 15 "ideally conceived educational practices" or Program Requirements, which subdivide into the five Key Features (general areas) in Table 17.1. Part III consists of Basic Information Forms, ". . . a comprehensive inventory of factual information about all aspects of a program . . . organized and keyed . . . to each of the five Key Features. . . ." These aid in the objective collection of data. Part IV is the Evaluator's Workbook, designed to aid the evaluator in handling the information derived from the Basic Information Forms and from observations. Part V is the Summary Report which (1) permits the evaluator to transfer numerical data to statistical and graphic summary sheets, and (2) aids in the creation of a summary narrative related to each Program Requirement.

It can be seen even in these sketchy outlines that the evaluation of education programs, including G/T programs, can be approached from many

TABLE 17.1   The DESDEG Model

Key Feature A: Philosophy and Objectives
    Program Requirement 1:   Existence and Adequacy of a Document
    Program Requirement 2:   Application of the Document
Key Feature B: Student Identification and Placement
    Program Requirement 3:   Validity of Conception and Adequacy of Procedures
    Program Requirement 4:   Appropriateness of Relationship Between Capacity and Curriculum
Key Feature C: The Curriculum
    Program Requirement 5:   Relevance of Conception
    Program Requirement 6:   Comprehensiveness
    Program Requirement 7:   Articulation
    Program Requirement 8:   Adequacy of Instructional Facilities
Key Feature D: The Teacher
    Program Requirement 9:   Selection
    Program Requirement 10:   Training
Key Feature E: Program Organization and Operation
    Program Requirement 11:   General Staff Orientation
    Program Requirement 12:   Administrative Responsibility and Leadership
    Program Requirement 13:   Functional Adequacy of the Organization
    Program Requirement 14:   Financial Allocation
    Program Requirement 15:   Provision for Evaluation

Joseph S. Renzulli, DESDEG Model. Reprinted by permission.

different viewpoints, use different strategies, and can focus on a variety of dimensions and considerations. A recent review of educational evaluation which focuses on the definition and functions of evaluation, variables, and criteria that should be used, the process and methods of evaluation, and standards for judging the merit of an evaluation appear in Nevo (1983).

THE RIMM MODEL

Rimm's (1977) model both (1) structures program evaluation in a relatively easy-to-follow fashion, and (2) ties it to the initial program plan. To begin, summarizing a program in one picture is very helpful for conceptualizing program components and, therefore, for relating evaluation needs to those components (see Figure 17.1). The diagram demonstrates how the different parts of a program fit together and, importantly, how evaluation can

FIGURE 17.1 Framework for the Evaluation and Monitoring of a Gifted Program

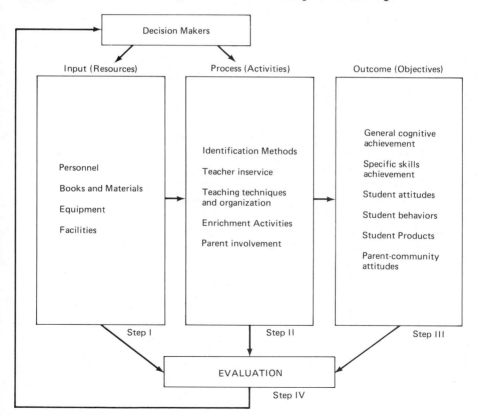

help one monitor all educational *Inputs* (*resources*), all *Processes* (*activities*), and all *Outcomes* (*goals and objectives*). Using the model has many advantages. First, it helps us understand the relationships among educational resources, processes, and outcomes. Second, using the model helps prevent the implementation of any activity without considering its eventual *evaluation*. Third, the model helps us become more sensitive to the close relationship of program decisions to the many student outcomes. Finally, and most importantly, the model itemizes on one page the program components that should be evaluated in regard to both (1) how well the component was implemented, and/or (2) how successfully that component helped achieve program goals.

The components within each of the three steps of the model reflect specific areas that should be evaluated. That is, each of the various types of input/resources (Step I), of processes/activities (Step II), and of outcomes/objectives (Step III) should be evaluated. Evaluation data (Step IV) from the components will present a comprehensive picture of the success and impact of a gifted program. This information is brought together and fed back to the decision makers who will use it for further planning—for modifying the input and process steps, which may include program expansion. Without the crucial evaluation step, there would be little clear basis for good decisions. Of course, the success of this approach depends heavily on the relevance and the clarity of the evaluation information obtained in Step IV.

Figure 17.2 provides a blank framework for the reader to outline his or her own program and evaluation model. The reader may wish to complete the diagram as this chapter is read.

Step I: *Input* represents resources. Resources typically include such program ingredients as teaching and support personnel, books, materials, equipment, and facilities. Resources may also include more specific categories such as community resource persons, specific student populations, or funding sources. Resources are the investments in the program and they usually are relatively easy to identify and list.

Step II: *Process* includes the activities of the program—everything that is planned to make the program effective. Typical categories of activities include identification procedures, teaching techniques, educational groupings, enrichment experiences, acceleration plans, teacher in-service training, and parent involvement activities. One may wish to itemize more specific curriculum activity components of the program, for example, creative-thinking instruction, creative writing, a computer mini-course, accelerated mathematics, Renzulli's (1977) enrichment triad, and so on. The list of categories of activities should be exhaustive, which means that each and every specific program activity would fit into a process category.

Step III: *Outcome* represents the goals and objectives of the gifted program. It actually may be easier to complete the list for Step III *before*

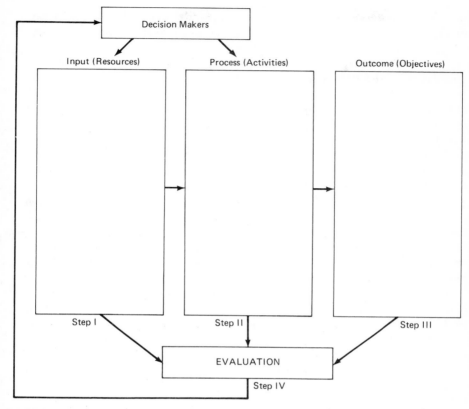

FIGURE 17.2 Framework for the Evaluation and Monitoring of Your Gifted Program

completing Steps I and II. What do you expect to accomplish? What are the purposes of the program? Some ideas for program goals were listed in Chapter 3.

Note that increased academic achievement is not necessarily a central outcome of a gifted program, although it may be an objective for gifted underachievers or, for example, for an accelerated math, biology, or reading program. More frequently, increases in specific *skills* are the intended outcomes of a program, for example, creative, critical, or evaluative thinking and independent study and research skills. Positive student *attitudes,* including self-concepts, attitudes toward education, and high career aspirations, are also frequently stated goals. In addition, scientific, literary, and artistic *products* are important and potentially measurable objectives. Parent and community attitudes toward the program and toward the needs of gifted children are further important outcomes to monitor.

Completing the model by inserting program components into each step should both (1) provide the reader with an overview of the entire program, and (2) assist with planning the necessary evaluations.

EVALUATING THE WRITTEN PLAN VERSUS ACTUAL ACTIVITIES

Outside persons (for example, the principal, members of the school board, the district superintendent, parents) may evaluate the results of a program strictly according to the written program plan, including the statement of philosophy, rationale, and goals (Davis, 1983b). This type of evaluation is relatively easy for outsiders to conduct and requires no particular measurement skills; the written goals and plans are simply compared with the actual apparent activities and outcomes. The Provus (1972) *discrepancy evaluation* concept mentioned earlier is a similar approach. The outsiders may ask such questions as: Were the identification procedures sensible, effective, and fair? Were the in-service workshops held as scheduled? Were the instructional strategies (grouping, acceleration, enrichment) carried out as planned? Did the planned field trips materialize? Were mentors/professionals in the community used as planned? Did students really become independent learners, thinkers, creators, and problem solvers? Were skills of analysis, synthesis, evaluation, critical thinking, and divergent thinking really strengthened? Were the evaluation and modification procedures carried out as planned?

Such questions clearly serve as a means of "checking up" on the program and its leaders, and may easily be perceived as threatening. However, the intent typically is constructive.

COMPLEXITY OF EVALUATION AND AUDIENCE: A HIERARCHY

The sophistication of an evaluation will be related to the intended audience—the persons who are the decision makers for a particular program. These decision makers can be placed in a *hierarchy* in terms of the quantity and the quality (statistical complexity) of the information they must have to carry out their own responsibilities. The goal should be to provide the appropriate information to match the information needs of these decision makers.

Briefly, (1) students and parents will need less information than (2) teachers and program directors, who in turn need less information than (3) administrators and school board members. (4) The state department of education will require still more technical information; and (5) the federal government, with its nationally selected and highly experienced grant reviewers, will require the greatest amount and the highest technical level of information.

Table 17.2 summarizes the relationship between levels of the decision-making hierarchy, components of the program emphasized (Rimm model), and the persons primarily responsible for the evaluation. Note that the teacher or program director can function as an evaluator at three levels of the hierarchy.

The hierarchy of decision makers is based on the different purposes or uses of the program evaluation information. A student or his or her parents may need to know only if the activity is generally interesting, challenging, motivating, and beneficial in very personal terms in order to decide if the student should continue in the program. A relatively small amount of information is needed for a decision that may have an important impact upon just one student, but no particular impact on the program as a whole. The student and his or her parents, with the help of the program teacher and/or coordinator, can assess the value of the program for that student.

The teacher or program director requires quite a bit more information than students and parents in order to modify, improve, and perhaps expand the program. This function of evaluation is called *formative evaluation.* Conducted throughout the school year, it is intended to provide immediate and continuous feedback to the staff regarding program strengths and weaknesses. The emphasis of formative evaluation will be on process (Figure 17.1); that is, on the value of various activities and experiences. Formative evaluation usually is conducted quite effectively by program staff, although observations of an independent (outside) evaluator usually add objectivity, insights, and ideas to the evaluation.

The school principal, district administrators, and members of the elected school board must decide whether to continue, change, or expand the gifted program, and hopefully not to fold it up. To make these kinds of

TABLE 17.2 Summary of the Relationship Between Hierarchy of Decision Making and Evaluation Plan

HIERARCHY OF DECISION MAKING	MODEL COMPONENT EMPHASIZED	STAFF RESPONSIBILITY
Individual Student or Parent	Individual Process and Outcome	Pupil, Teacher, and/or Parent
Teacher or Program Director	Process and Outcomes	Teacher, Program Director, or Administrator with some background in evaluation or independent evaluator
State or Federal Government	Input, Process, and Outcomes	Independent Evaluator with support of Program Staff

decisions, a *summative evaluation* must be conducted. The emphasis is on *outcomes*, and so a summative evaluation is conducted at the end of a unit, project, or most often, the school year. It "sums up" program success. Administrators and school board members may expect the staff to relate program input to outcomes in order to estimate some kind of cost-effectiveness. A teacher or program director with a small amount of advanced training in evaluation and statistics sometimes can successfully conduct such an evaluation. (However, if you happen to believe that a "t-test" is intended to compare the flavors of *teas* or is part of a golf game, it is time to call for help.) Board of education members primarily will want to know if a program has been "effective," and so the *how*'s and *why*'s of its effectiveness must be clearly and simply communicated.

Generally, local school people will feel their accountability obligation is met if one can prove that (1) the program was conducted as planned, (2) the students involved learned what was supposed to be taught, and (3) the process of learning was a positive one.

However, if a program is state or federally funded, a professional summative evaluation conducted by an experienced outside evaluator probably will be necessary. This evaluation typically includes a more technical, experimentally oriented evaluation. The teacher's role then becomes one of *cooperator*. The teacher need only inform the evaluator of the resources, activities, and objectives, and provide him or her with the needed data. Some test administration may be involved. Clear communication with the evaluator and full cooperation in gathering the necessary data will facilitate the accurate evaluation of the program. The outside evaluator should not be considered an adversary who is anxious to pounce on weaknesses. His or her role is to provide constructive feedback to the staff for program improvement, and to objectively report the reasonableness and effectiveness of the program plans, methods, activities, and so forth. Although the objectivity of outside evaluators may appear threatening during early program development, that same objectivity will be extraordinarily reinforcing when a program is stabilized and functioning well.

The outside evaluation may require the use of a *control group* of subjects (for example, students of similar ability in another school district where there is no program). Test scores from such a control group, when compared with scores of students in the program, would help determine if any improvements (for instance, in creativity scores, self-concept development, achievement) are actually due to the program and not due simply to maturation, the passage of time, or other educational experiences. Teacher-coordinators likely will drown in a sea of statistics if they attempt this type of evaluation on their own.

As emphasized earlier, an important first consideration for effective evaluation is outlining the evaluation design at the same time the rest of the program is planned, namely, before the program begins. Even an expert evaluator will be less able to do his or her job if the program begins without coordinating the program objectives with their eventual evaluation. Beginning a G/T program without an evaluation design is comparable to beginning one's classroom teaching without a curriculum plan. In both cases, the preplanning helps outline where you are going, how to get there, and what to do when you arrive.

In summary, no program for the gifted should be conducted without some evaluation. Whether the decision makers are students, parents, teachers, administrators, school board members, or state or federal agencies, they will want to know about the "success" and the particular "effects" of the program.

INSTRUMENT SELECTION

Some form of measurement is almost always necessary to determine the degree to which program objectives have been achieved (for example, those in the *outcome* rectangle of the Rimm model). Ideally, in order to reach sound conclusions one should try to obtain *two* measurements of each objective, particularly the most important ones. Also, whenever possible one should use instruments—tests, questionnaires, rating forms—already available. To do a proper job of developing one's own instruments requires a considerable amount of time, and usually requires training and experience in test construction.

Besides, with a little digging a teacher-coordinator most likely will discover that the test-building work already has been done. Many instruments for assessing innumerable aspects of G/T programs are available, for example, in Renzulli (1975), Renzulli, Reis, and Smith (1981), Sjogren, Hopkins, and Gooler (1975), and the Association for the Gifted Evaluation Committee (1979). For new evaluation ideas, check current journals on gifted education and creativity; they frequently describe instruments that have been recently developed and validated. Some sample instruments appear at the end of this chapter.

Tests with *norms* for different grades are desirable. Such information allows one to more easily interpret and communicate the performance of gifted students compared with students in the norm group. However, for a sensible comparison the students in the norm group must be similar to those in the gifted program. For example, they should not be from a higher or lower SES level or from a different cultural environment.

Although there are indeed many different tests for review, it can happen that an instrument exactly right for a specific purpose will not be found. Do not make the mistake of using an instrument—no matter how carefully designed—that measures something other than what the program plans to teach. It is essential that the *objectives* of the program activities, on one hand, be matched with the *purposes* and the *contents* of the tests and inventories, on the other. If test purposes or contents do not match program objectives and activities, one is not very likely to find a measurable effect of the program. This simple point may seem self-evident to the sensible reader. However, it is a very common error for G/T teachers and coordinators to teach one set of contents and skills (for example, advanced math), yet evaluate others (for example, creativity)—and then be surprised and disappointed to find "no effects" or "no transfer" of the training experience. Importantly, negative evaluation findings can easily be misused; they can readily, and logically, be interpreted as evidence that the program was ineffective.

Pilot Testing

A program evaluator may need to *pilot* a test, that is, try it out, with a few children to help decide if it is appropriate for the desired purpose. For example, suppose a program included accelerated reading or math and the evaluator wanted to determine if a particular norm-referenced test could be used to evaluate student achievement.[1] If the test is administered to two or three students and they "top out" near the maximum possible score, this would immediately signal that the test is not satisfactory. It would not assess the high achievement level of the gifted students. It may be necessary to pilot three or four tests to find an appropriate one. One strategy is to pilot several tests simultaneously with several small groups of students. This quickly provides plenty of information for test comparison and selection.

Topping Out and Regression Toward the Mean

As discussed earlier in this book, the topping-out phenomenon is a frequent occurrence when gifted students take standardized, norm-referenced achievement tests. The tests often are not difficult enough to discriminate among nor evaluate the learning of high-achieving gifted children. If we measure improvements from pretests to post-tests but students have already achieved ceiling scores on the pretests, it will appear that the students showed no measurable improvement. In fact, there simply was no place for the scores to go. Actual progress could not be measured.

A potentially more serious problem related to using too-easy achievement tests comes from the *regression toward the mean* effect. This simply means that given a first score that is extreme (either very high or very low), by chance alone the next score is likely to "regress" toward the mean. For

---

[1]A *norm-referenced* test is one of moderate difficulty that is designed to produce a normal, bell-curve distribution of scores—for example, a standardized achievement test. Norm-referenced tests contrast with *criterion-referenced* tests, which are designed to evaluate the mastery of specific objectives (criteria)—for example, a spelling test.

example, given an extremely tall boy, the father is likely to be shorter; given an extremely tall father, the son is likely to be shorter. Now if gifted students score near the very top of a pretest, their scores on the post-test by chance alone are likely to be lower—incorrectly suggesting that participation in the special G/T activities damaged students' learning. For example, with regressed scores on a basic skills test, an audience could conclude that the gifted program is having a negative effect on the basic skills of students. They probably would attribute this damage to students missing instructional time in the regular classroom. Since pulling out students from the regular classroom often is a controversial issue in the first place, such an interpretation could be devastating to an excellent program.

TEST CONSTRUCTION

There are times when a state or federal agency will require evidence for the effectiveness of a program, but the exactly appropriate tests and measures simply do not exist. It therefore may be necessary to construct original tests or questionnaires in order to evaluate specific student skills, information, attitudes, or abilities, the effectiveness of specific program components, or even the overall quality of the total program. Technical help from an evaluation expert at a university or private consulting firm, someone experienced in evaluating G/T programs and in constructing tests, probably will be needed.

To select a consultant, contact directors of other G/T programs and state or even national leaders in gifted education to find who in the area is available and qualified. When a consultant is recommended, one can elicit opinions of his or her work from teachers and program directors for whom the consultant has provided services. One also can ask to review tests and reports the consultant has prepared for other clients.

Competitive bidding can be misleading, since there is a considerable range of quality that fixed evaluation dollars can buy. Also, a poor instrument or evaluation is worse than none at all, even if the cost is lowest. Test construction may be expensive, so be prepared. The high cost of test construction is one very good reason to use established tests, as recommended earlier.

Rating Students' Products

Artistic, literary, scientific, or other types of student products may be outcomes of a program, and although they are difficult to evaluate reliably, their quality is measurable. Product evaluation usually involves either of two approaches. With the first *gain score* approach, samples of students' work obtained at the outset of the program (pretest products) are compared with students' products at the end of the educational experience (post-test products). Gain scores may be used to evaluate products that reflect the development of such skills and abilities as art, creative writing, divergent thinking, and others.

With the second *absolute* approach, individual students' products are evaluated according to their excellence without an objective comparison with earlier products. The absolute approach would be used if science or other major projects (for example, of the Renzulli Type III variety) are evaluated for which earlier comparison products are not available.

With either the gain score or the absolute method, rating scales may be used to quantify the judgments. As two examples, Renzulli (1975) recommended the scale in Appendix 17.1, developed by the Warwick, Rhode Island, Public Schools, for evaluating the quality of visual arts products. (This art scale includes a "growth" rating, which would make no sense in a pretest. Therefore, if this scale were used to assess gain scores the "growth" item would be omitted from both the pretest and the post-test). The scale in Appendix 4.4, developed by the state of Michigan Department of Education, may be used to evaluate the excellence of virtually any type of student product.

The rating scales in Appendixes 17.1 and 4.4 could serve as models for creating one's own product-rating scales. Alternatively, the following steps could be used to develop original rating scales:

Step 1. Determine the evaluation criteria (for example, creativeness, technical skill) and the specific scales for rating those criteria. The criteria should come from the teaching objectives. Note the objectives reflected in each scale in Appendixes 17.1 and 4.4. As for the rating scales themselves, while Appendix 17.1 uses six-point scales, a five-point scale as in Appendix 4.4 usually is most comfortable. It is best to describe the meaning of each point on the scale. The "low," "moderate," and "high" descriptions of Appendix 17.1 and the "To a great extent," "Somewhat," and "To a limited extent" of Appendix 4.4 are very minimal descriptions. For example, a scale for evaluating the use of *humor* in creative writing might be based on the following descriptors:

"1": No use of humor.

"2": One humorous comment, which does not appear original.

"3": Two or three humorous statements or paragraphs, which do not appear original.

"4": Two or three statements or paragraphs that do appear original.

"5": Original humorous themes are skillfully integrated into the entire story.

Such scale-point descriptions will improve the accuracy (reliability) of the raters' ratings.

Step 2. Collect pretest creative products from each child in the program. All products should be identified with code numbers so that the students' names and the date of collection will not be obvious to the raters.

Step 3. Select at least two raters. They may be teachers or community members. Train them to use the particular scales with extra products that will not be used as "official" data. After rating several products together, use a few more extra products for the individual raters each to rate separately.

Step 4. Calculate the percentage of rater agreement. With five-point scales, two raters should agree on at least 80 percent of the practice ratings before they begin rating the pretest and post-test products. If the raters do not agree at an 80-percent level, they need more training, including a discussion of the reasons for their disagreements.

Step 5. After interrater reliability is established, to minimize bias raters should rate all products. This should be done without knowing the names of the children and without knowing which are pretest products and which are post-test products.

Step 6. Calculate the average pretest ratings for the group and compare them with the average post-test ratings. If a program is effective, the average post-test rating should be higher, indicating that skill development increased since the pretest products were created. Statistics may be necessary in order to conclude that the overall increase is not due to chance. Also, as noted earlier, a control group may be necessary to prove that the improvement of your trained students was not due to the passage of time or to other educational experiences.

For information regarding the gains (or losses) of individual students, one would examine the differences between pretest and post-test ratings for each student.

Step 7. In reporting the findings, the means (and other statistics, if any) must be meaningful, reliable, and valid. If possible, include a few sample products (for example, samples of creative writing, scientific reports, photos of artwork) to illustrate the student gains. These sample products will help any audience understand the meaning of the ratings.

Classroom Observation Data

Parents, administrators, school board members, and government agencies usually like to know what happens in a gifted program, and so classroom observation data are good data to collect. A structured observation form can be developed for a program and used to describe "who is doing what with whom and when" in a very specific way. As one example, Appendix 17.2 (adapted from Rimm, 1981a) shows a structured observation form used for monitoring a reading program. The letters at the top of each column represent each of the ten students observed. Filling in a circle indicates that a student is involved in one of the activities listed in the rows. An objective observer would enter the classroom at random times of the day and observe ten randomly selected students, recording their activities on the checklist. Descriptive comments may be added to each observation to provide a richer description of the class environment.

A form such as the one in Appendix 17.2 could be adapted for use with any particular G/T program. Category headings could be modified or new ones created; each would have specific subcategories. For example, one might wish to record pupil's interest level, pupil's behavior, pupil's interactions, teacher's instructional activities, materials and equipment in use, or activities of other adults. Additional headings, each with specific subcategories, could be included depending upon the special activities of the program.

If desirable, at the end of the year summary forms can be tabulated and percentages calculated to describe the specific *type* and *extent* of the activities engaged in during that year. This summary provides objective documentation of the year's program activities. Thus if a school board member wanted to know how much time microcomputers were in use, how many students participated in the *Great Books* discussions, or what proportion of the G/T program time was spent in independent projects, exact numbers and percentages would be available to support personal observations and impressions. There is nothing quite so convincing as hard data.

Questionnaires

Activities in both the *process* and *outcomes* components of Rimm's model may be evaluated with questionnaires. While students, teachers, parents, board members, and administrators all find paperwork burdensome, the best way to find answers is to ask questions. Decision makers at all levels will want to know (and have a right to know) the effectiveness and special strengths of a program and its weaknesses as perceived by others. They also are interested in others' constructive suggestions for improving the program. If questionnaires are brief and require only that a few numbers be circled and/or a few questions be answered, most persons will respond. You can bet that those who are strongly enthusiastic and those who are most disappointed or critical will be certain to respond.

Questionnaires use various types of items. Objective items include *checklists, rating scales, rankings,* and *multiple-choice* statements. The advantages of objective items include ease of development, efficiency of administration, clear response options, easy and objective scoring, and ready quantifiability for statistical purposes. Some disadvantages include the limited nature of the response options, along with little or no information about the *reasons* for the judgments.

Because of these disadvantages, many objective questionnaires also include open-ended items. Open-ended items provide an opportunity for students, teachers, parents, principles, and even school board members to voice reasons for their opinions, as well as to contribute suggestions and potential solutions to problems. Information can indeed be rich and valuable. For formative evaluation purposes, open-ended items usually are more valuable than objective items. In the negative column, open-ended items are more time consuming for both respondents and scorers, interpretations may be ambiguous, and the answers are not readily quantifiable.

As examples of combining objective with open-ended questionnaires, Appendix 17.3 presents an example of a brief questionnaire that could be used by teacher participants in an in-service program. Appendix 17.4 shows a questionnaire that allows school board members to evaluate G/T services of a high school. Appendix 17.5 presents a nonobjective open-ended form that students could use to evaluate a learning center.

Generally, it is wise to set aside a few minutes in every program for teachers and students to complete the evaluation forms. If you create the time, persons will fill out the questionnaires on the spot; questionnaires taken home or mailed often are not returned.

DAILY LOGS

As a general principle, *log everything.* Each staff member should keep a notebook handy in which to make brief notes on daily activities. The value of the entries will far outweigh the few minutes invested each day. The kinds of information that could be logged include:

A description of activities
Preparation for the activities
Number of participants
Perceived effectiveness of the activities
Modifications for the future
Any data collected
Any anecdotal material

A personal log kept by each staff member can provide important program documentation serving at least three purposes. First and foremost, it can provide a description of the activities and accomplishments of the students, and therefore of the value of the specific learning activities and projects. Second, it can assure administration and board members that the staff member has indeed made critical contributions to the program. Third, it will serve to remind the teacher of the quantity and quality of his or her own contributions and accomplishments.

STUDENT SELF-EVALUATIONS

Student self-evaluations are important in G/T programs. Primarily, they provide individual students with a clear measure of accomplishment relative to their own goals and objectives. Positive feedback reinforces student motivation and commitment, while objectively documenting their personal progress. For program evaluators, when individual self-evaluations are combined they become important measures of student outcomes, some of which could not be obtained in any other way.

Independent self-monitoring usually can be conducted quite handily by students in junior and senior high school. Younger children also can take responsibility for self-evaluation, with a little help from their teachers. One example of a summative, end-of-the-year student self-evaluation form appears in Appendix 17.6.

Parke and Buescher (1982) recommended a seven-step model for student self-evaluation and self-documentation. Their model places the individual self-evaluation within the framework of the overall program evaluation; it thus begins with program planning.

Step 1 evolves around setting program *objectives.* Since this is a student model, individual student objectives must be set, jointly by the student and teacher, within the larger program objectives.

Step 2 involves determining program *standards.* This step includes jointly deciding on the individual behaviors that will be exhibited by the students as evidence of attaining program objectives.

Step 3 relates to determining the *preprogram knowledge and/or skill* level of individual students. This preassessment can involve diagnostic or norm-referenced achievement testing, or personality, self-concept, creativity, critical-thinking, leadership, or other assessment. Product evaluations, teacher observations, teacher logs, or student questionnaires also can be part of this initial assessment. All should relate to the specific objectives for the program and the individuals in it (Steps 1 and 2).

Step 4 is the initiation of *learning experiences,* the actual activities of the program as experienced by the individual student.

Step 5 is student *self-documentation* of growth. This step requires that students monitor their progress by collecting evidence of their personal accomplishments, including products, reports, logs, notes, or other reflections of their own learning experiences. Students may require teacher assistance in determining the kinds of relevant information to collect, but collecting the information can be mostly the students' responsibility.

Step 6 involves *assessing knowledge and/or skill levels* with objective tests.

Step 7 is the *comparison* of skill levels—information from Steps 5 and 6—with the originally set individual performance standards (Step 2). In this last step students determine the degree to which they have met the initial standards they set for themselves within the original program standards. They also can review this assessment information with their teacher and determine their next objectives and standards. The teacher or coordinator, in turn, can combine individual records of student attainment to determine if program objectives (Step 1) have been achieved.

PERFORMANCE CONTRACTING

Student *performance contracting* is another vehicle for individual student evaluation. Within the student contract, the teacher and the student spell out:

1. Specific *objectives*, including skills to be learned and final projects and papers to be completed.
2. The *activities* in which the student plans to engage to achieve these objectives.
3. The *deadline* by which these objectives will be completed.
4. The *materials* the student will produce (or collect) in support of his or her attainment of the objectives.
5. The *methods* and *criteria* by which the attainment of the objectives will be evaluated.

The student contract is a "study guide" for both the student and the teacher, as well as the basis for an evaluation and documentation of the student's personal performance. The emphasis of the contract should be on student responsibility, with the teacher as a facilitator. Performance contracts are a type of learning activity that encourages the independence and creativity that most gifted students thrive on. Thus individual student needs are served while providing program evaluation and accountability data.

COMMITMENT TO EVALUATION

Teachers and coordinators in gifted programs are likely to view evaluation as burdensome. Their time always is scarce, and time used for evaluation will be at the expense of time for students. It thus is very tempting simply to avoid evaluation altogether. However, skipping the evaluation process is a short-sighted decision for gifted programs—which, we repeat, have a history of being quickly cut from school, state, and federal budgets. Good evaluation is the only way to determine the most effective way to enhance the education of gifted learners. It also is the only way to prove to program sponsors and decision makers that the program has indeed accomplished its objectives.

SUMMARY

Evaluation in gifted education has been minimal. However, it is important both for demonstrating success to outsiders and for improving the program. Evaluation plans should be made at the outset of program planning.

Some objectives are difficult to evaluate, such as improvements in self-awareness, creativity, reasoning and analyzing, social responsibility, and others. Other outcomes are comparatively easy to assess, such as the success of acceleration or the improved quality of student products.

Stufflebeam's evaluation model included three steps, delineating the information to be collected, obtaining it, and providing it to decision makers. The information relates to planning decisions, structuring decisions (procedures), implementing decisions, and recycling (evaluation) decisions.

Provus's discrepancy includes five steps: Design, Installation, Process (activities), Product, and Product Comparison. At each step one compares the program reality with a standard and then corrects the discrepancy.

Eash's differential evaluation focuses on three considerations, Effort (activities), Effect (products and outcomes), and Efficiency (the relationships of effort and resources to the quality of the Effects).

Renzulli's DESDEQ model included five steps corresponding to five documents, the Manual, Evaluation Scales, Basic Information Forms, Evaluator's Workbook, and the Summary Report.

Rimm's model structures the program evaluation and ties it to the initial program plan. The three steps of Input (resources), Process (activities), and Outcome (objectives), each with specific subcategories, all may be evaluated.

Increased academic achievement may or may not be a central outcome. Rather, improvements in process skills and attitudes are usual goals of G/T programs.

Outside persons may evaluate a program simply by comparing the actual activities and outcomes with the original written plan.

Audiences form a hierarchy in the quality and quantity of needed evaluation information. Students and parents need relatively little information to decide whether to continue in the program. Teachers and program directors require more information, particularly continuous, formative evaluation for program improvement. Administrators and school board members will require summative information to decide whether to continue or expand the program.

If the program is funded by state or federal sources, their decision makers will require considerable amounts of information, including test scores, some of which will involve statistical comparisons and perhaps control groups.

One should try to obtain two measurements of each important objective. It is usually easier and cheaper to locate already validated tests than to construct your own. It is important to be certain that the test measures the objectives that were the basis of the teaching. Using the wrong tests will produce negative results, creating a bad impression.

Pilot testing is advisable, for example, to cope with the topping-out problem common with gifted students. On a second testing, very high scores may regress toward the mean, creating the appearance that the program damaged, for example, basic skill development.

Ratings of student projects may use the gain-score approach; ratings of preprogram projects are compared with ratings of postprogram projects. With the absolute approach, complex projects are evaluated without a comparison to earlier projects.

In creating original rating scales, one would determine the evaluation criteria, collect pretest products, select and train at least two raters, determine rater agreement, use "blind" ratings," and compare average pretest ratings with average post-test ratings. It is desirable to include sample projects in final reports.

Classroom observation data present objective information regarding "what happens" in a gifted program.

The process (activities) and outcome (objectives) sections of Rimm's model may be evaluated with questionnaires.

Objective questionnaire items (for example, checklists, rating scales, multiple-choice questions) are easily administered and scored. They may be combined with less objective and more time-consuming—but highly imformative—open-ended questions.

Daily logs provide valuable records of activities, preparation, participants, perceived effectiveness, ideas for modifications, and anecdotal information.

Self-evaluations provide positive, motivating feedback to students. They also provide unique program evaluation data.

Parke and Buescher outlined a seven-step model for student self-evaluation.

Performance contracting can be used to individualize instruction and to document student accomplishments.

Good evaluation is absolutely essential for program continuity and program improvement.

RECOMMENDED READING

CALLAHAN, C. M., Issues in evaluating programs for the gifted. *Gifted Child Quarterly,* 1983, *27,* 3–7.

GUBA, E. G., & LINCOLN, Y. S. *Effective evaluation.* San Francisco, Calif.: Jossey-Bass, 1981.

NEVO, D. The conceptualization of educational evaluation: An analytical review of the literature. *Review of Educational Research,* 1983, *53,* 117–128.

PATTEN, M. S. *Qualitative evaluation methods.* Beverly Hills, Calif.: Sage, 1980.

POPHAM, W. J. *Educational evaluation.* Englewood Cliffs, N.J.: Prentice-Hall, 1975.

POPHAM, W. J. (ed.) *Evaluation in education.* Berkeley, Calif.: McCutchan, 1974.

PROVUS, M. M. *Discrepancy evaluation.* Berkeley, Calif.: McCutchan, 1971.

RENZULLI, J. S. The confession of a frustrated evaluator. *Measurement and Evaluation in Guidance,* 1972, 5, 298–305.

RENZULLI, J. S. *A guidebook for evaluating programs for the gifted and talented.* Ventura, Calif.: Office of the Ventura County Superintendent of Schools, 1975.

RENZULLI, J. S., & WARD, V. S. *Diagnostic and evaluative scales for differential education for the gifted.* Storrs, Conn.: University of Connecticut, 1969.

SCRIVEN, M. The methodology of evaluation. In R. E. Stake (ed.), *AERA monograph series on curriculum evaluation,* No. 1. Chicago: Rand McNally, 1967.

STUFFLEBEAM, D. L., FOLEY, W. J., GEPHART, W. J., GUBA, E. G., HAMMON, R. L., MERRIMAN, H. W., & PROVUS, M. M. *Educational evaluation and decision-making.* Itasca, Ill.: Peacock, 1971.

STUFFLEBEAM, D. W., & WEBSTER, W. J. An analysis of alternative approaches to evaluation. *Educational Evaluation and Policy Analysis,* 1980, 2(3), 5–20.

WORTHEN, B. R., & SANDERS, J. R. *Educational evaluation: Theory and practice.* Belmont, Calif.: Wadsworth, 1973.

APPENDIX 17.1 PROJECT GIFTED: EVALUATION SCALE
FOR VISUAL ARTS

Code No. _____ Age _____ Boy/Girl _____ TOTAL SCORE _____

Evaluator _____ Position _____ Date _____

Elements	Low		Moderate		High	
	1	2	3	4	5	6
1. Creative Expression, Imagination, Uniqueness						
2. Flexibility, Appreciation, and Adaptability to Various Media						
3. Fluency, Variety or Number of Ideas						
4. Sensitivity-Composition-Design						
5. Manipulative Skills: Construction, Weaving, etc.						
6. Growth						
Column Total						
Weight	1	2	3	4	5	6
Weighted Column Total						
TOTAL SCORE						

J. S. Renzulli, *An Evaluation of Project Gifted.* Storrs, University of Connecticut, 1973. Reprinted by permission.

APPENDIX 17.2 EXAMPLE OF A STRUCTURED OBSERVATION FORM

Date _____ a.m. _____ p.m. _____ Observer _____

1. Pupil's Location

	abc	def	ghij
Desk or table	000	000	0000
Carrel	000	000	0000
Open area	000	000	0000
Materials center	000	000	0000
Other (specify):	000	000	0000

2. Instructional Content

	abc	def	ghij
Readiness	000	000	0000
Decoding skills	000	000	0000
Comprehension	000	000	0000
Enjoyment or appreciation	000	000	0000
Vocabulary	000	000	0000
Spelling	000	000	0000
Grammar	000	000	0000
Composition	000	000	0000
Oral expression	000	000	0000
School library usage	000	000	0000
Speed reading	000	000	0000
Dictionary skills	000	000	0000
Other (specify):	000	000	0000

3. Pupil's Instructional Grouping

	abc	def	ghij
Whole-class group instruction	000	000	0000
Partial-class group instruction	000	000	0000
Tutorial (one to one) instruction	000	000	0000
Independent work on individually-assigned activity	000	000	0000
Independent work on a group-assigned activity	000	000	0000
Shared work on group-assigned activity	000	000	0000
Shifting group patterns	000	000	0000

4. Instructional and Audiovisual Materials and Equipment in Use

5. Pupil's Behavior

6. Person Relating to Pupil

7. Person's Instructional Role

S. Rimm, "Evaluation of gifted programs—as easy as ABC." In R. E. Clasen et al. (eds.), *Programming for the Gifted, Talented, and Creative* (Madison: University of Wisconsin, 1981).

APPENDIX 17.3 EVALUATION FORM FOR IN-SERVICE WORKSHOPS

Workshop Title: <u>CREATIVITY IN THE CLASSROOM</u>

Circle the appropriate numbers below.

1. I found this program to be . . .

1	2	3	4	5
Dull		Of average Interest		Very Interesting

2. I think that what I learned today will be . . .

1	2	3	4	5
Useless		Somewhat Useful		Very Useful

3. I would like to have more inservice programs on this topic.

1	2	3	4
No, not at all	Yes, but not for a while	Yes, more this year	Other (Explain Below):

   Explanation: _____

   _____

   _____

4. The things I liked most about this inservice were: _____

   _____

   _____

   _____

5. The things I liked least about this inservice were: _____

   _____

   _____

   _____

APPENDIX 17.4 SCHOOL BOARD QUESTIONNAIRE

SCHOOL BOARD QUESTIONNAIRE

We suggest you read the questionnaire before you start to answer.

   Please indicate the extent to which you agree or disagree with each of the following statements by circling the appropriate letter. The letters mean the following:

                    SA — Strongly agree
                    A — Generally agree
                    U — Undecided
                    D — Generally disagree
                    SD — Strongly disagree

   Please use the comment line if you want to explain your answer. Answer question 9 only if you have children in the high school.

1. School E High School provides a well-   SA   A   U   D   SD
    balanced educational program.

    Comment_____

2. This school has a good program·for the   SA   A   U   D   SD
    able students.

    Comment_____

3. Most parents feel School E is a good   SA   A   U   D   SD
    school.

    Comment_____

4. The School E program is mainly for the   SA   A   U   D   SD
    college-bound student.

    Comment_____

5. Students at School E are receiving a good   SA   A   U   D   SD
    education in the basics like math, English,
    history, science.

    Comment_____

6. There are too many frills in the School E   SA   A   U   D   SD
    program.

    Comment_____

7. School E has a good extra-curricular program, SA   A   U   D   SD
    i.e., athletics, music, school paper, drama,
    clubs, etc.

    Comment_____

8. School E should have more vocational courses. SA   A   U   D   SD

    Comment_____

9. Most of the teachers our child has had at   SA   A   U   D   SD
    School E have done a good job.

    Comment_____

D. Sjogren, T. Hopkins, & D. Gooler, *Evaluation Plans and Instruments: Illustrative Cases of Gifted Program Evaluation Techniques.* Center for Instructional Research and Curriculum Evaluation, Urbana-Champaign: University of Illinois. Reprinted by permission.

APPENDIX 17.5 STUDENT EVALUATION: LEARNING CENTER PROGRAM

```
                    STUDENT EVALUATION
                    LEARNING CENTER PROGRAM

For the past sixteen weeks you have been attending sessions at the
_____ County Learning Center.  We would like to know some
of your feelings about the program.  By answering questions and
completing the following sentences, you can help us in improving
the program.
```

1. Which class did you like best? _____

2. Why? _____

3. Of the classes I was not in, I wish I could have taken _____

   _____

4. Why? _____

5. I wish my classes at the Learning Center were longer _____,

   shorter _____, the same _____ (check one).

6. The Learning Center needs more _____

7. The class in which I learned or accomplished most was _____

   _____

8. If I could change three things about the Learning Center, I would

   a. _____
   b. _____
   c. _____

9. Has the Learning Center helped you in any way with things you do

   at school? _____

10. How? _____

11. Has the Learning Center helped you in any way with things you do

    at home? _____

12. How? _____

13. Has the Learning Center helped in any way with the way you get

    along with or feel about people? _____. If so, how? ___

    _____

From Florida's State Resource Manual for Gifted Child Education. State of Florida Department of Education, 1973. Reprinted by permission.

APPENDIX 17.6 PUPIL SELF-EVALUATION

PUPIL SELF-EVALUATION

Pupil's Name _____

Think of yourself at the present time in comparison to last year. As a result of <u>this year's</u> work, please rate yourself on the following items. Place the letters <u>a</u>, <u>b</u>, <u>c</u>, <u>d</u>, and <u>e</u> on the line following each item according to the scale below.

(a)	Much less	(d)	More
(b)	Less	(e)	Much more
(c)	About the same		

1. Ability to think things through for yourself _____

2. Knowledge of subject matter areas (science, social studies, and others I have taken) _____

3. Interest in school _____

4. Ability to see how things go together in a situation (see relationships) _____

5. Ability to find information _____

6. Ability to work well by myself _____

7. The liking and respect of other pupils for me _____

8. Ability to judge the usefulness of facts _____

9. Ability to get along with my teacher(s) _____

10. Enjoyment of learning _____

11. Knowledge of arithmetic, spelling, and other basic skills _____

12. Curiosity about learning new things _____

13. Ability to accept responsibility _____

14. Opportunity to make things, experiment, and use ideas _____

15. Knowledge of my strengths and weaknesses _____

16. Willingness to do work as a leader _____

Please answer the following questions:

17. Has the school year been helpful to you? Yes _____   No _____

    Please explain.

    _____

    _____

18. Has any part of the school work this year created any problems for you?   Yes _____   No _____

    Please explain.

    _____

    _____

R. E. Simpson, & R. A. Martinson, *Educational Program for Gifted Pupils.* Sacramento, Calif.: California State Department of Education, 1961. Reprinted by permission.

REFERENCES

ADAMS, M. The compassion trap. In V. Gomick & B. K. Moran (eds.), *Woman in sexist society: Studies in power and powerlessness*. New York: New American Library, 1971.

ADDISON, L. Simulation gaming and leadership training for gifted girls. *Gifted Child Quarterly*, 1979, *23*, 288–96.

_____. Attribution theory and gifted females. Presented at the CEC-TAG National Topical Conference on the Gifted and Talented Child, Orlando, Fla., December 1981.

ALBERT, R. S. Toward a behavioral definition of genius. *American Psychologist*, 1975, *30*, 140–51.

ALBRECHT, K. *Brain power: Learn to improve your thinking skills*. Englewood Cliffs, N.J.: Prentice-Hall, 1980.

_____. Brain power: The human mind as the next great frontier. Speech presented at the Third Annual Midwest Conference on Gifted and Talented Children, Milwaukee, Wis., April 1983.

ALEXAKOS, C. E., & ROTHNEY, J. W. M. Post high school preferences of superior students. *Personnel and Guidance Journal*, 1967, *46*, 150–55.

ALLAIN, V. A. Sexism in education. In T. C. Hunt (ed.), *Society, culture, and schools: The American approach*. Garrett Park, Md.: Garrett Park Press, 1979.

_____. Women in education: The future. *Educational Horizons*, 1981, *60*, 52–56.

ALLEN, M. S. *Morphological creativity*. Englewood Cliffs, N.J.: Prentice-Hall, 1962.

ALLEN, R. R., KAUFFELD, F. J., & O'BRIEN, W. R. A. *Semiprogrammed introduction to verbal argument*, Parts 1–4. Madison, Wis.: Wisconsin Research and Development Center for Cognitive Learning, 1968.

_____, & ROTT, R. K. The nature of critical thinking. Theoretical Paper No. 20, Wisconsin Research and Development Center for Cognitive Learning, University of Wisconsin, Madison, Wis., 1969.

ALMQUIST, E. M., & ANGRIST, S. Role model influences in college women's career aspirations. *Merrill-Palmer Quarterly*, 1971, *17*, 263–79.

ALPER, T. G. Achievement motivation in college women: A now-you-see-it-now-you-don't phenomenon. *American Psychologist*, 1974, *29*, 194–203.

ALSCHULER, A. S. *Developing achievement motivation in adolescents.* Englewood Cliffs, N. J.: Educational Technology Publications, 1973.

ALTMAN, S. L., & GROSSMAN, F. K. Women's career plans and maternal employment. *Psychology of Women Quarterly*, 1977, *1*, 365–76.

ALVINO, J., MCDONNEL, R. C., & RICHERT, S. National survey of identification practices in gifted and talented education. *Exceptional Children*, 1981, *48*, 124–32.

American Psychological Association. *Standards for educational and psychological tests.* Washington, D.C., 1974

ARMSTRONG, J. M. *A national assessment of achievement and participation of women in mathematics.* Final Report to the National Institute of Education on Grant No. NIE-G-77-0061. Denver, Colo.: Education Commission of the States, 1979.

ARONSON, E., BLANEY, N., SIKES, J., STEPHAN, C., & SNAPP, M. Busing and racial tension: The jigsaw route to learning and liking. *Psychology Today*, 1975, *8(9)*, 43–50.

ASIMOV, I. *Asimov's Guide to Shakespeare.* New York: Avenel Books, 1978.

Association for the Gifted Evaluation Committee. *Sample instruments for the evaluation of programs for the gifted and talented.* Storrs, Conn.: University of Connecticut, 1979.

ATKINSON, J. W. *Motives in fantasy, action, and society: A method of assessment and study.* New York: Van Nostrand, 1958.

———. The mainsprings of achievement-oriented activity. In G. A. Davis & T. F. Warren (eds.), *Psychology of education: New looks.* Lexington, Mass.: D.C. Heath, 1974.

AUSUBEL, D. P. In defense of advance organizers: A reply to the critics. *Review of Educational Research*, 1978, *48*, 251–57.

BANDURA, A., & WALTERS, R. H. *Social learning and personality development.* New York: Holt, 1963.

BANKS, W. *Teaching strategies for ethnic studies* (2nd ed.). Boston: Allyn & Bacon, 1979.

BARATZ, J. C. Teaching reading in an urban negro school system. In G. A. Davis & T. F. Warren (eds.), *Psychology of education: New looks.* Lexington, Mass.: D.C. Heath, 1974.

BARDWICK, J. M. *Psychology of women.* New York: Harper & Row, 1971.

BARRON, F. *Creative person and creative process.* New York: Holt, 1969.

———. An eye more fantastical. In G. A. Davis & J. A. Scott (eds.), *Training creative thinking.* Huntington, N.Y.: Krieger, 1978.

BARTELL, I. P. An investigation of depression in academically gifted children. Unpublished Masters Thesis, University of Wisconsin, Madison, Wis., 1983.

BARTKOVICH, K. G., & MEZYNSKI, K. Fast-paced precalculus mathematics for talented junior high students: Two recent SMPY programs. *Gifted Child Quarterly*, 1981, *25*, 73–80.

BEE, H. (ED.) *Social issues in developmental psychology.* New York: Harper & Row, 1974.

BEM, S. L. The measurement of psychological androgyny. *Journal of Consulting and Clinical Psychology*, 1974, *42*, 155–62.

BENBOW, C. P., & STANLEY, J. C. Sex differences in mathematical ability: Fact or artifact? *Science*, 1980, *210*, 1262–1264.

———, & STANLEY, J. C. Mathematical ability: Is sex a factor? *Science*, 1981, *212*, 4491.

———, & STANLEY, J. C. Intellectually talented boys and girls: Educational profiles. *Gifted Child Quarterly*, 1982, *26*, 82–88.

———, & STANLEY, J. C. Constructing educational bridges between high school and college. *Gifted Child Quarterly*, 1983, *27*, 111–13. (a)

———, & STANLEY, J. C. Sex differences in mathematical reasoning ability: More facts. *Science*, 1983, *222*, 1029–1031. (b)

BERLINER, D. C., & ROSENSHINE, B. The acquisition of knowledge in the classroom. In R. C. Anderson, R. J. Spiro & W. E. Montague (eds.), *Schooling and the acquisition of knowledge.* Hillsdale, N.J.: Erlbaum, 1977.

BERNARD, J. *The future of marriage.* New York: Bantam, 1972.

BERNAL, E. M. Alternative avenues for assessment of culturally different gifted. Speech presented to the Department of Educational Psychology, University of Georgia, February 1978.

———. The education of the culturally different gifted. In A. H. Passow (ed.), *The gifted and the talented.* Chicago: National Society for the Study of Education, 1979.

BERNDT, D. J., KAISER, G. F., & VAN AALST, F. Depression and self-actualization in gifted adolescents. *Journal of Clinical Psychology,* 1982, *38,* 142–50.

BESTOR, A. E. *Educational wastelands.* Urbana, Ill.: University of Illinois Press, 1953.

BILLER, H. B. *Father, child, and sex role.* Lexington, Mass.: D. C. Heath, 1971.

BINET, A., & SIMON, T. Methodes nouvelles pour le diagnostic du niveau intellectuel des anormaux. *L'Année Psychologique,* 1905, *11,* 191–244. (a)

———, & SIMON, T. Sur la necessité d'établir un diagnostic scientific des états inférieurs de l'intelligence. *L'Année Psychologique,* 1905, *11,* 163–90. (b)

BIRCH, J. W. Early school admission for mentally advanced children. *Exceptional Children,* 1954, *21(3),* 84–87.

BIRNBAUM, J. A. Life patterns and self-esteem in gifted family-oriented and career-committed women. In M. T. Mednick, S. S. Tangri, & L. W. Hoffman (eds.), *Women and achievement: Social and motivational analyses.* New York: Halsted Press, 1975.

BIRNEY, R. C., BURDICK, H., & TEEVAN, R. C. *Fear of failure.* New York: Van Nostrand, 1969.

BLANTON, M. Bloom's taxonomy revisited. *G/C/T,* Sept./Oct. 1982, 22.

BLOCK, J. H. Issues, problems, and pitfalls in assessing sex differences. *Merrill-Palmer Quarterly,* 1976, *22,* 283–308.

BLOOM, B. S. (ed.) *Taxonomy of educational objectives.* New York: McKay, 1974.

BLOOM, B. S. Affective outcomes of school learning. *Phi Delta Kappan,* 1977, *59,* 193–98.

———. The limits of learning. Presented at the CEC-TAG National Topical Conference on the Gifted and Talented Child, Orlando, Fla., December 1981. (b)

———, ENGLEHART, M. D., FURST, E. J., HILL, W. H., & KRATHWOHL, D. R. *Taxonomy of educational objectives, handbook I: Cognitive domain.* New York: Longmans Green, 1956.

———, & SOSNIAK, L. A. Talent development vs. schooling. *Educational Leadership,* 1981, *39,* 86–94.

BOSTON, B. *The sorcerer's apprentice.* Reston, Va.: Council for Exceptional Children, 1976.

BRODY, L., & FOX, L. H. An accelerative intervention program for mathematically gifted girls. In L. H. Fox, L. Brody, & D. Tobin (eds.), *Women and the mathematical mystique.* Baltimore, Md.: Johns Hopkins University Press, 1980.

BRONFENBRENNER, U. Developmental research and public policy and the ecology of childhood. *Child Development,* 1974, *45,* 1–5.

BRONSON, F. H., & DESJARDINS, C. Aggression in adult mice: Modification by neonatal injections of gonadal hormones. *Science,* 1968, *161,* 705–706.

BROPHY, J. E. Research on the self-fulfilling prophecy and teacher expectations. Presented at the American Educational Research Association, New York, April 1982.

———, & GOOD, T. L. Teacher's communication of differential behavioral data. *Journal of Educational Psychology,* 1970, *61,* 365–74.

BRUCH, C. B., & CURRY, J. A. Personal Learnings: A current synthesis on the culturally different gifted. *Gifted Child Quarterly,* 1978, *22,* 313–21.

BRUININKS, V. L. Peer status and personality characteristics of learning disabled and nondisabled students. *Journal of Learning Disabilities,* 1978, *11,* 484–89.

BRYAN, T. Social relationships and verbal interactions of learning disabled children. *Journal of Learning Disabilities,* 1978, *2,* 107–115.

BUCKMASTER, L., & DAVIS, G. A. ROSE: A measure of self-actualization and its relationship to creativity. *Journal of Creative Behavior,* in press.

BUDMEN, K. O. What do you think, teacher? Critical thinking, a partnership in learning. *Peabody Journal of Education,* 1967, *45,* 2–5.

BUFFERY, A. W. H., & GRAY, J. A. Sex differences in the development of spatial and linguistic skills. In C. Ounsted & D. C. Taylor (eds.), *General differences: Their ontogeny and significance.* Baltimore, Md.: Williams & Wilkins, 1972.

BURK, E. A. *Relationship of temperamental traits to achievement and adjustment in gifted children.* Ann Arbor, Mich.: University Microfilms International, 1980.

BUROS, O. K. *Mental measurements yearbook.* Highland Park, N.J.: Gryphon Press, 1982.

BURTON, N. W., & JONES, L. V. Recent trends in achievement levels of black and white youth. *Educational Researcher,* 1982, *10,* 10–14, 17.

BURTON, T. A., & HIRSHOREN, A. Some further thoughts and clarification on the education of severely and profoundly retarded children. *Exceptional Children,* 1979, *45,* 618–25.

BUSHMAN, J. H., & JONES, S. K. *Effective communication: A handbook of discussion skills.* Buffalo, N.Y.: DOK Publishers, 1977.

CALLAHAN, C. M. The gifted and talented woman. In A. H. Passow (ed.), *The gifted and the talented.* Chicago: National Society for the Study of Education, 1979.

CARELLI, A. O. Creative dramatics for the gifted: A multi-disciplinary approach. *Roeper Review,* 1981, *5(2),* 29–31.

———. Sex equity and the gifted. *G/C/T,* 1982, Nov./Dec., 2–7.

CARLSMITH, L. Effect of early father absence on scholastic aptitude. *Harvard Educational Review,* 1964, *34,* 3–21.

CASSERLY, P. L. Helping able young women take math and science seriously in school. In N. Colangelo & R. T. Zaffrann (eds.), *New voices in counseling the gifted.* Dubuque, Iowa: Kendall/Hunt, 1979.

CATTELL, J. M. Mental tests and measurements. *Mind,* 1890, *15,* 373–80.

CHAMBERS, J. A., & BARRON, F. The culturally different gifted student: Identifying the ablest. *Journal of Creative Behavor,* 1978, *12,* 72–74.

———, BARRON, F., & SPRECHER, J. W. Identifying gifted Mexican-American students. *Gifted Child Quarterly,* 1980, *24,* 123–28.

CHISHOLM, S. Address at the National Forum on the Culturally Disadvantaged Gifted Youth. *G/C/T,* Nov./Dec. 1978, 2–4, 40–41.

CLASEN, D. R. Meeting the rage to know: College for kids, an innovative enrichment program for gifted elementary children. Unpublished report, Department of Educational Psychology, University of Wisconsin, Madison, Wis., 1982.

CLASEN, R. E., & ROBINSON, B. (eds.) *Simple gifts.* Madison Wis.: University of Wisconsin–Extension, 1979.

———, ROBINSON, B., CLASEN, D. R., & LIBSTER, G. (eds.). *Programming for the gifted, talented and creative: Models and methods.* Madison, Wis.: University of Wisconsin-Extension, 1981.

CLIFFORD, M. M. *Practicing educational psychology.* Boston: Houghton Mifflin, 1981.

COHN, R. J. Thoughts on acceleration. *G/C/T,* Mar./Apr. 1980, 6–7.

COHN, S. J. Talent searches: A national and international effort. *Chronicle of Academic and Artistic Precocity,* 1983, *2,* 1–3. (a)

———. *1983 Summer classes sponsored by the Project for the Study of Academic Precocity.* Tempe, Ariz.: Department of Special Education, Arizona State University, 1983. (b)

COLANGELO, N., & KELLY, K. R. A study of student, parent, and teacher attitudes toward gifted programs and gifted students. *Gifted Child Quarterly,* 1983, *27,* 107–110.

COLEMAN, J. S. Public and private schools. Invited address to the American Educational Research Association, Los Angeles, April 1981.

COMBS, A. W. Humanistic goals of education. In D. A. Read & S. B. Simon (eds.), *Humanistic education sourcebook.* Englewood Cliffs, N.J.: Prentice-Hall, 1975.

CONNER, R. S., LEVINE, S., & WERTHEIM, G. S. Hormonal determinants of aggressive behavior. *Annals of the New York Academy of Science,* 1969, *159,* 760–776.

CONNOLLY, K. J., & BRUNER, J. S. Competence: Its nature and nurture. In K. J. Connolly & J. S. Bruner (eds.), *The growth of competence.* London: Academic Press, 1974.

COOPER, H. M. Pygmalion grows up. *Review of Educational Research,* 1979, *49,* 389–410.

COPLEY, F. *The American high school and the talented student.* Ann Arbor, Mich.: University of Michigan, 1961.

COSER, R. L., & ROKOFF, G. Women in the occupational world: Social disruption and conflict. *Social Problems,* 1971, *18,* 535–54.

COVINGTON, M. V., & BEERY, R. G. *Self-worth and school learning.* New York: Holt, 1976.

———, CRUTCHFIELD, R. S., OLTON, R. M., & DAVIES, L. *Productive thinking program.* Columbus, Ohio: Charles E. Merrill, 1972.

———, & OMELICH, C. L. It's best to be able and virtuous too: Student and teacher evaluative responses to successful effort. *Journal of Educational Psychology,* 1979, *71,* 688–700.

COX, C. M. *The early mental traits of three hundred geniuses. Volume II: Genetic studies of genius.* Stanford, Calif.: Stanford University Press, 1926.

COX, J., & DANIEL, N. Identification: Special problems and special populations. *G/C/T,* Nov./ Dec. 1983, 54–61. (a)

———, & DANIEL, N. The role of the mentor. *G/C/T,* Sept./Oct. 1983, 54–61. (b)

———, & DANIEL, N. Specialized schools for high ability students. *G/C/T,* May/June 1983, 2–9 (c)

CRABBE, A. B. The 1979 future problem solving bowl. *G/C/T,* Nov./Dec. 1979, 15–16.

———. Creating a brighter future: An update on the future problem solving problem. *Journal for the Education of the Gifted,* 1982, *5,* 2–9.

CRANDALL, V. Sex differences in expectancy of intellectual and academic reinforcement. In C. P. Smith (ed.), *Achievement-related motives in children.* New York: Russell Sage Foundation, 1969.

CRAWFORD, R. P. The techniques of creative thinking. In G. A. Davis & J. A. Scott (eds.), *Training creative thinking.* Huntington, N. Y.: Krieger, 1978.

CRONBACH, L. J., & SNOW, R. E. *Aptitude and instructional methods.* New York: Irving Publishers, 1977.

CUTTS, N. E., & MOSELY, N. *Teaching the bright and the gifted.* Englewood Cliffs, N.J.: Prentice-Hall, 1957.

DANIELS, P. R. *Teaching the gifted/learning disabled child.* Rockville, Md.: Aspen, 1983.

DAURIO, S. P. Educational enrichment vs. acceleration: A review of the literature. In W. C. George, S. J. Cohen, & J. C. Stanley (eds.), *Acceleration and enrichment: Strategies for educating the gifted.* Baltimore, Md.: Study of Mathematically Precocious Youth, Johns Hopkins University, 1979.

DAVIS, G. A. *Psychology of problem solving: Theory and practice.* New York: Basic Books, 1973.

———. In frumious pursuit of the creative person. *Journal of Creative Behavior,* 1975, *9,* 75–87.

———. Personal creative thinking techniques. *Gifted Child Quarterly,* 1981, *25,* 99–101. (a)

———. Review of the Revolving Door Identification Model. *Gifted Child Quarterly,* 1981, *25,* 185–86. (b)

———. A model for teaching for creative development. *Roeper Review,* 1982, *5(2),* 27–29.

———. *Creativity is forever.* Dubuque, Iowa: Kendall/Hunt, 1983. (a)

———. *Educational Psychology: Theory and practice.* Reading, Mass.: Addison-Wesley, 1983. (b)

———. *The good person book.* Cross Plains, Wis.: Badger Press, 1984, in preparation.

———, & BULL, K. S. Strengthening affective components of creativity in a college course. *Journal of Educational Psychology,* 1978, *70,* 833–36.

———, & DiPEGO, G. *Imagination express: Saturday subway ride.* Buffalo, N.Y.: DOK Publishers, 1973.

———, Helfert, C. J., & Shapiro, G. R. Let's be an ice cream machine!: Creative dramatics. *Journal of Creative Behavior*, 1973, *7*, 37–48.

———, & O'Sullivan, M. Taxonomy of creative objectives: The model AUTA. *Journal of Creative Behavior*, 1980, *14*, 149–60.

———, Peterson, J. M., & Farley, F. H. Attitudes, motivation, sensation seeking, and belief in ESP as predictors of real creative behavior. *Journal of Creative Behavior*, 1974, *8*, 31–39.

———, & Rimm, S. Identification and counseling of the creatively gifted. In N. Colangelo & R. T. Zaffrann (eds.), *New voices in counseling the gifted.* Dubuque, Iowa: Kendall/Hunt, 1979.

———, & Rimm, S. *GIFFI II: Group inventory for finding interests.* Watertown, Wis.: Educational Assessment Service, 1980.

———, & Rimm, S. Group inventory for finding interests (GIFFI) I and II: Instruments for identifying creative potential in the junior and senior high school. *Journal of Creative Behavior*, 1982, *16*, 50–57.

Dean, R. S. Effects of self-concept in learning with gifted children. *Journal of Educational Research*, 1975, *3*, 315–18.

Deaux, K. Ahhh, she was just lucky. *Psychology Today*, 1976, *10*, 70.

DeBono, E. *Opportunities.* New York: Penguin, 1980.

Delisle, J. R. Reaching towards tomorrow: Career education and guidance for the gifted and talented. *Roeper Review*, 1982, *5(2)*, 8–11.

———, & Renzulli, J. S. The revolving door identification and programming model: Correlates of creative production. *Gifted Child Quarterly*, 1982, *26*, 89–95.

DeMott, B. Mind-expanding teachers. *Psychology Today*, 1981, *4*, 110–19.

Department of Educational Research and Program Assessment. *ESEA Title VII bilingual/ bicultural education program, 1978–1979.* Milwaukee, Wis.: Milwaukee Public Schools, 1979.

Dettman, D. F., & Colangelo, N. A functional model for counseling parents of the gifted. *Gifted Child Quarterly*, 1980, *24*, 158–61.

Diessner, R. The relationship between cognitive abilities and moral development. *G/C/T*, May/June 1983, 15–17.

Dillon, J. T. Problem finding and solving. *Journal of Creative Behavior*, 1982, *16*, 97–111.

Donahue, T. J., & Costar, J. W. Counselor discrimination against young women in career selection. *Journal of Counseling Psychology*, 1977, *24*, 481–86.

Dressel, P. L., & Mayhew, L. B. *General education: Explorations in evaluation.* Washington, D.C.: American Council on Education, 1954.

Drews, E., & Teahan, J. Parental attitudes and academic achievement. *Journal of Clinical Psychology*, 1957, *13*, 328–32.

Durden-Smith, J., & DeSimone, D. Is there a superior sex? *Readers Digest*, Nov. 1982, 263–70.

Dweck, C. S., & Bush, E. S. Sex differences in learned helplessness: I. Differential debilitation with peer and adult evaluators. *Developmental Psychology*, 1976, *12*, 147–56.

Eash, M. *Issues in evaluation and accountability in special programs for gifted and talented children.* Chicago: University of Illinois–Chicago Circle, 1972.

Eberle, B. *Classroom cues: A flip book for cultivating multiple talent.* Buffalo, N.Y.: DOK Publishers, 1974.

Educational Policies Commission. *Education of the gifted.* Washington, D.C.: National Education Association, 1950.

Edwards, D. A. Early androgen stimulation and aggressive behavior in male and female mice. *Physiological Behavior*, 1969, *4*, 333–38.

Eisenberg, D., & Epstein, E. The discovery and development of giftedness in handicapped children. Paper presented at the CEC-TAG National Topical Conference on the Gifted and Talented Child, Orlando, Fla., December 1981.

Elashoff, J. D., & Snow, R. E. *Pygmalion reconsidered.* Worthington, Ohio: Charles E. Jones, 1971.

ELMAN, L. L., & ELMAN, D. Mainstreaming the gifted: An approach that works. *G/C/T*, Jan./Feb. 1983, 45–46.

ENNIS, R. H. A concept of critical thinking: A proposed basis for research in the teaching and evaluation of critical thinking ability. *Harvard Educational Review*, 1962, *32*, 83.

———. Critical thinking readiness in grades 1–12: Phase I. Deductive reasoning in adolescence. Project No. 1680, School of Education, Cornell University, 1964.

EPSTEIN, E. Learning disabilities mask giftedness. *Gifted Children Newletter*, 1981, *2(11)*.

EPSTEIN, J. *Masters: Portraits of great teachers*. New York: Basic Books, 1981.

ERIKSON, E. H. *Identity and the life cycle: Selected papers by Erik H. Erikson*. New York: International Universities Press, 1959.

ERIKSON, E. H. *Identity: Youth and crisis*. New York: Norton, 1968.

ERLICH, V. *Gifted children: A guide for parents and teachers*. Englewood Cliffs, N.J.: Prentice-Hall, 1982.

ERNEST, J. Mathematics and sex. *American Mathematical Monthly*, 1976, *83*, 595–614.

EXUM, H. Key issues in family counseling with gifted and talented black students. *Roeper Review*, 1983, *5(3)*, 28–31.

FABUN, D. *You and creativity*. New York: Macmillan, 1968.

FANTINI, M. D. A caring curriculum for gifted children. *Roeper Review*, 1981, *3(4)*, 3–4.

FARLEY, F. H. Basic process individual differences: A biologically based theory of individualization for cognitive, affective, and creative outcomes. In F. H. Farley & N. J. Gordon (eds.), *Psychology and education: The state of the union*. Berkeley, Calif.: McCutchan, 1981.

FARMER, H. S., & BOHN, M. J. Home career conflict reduction and the level of career interest in women. *Journal of Counseling Psychology*, 1970, *17*, 228–32.

FAUNCE, P. S. Personality characteristics and vocational interests related to the college persistence of academically gifted women. *Journal of Counseling Psychology*, 1968, *15*, 31–40.

FELD, S. RUHLAND, D., & GOLD, M. Developmental changes in achievement motivation. *Merrill-Palmer Quarterly*, 1979, *25*, 43–60.

FELDHUSEN, J. Teaching gifted, creative, and talented students in an individualized classroom. *Gifted Child Quarterly*, 1981, *25*, 108–111.

FELDHUSEN, J. F. Meeting the needs of gifted students through differentiated programming. *Gifted Child Quarterly*, 1982, *26*, 37–41.

———, & KOLLOFF, M. B. A three-stage model for gifted education. *G/C/T*, Jan./Feb. 1978, 3–5, 53–57.

———, & KOLLOFF, M. B. A three-stage model for gifted education. In R. E. Clasen, B. Robinson, D. R. Clasen, & G. Libster (eds.), *Programming for the gifted, talented and creative: Models and methods*. Madison, Wis.: University of Wisconsin–Extension, 1981.

———, & SOKOL, L. Extraschool programming to meet the needs of gifted youth: Super Saturday. *Gifted Child Quarterly*, 1982, *26*, 51–56.

———, & TREFFINGER, D. J. *Creative thinking and problem solving in gifted education*. Dubuque, Iowa: Kendall/Hunt, 1980.

———, & WYMAN, A. R. Super Saturday: Design and implementation of Purdue's special program for gifted children. *Gifted Child Quarterly*, 1980, *24*, 15–21.

FELDMAN, D. The mysterious case of extreme giftedness. In A. H. Passow (ed.), *The gifted and the talented*. Chicago: National Society for the Study of Education, 1979.

FELDMAN, R. D. *Whatever Happened to the Quiz Kids?* Chicago: Chicago Review Press, 1982.

FELTON, G. S., & BIGGS, B. E. *Up from underachievement*. Springfield, Ill.: Charles C. Thomas, 1977.

FENNEMA, E. Sex-related differences in mathematics achievement: Where and why. In L. H. Fox, L. Brody, & D. Tobin (eds.), *Women and the mathematical mystique*. Baltimore, Md.: Johns Hopkins University Press, 1980.

FEREE, M. M. The confused American housewife. *Psychology Today*, Sept. 1976, 76–80.

FIEDLER, E. D. The Kranz Talent Identification Instrument. Speech presented at the Wisconsin Council on Gifted and Talented, Madison, Wis., October 1982.

FINE, M. J., & PITTS, R. Intervention with underachieving gifted children: Rationale and strategies. *Gifted Child Quarterly,* 1980, *24,* 51–55.

First Official U.S. Education Mission to the USSR. *Soviet commitment to education, Bulletin 1959, No. 16.* Washington, D. C.: Office of Education, Department of Health, Education, and Welfare, 1959.

FITZGERALD, L. F., & CRITES, J. O. Toward a career psychology of women: What do we know? What do we need to know? *Journal of Counseling Psychology,* 1980, *27,* 44–62.

FLIEGLER, L. A., & BISH, C. E. The gifted and talented. *Review of Educational Research,* 1959, *29,* 408–442.

FOX, L. H. Facilitating the development of mathematical talent in young women. Unpublished Ph.d. thesis, Johns Hopkins University, 1974.

―――. The effects of sex-role socialization on mathematics participation and achievement. In J. Shoemaker (ed.), *Women and mathematics: Research perspectives for change.* Papers in Education and Work, No. 8. Washington, D.C.: National Institute of Education, U.S. Department of Health, Education and Welfare, 1977. (a)

―――. Sex differences: Implications for program planning for the academically gifted. In J. C. Stanley, W. C. George, and C. H. Solano (eds.), *The gifted and the creative: A fifty-year perspective.* Baltimore, Md.: Johns Hopkins University Press, 1977. (b)

―――. Programs for the gifted and talented: An overview. In A. H. Passow (ed.), *The gifted and the talented.* Chicago: National Society for the Study of Education, 1979.

―――. Mathematically able girls: A special challenge. *Arithmetic Teacher,* Feb. 1981, 22–23. (a)

―――. Preparing gifted girls for future leadership roles. *G/C/T,* Mar./Apr. 1981, 7–11. (b)

―――. Identification of the academically gifted. *American Psychologist,* 1981, *36,* 1103–11. (c)

―――. Bridging the transition from high school to college. *Chronicle of Academic and Artistic Precocity,* 1983, *2,* 4.

―――, BRODY, L., & TOBIN, D. (eds.). *Women and the mathematical mystique.* Baltimore, Md.: Johns Hopkins University Press, 1980.

FRANKS, B., & DOLAN, L. Affective characteristics of gifted children: Educational implications. *Gifted Child Quarterly,* 1982, *26* 172–78.

FRAZIER, A., PASSOW, A. H., & GOLDBERG, M. L. Curriculum research: Study of underachieving gifted. *Educational Leadership,* 1958, *16,* 121–25.

FRAZIER, N., & SADKER, M. *Sexism in school and society.* New York: Harper & Row, 1973.

FREEDMAN, D. G. *Human infancy: An evolutionary perspective.* Hillsdale, N.J.: Erlbaum, 1974.

FREEHILL, M. F., & MCDONALD, J. Zeal: Essential to superior intellectual achievements? *Gifted Child Quarterly,* 1981, *25,* 123–27.

FRENCH, J. L. *Educating the gifted: A book of readings.* New York: Holt, 1959.

FREUD, S. *An outline of psychoanalysis.* New York: Norton, 1949.

FREY, C. The resource room. *G/C/T,* May/June 1980, 26–27.

FRIEDMAN, J. M. & MASTER, D. School and museum: A partnership for learning. *Gifted Child Quarterly,* 1980, *25,* 43–48.

FRIEZE, I. H. Women's expectations for and causal attributions of success and failure. In M. T. Mednick, S. S. Tangri, & L. W. Hoffman (eds.), *Women and achievement: Social and motivational analyses.* New York: Halsted, 1975.

―――, PARSONS, J., & RUBLE, D. Some determinants of career aspirations in college women. Paper presented at the UCLA Symposium on Sex Roles and Sex Differences, Los Angeles, 1972.

FROST, D. The great debates: For enrichment. Presented at the CEC-TAG National Topical Conference on the Gifted and Talented Child, Orlando, Fla., December 1981.

FURST, E. J. Bloom's taxonomy of educational objectives for the cognitive domain: Philosophical and educational issues. *Review of Educational Research,* 1981, *51,* 441–53.

GAGE, N. L., & BERLINER, D. C. *Educational psychology* (2nd ed.). Chicago: Rand-McNally, 1979.

GALLAGHER, J. J. *The gifted child in the elementary school.* Washington, D.C.: National Education Association, 1959.

_____. *Research summary on gifted education.* Springfield, Ill.: State Department of Public Instruction, 1966.

GALTON, F. *Hereditary genius.* London: Macmillan, 1869.

GARTNER, A., KOHLER, M., & REISSMAN, F. *Children teach children.* New York: Harper & Row, 1971.

GAY, J. E. A proposed plan for identifying black gifted children. *Gifted Child Quarterly,* 1976, *22,* 353–57.

GEAR, G. H. Accuracy of teacher judgment in identifying intellectually gifted children: A review of the literature. *Gifted Child Quarterly,* 1976, *20,* 478–90.

GEARHEART, B. R., & WEISHAHN, M. W. *The handicapped child in the regular classroom.* St. Louis, Mo.: Mosby, 1976.

GENSLEY, J. The gifted child in the affective domain. *Gifted Child Quarterly,* 1977, *21,* 448–49.

GEORGE, W. C. Accelerating mathematics instruction for the mathematically talented. *Gifted Child Quarterly,* 1976, *20,* 246–61.

_____. The talent search concept: An identification strategy for the intellectually gifted. *Journal of Special Education,* 1979, *13,* 221–37. (a)

_____. The third D: Development of talent (fast-math classes). In N. Colangelo & R. T. Zaffrann (eds.), *New voices in counseling the gifted.* Dubuque, Iowa: Kendall/Hunt, 1979. (b)

GETZELS, J. W., & DILLON J. T. The nature of giftedness and the education of the gifted. In R. M. Travers (ed.), *Second handbook of research in training.* Chicago: Rand-McNally, 1973.

_____, & JACKSON, P. W. *Creativity and intelligence.* New York: Wiley, 1962.

_____, & JACKSON, P. W. The teacher's personality and characteristics. In N. L. Gage (ed.), *Handbook of research on teaching.* Chicago: Rand-McNally, 1963.

GIELE, J. Z. *Women and the future: Changing sex roles in modern America.* New York: Free Press, 1978.

GODDARD, H. H. Four hundred feebleminded children classified by the Binet method. *The Training School,* 1910, *6,* 146–55.

_____. Two thousand normal children measured by the Binet measuring scale of intelligence. *Pedagogical Seminary,* 1911, *18,* 232–59.

GOERTZEL, M. G., GOERTZEL, V., & GOERTZEL, T. G. *300 eminent personalities.* San Francisco: Jossey-Bass, 1978.

GOERTZEL, V., & GOERTZEL, M. G. *Cradles of eminence.* Boston: Little, Brown, 1962.

GOLDBERG, P. Are women prejudiced against women? *Transaction,* 1968, *4,* 28–30.

GOLDBERG, S. *The inevitability of patriarchy.* New York: Morrow, 1973.

GONSALVES, W. C., GRIMM, J., & WELSH, J. M. Leadership training: A lesson in living. *Roeper Review,* 1981, *3(3),* 16–19.

GORDON, W. J. J. *Synectics.* New York: Harper & Row, 1961.

_____. *Making it strange.* Books 1–4. New York: Harper & Row, 1974.

_____, & POZE, T. SES synectics and gifted education today. *Gifted Child Quarterly,* 1980, *24,* 147–51.

GOURLEY, T. J. Adapting the varsity sports model to nonpsychomotor gifted students. *Gifted Child Quarterly,* 1981, *25,* 164–66.

GOWAN, J. C. *Definitions of giftedness.* Simple gifts, Videotape No. 1. Madison, Wis.: University of Wisconsin–Extension, 1978.

_____. Introduction. In J. C. Gowan, J. Khatena, & E. P. Torrance (eds.), *Creativity: Its educational implications* (2nd ed.). Dubuque, Iowa: Kendall/Hunt, 1981.

GOY, R. W., & RESKO, J. A. Gonadal hormones and behavior of normal and pseudohermaphroditic nonhuman female primates. *Recent Progress in Hormone Research,* 1972, *28,* 707–33.

GRAHAM, P. A. Expansion and inclusion: A history of women in American higher education. *Signs,* 1978, *3,* 759–73.

GREGORY, A. Super Saturday: A description of Purdue University's special program for gifted children with special emphasis on the studio arts areas. *G/C/T,* Jan./Feb. 1982, 13–16.

GRIGGS, S. A., & PRICE, G. E. A comparison between the learning styles of gifted versus average suburban junior high school students. *Roeper Review,* 1980, *3,* 7–9.

GRONLUND, N. E. *Constructing achievement tests* (2nd ed.). Englewood Cliffs, N.J.: Prentice-Hall, 1977.

GUILFORD, J. P. Creativity: Its measurement and development. In S. J. Parnes & H. F. Harding (eds.), *A source book for creative thinking.* New York: Scribner's 1962.

———. *The nature of human intelligence.* New York: McGraw-Hill, 1967.

———. *Way beyond the IQ.* Buffalo, N.Y.: Creative Education Foundation, 1977.

———. Some incubated thoughts on incubation. *Journal of Creative Behavior,* 1979, *12,* 1–8. (a)

———. Varieties of creative giftedness, their measurement and development. In J. C. Gowan, J. Khatena, & E. P. Torrance (eds.), *Educating the ablest* (2nd ed.). Chicago: Peacock, 1979. (b)

———. Three faces of intellect. In W. B. Barbe & J. S. Renzulli (eds.), *Psychology and education of the gifted* (3rd ed.). New York: Irvington, 1981.

———. Transformation abilities or functions. *Journal of Creative Behavior,* 1983, *17,* 75–83.

GURCSIK, B. SOI: A foundation for gifted curriculum. *Roeper Review,* 1981, *4(1),* 27–28.

HADAMARD, J. *The psychology of invention in the mathematical field.* Princeton, N.J.: Princeton University Press, 1945.

HALL, E. J. Accelerating gifted girls. *G/C/T,* Nov./Dec. 1982, 49–50.

HALVERSON, C., & VICTOR, J. Minor physical anomalies and problem behavior in elementary school children. *Child Development,* 1976, *47,* 281–85.

HEBB, D. O. *Textbook of psychology* (3rd ed.). Philadelphia: W. B. Saunders, 1972.

HEILBRUN, A. B. *Aversive maternal control.* New York: Wiley, 1973.

———, HARRELL, S. N., & GILLARD, B. J. Perceived childrearing attitudes of fathers and cognitive control in daughters. *Journal of Genetic Psychology,* 1967, *111,* 29–40.

HEIST, P. (ed.) *The creative college student: An unmet challenge.* San Francisco: Jossey-Bass, 1968.

HELMAN, I. B., & LARSON, S. B. *Now what do I do?* Buffalo, N.Y.: DOK Publishers, 1979.

HELSON, R. Generality of sex differences in creative style. *Journal of Personality,* 1968, *36,* 33–48.

———. Women mathematicians and the creative personality. *Journal of Consulting and Clinical Psychology,* 1971, *36,* 210–11, 217–20.

HERMANN, K. E., & STANLEY, J. C. An exchange: Thoughts on nonrational precocity. *G/C/T,* Nov/Dec. 1983, 30–36.

HERR, E. L., & WATANABE, A. Counseling the gifted about career development. In N. Colangelo & R. T. Zaffrann (eds.), *New voices in counseling the gifted.* Dubuque, Iowa: Kendall/Hunt, 1979.

HERSBERGER, J., & ASHER, W. Comment on "A Quota System for Gifted Minority Children." *Gifted Child Quarterly,* 1980, *24,* 96.

HETHERINGTON, E. M. Effects of father-absence on personality development in adolescent daughters. *Developmental Psychology,* 1972, *7,* 313–26.

———, & FRANKIE, G. Effects of parental dominance, warmth, and conflict on imitation in children. *Journal of Personality and Social Psychology,* 1967, *6,* 119–25.

HILTON, T. L., & BERGLUND, G. W. Sex differences in mathematics achievement—a longitudinal study. *Journal of Educational Research,* 1974, *67,* 231–37.

HOBBS, N. (ed.) *Issues in the classification of the children.* Volume 2. San Francisco: Jossey-Bass, 1975.

HOBSON, J. R. Mental age as a workable criterion for school admission. *Elementary School Journal*, 1948, *48*, 312–21.

HOFFMAN, B. *The tyranny of testing*. New York: Collier Books, 1964.

HOFFMAN, E. Children's perceptions of their emotionally disturbed peers. *Dissertation Abstracts*, 1976, *37*, 952–B.

HOFFMAN, L. W. Early childhood experiences and women's achievement motives. *Journal of Social Issues*, 1972, *28(2)*, 129–56.

_____. Fear of success in males and females. *Journal of Consulting and Clinical Psychology*, 1974, 42, 353–358.

HOLLINGWORTH, L. S. *Gifted children: Their nature and nurture*. New York: Macmillan, 1926.

_____. *Children above 180 IQ Stanford-Binet: Origin and development*. New York: World Book Co., 1942.

HORNER, M. S. Fail: Bright women. *Psychology Today*, Nov. 1969, 36, 38, 62.

_____. The motive to avoid success and changing aspirations of college women. In J. Bardwick (ed.), *Readings on the psychology of women*. New York: Harper & Row, 1972. (a)

_____. Toward an understanding of achievement related conflicts in women. *Journal of Social Issues*, 1972, *28*, 155–75. (b)

HORWITZ, E. L. Educating the gifted child. *Gifted Child Quarterly*, 1974, *2*, 16–21.

HYRUM, G. H. An experiment in developing critical thinking in children. *Journal of Experimental Education*, 1957, *26*, 125–32.

IANO, R. P., AYERS, D., HELLER, H. B., McGETTIGAN, J. F., & WALKER, V. S. Sociometric status of retarded children in an integrative program. *Exceptional Children*, 1974, *40*, 267–71.

JACKSON, R. M., CLEVELAND, J. C., & MIRENDA, P. F. The longitudinal effects of early identification and counseling of underachievers. *Journal of School Psychology*, 1975, *13*, 119–28.

JENSEN, A. R. How much can we boost IQ and scholastic achievement? *Harvard Educational Review*, 1969, *39*, 1–123.

_____. *Educational Differences*. New York: Barnes & Noble, 1974.

_____. Test bias and construct validity. *Phi Delta Kappan*, 1976, *58*, 340–46.

_____. *Bias in mental testing*. New York: Free Press, 1980.

_____. Changing conceptions of intelligence. Presented at the American Educational Research Association, New York, April 1982.

JOHNSON, B. (ed.). *A new generation of leadership: Education for the gifted and talented*. Bethesda, Md.: ERIC Reproduction Services (ED 145601), 1977.

JONES, J. L. Women in science. *USA Today*, 1978, *107*, 4.

JORDON, T. J. Self-concepts, motivation, and academic achievement of black adolescents. *Journal of Educational Psychology*, 1981, *73*, 509–17.

JUNTUNE, J. *Successful programs for the gifted and talented*. Hot Springs, Ark.: National Association for the Gifted and Talented, 1981.

KAGAN, J. Impulsive and reflective children: Significance of conceptual tempo. In J. D. Krumboltz (ed.), *Learning and the educational process*. Chicago: Rand McNally, 1965.

_____, PEARSON, L., & WELCH, L. Conceptual impulsivity and inductive reasoning. *Child Development*, 1966, *37*, 583–94.

_____, & KOGAN, N. Individual variation in cognitive processes. In P. H. Mussen (ed.), *Carmichael's manual of child psychology* (3rd ed.). New York: Wiley, 1970.

KANOY, R. C., JOHNSON, B. W., & KANOY, K. W. Locus of control and self-concept in achieving bright elementary students. *Psychology in the Schools*, 1980, *17*, 395–99.

KAPLAN, S. N. *Providing programs for the gifted and talented*. Ventura, Calif.: Office of the Ventura County Superintendent of Schools, 1974.

KARAMESSINIS, N. P. Personality and perceptions of the gifted. *G/C/T*, May/June 1980, 11–13.

KARNES, F. A., & BROWN, K. E. Moral development and the gifted: An initial investigation. *Roeper Review*, 1981, *3(4)*, 8–10.

———, & CHAUVIN, J. C. Almost everything that parents and teachers of gifted secondary school students should know about early college enrollment and college credit by examination. *G/C/T*, Sept./Oct. 1982, 39–42. (a)

———, & CHAUVIN, J. C. A survey of early admission policies for younger than average students: Implications for gifted youth. *Gifted Child Quarterly*, 1982, *26*, 68–73. (b)

KARNES, M. B. Young handicapped children can be gifted and talented. *Journal for the Education of the Gifted*, 1979, *2*, 157–72.

———, & SHWEDEL, A. M. RAPYHT Project: Activities for talent identification. Mimeograph. Urbana, Ill.: University of Illinois, Institute for Child Behavior and Development, 1981.

———, SHWEDEL, A. M., & LEWIS, G. F. Long-term effects of early programming for the gifted/talented handicapped. *Journal for the Education of the Gifted*, 1983, *6*, 266–76.

KATZ, M. L. *Female motive to avoid success: A psychological barrier or a response to deviancy.* Princeton, N.J.: Educational Testing Service, 1973.

KEATING, D. P. Four faces of creativity: The continuing plight of the intellectually underserved. *Gifted Child Quarterly*, 1980, *24*, 56–61.

KESTER, E. S. The affective domain: A dialog not a monolog. *Creative Child and Adult Quarterly*, 1975, *3*, 173–77.

———. SOI: A qualitatively different program for the gifted. *G/C/T*, Jan./Feb. 1982, 21–25.

KILSON, M. The status of women in higher education. *Signal*, 1976, *4*, 935–42.

KLAUSMEIER, H. J., & GOODWIN, W. *Learning and human abilities* (4th ed.). New York: Harper & Row, 1975.

———, QUILLING, M. R., SORENSON, J. S., WAY, R. S., & GLASRUD, G. R. *Individually guided education and the multi-unit elementary school: Guidelines for implementation.* Madison, Wis.: Research and Development Center for Cognitive Learning, 1971.

KOHLBERG, L. *Stages in the development of moral thought and action.* New York: Holt, 1969.

———. The child as moral philosopher. In G. A. Davis & T. F. Warren (eds.), *Psychology of education: New looks.* Lexington, Mass.: D. C. Heath, 1974.

———. Moral stages and moralization: The cognitive developmental approach. In T. Lickona (ed.), *Moral development and behavior.* New York: Holt, Rinehart, & Winston, 1976.

KOLATA, G. Math genius may have hormonal basis. *Science*, 1983, *222*, 1312.

KOLLOFF, M. B., & FELDHUSEN, J. F. PACE (Program for Academic and Creative Enrichment): An application of the Purdue three-stage model. In R. E. Clasen, B. Robinson, D. R. Clasen, & G. Libster (eds.), *Programming for the gifted, talented and creative: Models and methods:* Madison, Wis.: University of Wisconsin–Extension, 1981.

KOVACS, M. Rating scales to assess depression in school-aged children. *Acta Paedopsychiatrica*, 1980, *40*, 305–315.

KRANZ, B. *Kranz talent identification instrument.* Moorhead, Minn.: Moorhead State College, 1981.

KRIPPNER, S. The creative person and non-ordinary reality. *Gifted Child Quarterly*, 1972, *16*, 203–228.

KRUEGER, M. L. *On being gifted.* New York: Walker & Company, 1978.

KRYANIUK, L. W., & DAS, J. P. Cognitive strategies in native children: Analysis and intervention. *Alberta Journal of Educational Research*, 1976, *22*, 271–80.

LABOV, W. Academic ignorance and black intelligence. In G. A. Davis & T. F. Warren (eds.), *Psychology of education: New Looks.* Lexington, Mass.: D. C. Heath, 1974.

LAJOIE, S. P., & SHORE, B. M. Three myths? The over-representation of the gifted among dropouts, delinquents and suicides. *Gifted Child Quarterly*, 1981, *25*, 138–41.

LAMB, M. E. *The role of the father in child development.* New York: Wiley, 1976.

LAMB, R. A., & BUSSE, C. A. Leadership beyond lip service. *Roeper Review*, 1983, *5(3)*, 21–23.

LANSDOWN, R., & POLAK, L. A study of the psychological effects of facial deformity in children. *Child Care, Health, and Development,* 1975, *1,* 85–91.

LAVACH, J. F., & LANIER, H. B. The motive to avoid success in 7th, 8th, 9th and 10th grade high-achieving girls. *Journal of Educational Research,* 1975, *68,* 216–18.

LEFKOWITZ, W. Communication grows in a "Magic Circle." In D. A. Read & S. B. Simon (eds.), *Humanistic education sourcebook.* Englewood Cliffs, N.J.: Prentice-Hall, 1975.

LEHMAN, E. B., & ERDWINS, C. J. The social and emotional adjustment of young intellectually gifted children. *Gifted Child Quarterly,* 1981, *25,* 134–37.

LEINHARDT, G., SEEWALD, A. M., & ENGEL, M. Learning what's taught: Sex differences in instruction. *Journal of Educational Psychology,* 1979, *71,* 432–39.

LEROSE, B. *The lighthouse design: A model for educating children.* Racine, Wis.: Racine Unified School District, 1977.

_____. A quota system for gifted minority children: A viable solution. *Gifted Child Quarterly,* 1978, *22,* 394–403.

_____. Accelerating gifted girls. *G/C/T,* Nov./Dec. 1982, 48–52.

LEVY-AGRESTI, J., & SPERRY, R. W. Differential perceptual capacities in major and minor hemispheres. *Proceedings of the National Academy of Sciences,* 1968, 61.

LIDDLE, G. W. The adrenal cortex. In R. H. Williams (ed.), *Textbook of endocrinology.* Philadelphia: Saunders, 1974.

LIPMAN, M. Philosophy for children. *Metaphilosophy,* 1976, *7(1),* 17–39.

_____. What is different about the education of the gifted? *Roeper Review,* 1981, *4(1),* 19–20.

_____, SHARP, A. M. & OSCANYAN, F. S. *Philosophy in the classroom* (2nd ed.). Philadelphia: Temple University Press, 1980.

LIPS, H. M., & COLWILL, N. L. *The psychology of sex differences.* Englewood Cliffs, N.J.: Prentice-Hall, 1978.

LYNN, D. B. *The father: His role in child development.* Monterey, Calif.: Brooks/Cole, 1974.

LYTLE, W. G., & CAMPBELL, N. J. Do special programs affect the social status of the gifted? *Elementary School Journal,* 1979, *80,* 93–97.

McCLELLAND, D. C. Toward a theory of motive acquisition. *American Psychologist,* 1965, *29,* 321–33.

_____. *The achieving society.* New York: Irvington, 1976.

_____, ATKINSON, J. W., CLARK, R. A., & LOWELL, E. I. *The achievement motive.* New York: Appleton, 1953.

MACCOBY, E. E., & JACKLIN, C. *Psychology of sex differences.* Stanford, Calif.: Stanford University Press, 1974.

MACKINNON, D. W. Educating for creativity: A modern myth? In G. A. Davis & J. A. Scott (eds.), *Training creative thinking.* Huntington, N.Y.: Krieger, 1978.

MAGOON, R. A. Developing leadership skills in the gifted, creative, and talented. *G/C/T,* Mar./Apr. 1980, 40–43.

_____. A proposed model for leadership development. *Roeper Review,* 1981, *3(3),* 7–9.

MAKER, C. J. *Providing programs for the handicapped gifted.* Reston, Va.: Council for Exceptional Children, 1977.

_____. *Curriculum development for the gifted.* Rockville, Md.: Aspen, 1982.

MARINI, M. M. Sex differences in the determination of adolescent aspirations: A review of research. *Sex Roles: A Journal of Research,* 1978, *4,* 723–54.

MARLAND, S. P., JR. *Education of the gifted and talented, Volume 1. Report to the Congress of the United States by the U.S. Commissioner of Education.* Washington, D.C.: U.S. Government Printing Office, 1972.

MARTINSON, R. A. *The identification of the gifted and talented.* Ventura, Calif.: Office of the Ventura County Superintendent of Schools, 1974.

MARX, J. L. Autoimmunity in left-handers. *Science,* 1982, *217,* 141–42, 144.

MASLOW, A. H. *Motivation and personality.* New York: Harper & Row, 1954.

―――. *Toward a psychology of being* (2nd ed.). Princeton, N.J.: Van Nostrand, 1968.

―――. *The farther reaches of human nature.* New York: Viking Press, 1971.

MATTSON, B. D. Mentors for the gifted and talented: Whom to seek and where to look. *G/C/T,* Mar./Apr. 1983, 10–11.

MEAD, M. Sex and achievement. *Forum,* 1935, *94,* 302.

MEEKER, M. *The structure of intellect: Its interpretation and uses.* Columbus, Ohio: Charles E. Merrill, 1969.

―――. *Basic teaching comprehension skills workbook.* Books 1–5. El Segundo, Calif.: SOI Institute, 1976.

―――. Is modern education really modern? In R. E. Clasen, B. Robinson, D. R. Clasen, & G. Libster (eds.), *Programming for the gifted, talented and creative: Models and methods.* Madison, Wis.: University of Wisconsin–Extension, 1981. (a)

―――. Teaching children to think—not parrot. In R. E. Clasen, B. Robinson, D. R. Clasen, & G. Libster (eds.), *Programming for the gifted, talented and creative: Models and methods.* Madison, Wis.: University of Wisconsin–Extension, 1981. (b)

―――. Other ways to identify giftedness. In R. E. Clasen, B. Robinson, D. R. Clasen, & G. Libster (eds.), *Programming for the gifted, talented and creative: Models and methods.* Madison, Wis.: University of Wisconsin–Extension, 1981. (c)

MEICHENBAUM, D. H. *Cognitive-behavior modification.* New York: Plenum, 1977.

MICKLUS, S., & GOURLEY, T. *Problems, problems, problems.* Glassboro, N.J.: Creative Competitions, 1982.

MILGRAM, R. M., & MILGRAM, N. A. Personality characteristics of gifted Israeli children. *Journal of Genetic Psychology,* 1976, *129,* 185–92. (a)

―――, & MILGRAM, N. A. Self-concept as a function of intelligence and creativity in gifted Israeli children. *Psychology in the Schools,* 1976, *13,* 91–96. (b)

MILTON, G. A. The effects of sex-role identification upon problem-solving skill. *Journal of Abnormal and Social Psychology,* 1957, *55, 208–212.*

MITCHELL, P. (ed.). *An advocate's guide to building support for gifted and talented education.* Washington, D.C.: National Association of State Boards of Education, 1981.

MONEY, J., HAMPSON, J. G., & HAMPSON, J. L. Hermaphroditism: Recommendations concerning assignment of sex, change of sex, and psychological management. *Bulletin of Johns Hopkins University Hospital,* 1973, *97,* 284–300.

―――, & SCHWARTZ, M. Biosocial determinants of gender identity differentiation and development. In J. B. Hutchinson (ed.), *Biological determinants of sexual behavior.* New York: Wiley, 1978.

MONTAGU, A. My idea of education. *Today's Education,* Feb./Mar. 1980, 49.

MOORE, B. A. A model career education program for gifted disadvantaged students. *Roeper Review,* 1979, *2*(2), 20–22.

MORROW, L. Home and school correlates of early interest in literature. Paper presented at the American Educational Research Association, Montreal, April, 1983.

MOSLEY, J. H. Ten suggestions to insure the brevity of your gifted program. *G/C/T,* Nov./Dec. 1982, 46.

MOSS, E. S. Mothers and gifted preschoolers—teaching and learning strategies. Paper presented at the American Educational Research Association, Montreal, April 1983.

MOYER, K. E. Sex differences in aggression. In R. C. Friedman, R. M. Richart, & R. L. Vande Weile (eds.), *Sex differences in behavior.* New York: Wiley, 1974.

MURPHY, S. Programming for the academically gifted: The Hard Day's Night model. *G/C/T* Mar./Apr. 1980, 20–21.

MUSSEN, P. H., & RUTHERFORD, E. Parent-child relations and parental personality in relation to young children's sex-role preferences. *Child Development,* 1963, *34,* 589–607.

NADELSON, T. & EISENBERG, L. On being married to a professional woman. *American Journal of Psychiatry*, 1977, *134*, 1071–1076.

National Advisory Committee on the Handicapped. *The unfinished revolution: Education for the handicapped.* Washington, D.C.: U.S. Government Printing Office, 1976.

National Assessment of Educational Progress. *Male-Female achievement in eight learning areas: A compilation of selected assessment results.* Denver, Colo.: Education Commission of the States, 1975.

NAVARRE, J. Is what is good for the gander, good for the goose: Should gifted girls receive differential treatment? *Roeper Review*, 1980, *3(2)*, 21–25.

———. How the teacher of the gifted can use the SOI. *G/C/T*, Jan./Feb. 1983, 16–17.

NEVO, D. The conceptualization of educational evaluation. *Review of Educational Research*, 1983, *53*, 117–28.

NEWBURG, N. A. *Affective education in Philadelphia.* Bloomington, Ind.: Phi Delta Kappa Educational Foundation, 1977.

NICHOLS, J. G. Development of perception of own attainment and causal attributions for success and failure in reading. *Journal of Educational Psychology*, 1979, *71*, 94–99.

NOVAK, D. Children's reactions to emotional disturbance in imaginary peers. *Journal of Consulting and Clinical Psychology*, 1974, *42*, 462.

NYQUIST, E. The gifted: The invisibly handicapped, or there is no heavier burden than a great potential. Paper presented at the National Conference on the Gifted, Albany, N.Y., 1973.

O'CONNELL, B. *Arts for the handicapped, ESEA Title IV-C Model Sites Project.* Sheboygan, Wis.: Wisconsin Department of Public Instruction, 1982.

OGBY, J. U. Origins of human competence: A cultural-ecological perspective. *Child Development*, 1981, *52*, 413–29.

Olympics of the Mind Association. *What is Olympics of the Mind?* Glassboro, N. J.: OM Association, 1983.

OSBORN, A. F. *Applied imagination* (3rd ed.). New York: Scribner's 1963.

PALLAS, A. M., & ALEXANDER, K. L. Sex differences in quantitative SAT performance: New evidence on the differential coursework hypothesis. *American Educational Research Journal*, 1983, *20*, 165–82.

PARISH, T. S., & NUNN, G. D. Locus of control as a function of family type and age at onset of father absence. Paper presented at the American Educational Research Association, Montreal, Canada, April 1983.

PARKE, B. N., & BUESCHER, T. M. Evaluating programs through student self-documentation. *Roeper Review*, 1982, 5(1), 15–17.

PARKER, J. The leadership training model. *G/C/T*, Sept./Oct. 1983, 8–13.

PARKER, M. Bright kids in trouble with the law. *G/C/T*, Sept./Oct. 1979, 62–63.

PARNES, S. J. Can creativity be increased? In G. A. Davis & J. A. Scott (eds.), *Training creative thinking.* Huntington, N.Y.: Krieger, 1978.

———. *The magic of your mind.* Buffalo, N.Y.: Creative Education Foundation, 1981.

———, NOLLER, R. B., & BIONDI, A. M. *Guide to creative action.* New York: Scribner's, 1977.

PARSONS, J. Women and mathematics: Synthesis of recent research. Paper presented at the American Educational Research Association, New York, April 1982.

PARSONS, J. E., FRIEZE, I. H., & RUBLE, D. M. Intrapsychic factors influencing career aspirations in college women. *Sex Roles: A Journal of Research*, 1978, *4*, 337–48.

PASSOW, A. H. Enrichment of education for the gifted. In N. B. Henry (ed.), *Education for the gifted*, Part II. Chicago: National Society for the Study of Education, 1958.

———. The nature of giftedness and talent. *Gifted Child Quarterly*, 1981, *25*, 5–10.

PAYNE, D., HALPIN, G., ELLET, C., & DALE, J. General personality correlates of creative personality in academic and artistically gifted students. *Journal of Special Education*, 1975, *9*, 105–108.

PERKINS, J. A., & WICAS, E. A. Group counseling bright underachievers and their mothers. *Journal of counseling psychology,* 1971, *18,* 273–78.

PERRONE, P. A., KARSHNER, W. W., & MALE, R. A. Identification of talented students. In N. Colangelo & R. T. Zaffrann (eds.), *New voices in counseling the gifted.* Dubuque, Iowa: Kendall/Hunt,1979.

————, & PULVINO, C. J. New directions in the guidance of the gifted and talented. In J. C. Gowan, J. Khatena, & E. P. Torrance (eds.), *Educating the ablest* (2nd ed.). Chicago: Peacock, 1979.

PETERSON, C. *Winning systems for accelerated schools.* Denver, Colo.: Accelerated Schools Foundation, 1978.

PETRO, C. S., & PUTNAM, B. A. Sex-role stereotypes: Issues of attitudinal changes. *Signs,* 1979, *5,* 1–4.

PFEIL, M. P. Fourth Street School's new claim to fame. *American Education,* Mar. 1978, 10–13.

PIAGET, J., & INHELDER, B. *The psychology of the child. (H. Weaver Trans.)* New York: Basic Books, 1969.

PIERCE, J. W., &BOWMAN, P. Motivation patterns of superior high school students. *Cooperative Research Monograph No. 2,* 1960, 33–66.

PINE, G. J., & BOY, A. V. *Learner-centered teaching: A humanistic view.* Denver, Colo.: Love Publishing Co., 1977.

PINEGREE, S. The effects of nonsexist television commercials and perceptions of reality on children's attitudes about women. *Psychology of Women Quarterly,* 1978, *2,* 262–77.

PLESE, S. An application of triad for gifted enrichment: The organization of a community resource center. *Roeper Review,* 1982, *5(2),* 5–8.

PLOWMAN, P. D. Training extraordinary leaders. *Roeper Review,* 1981, *3(3),* 13–16.

POLOMA, M. M. Role conflict and the married professional woman. In C. Safilios-Rothchild (ed.), *Toward a sociology of women.* Lexington, Mass.: Xerox College Publishing, 1972.

POST, R. D. Causal explanations of male and female academic performance as a function of sex-role biases. *Sex Roles,* 1981, *7,* 691–98.

POSTMAN, N. *Crazy talk, stupid talk.* New York: Dell, 1976.

PRINCE, G. *The practice of creativity.* New York: Collier Books, 1970.

PROVUS, M. M. *Discrepancy evaluation.* Berkeley, Calif.: McCutchan, 1972.

PULVINO, C. J., COLANGELO, N., & ZAFFRANN, R. T. *Laboratory counseling programs.* Madison, Wis.: Department of Counseling and Guidance, University of Wisconsin, 1976.

RADIN, N. Father-child interaction and the intellectual functioning of four-year-old boys. *Developmental Psychology,* 1972, *6,* 353–61.

————. Observed maternal behavior with four-year-old boys and girls in lower-class families. *Child Development,* 1974, *45,* 1126–1131.

————. The role of the father in cognitive, academic and intellectual development. In M. E. Lamb (ed.), *The role of the father in child development.* New York: Wiley, 1976.

————, & EPSTEIN, A. Observed paternal behavior and the intellectual functioning of preschool boys and girls. Paper presented at the Society for Research in Child Development, Denver, Colo., April 1975.

REIS, S. M. Creating ownership in gifted and talented programs. *Roeper Review,* 1983, *5(4),* 20–23.

————, & RENZULLI, J. S. A case for a broadened conception of giftedness. *Phi Delta Kappan,* 1982, *63,* 619–20.

RENZULLI, J. S. *A guidebook for evaluating programs for the gifted and talented.* Ventura, Calif.: Office of the Ventura County Superintendent of Schools, 1975.

————. *The enrichment triad model: A guide for developing defensible programs for the gifted and talented.* Mansfield, Conn.: Creative Learning Press, 1977.

————. What makes giftedness? Reexamining a definition. *Phi Delta Kappan,* 1978, 180–84.

————. The gifted constitute 3–5% of the population! *Gifted Child Quarterly,* 1982, *26,* 11–14.

————. Rating the behavioral characteristics of superior students. *G/C/T*, Sept./Oct. 1983, 30–35.

————, & HARTMAN, R. K. Scale for rating the behavior characteristics of superior students. *Exceptional Children*, 1971, *38*, 243–48.

————, & HARTMAN, R. K. Scale for rating the behavioral characteristics of superior students. In W. B. Barbe & J. S. Renzulli (eds.), *Psychology and education of the gifted* (3rd ed.). New York: Irvington, 1981.

————, REIS, S. M., & SMITH, L. H. *The revolving door identification model*. Mansfield, Conn.: Creative Learning Press, 1981.

————, & SMITH, L. H. Developing defensible programs for the gifted and talented. *Journal of Creative Behavior*, 1978, *12*, 21–29, 51.

————, & SMITH, L. H. Issues and procedures in evaluating gifted programs. In A. H. Passow (ed.), *The gifted and the talented*. Chicago: National Society for the Study of Education, 1979.

————, & WARD, V. S. *Diagnostic and evaluative scales for differential education for the gifted*. Storrs, Conn.: University of Connecticut, 1969.

REST, J. *Defining issues test*. Minneapolis, Minn.: University of Minnesota, 1972.

RESTAK, R. *The brain: The last frontier*. New York: Doubleday, 1979.

REYNOLDS, M. C. Acceleration. In E. P. Torrance (ed.), *Talent and education*. Minneapolis: University of Minnesota Press, 1960.

————, BIRCH, J. W., & TUSETH, A. A. Research on early admissions. In W. Dennis & M. Dennis (eds), *The intellectually gifted: An overview*. New York: Grune & Stratton, 1976.

RICHARDSON, S. Some social-psychological consequences of handicapping. *Pediatrics*, 1962, *32*, 291–97.

————. Handicap, appearance, and stigma. *Social Science and Medicine*, 1971, *5*, 621–28.

RIMM, S. *GIFT: Group inventory for finding creative talent*. Watertown, Wis.: Educational Assessment Service, 1976.

————. A comprehensive framework for total educational evaluation. Forward, *Journal of the Wisconsin Association for Supervision and Curriculum Development*, Fall 1977, 9–18.

————. Congratulations Miss Smithersteen, you have proved that Amy isn't gifted. *G/C/T*, Sept./Oct. 1980, 22–24.

————. Evaluation of gifted programs—as easy as ABC. In R. E. Clasen, B. Robinson, D. R. Clasen, & G. Libster (eds.), *Programming for the gifted, talented and creative: Models and methods*. Madison, Wis.: University of Wisconsin–Extension, 1981. (a)

————. Understanding underachievement. Presented at the Wisconsin Council for Gifted and Talented, LaCrosse, Wis., October 1981. (b)

————. *PRIDE: Preschool interest descriptor*. Watertown, Wis.: Educational Assessment Service, 1982.

————. Identifying creativity, Part 1. *G/C/T*, Mar./Apr. 1983, 34–37.

————. If God had meant gifted children to run our homes, she would have created them bigger. *G/C/T*, 1984, in press.

————. *Underachievers to Wonderachievers*. In preparation.

————, & DAVIS, G. A. GIFT: An instrument for the identification of creativity. *Journal of Creative Behavior*, 1976, *10*, 178–82.

————, & DAVIS, G. A. *GIFFI I: Group inventory for finding interests*. Watertown, Wis.: Educational Assessment Service, 1979.

————, & DAVIS, G. A. Five years of international research with GIFT: An instrument for the identification of creativity. *Journal of Creative Behavior*, 1980, *14*, 35–46.

————, & DAVIS, G. A. Identifying creativity, Part II. *G/C/T*, Sept./Oct. 1983, 19–23.

————, DAVIS, G. A., & BIEN, Y. Identifying creativity: A characteristics approach. *Gifted Child Quarterly*, 1982, *26*, 165–71.

ROBINSON, B. College for kids: The anatomy of a summer enrichment program for K–4 gifted children at the University of Wisconsin–Parkside. In R. E. Clasen, B. Robinson, D.

R. Clasen, & G. Libster, (eds.), *Programming for the gifted, talented and creative: Models and methods.* Madison, Wis.: University of Wisconsin–Extension, 1981.

———, DAVIS, G. A., FIEDLER, E. D., & HELMAN, I. B. *Education of the gifted and talented: A primer.* Madison, Wis.: Wisconsin Department of Public Instruction, 1982.

ROBINSON, H. B., ROEDELL, W. C., & JACKSON, N. E. Early identification and intervention. In A. H. Passow (ed.), *The gifted and the talented.* Chicago: National Society for the Study of Education, 1979.

RODENSTEIN, J. M., & GLICKAUF-HUGHES, C. Career and lifestyle determinants of gifted women. In N. Colangelo & R. T. Zaffrann (eds.), *New voices in counseling the gifted.* Dubuque, Iowa: Kendall/Hunt, 1979.

ROGERS, C. R. A coordinated research in psychotherapy: A non-objective introduction. *Journal of Consulting Psychology,* 1949, *13,* 49–51.

———. Toward a theory of creativity. In S. J. Parnes & H. F. Harding (eds.), *A source book for creative thinking.* New York: Scribner's, 1962.

ROSENTHAL, R. J., & JACOBSON, L. *Pygmalion in the classroom.* New York: Holt, 1968.

ROSS, A. O. *The exceptional child in the family.* New York: Grune & Stratton, 1964.

ROSS, A., & PARKER, H. Academic and social self-concepts of the academically gifted. *Exceptional Children,* 1980, *47,* 6–10.

ROYER, R. Creative writing assignment for the gifted. *G/C/T,* Jan./Feb. 1982, 29–30.

RUDD, N. A., & McKENRY, P. C. Working women: Issues and implications. *Journal of Home Economics,* 1980, *72(4),* 26–29.

RUHLAND, D., GOLD, M., & FELD, S. Role problems and the relationship of achievement to performance. *Journal of Educational Psychology,* 1978, *70,* 950–59.

RUSSELL, D. H. Higher mental processes. In C. W. Harris (ed.), *Encyclopedia of educational research.* New York: Macmillan, 1960.

SADKER, M. P., SADKER, D. M., & HICKS, T. The one-percent solution? Sexism in teacher education texts. *Phi Delta Kappan,* 1980, *61,* 550–53.

SANBORN, M. Career development: Problems of gifted and talented students. In N. Colangelo & R. T. Zaffrann (eds.), *New voices in counseling the gifted.* Dubuque, Iowa: Kendall/Hunt, 1979. (a)

———. Differential counseling needs of the gifted and talented. In N. Colangelo & R. T. Zaffrann (eds.), *New voices in counseling the gifted.* Dubuque, Iowa: Kendall/Hunt, 1979. (b)

———. Counseling and guidance needs of the gifted and talented. In A. H. Passow (ed.), *The gifted and the talented.* Chicago: National Society for the Study of Education, 1979. (c)

SANDERS, N. M. *Classroom questions: What kinds?* New York: Harper & Row, 1966.

SATO, I. S., BIRNBAUM, M., & LoCICERO, J. E. *Developing a written plan for the education of gifted and talented students.* Ventura, Calif.: Office of the Ventura County Superintendent of Schools, 1974.

SATO, I. S., & JOHNSON, B. Multifaceted training meets multidimensionally gifted. *Journal of Creative Behavior,* 1978, *12,* 63–71.

SCHAEFER, C. M. *Biographical inventory-creativity.* San Diego: Educational and Industrial Testing Service, 1970.

SCHAFER, M. *Die sprache des pferdes.* Munich: Nymfenburger Verlagshandlung, 1974.

SCHAUER, G. M. Emotional disturbances and giftedness. *Gifted Child Quarterly,* 1976, *20,* 470–77.

SCHNUR, J. O., & STEFANICH, G. P. Science for the handicapped gifted child. *Roeper Review,* 1979, *2(2),* 26–28.

SCHUBERT, J., & CROPLEY, A. J. Verbal regulation of behavior and IQ in Canadian Indian and white children. *Developmental Psychology,* 1972, *7,* 295–301.

SCHWARTZ, L. L. Women and their achievement motivation. *Pennsylvania Personnel and Guidance Association Journal,* Spring 1975, 11–16.

———. Advocacy for the neglected gifted: Females. *Gifted Child Quarterly,* 1980, *24,* 113–17.

SCRUGGS, T. E., COHN, S. J. A university-based summer program for a highly able but poorly achieving Indian child. *Gifted Child Quarterly,* 1983, *27,* 90–93.

SEARS, P. S. The Terman genetic studies of genius, 1922–1972. In A. H. Passow (ed.), *The gifted and the talented.* Chicago: National Society for the Study of Education, 1979.

_____, & BARBEE, A. H. Career and life satisfactions among Terman's gifted women. In J. C. Stanley, W. C. George, & C. H. Solano (eds.), *The gifted and the creative: A fifty-year perspective.* Baltimore, Md.: Johns Hopkins University Press, 1977.

SEARS, R. R. Sources of life satisfactions of the Terman gifted men. *American Psychologist,* 1977, *32,* 119–28.

SEGOE, M. V. *Terman and the gifted.* Los Altos, Calif.: Kaufman, 1975.

SELIGMAN, M. E. P. *Helplessness: On depression, development and death.* San Francisco: Freeman, 1975.

SELLS, L. W. Mathematics, minorities, and women. *ASA Footnotes,* 1976, *4(1),* 1, 3.

SERBIN, L., & O'LEARY, D. K. How nursery schools teach girls to shut up. *Psychology Today,* 1975, *9(12),* 56–58.

SHALLCROSS, D. J. *Teaching creative behavior.* Englewood Cliffs, N.J.: Prentice-Hall, 1981.

SHAVER, P., & FREEDMAN, J. Your pursuit of happiness. *Psychology Today,* 1976, *10(8),* 26–32.

SHAW, M. C., & WHITE, D. L. The relationship between child-parent identification and academic underachievement. *Journal of Clinical Psychology,* 1965, *21,* 10–13.

SHEEHY, G. *Pathfinders.* New York: Bantam Books, 1982.

SHEPARD, L. A. Self-acceptance: The evaluative component of the self-concept construct. *Journal of Educational Research,* 1979, *16,* 139–60.

SIMON, S. B., HOWE, L., & KIRSCHENBAUM, H. *Value clarification: A handbook of practical strategies for teachers and students.* New York: Hart, 1972.

_____, & MASSEY, S. Value clarification. *Educational Leadership,* 1973, *5,* 738–39.

SISK, D. Issues and future directions in gifted education. *Gifted Child Quarterly,* 1980, *24,* 29–36.

_____. The use of creative activities in leadership training. In W. B. Barbe & J. S., Renzulli (eds.), *Psychology and education of the gifted* (3rd ed.). New York: Irvington, 1981.

SJOGREN, D., HOPKINS, T., & GOOLER, D. *Evaluation plans and instruments: Illustrative cases of gifted program evaluation techniques.* Champaign, Ill.: Center for Instructional Research and Curriculum Evaluation, University of Illinois, 1975.

SMITH, J. M. *Setting conditions for creative teaching in the elementary school.* Boston: Allyn & Bacon, 1966.

SMITH, L. G. Centuries of educational inequities. *Educational Horizons,* 1981, *60,* 4–10.

SOLANO, C. Precocity and adult failure. Paper presented at the National Association for Gifted Children, 1976. (a)

_____. Teacher and pupil stereotypes of gifted boys and girls. Paper presented at the American Psychological Association, Washington, D. C., 1976. (b)

SOLOMON, A. O. Analysis of creative thinking of disadvantaged children. *Journal of Creative Behavior,* 1974, *8,* 293–95.

STAINES, G., TAVRIS, C., & JAYARATNE, C. The Queen Bee syndrome. *Psychology Today,* 1974, *7(8),* 55–60.

STAKE, J. E. The educator's role in fostering female career aspirations. *Journal of NAWDAC,* 1981, 3–10.

STAKE, R. W. The countenance of educational evaluation. *Teachers College Record,* 1967, *68,* 523–40.

STANKOWSKI, W. M. Definition. In R. E. Clasen & B. Robinson (eds.), *Simple gifts.* Madison, Wis.: University of Wisconsin–Extension, 1978.

STANLEY, J. C. Test better finder of great math talent than teachers are. *American Psychologist,* 1976, *31,* 313–14.

———. Rationale of the studies of mathematically precocious youth (SMPY) during its first five years of promoting educational acceleration. In J. C. Stanley, W. C. Solano, & C. H. George (eds.). *The gifted and the creative: A fifty-year perspective.* Baltimore, Md.: Johns Hopkins University Press, 1977.

———. Concern for intellectually talented youths: How it originated and fluctuated. In R. E. Clasen & B. Robinson (eds.), *Simple gifts.* Madison, Wis.: University of Wisconsin–Extension, 1978. (a)

———. Identifying and nurturing the intellectually gifted. In R. E. Clasen & B. Robinson (eds.), *Simple gifts.* Madison, Wis.: University of Wisconsin–Extension, 1978. (b)

———. The study and facilitation of talent for mathematics. In A. H. Passow (ed.), *The gifted and the talented.* Chicago: National Society for the Study of Education, 1979.

———. Finding intellectually talented youths and helping them greatly via educational acceleration. Speech to the Wisconsin Council on Gifted and Talented, Madison, Wis., October 1982. (a)

———. SMPY's "700M before age 13" national talent search. Paper presented at the National Association for Gifted Children, New Orleans, October 1982. (b)

———, & BENBOW, C. P. Educating mathematically precocious youths: Twelve policy recommendations. *Educational Researcher,* 1983, *11(5),* 4–9.

———, & GEORGE, W. C. SMPY's ever-increasing D4. *Gifted Child Quarterly,* 1980, *24,* 41–48.

STERNGLANZ, S. H., & SERBIN, L. A. Sex-role stereotyping in children's television programs. *Developmental Psychology,* 1974, *10,* 710–15.

STRYKOWSKI, B., & WALBERG, H. J. Psychological traits and childhood environments of eminent writers. *Roeper Review,* 1983, *6(2),* 102–105.

STUFFLEBEAM, D. L., FOLEY, W. J., GEPHART, W. J., GUBA, E. G., HAMMOND, R. L., MERRIMAN, H. O., & PROVUS, M. M. *Educational evaluation and decision making in education.* Itasca, Ill.: Peacock, 1971.

SUTHERLAND, S. L. The unambitious female: Women's low professional aspirations. *Signs: Journal of Women in Culture and Society,* 1978, *3,* 774–94.

SUTTON-SMITH, B., ROSENBERG, B. G., & LANDY, F. Father-absence effects in families of different sibling compositions. *Child Development,* 1968, *39,* 1213–21.

SWENSON, E. V. Teacher-assessment of creative behavior in disadvantaged children. *Gifted Child Quarterly,* 1978, *22,* 338–43.

SWING, E. S. Public school elitist education in a revolutionary era. *English Journal,* 1973, *62,* 1223–1224.

TANGRI, S. S. Determinants of occupational role innovation among college women. *Journal of Social Issues,* 1972, *28,* 177–99.

TANNENBAUM, A. J. Pre-Sputnik to post-Watergate concern about the gifted. In A. H. Passow (ed.), *The gifted and the talented.* Chicago: National Society for the Study of Education, 1979.

TAN-WILLMAN, C., & GUTTERIDGE, D. Creative thinking and moral reasoning of academically gifted secondary school adolescents. *Gifted Child Quarterly,* 1981, *25,* 149–53.

TAYLOR, C. W. How many types of giftedness can your program tolerate? *Journal of Creative Behavior,* 1978, *12,* 39–51.

TEAHAN, J. E. Parental attitudes and college success. *Journal of Educational Psychology,* 1963, *54,* 104–109.

TERMAN, L. M. The intelligence quotient of Francis Galton in childhood. *American Journal of Psychology,* 1917, *28,* 208–215.

———. The discovery and encouragement of exceptional talent. In W. B. Barbe & J. S., Renzulli (eds.), *Psychology and education of the gifted* (3rd ed.). New York: Irvington, 1981.

———, & ODEN, M. H. *Genetic studies of genius: Mental and physical traits of a thousand gifted children.* Stanford, Calif.: Stanford University Press, 1925.

———, & ODEN, M. H. *Genetic studies of genius: The gifted child grows up.* Stanford, Calif.: Stanford University Press, 1947.

_____, & ODEN, M. H. The Stanford studies of the gifted. In P. A. Witty (ed.), *The gifted child.* Boston: D. C. Heath, 1951.

_____, & ODEN, M. H. *Genetic studies of genius: The gifted at mid-life.* Stanford, Calif.: Stanford University Press, 1959.

TETENBAUM, T., & HOUTZ, J. The role of affective traits in the creative problem-solving performance of gifted urban children. *Psychology in the Schools,* 1978, *15,* 91–96.

THORNDIKE, R. S., & HAGEN, E. P. *Management and evaluation in psychology and education.* New York: Wiley, 1977.

TIDBALL, M. E. Perspective on academic women and affirmative action. *Educational Record,* 1973, *54,* 130–35.

TOBIN, D. Accelerated mathematics for the gifted. *G/C/T,* Sept./Oct. 1979, 48–50.

TONGUE, C., & SPERLING, C. *Parent nomination form.* Raleigh, N.C.: North Carolina Department of Public Instruction, 1976.

TORRANCE, E. P. *Guiding creative talent.* Englewood Cliffs, N.J.: Prentice-Hall, 1962.

_____. *Torrance tests of creative thinking.* Bensenville, Ill.: Scholastic Testing Service, 1966.

_____. Are the Torrance tests of creative thinking biased against or in favor of disadvantaged groups? *Gifted Child Quarterly,* 1971, *15,* 75–81.

_____. Creative young women in today's world. *Exceptional Children,* 1972, *38,* 597–603.

_____. Future careers for gifted and talented students. *Gifted Child Quarterly,* 1976, *20,* 142–56.

_____. Creatively gifted and disadvantaged gifted students. In J. C. Stanley, W. C. George, & C. H. Solano (eds.), *The gifted and the creative: A fifty-year perspective.* Baltimore, Md.: Johns Hopkins University Press, 1977. (a)

_____. *Creativity in the classroom.* Washington, D.C.: National Educational Association, 1977. (b)

_____. *The search for satori and creativity.* Buffalo, N.Y.: Creative Education Foundation, 1979.

_____. Assessing the further reaches of creative potential. *Journal of Creative Behavior,* 1980, *14,* 1–19.

_____. Creative teaching makes a difference. In J. C. Gowan, J. Khatena, & E. P. Torrance (eds.), *Creativity: Its educational implications* (2nd ed.). Dubuque, Iowa: Kendall/Hunt, 1981. (a)

_____. Non-test ways of identifying the creatively gifted. In J. C. Gowan, J. Khatena, & E. P. Torrance (eds.), *Creativity: Its educational implications* (2nd ed.). Dubuque, Iowa: Kendall/ Hunt, 1981. (b)

_____. Sociodrama as a creative problem-solving approach to studying the future. In J. C. Gowan, J. Khatena, & E. P. Torrance (eds.), *Creativity: Its educational implications* (2nd ed.). Dubuque, Iowa: Kendall/Hunt, 1981. (c)

_____. Teaching gifted and creative learners. In M. Wittrock (ed.), *Handbook of research on teaching* (3rd ed.). Chicago: Rand-McNally, 1984.

_____, & MYERS, R. E. *Creative learning and teaching.* New York: Dodd, Mead, 1970.

_____, & TORRANCE, J. P. The 1977–78 future problem-solving program: Interscholastic competition and curriculum project. *Journal of Creative Behavior,* 1978, *12,* 87–89.

_____, WILLIAMS, S. E., TORRANCE, J. P., & HORNG, R. *Handbook for training future problem-solving teams.* Athens, Ga.: Georgia Studies of Creative Behavior, University of Georgia, 1978.

TORRES, S. *A primer on individualized education programs for handicapped children.* Reston, Va.: Council for Exceptional Children, 1977.

TOWNSEND, J. W., TORRANCE, E. P., & WU, T. Role of creative ability in the production of humor. *Journal of Creative Behavior,* 1981, *15,* 280–81.

TREFFINGER, D. J. Teaching for self-directed learning: A priority of the gifted and talented. *Gifted Child Quarterly,* 1975, *19,* 46–59.

———. Guidelines for encouraging independence and self-direction among gifted students. *Journal of Creative Behavior,* 1978, *12,* 14–20.

———. *Encouraging creative learning for the gifted and talented: A handbook of methods and techniques.* Ventura, Calif.: Ventura County Superintendent of Schools, 1980.

———. *Blending gifted education with the total school program.* Williamsville, N.Y.: Center for Creative Learning, 1981.

———. Gifted students, regular students: Sixty ingredients for a better blend. *Elementary School Journal,* 1982, *82,* 267–73.

———. Creativity: Celebrating the vision. Speech presented at the Third Annual Midwest Conference on Gifted and Talented Children, Milwaukee, Wis., April 1983.

———, & BARTON, B. L. Fostering independent learning. *G/C/T,* Jan./Feb. 1979, 3–6.

———, ISAKSEN, S. G., & FIRESTIEN, R. L. *Handbook of creative learning.* Volume 1. Williamsville, N.Y.: Center for Creative Learning, 1982.

———, & PEREZ, G. S. Self-description of instructional style for encouraging self-directed learning. In H. W. Singleton (ed.), *Gifted/talented education: Perspectives on curriculum and instruction.* Toledo, Ohio: University of Toledo, College of Education, 1980.

TREMAINE, C. Do gifted programs make a difference? *Gifted Child Quarterly, 1979, 23,* 500–517.

TRIGG, L. J., & PERLMAN, D. Social influences on women's pursuit of a nontraditional career. *Psychology of Women Quarterly,* 1976, *1(2),* 138–50.

TUCKER, B. F. Providing for the mathematically gifted child in the regular classroom. *Roeper Review,* 1982, *4(4),* 11–12.

USISKIN, Z. Cognitive development and achievement in secondary school geometry. Presented at the American Educational Research Association, New York, April 1982.

VAN TASSEL-BASKA, J. Review of the revolving door identification model. *Gifted Child Quarterly,* 1981, *25,* 187–88. (a)

———. The great debates: For acceleration. CEC/TAG National Topical Conference on the Gifted and Talented Child, Orlando, Fla., December 1981. (b)

———. Purdue offers summer programs. *Midwest Talent Search Quarterly,* 1983, *1(1),* 11.

VANTOUR, J. A. C. Discovering and motivating the artistically gifted LD child. *Teaching Exceptional Children,* 1976, *8,* 92–96.

VELLE, W. Sex hormones and behavior in animals and man. *Perspectives in Biology and Medicine,* 1982, *25,* 295–315.

VEROFF, J. Social comparison and the development of achievement motivation. In C. P. Smith (ed.), *Achievement-related motives in children.* New York: Russel Sage Foundation, 1969.

VETTER, B. M., & BABCO, E. L. *Professional women and minorities: A manpower data resource service.* Washington, D.C.: Scientific Manpower Commission, 1975.

WALBERG, H. J., TSAI, T., WEINSTEIN, T., GABRIEL, C. L., RASHER, S. P., ROSECRANS, T., ROVAI, E., IDE, J., TRUJILLO, M., & VUKOSAVICH, P. Childhood traits and environmental conditions of highly eminent adults. *Gifted Child Quarterly,* 1981, *25,* 103–107.

WALLACH, M. A. Creativity. In P. H. Mussen (ed.), *Carmichael's manual of child psychology* (3rd ed.). New York: John Wiley, 1970.

———, & KOGAN, N. *Modes of thinking in young children.* New York: Holt, 1965.

WALLAS, G. *The art of thought.* New York: Harcourt, Brace & World, 1926.

WAY, B. *Development through drama.* London: Longman, 1967.

WEBB, J. T., MECKERSTROTH, E. A., & TOLAN, S. S. *Guiding the gifted child.* Columbus, Ohio: Psychology Publishing Company, 1982.

WEBER, J. Moral dilemmas in the classroom. *Roeper Review,* 1981, *3(4),* 11–13.

WEINER, B. *Achievement motivation and attribution theory.* Morristown, N.J.: General Learning press, 1974.

———. *Human motivation.* New York: Holt, 1980.

WEINSTEIN, J., & LAUFMAN, L. The fourth R: Reasoning. *Roeper Review,* 1981, *4(1),* 20–22.

WEISS, P., & Gallagher J. J. Parental expectations for gifted children. *G/C/T,* Nov./Dec. 1983, 2–6.

WEITZMAN, L. J., & RIZZO, D. Images of males and females in elementary school textbooks in five subject areas. In *Biased textbooks*. Washington, D.C.: National Foundation for the Improvement of Education, 1974.

WELSH, G. S., & BARRON, F. *Barron-Welsh art scale*. Palo Alto, Calif.: Consulting Psychologists Press, 1963.

WHITE, B. L., KABAN, B. T., & ATTANUCCI, J. S. *The origins of human competence: Final report of the Harvard Preschool Project*. Lexington, Mass.: D.C. Heath, 1979.

WHITMORE, J. R. *Giftedness, conflict, and underachievement*. Boston: Allyn & Bacon, 1980.

WILLIAMS, F. E. *Classroom ideas for encouraging thinking and feeling*. Buffalo, N.Y.: DOK Publishers, 1970.

————. *A total creativity program for individualizing and humanizing the learning process*. Englewood Cliffs, N.J.: Educational Technology Publications, 1972.

————. Williams' strategies to orchestrate Renzulli's triad. *G/C/T*, Sept./Oct. 1979, 2–6, 10.

————. *Classroom ideas for encouraging thinking and feeling*. Volume 2. Buffalo, N.Y.: DOK Publishers, 1982.

WILLIS, B. C., et al. *The central purpose of American education*. Washington, D.C.: National Education Association, 1961.

WITTY, P. A. Evaluation of some research in the education of academically gifted children. In W. B. Barbe (ed.), *Psychology and education of the gifted*. New York: Appleton, 1965.

————. Equal educational opportunity for gifted minority group children: Promise or possibility? *Gifted Child Quarterly*, 1978, *22*, 344–51.

————, & GROTBERG, E. H. *Helping the gifted child*. Chicago: Science Research Associates, 1970.

WOLFLE, D. *America's resources of specialized talent*. New York: Harper & Row, 1954.

WOLLEAT, P. L. Guiding the career development of gifted females. In N. Colangelo and R. T. Zaffrann (eds.), *New voices in counseling the gifted*. Dubuque, Iowa: Kendall/Hunt, 1979.

YALOM, I. D., GREEN, R., & FISK, N. Prenatal exposure to female hormones: Effect on psychosexual development in boys. *Archives of General Psychiatry*, 1973, *28*, 554–61.

YAMAMOTO, K. Do creativity tests really measure creativity? *Theory into Practice*, 1966, *5*, 194–97.

YSSELDYKE, J. E., ALGOZZINE, B., & RICHEY, L. Judgment under uncertainty: How many children are handicapped? *Exceptional Children*, 1982, *48*, 531–34.

ZACHARIAS, J. R. The trouble with IQ tests. In P. L. Houts (ed.), *The myth of measurability*. New York: Hart, 1977.

ZAFFRANN, R. T., & COLANGELO, N. Counseling with gifted and talented students. In N. Colangelo and R. T. Zaffrann (eds.), *New voices in counseling the gifted*. Dubuque, Iowa: Kendall/Hunt, 1979.

ZIGLER, E., & MUENCHOW, S. Mainstreaming: The proof is in the implementation. *American Psychologist*, 1970, *34*, 993–96.

ZILLI, M. G. Reasons why the gifted adolescent underachieves and some of the implications of guidance and counseling to this problem. *Gifted Child Quarterly*, 1971, *15*, 279–92.

ZINBERG, D. College: When the future becomes the present. In R. B. Kundsin (ed.), *Women and success: The anatomy of achievement*. New York: William Morrow, 1974.

ZIV, A. *Counseling the intellectually gifted child*. Toronto, Canada: Governing Counsel of the University of Toronto, 1977.

AUTHOR INDEX

SUBJECT INDEX